Withdrawn from stock

UCC Library

CITY THAT NEVER SLEEPS

D1471729

Withdrawn from stock
UCC Library

791.43 POME

Withdrawn from stock
UCC Library

CITY THAT NEVER SLEEPS

New York and the Filmic Imagination

EDITED BY MURRAY POMERANCE

RUTGERS UNIVERSITY PRESS

New Brunswick, New Jersey, and London

Library of Congress Cataloging-in-Publication Data

City that never sleeps : New York and the filmic imagination / edited by Murray Pomerance.

    p.   cm.

Includes bibliographical references and index.

ISBN-13: 978–0–8135–4031–3 (hardcover: alk. paper)

ISBN-13: 978–0–8135–4032–0 (pbk.: alk. paper)

1. New York (N.Y.)—In motion pictures. I. Pomerance, Murray, 1946–

PN1995.9.N49C58 2007

791.43′627471—dc22

2006021862

A British Cataloging-in-Publication record for this book is available from the British Library.

New York skyline chapter opening ornament used by permission. Copyright Art Parts / Ron and Joe, Inc.

Images on pages 21, 63, and 121 are digital frame enlargements from *Manhattan* (Woody Allen, Jack Rollins & Charles H. Joffe / United Artists, 1979).

This collection copyright © 2007 by Rutgers, The State University

Individual chapters copyright © 2007 in the names of their authors

All rights reserved

No part of this book may be reproduced or utilized in any form or by any means, electronic or mechanical, or by any information storage and retrieval system, without written permission from the publisher. Please contact Rutgers University Press, 100 Joyce Kilmer Avenue, Piscataway, NJ 08854–8099. The only exception to this prohibition is "fair use" as defined by U.S. copyright law.

Manufactured in the United States of America

To Nellie, always,

and to Ariel, who has made New York his own

"Driver! Has this a peer in Europe or the East?"

"No no!" he said. Home! Home!

—*Paul Goodman, "The Lordly Hudson"*

Contents

Stayin' Alive: City of Danger and Adjustment

Acknowledgments

Nellie Perret and Ariel Pomerance inspired and supported this project of mine, as they have so many others, with patience, love, and—most importantly of all—quick wit. My knowledge of, and feeling for, New York City began in December of 1958 and over almost fifty years has been cultivated and tended by the best of urban gardeners, including:

Leslie Barker (Southampton); the late Wayne Barker and Susan Burgwyn Barker (Amagansett); Elliot Bien (Scarsdale and Novato); the late Heywood Hale Broun (Woodstock); the late Craig Claiborne (East Hampton); Larry Fine (Brooklyn); Krin Gabbard (New York); Peter Geffen (Forest Hills); Peter Glassgold (New York); the late Robert Gooblar (Hamilton and Toronto); Sally Goodman and the late Paul Goodman (New York and North Stratford, N.H.); the late Hoffman and Juliet Hays (East Hampton); Dave Heath (Toronto); the late Paul Levy (Hamilton and Toronto); the late Teresa Liss (Amagansett); Judith Lowry (New York); William Luhr (Floral Park); Ron and Howard Mandelbaum (New York); Mark Crispin Miller (New York); Stephen Miller (New York and Cape May); Mordecai Newman (New York); Jonathan Panitz (Paterson); the late Claironel Foster Perret, George Albert Perret, and Gabriel Aimé Perret (Amagansett and New York); Helen Selden Rattray and the late Everett T. Rattray (Amagansett); Peter and Mercedes Ribicoff (New York); Ken Robbins (New York and Springs); Ron and Joe (Santa Ana); William Rothman (Miami); Tom Rush (New York); Murray Rutner (New York); Steven Schneider (New York and Los Angeles); the late John and Margit Slade (East Hampton and New York); J. David Slocum (New York); Theodore Solotaroff (New York); Claire Smith (Brooklyn); David Sterritt (Baltimore); Jane White and the late Alfredo Viazzi (New York); Anita Herzog Weiner and the late Eugene Weiner (Hamilton, New York, Haifa); Burton Weiss (New York).

To make a book requires loving collaborators, such as my talented and committed friends at Rutgers University Press: Arlene Bacher, Christina Brianik, Marilyn Campbell, Gary Fitzgerald, Trudi Gershenov, Alison Hack, Anne Hegeman, Kenya Henderson, Adi Hovav, Donna Liese, Leslie Mitchner, Alicia Nadkarni, Eric Schramm, J'Aime Wells, and Winnie Westcott. Further, a measureless gratitude is owed my skilled and ingenuous assistants Nathan Holmes, David Kerr, and Nay Laywine for the myriad searches, inspections, verifications, and appraisals I have needed from them. I have received generous support from

Dr. Carla Cassidy, Dean of Arts, Ryerson University, and I have been sweetly assisted by Prof. Taylor Stoehr (Boston).

To the many very, very loyal contributors whose work speaks here, a special thanks for persisting so courteously with my mania and my eccentric vision. I fondly hope that this book touches the New Yorker in all of you as much as it springs from the New Yorker I have always longed to be.

Murray Pomerance
Toronto
October 2006

CITY THAT NEVER SLEEPS

A dream, not a place. The Jets warm up off-camera for *West Side Story* (Robert Wise, Mirisch/Seven Arts, 1961). Russ Tamblyn is at the head of the line at right. Courtesy Photofest New York.

Prelude

TO WAKE UP IN THE CITY
THAT NEVER SLEEPS

MURRAY POMERANCE

A Dream and Not a Place

Writing of New York as "cinema city," Richard A. Blake points to Jean Baudrillard's "amazed" insight that New York seems to have been engendered by its image on the big screen, that to grasp it "you should not . . . begin with the city and move inwards to the screen; you should begin with the screen and move outwards to the city." Such a commentary, he notes, says more about Baudrillard himself "as observer" than about the city (Blake 5). Although Baudrillard cannot really be said to inhabit the book you are about to read in the way his most adoring readers would wish, these pages start from the perspective that he is essentially right: to be in love with the movies, and also in love with New York, requires an affinity with his point of view. New York onscreen *is* New York, for those of us who have needed not only to walk its sidewalks but also to watch it in the dark. And it is true that for lovers of this screened New York, we travel from it to the city and not the other way around.

It is worth saying a little more about this perspective of Baudrillard, and the one we will adopt here, by and large. New York can certainly be subjected to an utterly different kind of investigation than these essays represent, one in which it is taken as a geographic entity (see Vernon *Metropolis 1985*), a cultural production with a history and power structure (see Goodman *Communitas*), a political residue (see Caro *Power Broker*), or even a single case study of a broader phenomenon, urbanization, that marked the period of modernity and that has effected shocking changes around the world (see Simmel "Metropolis and Mental Life"). But this book has no particular intention of looking at New York this way: of seeing it merely as a "typical city," or a political amalgamation, or the result of a set of historical and political forces set in motion by such as Boss Tweed, Fiorello La Guardia, Robert Moses, Robert Wagner, John Lindsay, Rudy Giuliani, or Donald Trump. These musings do not consider that New York onscreen is an attempted representation of these bedrock realities. And while it would certainly be possible and interesting to reflect upon ways that New York as a city—and as a cinematically represented city—differs from less urban centers, such as Schenectady (the home of Henry James's Daisy Miller) or Rapid City, South Dakota (where Roger O. Thornhill has an escapade), or any of a thousand others; or upon ways that it differs from how other major cities look onscreen—the Boston of *The Departed* (2006) or *Mystic River* (2003), the Chicago of *Risky Business* (1983) or *The Fugitive* (1993), the Los Angeles of *Colors* (1988) or *Grease* (1976)—these would, from a certain point of view, be meaningless comparisons, articulating some very arbitrary points of measurement and contrast instead of others and giving little by way of a portrait of either New York or any other place.

We could say, for example, that in Sydney Pollack's *Tootsie* (1982), when Dustin Hoffman stands on the sidewalk in front of the Russian Tea Room (formerly on West Fifty-seventh Street, next to Carnegie Hall), we are seeing an authentic picture of a part of historically actual New York; and we could try to use that as a way of looking at this city, at cities in general, at cities compared with one another: that this is not, for instance, North Clark Street in Chicago in front of Maggiano's, or La Cienega Boulevard in Beverly Hills in front of Matsuhisa. But equally important in cinema—and, I would argue, far more profound—is the oneiric moment at the beginning of *Manhattan* (1979) when Woody Allen treats us to a fireworks show over the East Side: here we are looking at something that is only mythical, that is splendid but not real as an urban datum. Equally galvanizing is the Manhattan of *Spider-Man 2* (2004), as our hero swings hysterically from building to building to catch a racing elevated train that seems to be hurtling off to nowhere. Images do not have to be factual in order to summon a taste of experience.

The point of view from which this arrangement of essays has been constructed is, to be sure, neither explicitly historiographical nor explicitly semantic. The process here does not involve the decoding of signs, but rather their contemplation. And therefore, there seems little point in hesitating to say that this book is something of a rhapsody and also something of a meditation. New York here is not exactly a place, since we are looking at what it is onscreen. We are looking at an evanescent, but also a lingering, New York. That New York is an eidolon, surely—an image that is possessed of a phantasmatic, apparitional, haunting quality, and that rests out of history as a mark of aspiration, memory, and direct experience. What makes all the New Yorks written about by these authors worth their presentation here is exactly that they have gripped and configured our imagination of place, not that they have mapped place or analyzed our relation to it successfully. The New York we write about is the New York of our screen dreams.

This book is therefore a contribution to a body of cinematic scholarship that intends boldly to break with a particularly debilitating tradition, in which cinema must be taken as an outgrowth of a preeminent, principal, and dominating precinematic reality. In this tradition (that burgeoned in the 1980s), as William Rothman writes,

> Academic film study was in the grip of the doctrine that its legitimacy could be established by only the "higher authority," the field called "theory." The reign of theoretical systematizing over film study . . . was at its most repressive. Students were taught that, to think seriously about film, they first had to break their attachments to the films they loved. It was an unquestioned doctrine within the field that movies were pernicious ideological representations to be resisted and decoded, not treated with the respect that is due to works of art capable of instructing us how to think about them. It was another dogma that . . . the world projected on the screen was itself an ideological construct, not real; and, indeed, that so-called reality was such a construct, too. (*Camera*, xii)

Missing (obligatorily) from such a deconstructionist approach as that is anybody's real *view* of the screen, in this case a view of screened New York. One's thrill in the image of New York, the exact pleasures it provides, its incitements to terror and exhilaration, its confusions of place and time—all of these must apparently take second place to a suspicion that what can be seen onscreen is, here with this material as elsewhere with the rest of what is in cinema, entirely bogus: contrived by the most craven of profiteers to trick us out of what is taken to be a position of authenticity, warped by comparison with the world in which we view it, aesthetically either ugly or only seductively beautiful, and therefore always in some way dangerous. But surely a serious and devoted philosophy of film, of the filmic image, can be based on affection for, even love of the screen and this delicious and challenging falsity. Feeling need not impair the serious viewer from considering the experience of watching, and indeed part of the intent here is to examine the screen New York as a way of finding what Herbert Read called a "true voice of feeling." As such, *City That Never Sleeps* is, as Rothman says, an alternative to skeptical views.

Because the city configured here is a kind of dream and not exactly a place, an inspiration and not exactly a polis, the book is called exactly what it is.

New York Is Alive

New York City has starred in movies for a long time. In the first years of the twentieth century, the Edison Manufacturing Company had a number of items in its catalogue representing the city onscreen, one particularly revealing example being the well-known *Skyscrapers of New York City, from the North River* (1903). This three-minute film is shot from a boat or barge moving downstream from around Fourteenth Street toward the Bowery. As we pass wharf after wharf, seeing steamers and ferries and tugs at their moorings, a long array of striking buildings graces the skyline, each a kind of silent cache holding the lives, stories, and fates of thousands of New Yorkers. While in the foreground the waterfront is busy with smoking ships, railway cars drawn up at piers, and some pedestrians, the buildings in their majestic silence and stolidity constitute together an elaborate wall of potentiality. This is the place where everything may happen; where everything may now be happening; where the future will unfold. And the smooth southward passage of the camera allows for what seems an endless chain of these structures, no two shaped alike, no two erected by the same human spirit. Watching them drift past us, we have a sense that the city continues and will continue forever. Financial potency, architectural boldness, the energy of commerce and entrepreneurship, the mystery of the vast population: all these appear together and seem to expand in a spirit of unlimited optimism as the film unwinds.

New York has hardly been a single unchanging entity in film. I would argue that at least since the birth of the talkies, at least three different New Yorks have come to light there. In one, tough-minded and aggressive explorers work their way through an urbanized jungle that is flooded with beams of arc light, flickering with neon or with the luminescence of fast-moving traffic at night or in a shadowy constant twilight—all this raised up as far as the eye can see with monuments to a sleek and arching modernism, vast avenues, countless eager windows and vitrines (as in *Miracle on 34th Street* [1947]), where multitudes seem always to be scrambling out of what Betty Comden and Adolph Green aptly called "a hole in the ground," where elevators seem always to be whisking the dignified and the stylish to private aeries halfway to the clouds (Janoth's office in *The Big Clock* [1948]), where business everywhere accelerates zeal, pressure, movement, and rhythm, where endless riveting is piously undertaken to make endless miles of skyscrapers, and where a burgeoning traffic wafts up and down the proud rivers moving the spirit of the place outward, over the ocean, until it meets the world. This is primarily the New York of the 1920s and 1930s, the New York of Paul Goodman's majestic book of poems, *The Lordly Hudson*, the New York of constant optimism in the face of poverty, the Depression, war, class war, floods of immigration, upshocks of crime. It is—seen today—the New York of "olden" glamorous days, the golden New York, if not the tranquil European cultivation we find in *The Age of Innocence* (1993), then still a locus of the chic and the jazzy, the New York where Hildy Johnson gabs at Walter Burns (in *His Girl Friday* [1940]), where C. K. Dexter Haven and Liz Imbrie prepare to steal down and meet Tracy Samantha Lord and all the other Lords (in *The Philadelphia Story* [1942]), where Jimmy Cagney as George M. Cohan opens on Broadway in one hit after another, hoofing and pounding and expostulating and singing from the bottom of his heart (in *Yankee Doodle Dandy* [1942]). This is the titanic New York of *The Fountainhead* (1949), the chivalrous New York of Linus Larabee's skyscraper empire in *Sabrina* (1954), the enticing New York of Tony Hunter dancing in the dark with Gabrielle Gerard in *The Band Wagon* (1953). It is the vivacious, glittering New York of the consummate fling, celebrated in *Nothing Sacred* (1937) and *Living It Up* (1954). Even very recent films celebrate this archaic New York: in 2005, Peter Jackson's great ape Kong still finds passage to it, and Times Square is still radiant and magical, yellow cabs are like bees at a picnic, theatergoers are every one sophisticated, tenements in dark side streets glower with hope and loss.

A number of icons tend to symbolize this particular New York, this New York as crucible: the grand Empire State Building (from 1931), Times Square with its multicolored stuttering invocation of ebullience, carriage rides through Central Park at night, the curtain going up on a Broadway play, an opulent hotel lobby, as in *Grand Hotel* (1932) or even *Spellbound* (1945), some vast quivering desperate mass moving through the commuter hub of Grand Central or old Penn Station, as in Alfred Hitchcock's *North by Northwest* (1959) or Vincente Minnelli's *The Clock* (1945).

In a second screened New York, that of the 1960s, 1970s, and 1980s, earlier landmarks, styles, sensibilities, and perspectives are going or gone: the automat, the Stork Club (from *The Wrong Man* [1956]), old Madison Square Garden (from *The Manchurian Candidate* [1962]), the dingy, narrow cave of the old Metropolitan Opera. In a newly gentrified city, masterpieces of architecture, such as the Pan Am building that looms over Grand Central Station, came to boast crass indomitability, endless aspiration, cold technical proficiency, cold capitalist logic. This New York is a diurnal city, not a nocturnal one; a New York in which shadowy noir eventfulness is replaced by obsessively illuminated crime drama procedure and ravaging business zeal, monsters displaced by detectives and stock brokers. A film like *Scandal Sheet* (1952), written about here chillingly by Wheeler Winston Dixon, becomes *The Detective* (1968) or *Wall Street* (1987). *Gold Diggers of 1933* (1933) becomes *All That Jazz* (1979). Such comedies as *Barefoot in the Park* (1967), *Plaza Suite* (1971), and *Annie Hall* (1977) all echo, in one way or another, the sure-footedness of this urban culture in which the collision of moving particles, no longer exciting or amusing in and of itself, has become a mere background ether, against which a romance of fragmented relationships, typically involving highly conventionalized and systematized modes of telecommunication, is played out in tedious routine. *The Anderson Tapes* (1971) shows this, as do *The Taking of Pelham One Two Three* (1974), *Falling in Love* (1984), or *The Interpreter* (2005). Glamour is replaced by pressure.

In this particular New York, a serious New York, which is not a nostalgic New York but one of anticipation and calculation, a kind of teleological nightmare, old monuments may die a strange death. Take Times Square, for example. It was once a place where, Marshall Berman remembers, "we would go to the Paramount and the Palace theatres and Lindy's and Tofinetti's restaurants and the lobby and café of the Astor Hotel. Afterwards, we would hang around the streets and check out the people and the signs. . . . All those places and spaces were magical" ("Too

Much" 42). But now that the Police Department generally portrayed it as "the unsafest place in the city" and in press releases "actually advised people to stay away," the Square was transformed. Berman writes:

> Many old-timers felt, over the years, police presence on the spot receding, like an army occupation that was being surreptitiously withdrawn. In the spring of 1980, right in the middle of 42nd Street, around twilight, I saw a man come up behind another man with a club, and smash his head. . . . No uniform was in sight. I had to try three stores before somebody—a pornographic theatre, as it happened—let me use the phone to call 911. (58)

Monuments also die by falling into the background, becoming scenery. In *On the Town* (1949), discussed here by Scott Bukatman, the Empire State Building was celebrated as a kind of holy place; in *Hannah and Her Sisters* (1986), Woody Allen glides past characteristic locales, like the Little Church Around the Corner, with a zealous concentration on the faces of his protagonists, as though the New York they inhabit is *only* a place.

There is, lastly, a very contemporary New York which is all close-up experience and diffuse stress, a decadent New York to be sure but one in which the city as scape recedes into a dark and foreboding perimeter and our consciousness is focused instead on the facial expressions, fashionable clothing, witty talk, and psychological neuroses of people trying to get through the day in what seems an interminable and indefinable war. The confrontation of the Kittredges (Donald Sutherland, Stockard Channing) with Geoffrey Miller (Ian McKellen) from South Africa in *Six Degrees of Separation* (1993), for example, takes place in close-up and medium shot inside their red-velvet plush Upper East Side apartment, through the vast picture windows of which, far in the background and as nothing more than an intimation, we can dimly discern the black sea which is the city and the twinkles which are the signal of its life forms. In *Birth* (2004), we are locked inside a family, tormented by relationships and fears, proprieties and manners, except for the opening sequence as a jogger dies in Central Park; this place, just like the death, is soon swallowed in personalities, conflicts, and revelations that are all shown as *views from the inside*, not visions of the city at all. *Rosemary's Baby* (1968), written of here by Joe McElhaney and by Elisabeth Weis and Randy Thom, was in many ways one harbinger of this New York, a New York of anxieties more than spaces, psychological drives more than social vectors, a New York also nicely typified by *Marathon Man* (1976), where as Dr. Szell (Laurence Olivier) examines Babe Levy's (Dustin Hoffman) teeth all the skyscrapers and avenues and rivers and boroughs of the city seem to disappear in a frantic mist of personal agony. Another harbinger, to be sure, was the 1980s and 1990s work of Woody Allen (written about here by William Rothman), who used the city routinely as an arbitrary stage setting against which to pose the more significant drama of the personalities and faces that populate it. (His two principal designers, Mel Bourne and Santo Loquasto, both started working, indeed, on the stage.)

These three urban visions—nostalgic New York, serious New York, and anxious New York—constitute a set of nodes in the long progression of filmic treatments of a great, and very specific, urban world. Thus, New York is far from an isolated, fixed, and readily discernable entity, shape, form, or spirit. It has a kind of biography, and therefore a kind of heartbeat and even, perhaps, a lifespan, so that any filmic treatment of it becomes something of a portrait. A portrait of New York, however revealing, can have its own peculiarity. Consider Ben Younger's *Prime* (2005), a love story with complications, set, like hundreds of other lighthearted comedies, in New York City. The opening credits predictably enough show a collage of exceptionally typical Manhattan street scenes, not a single one of them revealing where the action of the story later occurs; and the story itself proceeds to bounce from apartment to apartment, shuttling across the East River and ensconcing itself in galleries, restaurants, lobbies, and upon sidewalks. But while everything we see in this unremarkable film is absolutely generic to New York—that is, while the film was shot in New York and while at every moment it feels like a New York of the imagination rather than any other place—it is true that at only three brief moments in the film—and these not dramatic highlights—is it possible to actually pinpoint a precise, actual New York (or New York area) location: once, when the protagonists walk away from a pick-up basketball game in Madison Square Park; once when, voyaging out to the Hamptons, they are discernably speeding down Route 111 toward the Montauk Highway; and once when they spy one another in Dean and Deluca on West Broadway. The rest of *Prime* could have been shot on a back lot for all of its attention to the details of location; and yet, somehow, the aura of New York manages to permeate everything we see.

I can think of no other city which can withstand this kind of abstract and universalizing view and still so powerfully remain itself onscreen. When the recognizable landmarks of Paris or London or Rome are elided, quite as intentionally as New York landmarks are in *Prime*, it is any city in France, any city in England, any city in Italy that we see. But there is no place *like* New York that is also not in fact New York. New York City, then, is a true personality of the silver screen, even more than a star. As there is no one so quintessentially Gable-like as Gable, no one so Garboesque as Garbo, no King Kong but King Kong, so nowhere but New York is New York. Because the City is a star in its own right, no study of it in film can be sufficient that treats it as nothing other than a setting or a location. New York participates actively in the films that show it. Cinematically, New York is alive.

An Outside View

New York is, of course, New Yorkers—those mingled masses among whom one finds a certain civic pride and also a conviction of having been given some special blessing by virtue of this rocky seaside place that is their home. The *New Yorker* ran a cover cartoon on March 7, 2005: Adam and Eve, naked and panicky, were stumbling across the Brooklyn Bridge away from Manhattan, with a great Godly hand in the sky sternly pointing them the way. This was surely a comment about skyrocketing Manhattan real estate values and the new yuppie exodus to the Arcadian quietudes of Brooklyn. And yet, the cartoon said more. There was no reason at all to suppose, looking at this static moment, that Adam and Eve would be stopping on the other side of the East River. Might they not have to wend their way all the way out the L.I.E., into Nassau, and then Suffolk Counties, and thence maybe by ferry into the upper reaches of Connecticut, even Massachusetts? For this image showed nothing if not an ultimate horror, banishment from New York for exile on the outside. And looking at it, suddenly, I could remember what I had long known, that for New Yorkers, the City is "in," indeed a kind of womb, and every other place in the world is beyond the pale. This, after all, was the meaning of that great Saul Steinberg *New Yorker* cover, too (March 29, 1976), in which, past Ninth and Tenth Avenues and the Hudson River (60 percent of the image) was . . . well, the world: New Jersey, Kansas City, Los Angeles, the Pacific, and then, in a thin strip way at the back, Japan, Russia, and China. In this sense, New York is not only America's biggest and most central city, it is America. New Yorkers are not merely its denizens: they are Americans, quintessentially.

But typically, New Yorkers do not possess a traveled and analytical view of their city. The New Yorker, far less than a visionary with an ideal point of view—whichever his view in life—lives on a block, and knows his neighborhood, not at all unlike Jeff Jefferies in *Rear Window* (1954) who surely, even when his legs are healed, doesn't scramble around so very much unless he's on assignment. Perhaps the New Yorker shops for vegetables in a tiny market that comes alight like a carnival at night—mine was once on West End Avenue just below Eighty-sixth Street. Perhaps he can be found, when he dines out, at favorite haunts, not fancy tourist lures hyped on the Food Network: in the "old" days, gulping moussaka at Molfetas Bros. on Forty-seventh Street West; inhaling rarebit at Elizabeth's across from the Public Library; nibbling mocha éclairs at Patisserie Lanciani on West Fourth Street; or ogling the fettuccine at Trattoria da Alfredo, with bowls of lemons sitting on the sideboard behind his shoulder. For celebration he might have gone to Luchow's or the Coach House or even, once in a rare, rare while, The Four Seasons. Before it moved, the New Yorker would have shopped for his reading at the Gotham Book Mart on West Forty-seventh Street, chatting with Frances Steloff in the old days or with Andy Brown or Phil Lyman later on; or perhaps would frequent—still frequents—the Strand on West Broadway for pristine remainders. For delicacies, Zabar's on Broadway, or else Murray the Sturgeon King. Every year the neighborhoods shift and grow, but also remain neighborhoods, which is precisely what they have seemingly always been. For the tourist, each moment in New York is, at least potentially, a sparkling treasure, an immensity of experience; for the New Yorker, there is a comforting mundanity to everyday life, a predictability and a delicious smallness. The deliciousness of the smallness, its familiarity, cannot be shown onscreen; onscreen everything is treasure, and every screen view of New York is therefore a view from the outside.

However, having adjusted to this perspective we might wonder how the City has figured, in fact, in various treatments onscreen.

Types of Rendition: "New York" on Film

Since on film, no less than in real life, New York has been a creature of many personalities and natures, no one system of typification suffices to grasp and hold it all. Something of the dense variety of film treatments of the city can be discerned if we think merely of different ways New York can function as a setting or principal element in a filmic exposition. This is not exactly a map of *City That Never Sleeps*, but it does depict something of a pretext for the kinds of approaches to be found here.

a. *New York as "actual" location*: The city has occasionally been a precise location for a precise story of and about New York, a story that could never be realized elsewhere any more than a tale of two people falling in love on the Eiffel Tower could be realized outside Paris. Take Francis Ford Coppola's *Life without Zoe* (1988), which is about a little girl who grows up in the Sherry-Netherland Hotel (at Fifty-ninth Street and Fifth Avenue) and frequently goes outside to play in her "yard," Central Park; or Spike Lee's *Do the Right Thing* (1989), set in Bedford-Stuyvesant (and addressed here by David Sterritt). For these films, New York is not only a good location, it is the only imaginable location, and no other city, no other atmosphere, will do. In this volume we find Peter Lehman and William Luhr writing about Blake Edwards's *Breakfast at Tiffany's*, another film which could not, at the time of its making (1961), have been set anywhere else because in that era-before-franchises Tiffany's *was* New York just as New York *was* Tiffany's. *Breakfast* was, I might say, an *Eloise* for grown-ups, with a pretty girl localized in respect to, and identified with, a vibrant New York landmark. David Desser's essay here shows that Walter Hill's *The Warriors* (1979) localizes the city in the same way, if not always with geographical accuracy. Robert Wise's *West Side Story* (1961), from the Broadway musical by Leonard Bernstein and Stephen Sondheim, is about gang rivalry on the West Side—of not just any city but specifically, and rhapsodically, New York; and although the play was adapted from Shakespeare's *Romeo and Juliet* the fact is that the adaptation is so authentically entrenched in Manhattan that no other location could have done for the film. Or we could consider Frank Perry's *Diary of a Mad Housewife* (1970), in which we follow the marital woes of Jonathan and Tina Balser (Richard Benjamin, Carrie Snodgress), a couple who could live nowhere but on Central Park West. The foibles, too, of Martin Scorsese's Jerry Langford (Jerry Lewis) in *The King of Comedy* (1983) could take place nowhere but in New York. Nor could Sidney Lumet's *A Stranger among Us* (1992), with Melanie Griffith as a New York cop infiltrating the Lubavitcher Hasidim of Brooklyn, work in any other environment. One could also include in this group Lumet's *Serpico* (1973) (written about here by Pamela Grace) and *Prince of the City* (1981), both films about police corruption in general, to be sure, but spelled out in fact as biographical reconstructions of actual New York Police Department cases which, for maximal verisimilitude, needed to be set in real locations. Such verisimilitude is also central to Scorsese's *Gangs of New York* (2002) and much of his *Goodfellas* (1990).

At this writing, the most universally known contemporary tragic vision of New York—the city as vulnerable target of terrorist bombing on September 11, 2001—has not substantially been addressed by popular film, but Oliver Stone's *World Trade Center*, with Nicolas Cage, manifests the director's struggle to replicate as closely as possible the visions that were broadcast at the time in news transmissions that often made use of footage shot by amateurs with video or cell cameras on the scene. One startling effect is the audience's placement inside the Trade Center as the building comes down all around, a standard convention of disaster film, to be sure, yet one with an additional, and profound, frisson because of the shock of the event itself. New York as a mythical city was titanic; it seemed untouchable, indomitable—just as Mayor Rudy Giuliani promised it would turn out to be. This particular actual New York, it is interesting to note, is, at least as a vision, very widely shared; New York belongs to—is inhabited by—all those who felt the pain of the attack, all those who with Barry Pepper and Philip Seymour Hoffman stare out a window in Spike Lee's *25th Hour*, looking down in horror and emptiness at the dark site where the proud towers used to stand.

b. *New York by affiliation:*   In some films, however, New York provides a pungent backdrop for characters who gain an edge of personality and a charming idiosyncrasy by being identified as New Yorkers, when the details of the story really do not necessitate shooting in New York and when the characters could as well come from somewhere else without their tale being shifted in any essential way. "New York" is thus a kind of costume, a spice, an icing that decorates the cake of the diegesis. Take that central duo, Flan and Ouisa in *Six Degrees of Separation*, nouveau riche, connected with the art world, the parents of children who go to private school in New England, and involved with a young man who spends considerable time in the nearby Park and is connected with the film star Sidney Poitier. They could live in Boston or Chicago or, for that matter, London. What is added to this story by the view of New York at night from the windows of their apartment, by the setting of a homosexual encounter in a horse-drawn hack in Central Park, and by the flamboyant Upper East Side characters drawn by Sutherland and Channing is a thrilling élan, a sense of being on the cusp of a turn in great fortunes, exactly the kind of sophisticated and middle-class kick the Kittredges are themselves searching after in every aspect of their lives and that we have taken to be a hallmark of, as I called it, "anxious New York." Perhaps the Kittredges typify a new population of New Yorkers, anxious in their anxious city exactly because they must strain as strangers to navigate their every move there. But if these two are *arrivistes*, they have, indeed, arrived: the veneer with which they seem to be coated reeks of what we would call "New Yorkishness." Setting the film in New York allows us to feel that we have become the Kittredges, then— that, also strangers, we are inside their experience since (perhaps like them, but even more directly) we are so affected by the glitter the setting provides. It gives us a nice narrative angle, but it does not permit that the Kittredge story be recounted more thoroughly than it otherwise might have been. Or consider a light comedy like Michael Hoffman's *One Fine Day* (1996), the vapid plot of which is summarized on the Internet Movie Database, accurately, like this:

> Melanie Parker, an architect and mother of Sammy, and Jack Taylor, a news-paper columnist and father of Maggie, are both divorced. They meet one morning when overwhelmed Jack is left unexpectedly with Maggie and for-gets that Melanie was to take her to school. As a result, both children miss their school field trip and are stuck with the parents.

Set in New York, this film gains a certain tense and bubbly energy, a contemporaneity, an extreme urbanity, and a directness because these qualities, typically associated with New York at least onscreen, are transferred to the characterizations by Michelle Pfeiffer and George Clooney. But a dozen other cities would have worked as well, and New York has no special role to play on the screen.

c. *New York as "cultural spirit"*:   Beyond generic New York films and decorative New York films, there are films in which the story that is told is not factually based on events that occurred, or must be seen to occur, in New York but where, still, the story points up some aspect of a social tendency or a cultural spirit that is endemic to New York in some special way. Wherever the story takes place, it's a New York story, whether or not the camera explicitly says so, and filming against a different recognizable backdrop might impair the telling. Scorsese's *Mean Streets* (1973), a generic New York film, has to be shot in Little Italy: but his *Goodfellas* is about criminal conspiracy (the Mafia) more generally, and its economic relation to the urban economy. Baltimore or Philadelphia could also have worked, and so might Chicago, but something cozy, protective, neighborly, knowledgeable, tough-minded, and yet gentle-hearted is added to the story and the characterizations by setting them all in New York. Much the same can be said for many other crime films. It would seem these "falsely authentic" New York tales,

tales that are not explicitly about New York life but somehow reflect upon some received and imaginary New York that we possess and are enriched for us in this reflection, borrow not so much from the reality of New York City as from the screen image of New York that has become conventionalized in our culture. Cops on the take, cops on the make, cops who don't give up no matter what the obstructions; millionaires in penthouses, millionaires with lavish taste, millionaires who aren't satisfied no matter what the developments; streetwise, canny, witty, philosophical workers; bustling traffic; resigned and philosophical cab drivers; an economy where everyone is dealing for everything all of the time; a topography of neon and speed, of false fronts and high hopes—all this can be found in New York, to be sure; but not only in New York. Yet we have come to accept it all as being the character of the city, and the "cultural spirit" New York film plays up this character, borrowing it again and again and accentuating it differently every time. Very typical of such presentations are *Bright Lights, Big City* (1988) and *The Bonfire of the Vanities* (1990), which are absolutely big-city dramas, but not necessarily New York ones. More recently, we have *The Devil Wears Prada* (2006).

   d. *"Imaginary" New York*:   A city of extremes, New York has become, in the cultural imagination, the quintessence of a certain kind of topos, which I would hardly describe as the city of the future (that is Los Angeles, even given the bleak, spectacular vision of that place we are afforded by Mike Davis) but which is either the City Engine in which America was made, the American Metropolis— that Metropolis being a nexus of both energy and style, of both tenacity and groundedness and desire—or else the City Playground in which languages, vectors, motivations, and impulses travel against one another and collide. New York as Metropolis is a static and monolithic place, a place of steam and grime, of metal and concrete, of shadow and determination, of ethnicity and hunger and fleeting glory. New York as Playground is vibrant and electronic, a place of signals and heartbeats, furtive glances and brief contacts, flashes of light and confusion. Monolithic New York is *Citizen Kane* (1941) and *The Thin Man* (1934), *The Hudsucker Proxy* (1994) and *The Big Clock*, *The World, the Flesh* and *the Devil* (1959) and *Vanilla Sky* (2001). Electronic New York is *Spider-Man* (2002; 2004) and *Taxi Driver* (1976), *The Fifth Element* (1995) and *Just Imagine* (1930), *The Clock* and *New York, New York* (1977). What makes the New York of these films "imaginary" is some use of the lens or the writer's pen—the wide-angle views in *Kane*; the cartoony plasticity in *Spider-Man*; the effortless and magical continuity of feeling in *The Clock*.

   e. *"Transplanted" New York*:   There are also what might be thought to be "New Yorker" films (rather than New Yorker films), since they need not take place in or anywhere near New York but are centered nevertheless upon the traces of the New York experience as embedded now in the personality and performance of a type who could come, *as we imagine him*, only from New York. Some of these personifications have been embedded, in fact, in particular performers—Robert De Niro, Billy Crystal, Woody Allen, Maureen Stapleton, Zero Mostel, Gene Wilder, Bette Midler, James Caan, Harvey Keitel, Al Pacino, Ethel Merman, Walter Matthau—and some have been performed by outsiders who gain some truth in, but only in, the characterizations. Of the latter, excellent examples are Johnny Depp's performance in *Donnie Brasco* (1995), Sean Connery's in *The Anderson Tapes*, Michael Douglas's in *Wall Street*, and Faye Dunaway's in *The Eyes of Laura Mars* (1978). In "New Yorker" films, characters seem to have been transplanted from real New York with the original pavement still burning their feet. *My Dinner with Andre* (1981) qualifies fully as a "transplanted" film, since for almost its entire duration we are sitting in rather close focus in a secluded restaurant (that might be anywhere) watching two men have dinner; and yet the two men, Wallace Shawn and Andre Gregory, are absolute epitomes of the Manhattanite: urbane, sophisticated, personable, polite, warm, and utterly of the world of their own memory and experience. At the end, we are reminded that we *are in* New York, have never been anywhere else: Shawn speeds in a cab down Fifth Avenue under the credits, the locations of his boyhood sweetly, glimmeringly passing him by. In New York, the past both lingers and dissolves, leaving its traces on the human spirit. During the film, however, we were guided by these New York personalities to a completely different space. The "New York" personality often shows up in a World War II combat film platoon, or in the population of an airliner, ship, skyscraper, or planet bound for destruction in a disaster film. See, for example, Judd Hirsch in *Independence Day* (1996) or Robert Carradine in *The Big Red One* (1980). And often, the New York personality is transplanted to Hollywood (as, in the early 1930s with sound film coming in, it actually was): John Turturro in *Barton Fink* (1991); Jean Hagen, whining "I can't stand 'im!" in Brooklynese in *Singin' in the Rain* (1952).

f. *New York as "asylum"*:   In a number of films, such as Rob Reiner's *Rumor Has It . . .* (2005), Wes Anderson's *The Royal Tenenbaums* (2001), or Barry Sonnenfeld's *Men in Black* (1997), New York is configured as a kind of asylum or nest, in which a concatenation of truly bizarre human or non-human types reside in cozy familiarity and complete adaptation. Indeed, so weird are the types that no place outside of New York is imaginable as a repository for them. Such films work upon New York's longstanding attraction for strangers (its being home to the Statue of Liberty, for example) to play up a conceit that New York is a magnet for the desperate, the bizarre, the unshapely, the gargantuan—all those unmeasurable forms of the spirit that don't fit everyday civilization; that New York is the berthing place for the great Narrenschiff of the imagination. Not only immigration, then, but insanity and borderline personality; not only insanity but artistic excess and marginality are imagined to be at home here, and at home in a way that no other place could make possible. *Men in Black* makes a joke of this. The lunatic passion we see in Fred Coe's *A Thousand Clowns* (1965), the eccentricity that riddles

Ghost Busters (1984), the ferocity and extremity of both anguish and control we find in *Marathon Man*, the zeal we see in *Tootsie*, the disconnected weirdness that populates *They Might Be Giants* (1971)—all these qualities, outrageous or socially problematic in the light of both classically Eastern (European) and classically Western models, are somehow normalized in New York. Imagine Sidney Falco (Tony Curtis) or J. J. Hunsecker (Burt Lancaster) peopling *Sweet Smell of Success* (1957) in Indianapolis, Portland, Detroit, St. Louis! Even the typical Borscht Belt comedian, a staple of New York, is unthinkable in another setting, as we clearly see watching the gag men schmoozing and nibbling in the back room of the Carnegie Delicatessen in Woody Allen's *Broadway Danny Rose* (1984).

g. *"Magnificent" New York:*   And then there are films that celebrate New York as a borderless testament to power, privilege, and perspective, in which we see grandiosity, munificence, brilliant illumination, enormous height: New York as a work of art. The concluding sequences from *King Kong* surely illustrate this particular New York, as do virtually all the paeans of Woody Allen but most spectacularly the opening credit scenes of *Manhattan* and the Upper West Side apartment inhabited by Maureen O'Sullivan in *Hannah and Her Sisters*. Magnificent New York is Fred Astaire's Plaza Suite in *The Band Wagon*, Roger O. Thornhill's cocktail experience at the Oak Bar in *North by Northwest*, Rosemary's apartment in The Dakota (fictionalized as The Bramford) in *Rosemary's Baby*.

These essays are statements from a number of scholars of the cinema, people, it must be said, who work from various analytical perspectives and in various traditions, and who are thinking at the same time of what it means to see New York in film. The essays acknowledge the range of approaches to New York as both a situation and an experience that have been taken by the filmmakers most known as celebrants of the city and its peculiar life. While a far more exhaustive compendium of such filmmaking stances can be found in James Sanders's *Celluloid Skyline*, something of a catalogue raisonnée of New York filmmaking, that book is less variant in its treatment, and also less meditative in many ways, than what readers will find here; it starts with New York as a social history, and proceeds thence to the screen, moving in a direction this book explicitly reverses. Blake's *Street Smart*, a recent volume, treats Lumet, Allen, Scorsese, and Lee, although not, to be sure, with the perspectives one will find here, where our cultural differences as authors will permit us more motion, in a way, and thus allow us to achieve a meditation that is, I think, in tune with its subject.

The essays in this book are something like neighborhoods themselves, each exploring a territory that is exceptionally significant for the author and yet far less, in every dimension, than the totality that is New York. As every New Yorker must fail spectacularly to appreciate the whole of New York, so every author here makes only a bounded contribution to a project that could have gone in thousands of other directions. What is not here, then, is surely as interesting as what is. *King Kong* (1933) is not written about in these pages, although its great ape is an icon of Hollywood's vision of New York. The obsessive personality that we can see in *A Thousand Clowns*, the canyons of capitalism that so stagger the imagination in *Spider-Man* or *Godzilla* (1998), the frenzied New York of either version of *The Manchurian Candidate*, the seamy just-beyond-New-York of *On the Waterfront* (1954), the dangerous jungle of *Donnie Brasco*, the eroding distant pinnacles of *The Naked City* (1948), the caricatures to be found in *The Seven Year Itch* or *Artists and Models* (both 1955), the cloistered velvet caverns of *Holiday* (1938), the colorful hovels of *Bells Are Ringing* (1960), the charged financial environment of *The Solid Gold Cadillac* (1956), the bouncy coteries of *The Thin Man*, the nervosity of *The Anderson Tapes*, the jiving pulsions of *Tootsie* or *Three Days of the Condor* (1975)—all this and more is absent here. There is no *Fountainhead*, no *Hudsucker Proxy*, no *Marathon Man*, no *Odd Couple* (1968).

Indeed, if the real geographical space of New York sits in the five boroughs, chiseled into the granite island and its surround; if it stretches out to Paumanok Shores and gapes over to New Jersey; if it dreams northward to Westchester and Bear Mountain or southward into the sea; still in all this it is bounded and therefore, ultimately through some rhetoric and method, comprehensible. But the New York of the screen is another thing, drifting and evanescing, shifting in a myriad directions without cease. There are so many films about New York one could never hope to see them all, let alone capture them. And perhaps each one of these is so redolent and powerful even to grasp it takes us on a journey without limit and without measurement.

The hope is that these essays will stimulate us to gaze at that New York of the screen more intentfully, more hungrily. And that they will enrich our understanding of film generally, just as they open to us a New York we may well not have known. Regardless, they will show how New York really does exist on the screen in an utterly primary way, and how in watching its constant reilluminations we might find our way, curiously, home.

MEMORY ALL ALONE IN THE MOONLIGHT
City of Experience

New York onscreen is a locus of special, exhilarating, transcendent, oneiric experience. Here, the world is reduced to a galvanizing glow of black and white, while fireworks seem to explode irrepressibly into the heavens, as in *Manhattan*. Here, strangers meet and lives are profoundly changed, as in *Rosemary's Baby* or *The King of Comedy*. Here one is made increasingly sensitive to the sounds and sights of daily life, because the lights are so much brighter; because eventfulness seems to be exploding continuously all around, as we see in Robert Walker's initial reaction to seeing the crowds at Penn Station in *The Clock*.

To begin this section on New York as a City of Experience, Peter Lehman and William Luhr's "I Love New York!" is a rhapsody on Blake Edwards's *Breakfast at Tiffany's*, beautifully showing how this testament to an ultimate urban landmark, to a certain view of the city as home to the sophisticated and the always climbing, also functions to reveal the emotional bankruptcy of a vast metropolis in the face of human vulnerability. Holly Golightly's adventures in the wonderland of midtown reflect a past in an altogether different kind of world, a strangeness and hollow loneliness which are articulated in the director's artful staging of a key encounter in the empty bandshell area of Central Park, at a time when the bustling throng has been evacuated and there remains nothing but the shell of a place for social experience. For Edwards, New York is both "a chic center of cosmopolitan style, energy, exuberance, and attractive nonconformist behavior" and a setting for "menacing suspense." Holly's salvation here lies essentially in getting away from the crowd.

Scott Bukatman offers a meticulous and passionate analysis of two quite different filmic treatments in "A Day in New York," both of which try to answer the question of what can happen to you in just one day in this energetic city. Against a rich backdrop of musical treatments, in which "the opportunities that New York presents are stylistically marked by daring perceptual transformations" and "the stars who sing and dance are figures of sublime agency," Gene Kelly and Stanley Donen's *On the Town* is seen as a disappointing dilution of a taut and elegiac Broadway musical. With simpler, "stupider" songs, this tale of three sailors on shore leave in the city had to be "de-newyorkicized" to play to the vast audience Hollywood demanded. Gone is a sense of recognition among the characters, who in the Broadway version were lost in the urban jungle yet excited by the aromas of strangeness everywhere. Onscreen they became people who don't know each other: "their sense of blissful communion need never be tested against the gritty practical reality of sustained love." By contrast, Vincente Minnelli's *The Clock* is a poetic statement of love and imminency measured against the boy's need to depart (for the war) and played out to a climax in the pressure-chamber of state bureaucracy which is mitigating against the lovers' need to quickly wed.

And in "Paradise Lost and Found: A Bronx Tale," Barry Keith Grant reminisces about the 1950s movie theaters of the Bronx where he grew up and where some of his filmgoing sensibilities were grounded, especially in films such as *The Beast from 20,000 Fathoms*. A particular tabernacle of filmgoing here was the Paradise, a Loew's flagship theater "that stood apart as the grandest of them all." In his essay, Grant fuses a careful historiographical concern for 1950s exhibition venues and a keen appreciation of films shown in, or telling stories of, the Bronx to his memory of what life in the Bronx actually was when he was learning to love film. Seeing DeMille's *The Ten Commandments* (1956) at the Paradise, for instance, produced a profound impression on Grant: "I was thunderstruck not only by the epic sweep of the movie but also by the magnificent opulence of the theater (like the monumental pyramids that Ramses constructs within the film). [The Paradise] was one of those 'emporiums to the illusive God of movies,' and somehow I understood it to represent for better or worse what movies (at least Hollywood movies) were all about."

A mysterious stranger (Buddy Ebsen, r.) meekly solicits the help of a New Yorker
(George Peppard) in *Breakfast at Tiffany's* (Blake Edwards, Paramount, 1961). Digital
frame enlargement.

"I Love New York!"

BREAKFAST AT TIFFANY'S

PETER LEHMAN AND WILLIAM LUHR

Since its debut in 1961, Blake Edwards's *Breakfast at Tiffany's* has been considered one of the preeminent films celebrating New York City. Its first image of Audrey Hepburn as the elegantly dressed Holly Golightly standing at dawn before Tiffany's on Fifth Avenue defines carefree New York sophistication for many. In acknowledgment of this, one Manhattan cinema, The Screening Room, showed the film every Sunday for the run of its existence from July 1996 through October 2003.

On one level, it is odd that this, among the thousands of films that have been set there, has achieved the "New York City film" status it holds. It does not focus on the internationally recognized, iconic sights most associated with the city in 1961, like the Statue of Liberty, the Empire State Building, the United Nations, Lower East Side tenements, the George Washington or the Brooklyn Bridge, or the arch in Washington Square Park. Neither Edwards nor the film's stars, Hepburn and George Peppard, are figures whose careers are particularly associated with New York City. Until the film appeared, Tiffany's jewelry store never had the tourist attraction status it has held since.[1] The film's hugely popular, Academy Award–winning song, Henry Mancini's "Moon River," has nothing whatsoever to do with New York City and, indeed, invokes a rural rather than an urban landscape.

One aspect of the film that helps to account for its New York identity involves its celebration of the city as a place to which people who are unhappy with their lives come to reinvent themselves, a place where dreams come true. This element of fantasy is evident in both the film's title and its opening sequence. As the film opens, Holly arrives at Tiffany's alone at dawn with a bag of take-out coffee and a cruller and quietly, reverently, peers into its windows. Tiffany's is an expensive jewelry store. One cannot have breakfast there (although reportedly even now, nearly half a century after the film appeared, the store still gets requests for breakfast reservations). For Holly, this impromptu breakfast is the perfect way to end, or begin, a day. As she looks at the jewelry she would love to be able to afford, she herself looks like the wealthy, elegant socialite that she dreams of becoming. It is all fantasy, of course, but during the times when the central characters feel they are on the verge of fulfilling their fantasies, the film represents their joy by having them take exuberant pleasure in the city itself.

At one such point, Paul Varjak (Peppard) receives a fifty-dollar check from a literary magazine, verifying that it will publish one of his short stories. Although he had published a respected short story collection some years earlier and maintains literary aspirations, he has written nothing since then and has been living as the "kept man" of a wealthy society matron (Patricia Neal). This check signifies a new, respectable life for him and he asks his neighbor Holly to celebrate with him. She suggests that they spend the day doing things they have never done before. In keeping with the film's vision of New York City, this instantly translates into spending the day enjoying Fifth Avenue. They wander into the New York Public Library, a five-and-ten-cent store, and Tiffany's itself, having a carefree, almost childlike time. Later in the film when, due to her involvement with a rich suitor, Holly is about to leave New York for Brazil, she and Paul again go out to celebrate. As they sit near a small fountain, she talks of her plans to return in years to come, exuberantly bursting out, "Oh, I love New York!"

Holly has also come to New York to reinvent herself. At thirteen, as Lulamae Barnes, she married Doc Golightly, a much older horse doctor in rural Tulip, Texas, in order to provide for herself and her mentally disadvantaged brother. After the brother joined the army and no longer needed her support, she fled her backwoods life, and eventually earned her living in Manhattan as a social escort for wealthy men (which the film can only imply, in accordance with the production code of the times, involves prostitution) and as a naive courier for a gangster. Her unapologetic goal is to become an urban sophisticate and marry a rich man, thereby assuring security for herself and her brother.

New York has long been seen as "The Big Time" in Broadway Theater, Wall Street finance, fashion, and sports. As the song "New York, New York" would later brag, "If I can make it there, I'll make it anywhere." It is a city to which people from all over the country come to seek success, and this partly accounts for its image as a place to which out-of-towners come to reinvent themselves. An old cliché about the city is that the quintessential New Yorkers come from out of town. Novelist F. Scott Fitzgerald, although raised in St. Paul, Minnesota, was well known as a dashing New York sophisticate in the Roaring Twenties. Joe Namath, from Beaver Falls, Pennsylvania, is forever remembered as "Broadway Joe." Truman Capote, the author of the novella upon which *Breakfast at Tiffany's* is based, was from New Orleans but became widely considered a classic New Yorker. Andy Warhol, from Pittsburgh, Pennsylvania, became by the time of his death an iconic New York personality. And Yankee Stadium is still called "the house that Ruth built," though the Babe was born in Baltimore.

The film's image of New York City as a glamorous magnet for people who reinvent themselves and find success draws upon relatively recent (post-eighteenth century) presumptions, ones in which rootlessness can be seen as a valuable and not a pathetic thing. Traditionally, social prestige in cities such as Paris or Vienna was associated with the land-based aristocracy, a long family line, and the continuity of one's name. Within such social contexts, people like Holly who change their names or the place with which they identify (like Warhol, Capote, or Fitzgerald) would have been disdained as parvenus. In the New York of this film, however, the fact that Holly and Paul trade upon their youth and style and are not instantly rendered contemptible for doing so is indicative of changing social assumptions and of New York City in the mid-twentieth century as embodying those changes. And in contrast, the film presents Holly's former husband, Doc Golightly (Buddy Ebsen), a man of roots and a firm, established identity, as pathetic; his era is over.

Holly's and Paul's self-reinventions do, however, involve moral compromise since both trade upon their youth and sexual attractiveness to survive. The film portrays New York City as a place where "such things happen" but, in contrast to many earlier films dealing with transgressors against mainstream morality, it does not adopt a posture of censure toward Holly and Paul. Furthermore, it presents New York City itself as providing a tolerant environment in which they can work out their problems because they do not stick out there as they would in Baltimore or Tulip, Texas. New York's demimonde culture accommodates them; there are others like them.

The film presents their bohemian behavior as a transient stage from which they can emerge without taint or permanent damage. Its ending indicates that they will survive because they have abandoned their compromised lifestyle for a middle-class one. Paul leaves his rich benefactress, begins publishing his fiction again, and gets a job. When Holly's role as a gangster's courier is exposed, the ensuing, highly publicized scandal dooms her career as a social escort as well as her hopes for a quick marriage to a fabulously wealthy man. In addition, her recent trauma of learning about the accidental death of her brother makes her receptive to the value of Paul's love for her, and the film ends with them in a romantic embrace, in an alley far removed from the glitz and glamour of Fifth Avenue.

The narrative trajectory of the film, by which the central couple abandons a demimondaine lifestyle and adopts middle-class values, rescues them from any negative consequences for their traditionally perceived immoral behavior. A Hollywood agent's (Martin Balsam) endearing description of her as "a phony, but a real phony" implies that Holly's wacky, screwball behavior is something that is naively natural to her rather than an indication of fundamental immorality.

The film uses such strategies as the couple's adoption of middle-class values and the emphasis on Holly's naivete to insulate from viewer condemnation the potentially censorable aspects of Holly's behavior, such as prostitution. Furthermore, such behavior is ultimately overwhelmed by the film's jubilation in the joys of chic New York-style sexual attractiveness, fine clothes, youthful exuberance, amoral behavior, and a demimondaine lifestyle. This is highlighted by the pathetic figure of Doc Golightly. He comes to New York to retrieve Holly; she claims their marriage was annulled years ago and that he simply cannot accept this fact. Doc appears to be a decent man who knows that the much younger Holly married him only for protection of herself and her brother. He is neither angry nor bitter but rather a lost soul seeking to reestablish a relationship whose failure he cannot comprehend. In another movie he might be a highly sympathetic character, but in this one his shabby, unfashionable suit, battered fedora, and shambling presence, when contrasted with Holly's designer clothes and Paul's expensive suits, as well as the buoyant youth and attractiveness of those characters, render Doc hopelessly passé, a relic not only of a world gone by but also of a world that, even now, is alien to the lifestyle of urban sophisticates. The right or wrong of his claim simply does not matter. While the film represents this lonely, rustic man with compassion, it also represents him as irrelevant to New York City, and does not lament his sad, lonely departure.

The latitude that the film allows for the morally questionable behavior of Holly and Paul is indicative of major changes in the film industry at the time. In 1961 the Hollywood studio system was in a state of precipitous decline and censorship controls over mainstream films were dramatically loosening. Considerable press coverage was given to numerous films that challenged traditional censorship boundaries as well as to the fact that those films were becoming widely available to and attended by mainstream audiences. A year earlier, the fact that *The World of Suzie Wong* was categorized as a "prostitute with a heart of gold movie" did not prevent it from premiering at Radio City Music Hall, New York's prestigious showcase for family entertainment. (*Breakfast at Tiffany's* would premiere there a year later.) A U.S. Roman Catholic Bishops committee issued a report decrying the moral decline of contemporary Hollywood movies and, in response, industry spokespeople issued a rejoinder claiming that mainstream cultural values were dynamic and ever-changing, and that many controversial films were based upon prestigious literary works (see Hill). Some controversial films of 1961 included *The Children's Hour*, dealing with accusations of lesbianism; *Splendor in the Grass*, concerning teenage sexuality; *Back Street*, depicting long-term adultery; *Town Without Pity*, depicting a rape trial; and *By Love Possessed*, presenting adultery in a sympathetic light.

In *By Love Possessed*, for example, a respectable Massachusetts attorney (Efrem Zimbalist Jr.) has an affair with his partner's wife (Lana Turner). In the end, both return to their spouses and the film indicates that the affair has rejuvenated and not harmed their marriages. The happy ending and lack of censure for the couple's behavior was a clear violation of Hollywood's Production Code, but the traditions of classical Hollywood as well as its Code were crumbling at the time, making films like this and *Breakfast at Tiffany's* possible.

The 1961 context points to another important aspect of *Breakfast at Tiffany's* that has much less to do with Hollywood and the Production Code than with U.S. capitalism. To refer to Tiffany's in 2007 is both literally and connotatively a different thing than it was in 1961. In 1961 prestigious shops and restaurants were exclusively one-of-a-kind places; to go to Tiffany's meant to go to New York City and glamorous Fifth Avenue. Today, however, it might mean going to one of the Tiffany's franchise stores such as the one in Los Angeles on Rodeo Drive or the one in Scottsdale, Arizona. Comparably, the days of having to travel to Manhattan to visit Sak's Fifth Avenue are long gone.

By definition then, in 1961 *Breakfast at Tiffany's* invoked a quintessential New York experience in ways that many today might either have forgotten about or never have known in the first place. Tiffany's was exclusive not only in the sense of economic class (only the wealthy could afford to shop there) but also in the geographic sense: it was exclusive to New York. Other exclusive New York locations in the film are Fifth Avenue itself and the Central Park band shell. A look at the film's use of these locations reveals much about the film and its representation of the city in which it is exclusively set, exclusively in yet another sense of the word: every scene with the exception of Holly's visit to a nearby New York State prison takes place in the city.

We have already remarked upon the film's use of Fifth Avenue. It becomes a virtual synecdoche for the entire city of New York: ranging from Tiffany's to the Fifth Avenue Branch of the New York Public Library. Within the limited class context of this film, that represents the "full" spectrum, since poverty and ghettos are entirely repressed: the New York City celebrated in this film is one of jubilance and vitality, a place where true unemployment and poverty, with its racial dimension (as opposed to the fashionably attractive white "poverty" of social escorts and struggling writers), have "no place."

Within this notion of New York City and the centrality of Fifth Avenue, the film's use of the Central Park band shell raises a profound insight into modern urban life. The scene in question breaks markedly in tone with the rest of the film. Looking out of his apartment window, Paul spots a mysterious man who he fears is a detective hired by the husband of his "benefactress." Determined to uncover the man's identity, he leaves the apartment and walks toward Central Park to see if the man will follow him. The man does, and the ensuing sequence is one not of romantic comedy or romance but of mystery and ominous danger. The ominous music, the editing (with Paul repeatedly checking to see if the mysterious man is following him), the emotionally intense acting, and the narrative ambiguity combine to make the scene consistent in tone with a mystery thriller. Paul stops before the empty band shell to confront the ominous stranger, only to be surprised when the man comes up to him and meekly solicits his help. He reveals that he is Holly's husband, Doc Golightly, and has come to claim her. A painfully intimate scene ensues as Doc pathetically tells his story of having been abandoned by Lulamae and of his yearning to have her back.

This simple figure from the rural Southwest is clearly out of place in New York City, and the empty band shell amplifies his isolation. Why doesn't Paul confront Doc on the street when it becomes evident that he is being followed? Or in Central Park with its trees and many visitors? Why a band shell? And why one that is entirely empty? Not a soul is in sight as Doc and Paul talk.

The poignant scene derives much of its intensity from this unusual setting. Central Park is normally thought of as *the* outdoors gathering spot for New Yorkers to enjoy nature, relax, socialize, listen to concerts and plays, go to the zoo, and savor an ice cream cone—in short, to have a good time. The band shell in particular points to the social dimension of the park. Edwards creates the equivalent of a visual oxymoron here. The palpable absence of a band or any spectators becomes an uncanny presence within which unfolds the intense personal drama of this man who does not belong here. Devoid of the music that we should be hearing and the appreciative audience that we should be seeing, this empty space magnifies the sadness of the intimate drama that takes place in it.

While this event suggests something of the fascination that the Central Park setting supplies when a private event unfolds there, the film's variation points to a related though different dynamic. What if the public that should be having a good time is absent, not just physically and momentarily, but in a deeper, more emblematic way? What if, for the moment, the public space is abandoned—a mere shell of its designated social function? What if New York as a thriving model of social vitality is suddenly erased? Then the private drama unfolds amidst an eerie absence.[2]

After the explosion in urban populations following the Industrial Revolution, urban designers, attempting to compensate for the potentially isolating and alienating fragmentation of modern urban life, designed natural sites like Central Park into cities so that people might seek solace from and alleviate the cramped pressures of modern life. In earlier times, grand spaces such as Versailles tended to be accessible only to the privileged, but the democratic imperatives of the Enlightenment laid the groundwork for allowing all classes to avail themselves of such recreational spaces. This also extended to grand public buildings such as museums. In addition, sites like Central Park incorporate spaces particularly designed for diverse forms of public recreation, such as baseball fields, walking paths, lakes designed for boating, children's playgrounds, and the band shell. Holly intuitively grasps this aspect of modern urban life and takes gleeful pleasure in the wholly public space of Fifth Avenue, which includes places for the wealthy like Tiffany's, places for people of lower income like the five-and-ten-cent store, and monumental buildings like the Forty-second Street Branch of the New York Public Library, all of which are fully available to the public.

Although the city can bring joy, it can also bring desolation. *Breakfast at Tiffany's* appeared at a time when many had a profound concern about the dangers of alienation in modern life, regardless of population density or plenitude, a concern underscored by recently published books such as David Riesman's *The Lonely Crowd* and William H. Whyte's *The Organization Man*. Things like Central Park and band shells were designed to provide antidotes for modern urban alienation and pressures, but what if those antidotes might fail? What if the band shell has no band, no music, no audience? Then it all becomes revealing of the failure of modern life, of a dream gone wrong. At this point in the film, Doc's life has failed. Paul and Holly are also headed for failure but they don't know it yet. In *Breakfast at Tiffany's*, however, these places of communal celebration become the sites of intensely private moments in which something gone wrong plays itself out in deathly silence where once the roar of the crowd and the music of the band were heard. Despite the exclamation, "I love New York," then, at the center of *Breakfast at Tiffany's* is an ominous silence that suggests that all is not well in the metropolis the film celebrates. Indeed, the apartment house in which Paul and Holly live contrasts with the deserted band shell just a short walk away. People as diverse as Paul, his "benefactress," Holly, and their neighbor Yunioshi all gather in this apparently vibrant place. Even the offensive racial stereotyping of Yunioshi and his relationship with Holly points to such interaction, and an examination of it sheds light on Edwards's conception of New York.

Much has quite rightly been made of the buffoonish Asian character, Mr. Yunioshi, with his exaggerated slanted eyes, buck teeth, extreme accent, and sexual perversity. The stereotype is so offensive that George Axelrod, who wrote the screenplay based on Capote's novel, has continually stated that it was Edwards who created and added the character of Yunioshi, which Edwards has confirmed. Indeed, one dimension of the offensive stereotype is that a white actor, Mickey Rooney, plays Yunioshi. Right down to the casting, everything about Yunioshi points to Edwards.

What can account for this offensive portrayal of Yunioshi? Edwards typically interjects some elements of physical comedy into his films, and Yunioshi and the party scene, discussed below, clearly fit that pattern. But they both also contribute strongly to how the film shapes its representation of New York City. Yunioshi is marked as exotically other in that his clothing and apartment style are all Japanese, right down to his kimono and hanging lamp with a rice-paper shade. As such he is simultaneously a sign of "otherness" and also of New York as "melting pot"; he lives in the same apartment house as Holly and Paul. The racism in the film at one and the same time celebrates his otherness and mocks it—he is part of the film's sadly limited notion of "diversity" in New York and ridiculed for that very diversity.

It is instructive to briefly compare him with José da Silva Pereira (Vilallonga), the rich South American businessman whom Holly almost marries. Unlike Yunioshi,

Silva Pereira does not live in New York but, more to the point, he dresses and behaves in a manner that is entirely both European and American in style. Cultural and physical difference is thus minimized and his presence in New York just marks the city as very cosmopolitan. His wealth also makes him a perfect fit for the chic aspect of New York that the film celebrates. Compare this with the representation of race and ethnicity in *West Side Story*, also released in 1961. *Breakfast at Tiffany's* concentrates on the chic and wealthy, while *West Side Story* focuses just as exclusively on poor ethnic neighborhoods with gang violence. *West Side Story* is a modern-day retelling of the Romeo and Juliet story, with the rivalries taking place between two gangs, the Jets composed of the children of previous generations of European immigrants and the Sharks composed of first-generation Puerto Rican immigrants from a U.S. territory. Its emphasis on immigrants is far different from that in *Breakfast at Tiffany's*. It acknowledges patterns of immigration as a major influence on the city, defining entire neighborhoods by ethnicity and acknowledging the racial tensions and disturbances among such neighborhoods. Even though Japanese immigrants were not perceived as a major social or cultural problem in early 1960s New York, Edwards does not even place Yunioshi within a larger context of Japanese Americans living in New York. He is an isolated buffoon who seems to signify that New York City is a melting pot, but this racist representation is in part premised upon the repression of racial and ethnic neighborhoods and ghettos and the social and cultural problems resulting from such immigration and housing patterns. Indeed, the only Latin character in the film does not even live in New York and he is one of the world's richest men, a far cry from the Jets or the Sharks.

The chic New York City that lies at the center of *Breakfast at Tiffany's* is one perhaps best illustrated in the film's party scene, the other major addition that Edwards made to Axelrod's script, which brings together a bewildering variety of people who, while congenial and energetic, seem to have little or no depth or continuity in their relationships. Some of the guests at the party are drunk to the point of accidentally setting someone's hair on fire and then accidentally putting it out by spilling a drink, all the while nobody noticing anything; a couple seeks refuge in the bathroom and makes out in the bathtub behind the shower curtain. When they are discovered they restore their privacy by simply closing the curtain again. No one seems to know who anyone really is, and no one cares; it is all about being there and partying to excess, engaging other partiers in only the most superficial manner. In a similar display of superficiality, when Holly gets caught up in a scandal at the end of the film, all her New York friends desert her. Certainly none would travel across the country for her as Doc does.

The deserted dark alley in which the film ends, in stark contrast to the exuberant party at its center, is crucial to its representation of New York. Here the film celebrates Paul and Holly turning way from a chic, urban lifestyle such as that of the party toward becoming a middle-class couple on the way to having a family. The alley recalls the empty band shell, but this time there is no expectation of an audience and a performance. The scene in the band shell momentarily turns a romantic comedy into a film of menacing suspense. All the vibrancy of Fifth Avenue and New York City momentarily disappears as the site of a celebrated New York City landmark becomes the site of personal failure and rejection. *Breakfast at Tiffany's*, then, expresses an ambiguous, contradictory attitude toward New York City. On the one hand, it is a chic center of cosmopolitan style, energy, exuberance, and attractive nonconformist behavior of the kind that escapes the implied, oppressive morality of the straitlaced American heartland. It is a place where anything goes. On the other hand, this freewheeling lifestyle is superficial and the main characters have to escape it in order to mature and develop a growing relationship that leads them toward true love and union as a couple. Their salvation lies in removing themselves from the crowd of which they have been a part and from the city that much of the film has been celebrating. At the end, we find them embracing in a dark, rainy alley far from Fifth Avenue and Tiffany's, as the camera pulls up and away.

NOTES

1. One indication of such celebrity appears in an uncredited *New York Times* article (December 8, 1969, p. 67) entitled "Skating Party for Eye, Ear Infirmary." The article announces the sold-out, second annual Breakfast at Tiffany's Children Skating Party to be held at Rockefeller Center's ice skating rink the following Saturday. The party, a benefit for the Eye and Ear Infirmary, was underwritten by Tiffany's and hosted by Tiffany's head, Walter Hoving. It is not possible to order breakfast at Tiffany's since it is a jewelry store, so the rationale behind this annual event clearly involves good-will publicity for Tiffany's that draws upon the popularity of the film. The fact that the party was held not in Tiffany's but at the Rockefeller Center Skating Rink, which has nothing to do with Tiffany's, further enhances the association of Tiffany's with popular New York City landmarks.

2. As early as 1961, when he was also working on *Experiment in Terror*, which places an important scene in an eerily deserted baseball stadium, Edwards sensed an intensely alienating aspect of modern urban life that he linked to deserted public spaces. See Luhr and Lehman, *"Experiment."*

Gene Kelly (c.) in one of the balletic interludes against which the urban bustle of New York jostles. *On the Town* (Stanley Donen and Gene Kelly, MGM, 1949). Digital frame enlargement.

A Day in New York

ON THE TOWN AND THE CLOCK

SCOTT BUKATMAN

"We never been here before!"
"We only got 24 hours!"
"Aw, what can happen to you in just one day?"
—*On the Town*

What *can* happen in a day in New York City? Plenty. A day in the life of the city is a trope familiar in both the journalism of the nineteenth century and the city symphony films of the 1920s. The city is anthropomorphized, given a life, and it is at the same time delimited and made manageable. Boundaries are drawn, rhythms are established, and the myriad comings and goings of the urban multitudes are endowed with swirling coherence. Louis Marin has explored the paradoxical spatial demands of utopia narratives, which must present a space both bounded and infinite. The map makes visible the limits, while narrative opens the possibility of infinite trajectories, inexhaustible plenitude (Marin). There are, indeed, eight million stories in the naked city.

This essay concentrates on two stories that exist in the shadow of World War II. New York's economy "exploded" during the war. According to one source, three million soldiers and sixty-three million tons of supplies would pass through the Port of New York. The New York Navy Yard in Brooklyn "was swiftly expanded from forty to three hundred acres to become the largest shipyard in the world." And the increase in production was matched by an intensification of New York's nightlife: "At night . . . with the world on fire, New York seemed to turn at an even faster pace, the mood of hectic gaiety made all the more urgent by the war." Rationing of goods meant more money for entertainment; nightclubs, restaurants, and Broadway boomed, "while each night servicemen by the thousands swarmed through Times Square, looking for escape or a good time" (Burns and Sanders 471–72).

New York City was a major embarkation point for the European theater, and both of these stories concern servicemen on leave, strangers in a city of strangers, en route to horrors that were no less real for being left unspoken. These New York stories are structured by arrival and departure; compressed narratives of discovery, love, loss, and uncertainty in the most densely congested of modern environments, at a prolonged moment of heightened tension.[1] *On the Town*, the 1944 stage musical written by Betty Comden and Adolph Green with music by Leonard Bernstein, and staged by Jerome Robbins, is alive with an exuberance that practically defines the genre, while *The Clock*, Vincente Minnelli's film from the following year, rewrites the earlier musical in the terms of melodrama, replacing the musical's public euphoria with a more traumatic knowledge of the personal cost of war. The strong relation between these works has been somewhat obscured by the postwar film version of *On the Town* (Gene Kelly and Stanley Donen, 1949), which removes the wartime context along with the songs and most of the emotional resonance. Sections of the film version are worth reviewing, to praise what is preserved from the Broadway production, but mostly to count the ways by which the original significance is neatly obliterated. When the Minnelli film and the show are properly situated in relation to one another, *The Clock* points clearly to the darker undertones of the original *On the Town*, even as Minnelli's direction preserves within the melodrama some of the giddy promise of the musical comedy.

On the Town

In the Broadway musical *On the Town*, one feels the exuberance of the young collaborators, entering the history of the Broadway musical at an opportune moment when the form was proving itself capable of narrative and compositional depth alongside its native effervescence. The show bursts forth with a power that still retains its force.[2] Its main purpose is to capture the city (in both senses of the word "capture"). The public spaces of Times Square and Coney Island are the sites for its balletic interludes. The bustle and compressed sprawl of the city is the kaleidoscopic precondition for the narrative action; it seduces its ostensible seducers. *On the Town* is the exemplary narrative of arrival. Using the language of Gilles Deleuze, one could regard narratives of arrival as emblematic movement-images, as protagonists explore and possess a set of new spaces. And film musicals are themselves replete with movement-images of dancers soaring in unfettered space, furthering the utopian cinematic sensibility of 1920s cinema.[3]

New York City has served as inspiration throughout the history of the musical. New York musicals speak to the exuberant possibilities latent in the metropolis, commingling voices and styles with promiscuous grace. The careless hybridity of the form, with its mix of dialogue, song, and dance, its narrative interruptions and syncopated excurses, is perfectly suited to the character of twentieth-century New York.[4] The streets and skyscrapers, parks, plazas, and theaters exert their pull, proclaiming the fact of the musical's modernity from high (the rooftop nightclubs of *Swing Time* [1936]) and low (the crap game in the sewer from *Guys and Dolls* [1955]) and in-between (Gene Kelly stomping along the puddled street, singin' and dancin' in the rain).[5] Musicals organize the clamor of the streets into rhythms and rhymes, what Comden and Green called "The Throb of Manhattan."[6]

The genius of the form, however, is that it never *over*-organizes the city, respecting, rather than repressing its manic, randomizing energies. Only a semblance of control could ever be superimposed upon the life of the street, and here the musical has danced far ahead of modernist urban planners.[7]

New York is presented as a place not without its risks, but which still teems with opportunity. The city figured in *42nd Street* (1933) is a place where a young woman could move about on her own and make choices without fear of her community's reproach, a place to grow up and discover adult desires. The "city of strangers," as Sondheim later called it, is not in itself a bad thing, because the city, with its crisscrossing citizens, visitors, streets, and purposes, becomes a site of contingency, random encounter, the sudden emergence of new communities or the discovery of communities that were already there. Anything can happen and did— often to Ruby Keeler: go out a youngster, come back a star.

The opportunities that New York presents are stylistically marked by daring perceptual transformations on both stage and screen. The city is boldly abstracted in set design, and awash in color and music. And if the real Manhattan insists upon the superficial order of gridded streets and the instrumental reason of commerce, the urban musical, armed with montage and mobility and freed from the straitjacket of narrative plausibility, can cut, glide, or fly across it.

The stars who sing and dance are figures of sublime agency, whether first learning to negotiate the "urban jungle" like Peggy Sawyer (Keeler) in *42nd Street*, or relearning the town like Tony Hunter (Fred Astaire), planning his comeback in *The Band Wagon* (1953), or already its master, like Sky Masterson (Marlon Brando) laying claim to Times Square in *Guys and Dolls*. Gene Kelly is, of course, the great street performer of the musical, whether alone (*Singin' in the Rain* [1952], *It's Always Fair Weather* [1955]), with his buddies (*It's Always Fair Weather, Cover Girl* [1944]), or entertaining the kids (*An American in Paris* [1951], *Les Demoiselles de Rochefort* [1967]). The city and its spaces, all those encounters, these movements of world, lie immanent until activated by performers who, astonishingly, seem to channel the city's liberating energy through their very bodies.

On the Town is so fundamental to the idea of the New York musical that it's almost beside the point that the film based upon it is so lousy. After MGM bought the rights, Louis B. Mayer saw the show and hated it. Bernstein, Comden, and Green had produced a torrent of songs, symphonies, slapstick, frank sexuality mingling with romantic longing, urban bustle jostling up against balletic interludes. Nearly all of that original score was jettisoned and replaced with simpler, stupider songs thrown together by Comden and Green with Roger Edens, songs that are so poor that one is actively embarrassed for the performers. A perfect example is "Prehistoric Man," in which poor Betty Garrett must lurch around like an ape.

The play *On the Town* was based on *Fancy Free*, a ballet conceived and choreographed by Robbins and scored by Bernstein. The piece was somewhat inspired by several paintings by Paul Cadmus, primarily "The Fleet's In" (1934): beefcake sailors leering at girls. Apart from the subject matter, these works highlight "a refreshing lustiness and a naturalness of gesture" that Deborah Jowitt suggests might have been of interest to Robbins (Jowitt 74–75). Three sailors compete for two girls, showing off in a giddy series of dance solos before deciding that friendship means more to them than dames. Along with Agnes de Mille's *Rodeo*, *Fancy Free* was a milestone in the development of an American style of choreography rooted in a more colloquial idiom. Both *Rodeo* and *Fancy Free* used sets designed by Oliver Smith, who suggested basing a Broadway musical on *Fancy Free*.

Part of the tragedy of the film was how close it came to getting it right. The opening sequence with Frank Sinatra, Gene Kelly, and Jules Munshin, the only one filmed on location in New York, has been justifiably celebrated, perhaps more than any musical number apart from "Singin' in the Rain." Donen and Kelly blast their way through Arthur Freed's domestic mustiness, virtually reinventing the film musical for a new era. (It would take more than a decade for someone to effectively pick up the baton: Richard Lester in *A Hard Day's Night* [1964].) "New York, New York" constitutes the most dynamic urban portrait since the city symphonies of the 1920s and Busby Berkeley's excursions of the 1930s. City symphonies were often structured around "a day in the life" of the metropolis, beginning with empty streets and shuttered windows, moving through the routine of work, culminating in the accelerated frenzy of nightlife. The "typical" day becomes exceptional because it is enshrined through the "adventure of perception" that is the cinema (see Brakhage). Donen and Kelly respect the number's original theatricality by presenting the vocal sections in single long takes, while responding to the tempo and structure of the music by interpolating rapid montage sequences. The long crane shot of the dock worker lazily meandering toward the start of another work day, daydreaming of bed and bride, becomes a counterpoint for frenetic sensations of untethered motion: the jubilant explosion of sailors from the quiescent ship is carried forward by the bold montage of city streets and sites. This is not any day, or the everyday, but a singular day. "We can safely say the most beautiful sight is New York in the light of the day. Our only day." The editing replaces Robbins's original choreography, and unlike Berkeley's cutting on movement, "New York, New York" is edited to accentuate the brassy, surging score.

June 1944. The country at war . . . New York . . . the Brooklyn Navy Yard, a major embarkation point for the European theater. Three sailors on shore leave. Twenty-four hours for three sailors to taste the big city, its freedom and its depth. One of them has lugged along an out-of-date guidebook, wants to see the Hippodrome and the Woolworth Tower. But this isn't a city to see, it's a city to be in. Total immersion. The kind of commitment one can only make because it's limited—the rhythms of real life have no chance to intrude, sleep is a literal waste of time. Be here now.

Think of the phrase "fancy free." It capitalizes on an Irving Berlin song ("No Strings") that Fred Astaire introduced in *Top Hat* (1935). The song's refrain, "I'm fancy free and free for anything fancy," certainly captures the attitude of the sailors in both *Fancy Free* and *On the Town*. "I start out every morning just as free as the breeze," Berlin's protagonist sings; in *On the Town*, Gabey (John Battles onstage, Gene Kelly onscreen), Ozzie (Adolph Green/Jules Munshin), and Chip (Cris Alexander/Frank Sinatra) have only this one day, but they, too, are light as air. To be free for anything fancy doesn't speak to a desire for excessive ornament. What the lyric really means is, I'm free for anything [*that I*] fancy; I'm free and therefore present to all the imaginative possibilities I can conjure out of the world. But to be "fancy free" also means to be free of love: there are "no strings and no connections/No ties to my affections." Yet Berlin's singer is "feeling romancy": this isn't a song about living contentedly without love; no, it's about being *ready* for love:[8] "Bring on the big attraction/My decks are cleared for action." This last sure sounds like something the protagonists of *On The Town* might declare before storming the city.

None of these guys has ever seen a place like New York City before. Gabey's from a small town, but he's good with the ladies and wants to try his line on a cosmopolitan gal. Before he knows it, though, he's lost his heart to a picture of this month's Miss Turnstiles, Ivy Smith (Sono Osato/Vera-Ellen). Here the show and the film begin to diverge. A dance interlude in the show illustrates the PR flack that makes Ivy into an impossible amalgam, someone for everyone. But the film dance ends on a note of triumph, Ivy resplendent atop a pile of decimated footballers. In the show, her fate is to be replaced by next month's Miss Turnstiles, to melt back into the anonymity of the line of straphangers. She, too, has only a small window of opportunity, thirty days, to make her mark, to be someone.

The sailors examine the poster. She dances here, she studies there—how hard can it be to find this perfect woman in this perfect city on this perfect day? First, a cab, operated by one Brunhilde Eszterhazy (Nancy Walker). The city is alive with women who are alive to their own desires. Perhaps the war has made everyone aware of the clock, time, the end of time. Hilde is surely the cousin of the libidinous cabbie who chauffeurs Bogart in *The Big Sleep* (1946). But at this point again, the film gets it wrong. Chip wants to know why there's a lady cab driver (Betty Garrett) even though the war is over. Since the film is set in the postwar world of 1949, the city doesn't live under the shadow of the clock. Time is not as precious. And if the sailors aren't shipping out to war, where is the urgency of this day?

First stop, the American Museum of Natural History, where in the show Claire DeLoone (Betty Comden) is studying prehistoric man to sublimate her desire for the modern kind. She and Ozzie get "carried away," over-invested in momentary excitements. (Ozzie sings about attacking the onscreen villain at the "moving picture show," just like [his?] Uncle Josh.) "I Get Carried Away" and "Come Up to My Place" continue what "New York, New York" began—these are songs about desire, abundance, and the magic of the here and now.[9]

Splitting up into pairs (Ozzie and Claire, Chip and Hilde) is the only rational thing to do, but it leaves Gabey bereft and alone. He asks a passerby for directions but gets nowhere. "Gabey's comin' to town," he sings. "So what? Who cares?" The lyric is conversational and intimate, the kind of song that marks American popular music in the first half of the century. "A town's a lonely town, when you pass through and there is no one waiting there for you." Luckily, it doesn't take Gabey long to find Ivy. She's studying voice at Carnegie Hall with Madame Dilly (Susan Steell), "the best teacher on this side of the corridor," but not for much longer; she's working as a cooch dancer, but is still behind on her payments. The poor guy is so bedazzled that Ivy can't bring herself to tell him that being Miss Turnstiles isn't that big a deal. But it's also her fantasy of herself; it's not so easy to deny what he thinks he's found in her.

With Gabey and Ivy the film version goes completely off the rails. Ivy realizes that they're both from the same small town, had the same history teacher, whatever. Nostalgic for home, she asks him about his (their) hometown, which leads to their only shared number (aside from the dream ballet), the egregious bit of "hackwork" (as Mast calls it [239]) "Main Street." Some of the new songs by Comden, Green, and Edens offer dumbed-down versions of the originals, but "Main Street" demonstrates more than MGM's inability to "get it"; it clearly indicates that they didn't *want* it. The ultimate New York musical clearly had to be de-newyorkicized (much as Henry Jenkins demonstrates how Eddie Cantor was de-Semitized) for the hinterlands beyond Eleventh Avenue.[10] But if Gabey and Ivy are from the same small town, then they actually didn't even *need* New York to meet. Just stay home, stay put right there, right there where you live (a recurrent theme in Freed's films; recall the demonization of New York City in *Meet Me in St. Louis* [1944]). In the show, Gabey and Ivy may both be small-town kids, but they're from *different towns*. The metropolis offers the opportunity to bring even similar people together. Think of Paul Fejos's *Lonesome* (1929), where John and Mary, thrown together at Coney Island only to lose one another again, turn out to live in adjacent apartments. New York may look huge and anonymous, but it isn't as unmanageable as all that. (*The Clock* goes even further in transforming New York into something of a small town, as we will see.)[11]

Feeling a bit—but not too—guilty about leaving Gabey in the lurch, Ozzie, Chip, and their new girls try to get in some serious smooching before they all meet up to begin a night on the town. But privacy is hard to come by in the chaos of New York. Hilde's roommate, the adenoidal Lucy Schmeeler, is taking a sick day, and Claire's fiancé, a remarkably understanding bloke, keeps turning up to celebrate the couple's impending matrimony. Still, the romances have room to develop. Gabey's on his own, doesn't know that Ivy won't be able to make their date tonight because she has to do her cooch act at Coney Island. Act one ends with Gabey's being stood up, and a good chunk of act two is spent trying to cheer him up. They drag him from nightclub to nightclub until they finally find Madame Dilly, who spills the beans. Gabey heads for the subway and Coney Island, with the other couples close behind.

Bound for Coney Island, Gabey falls asleep. The subway car pulls apart to reveal Oliver Smith's set for the "imaginary Coney Island," the setting for Gabey's

"Great Lover" dream ballet. The dream ballet in the film version, titled "A Day In New York: A Comedy in Three Acts," begins by quoting the original *Fancy Free*—three exuberant sailors compete for two girls (including the wondrous Carol Haney). In the tried-and-true tradition of dream ballets since *Oklahoma*, the dream ballet in the film recapitulates much of the action we've already seen but without deeper resonance: Gabey falls in love with Ivy's portrait (we know this because he blows kisses to it, dances with it, and points back and forth from the picture to himself), and manages a brief *pas de deux* with her before she disappears, leaving him bereft and alone. (Kelly will never tire of this nonsense, which will also swamp *An American in Paris* the following year.) In the original show, the dream ballet presents Gabey as the Great Lover who is no match for Ivy Smith, who bests him in the boxing ring. Perhaps this athleticism is what the film was trying to evoke in the earlier Miss Turnstiles ballet.

On the next train, Chip and Hilde and Claire and Ozzie are settling in for the long trek from midtown Manhattan to Coney ("Relax. You've got one hundred and ninety six stops to go!"). The press of time begins to make itself felt. "Twenty-four hours can go so fast / You look around, the day has passed." The song is the quiet, devastating "Some Other Time," as moving a song as the genre has produced and, needless to say, omitted from the film. "Where has the time all gone to? Haven't done half the things we want to." The utopia of the perfect day, the perfect romance: is it undermined or enhanced by this evocation of loss? These people don't really know each other—their sense of blissful communion need never be tested against the gritty practical reality of sustained love. "Haven't got half my wishes / Never have seen you do the dishes." The ideal can only exist as a lost idea. There is always the possibility that it could have been more. Yet it's extraordinary how the song, which merits the word "bittersweet" more than anything I know, acknowledges that real love demands the time it takes to become banal: "Haven't had time to wake up / Seeing you there without your makeup" is more than a wistful desire for a quiet, private moment within the whirlwind of this romance; it admits the possibility they might not even have seen the real person underlying the other's public face. The even beat of the lyric, with its brief phrases and simple rhymes, ticks like an invisible clock. "Oh well," a shrug, "We'll catch up some other time." *We'll catch up* is possibly the least romantic of phrases—the singer has already begun to detach, but this forced casualness is belied by the repeated refrain and the aching litany of things that never will be.

The rest is anticlimax: they find Ivy doing her cooch dance, Gabey loves her anyway, the cops come to sort out the mess, and the gals are allowed to say goodbye to their men as they board their ship. It's uncertain whether any of them will see each other again. No promises have been made. Perhaps this day was singular. Perhaps real life will reassert itself. For now, though, there are three new sailors, three fresh sailors alive and loose for twenty-four hours in the city of infinite possibility. It's a helluva town.

The Clock

"A town's a lonely town/When you pass through/And there is no one waiting there for you." Gabey's song could also serve to introduce Joe (Robert Walker), the soldier on leave in Vincente Minnelli's *The Clock*. The film foregrounds the anxiety about the future that lurked behind the euphoria of *On the Town*. While Minnelli's film is often regarded as a follow-up to *Meet Me in St. Louis*—they share a complex nostalgia for the sanctuary of family and community, not to mention Judy Garland—it is also a kind of remake of *On the Town*, restaging the narrative in a different key. Minnelli decided to make New York "a character in the story" despite his inability to work on location (because of wartime economy cutbacks). Many of its themes and structures derive from *On the Town*: a serviceman on a brief leave in New York, a chance encounter that builds to love, the twin possibilities of love and loss, the balancing of typicality and uniqueness, the symmetries of structure that end where we began, with another cycle about to begin. As in *On the Town*, the lives of the characters exist beneath the clock (*Under the Clock* was the British title, in fact): time's passage is inexorable, even (especially?) in the presence of new love. *On the Town* celebrates arrival, while everything in *The Clock* is measured against Joe's imminent departure.

A recent symposium organized by Pavle Levi and myself explored responses to recent urban trauma in popular media (Polan). The destruction of the World Trade Center was seen to represent one kind of traumatic event—a sudden catastrophe—while the history of Sarajevo was emblematic of the more sustained experience of a state of siege. In his talk, Dana Polan proposed that these two temporal modes have analogs in narrative. The shock of violence ("the sudden arrival of the horrific") that changes everything (in, for example, the violence of noir) is different from the protracted experience of unrelenting, or slowly building, horror (Polan's example was the "gaslight" subgenre of domestic melodrama). Frequently the two are linked: the shock of an initial catastrophe yields to the tortuous task of assimilating trauma into the everyday.

Polan suggests that the traumatic can become the banal: the daily struggle to find water, or the wait for food rations, characterized not only the battle for Sarajevo but the aftermath of Hurricane Katrina in the Gulf States. In recognizing the intertwining of trauma and banality, Polan also located instances in which the banality of everyday urban life itself comes to constitute its own kind of trauma: the blankness of the blasted cityscapes encountered in postwar European cinema (in a film like *Germany Year Zero* [1948]) bleeds easily into the blankness of international-style urbanism (in films like *Play Time* [1967] or *Point Blank* [1967]). Urban experience, Polan notes, is comprised of "both singular and exceptional events *and* the regularity of a frequently deadening ordinariness. The possibility of nothing ever happening can be as traumatic as the risk of apocalyptic change." This trauma is registered through purposeless and ineffectual movement, highlighted by Gilles Deleuze, claims Polan, "as a key initial step in the refinement of what he termed the time-image in its concentration on reactive, rather than active, figures who wander slowly through an urban space whose ravages they register optically" (xi-xiii).

Something of this intertwining of trauma and banality is evident in *The Clock*. We move from the active movement-images of the Broadway/Hollywood musical to the time-image of postwar (or late-war) powerlessness. "For all the fitful oblivion and frenzied fun," write Ric Burns and James Sanders, "nothing could dispel for long the chilling arithmetic of the war" (472). By 1945, the early optimism of an Allied victory had yielded to the desperate reality of casualties and apocalyptic destruction; the evidence onscreen suggests that Americans were more willing to confront the grim realities of war. *The Clock*, an MGM melodrama, might "leave one with a warm feeling," as it did the critic from the *New York Times*, but its warmth is leavened by, or perhaps predicated upon, darker possibilities, including the possibility that the two young lovers are not, in fact, "meant" for each other. In keeping with the more realist conventions of the period, the film centers on normal, nonheroic people. Shot in understated black and white, many of the performances have a spontaneous, improvised feel (Garland, James and Lucile Gleason). The film's subtleties startle student audiences today, and I can hardly begin to imagine the emotional wallop it packed in 1945, in the context of newsreels and photojournalism. Much of the film's power comes from its context, which is everywhere implicit.

The film begins, like *On the Town*, with a shot of the Manhattan skyline: not an unusual establishing shot, but it helps establish New York as not just the setting but also the occasion for the drama (also not unlike the openings of *Broadway Melody* [1929] and *42nd Street*). Three shots bring us to Penn Station. A slow crane shot traverses the vast open space of the terminal, the scurrying crowd. The camera follows a serviceman, ambling a bit hesitantly; it loses him briefly, then moves in as he asks first one person, then another, for help: not just for directions, but for direction: "What are some of the things to see? What do you think would be the best thing to do on a Sunday?" Joe is kind of a hick, judging from his fascination with escalators, but the music is sympathetic rather than mocking. In a jauntier mood he steps outside, only to confront some of the most geometrically constricting urban compositions this side of Berenice Abbott or King Vidor. The buildings loom, if not menacingly, then at least heavily, and Joe ducks back into the relative safety of the station. Unlike the sailors in *On the Town*, this guy is on his own, by himself, with no buddies to back him up, none of that safety in numbers that means that you're never really alone in the big bad city. And Joe is army, rather than navy, a grunt, a GI Joe (or Jack or Willie), destined to slog through the mud, hide in holes, take a hill, lose a hill, take it back. No jaunty, sparkling whites, no romance of the open sea for Joe; just a drab and diminutive anonymity that is already making itself felt here in New York City. What can happen to this guy on a two-day pass?

At last, the cute meeting: Alice (Garland) trips over Joe's feet and breaks her heel. It's safe to say that he doesn't make a very good first impression, not by pretending to a smug overconfidence like Gabey, but just by his general lack of fit. He's, as he puts it, "green as grass." Yet he's not completely helpless: he gets her shoe fixed and joins her for a bus ride up Fifth Avenue. "Oh, say, this is a city! These buildings—the way they go right up!" She's rather amused, having had three whole years to become a seasoned and somewhat cynical New Yorker. Joe has trouble grasping that she's a girl on her own: no family, no husband, just a job in the city working as a secretary in an office. "What kind of office?" he wants to know, but she brushes off the personal questions with a level gaze and steady tone, "*Just* an office."[12]

He wants her company; perhaps she'd like to walk with him through the park? Out of the question. But then comes the second accident: she sneezes, not twice as per usual, but an unprecedented third time. Before we know it, they're in the park. Something is happening here. There will be a lot of talk in the film about their being fated to meet, and perhaps these accidents are signs of such predestination.

Alice, pragmatic about romances with servicemen, is undeniably drawn to Joe. They wind up in the park, alive to the possibility that they were fated to meet. As they listen to the sounds of the city, the background score becomes poundingly loud and ornate, building to a crescendo of heavenly choirs. The scene plays very much like a musical sequence without singing—"Dancing in the Dark" from Minnelli's *The Band Wagon*—alternating close-ups, synchronized movement, musical crescendos. It even ends with them walking away as the camera cranes up (a typical Minnelli/Freed finale). The rhetoric of the musical provides a language of transcendence, suggesting that Alice's surrender to "fate" is an almost conscious surrender to possibility; a willingness to trust the dream of love that the city has offered. The rest of the film will work against the "transcendence" of this scene: the real world will constantly intrude upon the romantic fantasy. *The Clock* is poised somewhere between the utopian possibility of a musical and the grim determinism of something else. Dreams in Minnelli's films are fragile, lovely illusions shattered as easily as Tootie's snow people in *Meet Me in St. Louis*. But dreams are no less necessary for their precariousness. They—and we—want it to be true. Back in St. Louis, Esther/Judy sang, "Through the years we all will be together, if the fates allow." In 1945 I daresay Alice and Joe, and viewers with them, needed the possibility of that truth. "Until then we'll have to muddle through somehow." So there they are.

They miss the last bus, but are given a lift by Al Henry (James Gleason), a garrulous milkman who unfortunately gets punched out by an even more garrulous drunk. Joe and Alice help out by delivering the milk and afterward Al's wife (Lucile Gleason) rewards them with a grand breakfast. Later on it will be Al's cousin who will help Alice and Joe cut through the red tape that prevents their marriage. New York, this vast, unknowable urban space, has been transformed into a small town, the kind of town where people know their milkman, everyone is welcome, and family is always close at hand.

But the light of dawn brings a seemingly more clear-eyed view of things. Couples shouldn't rush into marriage, after all, especially when one is a serviceman with an uncertain future. Of course not, no. They understand these things, and all things being equal, this might be where the story ends, on the verge of love in a time of war, a time of careful rationing and necessary regrets.

Then comes the urban trauma. Buffeted by the bustling subway crowds, they are separated. Joe tries to follow, but takes the express train, not the local (rube!). The city, the unlikely site of their small-town idyll, has reasserted itself as a dehumanizing metropolis. Trains thunder into stations; Alice and Joe pass one another without even noticing. (The same thing happens early in the film version of *On the Town*.) Alice is forced to ask around about a soldier she spent the night with that she knows only as "Joe." The woman at the USO advises her not to tell that story too widely. "You don't understand," Alice murmurs, but it could be that she understands all too well, perhaps better than Alice. Despite their quest to find one another, their traversal of the city becomes aimless, a criss-crossing of undifferentiated and unconnected spaces.

Here *The Clock* anticipates neorealism, but a neorealism tinged with noir; noir and neorealism will be the two paradigmatic expressions of postwar cinema. New York is not visibly ravaged by war as were London, Berlin, Dresden, Rome, or Hiroshima, but it cannot be other than ravaged by a war that may seem displaced but is everywhere present. The horror of separation, and the experience of the city that can disintegrate as easily as it can unify, recalls very clearly the terror experienced by the protagonists of *Lonesome*, but now the war adds a terrifying finality to the sense of loss. Alice and Joe had so little time anyway; it is especially horrific that even this small dispensation should be taken away so abruptly. The horror of loss becomes a synecdoche for the grief suffered by families across the country, whose grasp on their own loved ones was becoming increasingly unsteady.

But they are finally reunited, not beneath the clock at the Astor Hotel on Times Square where they first arranged to meet, but in Pennsylvania Station, where a morose Joe is getting ready to head back to camp. Their relief borders on hysteria, their desperate embrace a recuperative miracle that speaks to all those servicemen who ship out and never return, the lovers and family who never do, truly, manage to say goodbye (and this recalls the aching, unspoken farewell between the clandestine lovers of David Lean's *Brief Encounter*, from the same year as *The Clock*).[13] Alice and Joe breathlessly exchange last names, and in the next moment, agree to wed; it wouldn't be right not to. This taste of loss has been unbearable, but has yielded the knowledge that, especially in times of war and trauma, love is too precious to delay or rationalize out of existence. One must hold onto the certainties one has, despite the uncertainties to follow.

A day is gone, only one remains. Time enough to wed, but now a second trauma unfolds: the bureaucracy of the state mitigates against the haste Alice and Joe properly feel. Forms must be filled out, blood tests taken, approvals given, vows exchanged. And superimposed over everything is the clock that points to the moment of separation, perhaps forever. The city does not care about these two. "In neorealism," Dana Polan writes, "several urban temporalities come together: the calamity of war but also the sameness of postwar everydayness, the consequential event, for example, the theft of a bike, the disappearance of a woman on an island, but also the regularization of event, its re-inscription in bureaucracy, the generalization of the singular so that it is seen as everyone's common condition." The consequential event, Alice and Joe's meeting, their romance, their separation, all is subsumed by the regularization of an event that is "re-inscribed in bureaucracy."

Another trauma, another miracle: the city once again turns benign, as Al's cousin, the clerk of the court, turns up to help the couple. The wedding ceremony is a rush job, with janitors cleaning inside, trains rattling by outside, and a harried justice trying to get out of town for the weekend.[14] And that's it. They're married. The sustained hysteria that suffused their separation and search, the frantic struggle to get married, it all stops dead. The empty hallways emphasize the lack of family and friends, the unreality of a new life that seems so detached from the old. Alice is beginning to fall apart, but Joe is too preoccupied to notice. They go around the corner to a cafeteria to grab a bite, a bowl of soup, but here, too, the scene is marked by its institutional quality. No longer does their romance afford them a bubble of privacy. They calmly discuss writing to one another's folks (are they . . . living?). The man at the next table is far too interested in their conversation, but his urban survival skills are unbeatable: he registers sublime disinterest whenever Alice looks his way.

This was a civil ceremony, in a cold city, for two people with no shared past and only the possibility of a shared future. In the cafeteria, Alice finally breaks down, sobbing, choking for air as she confronts the ugliness of it. The trauma of banality has crushed the fantasy of romance, leaving only some signed and stamped documents behind, along with a bowl of not very good soup. Differently than in his scenes of breakdown in *The Bad and the Beautiful* (1952), *Lust for Life* (1956), *Meet Me in St. Louis*, or the nightmare in *Father of the Bride* (1950), Minnelli here never breaks with the realist aesthetic of the cafeteria. New York is not transformed by Alice's anguish; it is untouched, perhaps voyeuristically interested, but otherwise unaffected. There are a few million other stories in this city, some sadder even than this.

Alexander Nemerov has written about the impact of bit players and minor characters in the cinema, and among his examples is the nameless actor who plays this man at the next table. "Increasingly coming between" Alice and Joe, "he chomps his food and eavesdrops on their excruciating conversation." In characters like these, the "'slatelike hardness' [Manny Farber's term] of life itself might intrude its irreducible singularity into the otherwise generalized worlds of stars, glamour, and conventional plots" (Nemerov 68). At the same time, Nemerov maps, in Val Lewton's wartime horror films, a turn from movement toward moments of prolonged stasis, arguing that this stasis acknowledges, as home-front culture rarely did, the grim reality of ongoing death beyond American shores. These "icons of grief," as he calls them, constitute Lewton's attempts "to show a carefree American audience the nature of tragedy" (Nemerov 151). In the cafeteria in *The Clock* one also feels the cessation of movement, an inversion of the kinetic valence of the musical, as the characters suddenly begin to face the consequences of what they've done and what the future might hold. The hard-edged presence of the intrusive eavesdropper within this prolonged moment of uncertainty and irresolution, then, works against the utopian sense of control allowed movie stars and musicals, and further signals, against the background of an uncaring city, the repressed reality of a country at war. Even in *On the Town*, the moment of enforced stasis on the subway ride to Coney Island becomes the occasion for the reflective, quietly grieving "Some Other Time."

Leaving the cafeteria, Alice and Joe pass before a church as a happy pair of newlyweds emerges to a shower of shoes and rice and felicitations. Alice edges up to the door, peeks in. She and Joe go inside. Slowly walking up the aisle in the dark and deserted hall, they feel something. They slide into a pew, pick up a hymnal and read the wedding vows, softly, to each other, for each other. They might now be in a hallowed place, but they are also, finally, in a private place, so different from the municipal buildings, offices, and cafeterias that devalued the still tentative bond between them. Most of their relationship has taken place in public: crowded streets, zoos, museums, subways. Even seemingly private spaces remain connected to the world: windows puncture the space of their romantic restaurant and even, later, their hotel. But the church scene, so reminiscent of the scene in *Sunrise* (1927) when the husband and wife reaffirm their vows, is much more about carving out a private, intimate space than it is about religion. The camera frames them, and only them, as they perform the wedding ceremony themselves (incidentally turning the audience into *de facto* witnesses).

Cut to the morning after, the two of them high above the city in their nuptial hotel room. What does the cold light of morning reveal? Joe moves about a little uncertainly, his boyishness still evident, but Alice! A grown woman now, she sits with the most satisfied, proprietary look on her face, sassily flicking his lighter and snapping it closed, flick snap flick snap. He lights his cigarette, but when he makes a move to keep his lighter she tightens her claim. It's hers, now. No words are necessary. He begins to talk about the uncertain future, but she won't have it. "You're coming back," she tells him. She knows because all of this couldn't have happened by accident, this had to be fate, and if it's fate, then he's fated to return, for they were fated to find each other. It's tempting to trust Alice/Judy in this mode. Her certainty, the conventions of Hollywood romance, the transcendence of the nocturnal musical interlude in the park, everything seems to indicate that, at least within the terms of this fiction, he will, in fact, come back to her.

But *The Clock* raises the question: are they *really* desperately meant for each other? Or are they two people whom circumstances have brought together? As they waded through the bureaucracy to get their marriage license, Alice noticed another couple waiting to be married . . . another serviceman, another . . . pickup? She's clearly thinking it over: are *they* really in love or is this just a typical wartime circumstance? And, the film dares to ask, *so what if it is?* The script insists on fate, yet Minnelli's style continually emphasizes contingency, happenstance, and the anonymity of the city. If her heel hadn't broken; if she didn't sneeze the unprecedented third sneeze that required Joe's handkerchief; if they hadn't encountered the broken-down milk wagon: these things could be either the manifestations of fate or signs of a randomness that is fate's complete opposite.

As she accompanies him back to Penn Station to see him off, the cycle of arrivals and departures continues, as it did in *On the Town*. Minnelli's camera tracks over a few other family partings, including African Americans and Jewish Americans. This war has been a great democratizer. It's a bit comical to see all these stereotypical goodbyes with admonitions from parents and tears from spouses. But, we wonder, will *all* of these soldiers be coming back? Audiences in 1945 couldn't help but know that some of them simply wouldn't.[15] The possibility of death accompanies the possibility of love. Earlier, in the milk truck, Alice sleepily wondered about the direction of morning and the location of the sun: "Before that it's out in the sea, and before that . . ."—well, before that it's in Europe. "Joe," she suddenly asks. "Where are they sending you, do you know?" The comforting illusion of a benign fate is something the film's aesthetic belies. As they whispered their wedding vows in the church, a choirboy slowly snuffed out a row of candles, one after another. "Thy will be done."

Despite the hopeful talk of fate, the film continually acknowledges the provisional, accidental nature of their meeting, their slowly developing rapport, the fragility of their relationship. The ultimate significance of *The Clock* depends upon these being two ordinary people with no special claim on fate at all. Anything can happen from here, and we can certainly hope, along with Alice, that Joe will come back. There is indeed a fantasy of romance that Alice finds comforting, as does the audience; it's a fragile fantasy, though, and as is so often the case in Minnelli, there is something real in the fragility, the ephemerality, of fantasy. If not for the fantasy, they never would have fallen in love, third sneeze or no third sneeze. Minnelli's aesthetic does subvert the narrative of fated meetings and the promise of happy endings—this isn't *Madame Bovary*—but it does point to the characters' (and audiences') own necessary investment in the tenuous necessity of belief. Thus Alice can leave Joe to whatever the future may hold, walking back across the great expanse of the main terminal, strong enough to melt back into the crowd of people, people who have no greater claim to fate than she or anyone else. *The Clock* acknowledges darker, more complex possibilities. Death, yes, but also the necessary uncertainty that is adulthood's most difficult precondition.

That's what can happen in a day in New York.

NOTES

1. Dana Polan has discussed narratives in which characters find themselves "turning around and zigzagging across a space of a city that one knows only too well," and many of these, he notes, "take place over one 24 hour period as if to match unity of place by unity of time and impose a classical rigor on one's confinement to the city." For Polan, there are narratives of arrival, narratives of departure, and narratives of what happens in between. His own emphasis was on the last of these.

2. I saw the splendid production of *On the Town* staged by the English National Opera in London in March 2005.

3. Peter Wollen has linked the full-bodied performance of musical films with silent film performance (*Singin'*).

4. For more on urban musicals, see my "Syncopated City."

5. All right, the last one isn't set in New York, but Kelly, Dan Dailey, and Michael Kidd raise a ruckus on the streets of New York in *It's Always Fair Weather* (1955). In "Syncopated City," I mistakenly referred to Dan *Dailey* as Dan *Duryea*. Thanks and a big tip of the hat to my father, Jerry Bukatman, who was the only person to spot the error.

6. In *It's Always Fair Weather*.

7. For a sustained discussion of ways that urban cinema has outpaced urban planning, see Sanders.

8. "The sun's in my heart / And I'm ready for love," Gene sings in "Singin' in the Rain."

9. The film's substitution of "Prehistoric Man" for "I Get Carried Away" at least preserves the idea if not the wit—"I *really* like bearskin," puns Ann Miller, flirting with the camera as only she can. It should also be noted that the chemistry between Miller and Munshin prior to the song nails the original dynamic between Comden and Green, who played these roles on stage.

10. Hilde explains to Chip, and incidentally all those folks in the hinterlands, that big cities change all the time; guidebooks go out of date. As a New Yorker, it scares me that an audience would need to be told this. See Jenkins 153–84.

11. Gerald Mast has written that *On the Town* is about how great New York is as a place to visit, while Comden, Green, and Bernstein's later *Wonderful Town* is about how great a place it is to *live* in (298).

12. The casting of Judy Garland gives the film an odd relation to "The Trolley Song." The chance erotic encounter on a public conveyance she describes in the song is actually staged here in *The Clock*, but now she's resistant to it. And the casting of Robert Walker anticipates, even more oddly, *Strangers on a Train* (1951). As Joe peppers Alice with personal questions, undistracted by her guided tour of Fifth Avenue, it's difficult not to see Bruno ferreting out the dirty details from Guy Haines, and his unblinking, unwavering gaze at Guy playing tennis.

13. Thanks to Murray Pomerance and Alex Nemerov for sharing their insights of this scene with me. The feeling that Joe has, in a sense, returned from the dead, recalls the small wave of wartime films, such as *Here Comes Mr. Jordan* (1941) or Powell and Pressburger's *A Matter of Life and Death* (1946), in which the protagonists are indeed granted a reprieve from the finality of death.

14. It even recalls the ill-fated wedding in Stroheim's *Greed* (1924).

15. *The Clock* would pair well with Wyler's *The Best Years of Our Lives* (1946), an explicitly darker film about returning veterans.

"Am I in the Pharaoh's palace in Egypt . . . or the lobby of the Paradise in the Bronx?" Moses (Charlton Heston) muses in *The Ten Commandments* (Cecil B. DeMille, Paramount, 1956). Collection Barry Keith Grant.

Paradise Lost and Found

A BRONX TALE

BARRY KEITH GRANT

It would require a statistician of the cinema on the order of Barry Salt to count the number of Hollywood movies that begin with an aerial shot of Manhattan to set the story. Billy Wilder begins *The Lost Weekend* (1945) with the camera panning across a New York cityscape, selecting one window, tracking in and penetrating its secrets rather as Hitchcock would in Phoenix with *Psycho* fifteen years later. After all, there were eight million stories in the Naked City, as the opening voiceover of the popular television series, based on the 1948 Jules Dassin film, informed us every week in the late 1950s.

As a child growing up simultaneously in New York City and with the movies, another one of those eight million stories, it seemed natural to me that so many movies were set in the city where I lived or in some unnamed generic city that everyone was supposed to take for granted was New York (okay, possibly Chicago, also a big northern city with an elevated subway). After all, I saw many of these eight million stories on a daily basis through the countless windows in the apartment buildings adjacent to mine and sharing a common courtyard, like a serialized version of *Rear Window* (1954). In *The Beast from 20,000 Fathoms* (1953), which I saw at the old Zenith Theater in the South Bronx neighborhood where I grew up, a Rhedosaurus awakened by nuclear testing comes ashore in New York and rampages through the city. With the same Hollywood logic that dictates that aliens will always land in or attack the United States as their primary target, why would the Beast go anywhere else when it can be lured by the lights of the biggest city? There was no question that the Beast would come to New York; at a time when "Made in Japan" was a joke in the United States, only Japanese monsters would bother attacking Tokyo.

Watching *The Beast from 20,000 Fathoms* as a child, even while I could distinguish the location shots from the process shots and miniatures, I appreciated that it was at least a semblance of the city's distinctive wrought iron street lamps of the period being crumpled by the dinosaur in the miniature shots, almost matching the actual ones in the few location shots; where I lived, as soon as I stepped outside my door, these wrought iron lamps were everywhere. Even the seasonal pea coats worn by New York's Finest—including the cop lifted and swallowed whole by the dinosaur—were right. This attention to detail comes as no surprise, given that the film, as I learned years later, was designed and directed by Eugène Lourié, who worked as art director or production designer for Jean Renoir (*Les Bas-fonds* [1936]; *La Grande Illusion* [1937]), Charles Chaplin (*Limelight* [1952]), and Samuel Fuller (*Shock Corridor* [1963], *The Naked Kiss* [1964]). During the dinosaur's attack on New York in *Beast*, the only egregiously false note is that as the beast advances through the city, a policeman shouts into a call box that it is headed for "National and Pine"—a pair of streets that might exist in Anytown, U.S.A., but that do not, alas, in Manhattan. After the irradiated Beast's rampage, it disappears, apparently slipping away unnoticed (how else would such a beast disappear?), and the streets are deserted and disquietingly quiet. This plot improbability only enhances the sense of the creature as a dreamlike horror that can materialize anywhere. As troops are deployed in search of it, there is a location shot of Times Square, empty, except for the forlorn fluttering of pigeons—disturbed, presumably, by the second unit camera crew taking the shot, but nonetheless an effectively melancholic image of urban desolation that also pops up in the post-apocalyptic *The World, the Flesh and the Devil* (1959), in which Harry Belafonte wanders through the silent streets of Manhattan before finding other survivors of a holocaust (see Knight). In *Beast*, the preternatural calm of the back lot and studio sets through which the soldiers march adds to the film's eerie vision of the city that normally never sleeps.

Eventually, the creature is found and cornered at the famous Cyclone Roller Coaster in Coney Island. The setting provides an added thrill to the climax (I'd been on that very coaster many times before, knew its contours well). But just as it was only later that I could watch *Beast* and be fascinated by the fact that the marksman sent up on the roller coaster with the new weapon is Lee Van Cleef— with hair!—so it was that only when viewing the film again as an adult did I understand the roller coaster climax as a reflexive metaphor for the way popular movies such as *Beast* themselves provide us with a series of coordinated and controlled thrills, anticipating the supposedly more postmodern *Jurassic Park* (1993) forty years later. Such a perspective, of course, came only after I learned about film theory and the possibilities of interpretation. When I watched as a boy, subtext did not exist for me, and what I most admired about the movie was what Godard would call the reality of its illusion rather than the illusion of reality. As I suggested, *The Beast from 20,000 Fathoms* does retain some of the moody atmosphere for which Ray Bradbury's source story "The Foghorn" (1951) is well known, but my initial enjoyment of the movie as a young boy was as an effective preadolescent fantasy of wreaking destruction on the world ("This is full scale war against a terrible enemy such as modern man has never before faced," explains the news announcer during the post-rampage montage)—that is, on *my* world, precisely the world I knew. (Note: In her story "Attack of the Giant Baby," Kit Reed humorously comments on the preadolescent pleasure of such scenes, following the narrative conventions of the monster movie outlined by Susan Sontag [209–12], but replaces the enlarged dinosaur with an oversized toddler named Leonard who accidentally drank his scientist/father's experimental growth serum [Reed 178–86]).

Truth be told, *Beast* really doesn't show much of New York City. The film adeptly mixes in a few location shots of Times Square, Wall Street, Herald Square, and Thirty-fourth Street, but it's mostly backlot and model work. It works by a kind of Kuleshov effect, enhanced by my personal sense of place. I suppose there was something like pride of ownership involved: New York was my town, after all. Susan Sontag accurately locates the appeal of monster movies as being rooted in an "aesthetics of destruction"—"the peculiar beauties to be found in wreaking havoc, making a mess," as she puts it—but she is wrong in describing this pleasure as "dispassionate" (213–16). Audiences always enjoy seeing their own places represented in movies (even if they are being destroyed!), and their pleasure in films with such personal resonance is inevitably greater. Surely my youthful experience of the film was enhanced by seeing Ray Harryhausen's Rhedosaurus rumble down streets that were familiar to me on a personal level.

Yet, where was the Bronx, my part of New York, in all of this? For the Bronx was definitively not Manhattan—nor even, in the popular imagination, it seemed, New York City. The Bronx was a world apart, separated by a divide as great as the one that would, in 1977, confront Brooklynite Tony Manero (John Travolta) in *Saturday Night Fever* or, in 1988, daunt that ambitious secretary from Queens, Tess McGill (Melanie Griffith), in *Working Girl*. Most of the time in the movies, it seemed, Manhattan and New York City were synonymous, even though "the Bronx is up and the Battery down," as they sing in *On the Town* (1949), and never the two shall meet. In Hollywood films, blondes, nurses, and vampires come from or go to Brooklyn, but their travels never take them to the Bronx. Trees grow in Brooklyn, where there also are metaphorically resonant last exits. Béla Lugosi even met a gorilla from Brooklyn (1952), not the Bronx (even though a cottage once lived in by Edgar Allan Poe, author of "The Murders in the Rue Morgue," about a killer gorilla, still stands as a heritage site near Fordham Road). There is an identifiable Brooklyn type—fast-talking, gum-chewing, and wise-cracking, with an identifiable accent, like Eve Arden in virtually any role—but the Bronx conjures no such distinctive image. While *It Happened in Brooklyn* in 1947, in the movies nothing much happens in the Bronx, where *Marty* (1955), a self-effacing butcher (Ernest Borgnine), spends his days emptily wondering what to do. True, *Quackser Fortune Has a Cousin in the Bronx* (1970), but in the movie the eponymous protagonist, played by Gene Wilder, never gets out of Dublin. And in *Rumble in the Bronx* (*Hong faan qui* [1995]), Jackie Chan fights not only street gangs but also a runway hovercraft, the mountains of Vancouver (Brooklyn Heights?), where the film was shot, clearly visible in the background. In short, the mythology of the Bronx is in baseball, with the Bronx Bombers in the House that Ruth Built, not in movies.

Looking at those aerial establishing shots of New York, I had always hoped to catch a glimpse of the southern end of the Bronx, marginalized in the upper right corner of the frame (the shots always looked north from the harbor, showing the lower Manhattan skyline) as it was in the stories on the screen. If I didn't see it in those opening shots in movies I saw as a child, though, I did get to see my old neighborhood in a few movies later on, as an adult and only after the borough had succumbed to the growing crime rate of inner-city America in the 1970s and 1980s and became famous as the prime example of urban decay. So, in *The Bonfire of the Vanities* (1990), wealthy stockbroker Sherman McCoy's fall from the height of financial success with a "six million dollar apartment" in Manhattan to the lower depths of personal and professional despair is represented by him being confined to a dark underpass of a highway ramp in the South Bronx. *Fort Apache the Bronx* (1981) is a not-very-disguised western about cops in the same area. The film's generic logic works to depict civilization in the precinct neighborhood as having decayed to the point that it is more like the wilderness of westerns like *Stagecoach* (1939) or, for that matter, *Fort Apache* (1948)—that is, as the antithesis rather than the logical outcome of late capitalism. In John Cassavetes's *Gloria* (1980), Gena Rowlands and a young boy are pursued by mobsters through the South Bronx, in some of the same locations as in *Fort Apache the Bronx*. They flee through the fleabag remnants of the Concourse Plaza Hotel that, only a few blocks from Yankee Stadium, was once the ritziest in the Bronx, where many baseball players stayed when they were in town to lose to the Yankees. Knowing that across the street from this hotel was the stately borough criminal courthouse, boasting an impressive exterior marble facade with steps like the ones James Cagney dies on in *The Roaring Twenties* (1939) and massive Doric columns bespeaking the stately stability of Law, was extra-textual knowledge that gave the film's scenes of violence in the surrounding streets a poignant irony for me.

These films were preceded by a pair of movies, both released in 1979, that made it clear that the Bronx of my youth was a bygone Bronx. Philip Kaufman's *The Wanderers*, set in 1963, about a group of high school friends who must band together when various ethnic gangs compete for neighborhood turf, does evoke the true racist tensions that emerged during the period when the Bronx, then predominantly white (Italian, Irish, and Jewish), witnessed a migration of blacks and Latino/as from Manhattan. But in the film the gangs (including the Fordham Baldies, an actual gang and, for my social group then, a name spoken with muted terror), seem closer to Henry Winkler's genial Fonzie from television's "Happy Days" than to the real hoods from this 'hood. *The Wanderers* is ultimately a stylized *American Graffiti*-in-da-Bronx, with its conflicts resolved on the high school football field. The film's vision of the Bronx is tinged with a nostalgia that could not help but reveal the gap between its idealized past and the grim realities of the contemporary Bronx in 1979. In Walter Hill's more overtly expressionist *The Warriors*, a Coney Island gang is framed for the death of an influential and respected gang member at a meeting in the north Bronx, and pursued by other gangs from all over the city seeking revenge while trying to make it back to their home turf. The film uses some actual locations in the Bronx, but its overt stylization—"a comic strip world, with its bright colors, rapid fire editing, thinly drawn characters, neon signs, spray paint graffiti covering nearly every visible surface" (Sobchack 83)—makes *The Warriors* less about the real Bronx than a genre fantasy, a hybrid war film in which the gang is the lost patrol trying to return safely through enemy lines in the urban jungle.[1]

Martin Scorsese's *Raging Bull* (1980), starring Robert De Niro as boxer Jake LaMotta, does offer a greater sense of verisimilitude (or, perhaps more accurately, a different kind of stylization) in its Bronx scenes, but De Niro's own *A Bronx Tale* (1993) is decidedly more nostalgic. Set in the early 1960s on Belmont Avenue, just east of Fordham Road, the home of Dion and the Belmonts, the Bronx's most successful doo-wop group of the time,[2] the film's coming-of-age story involves a boy (Francis Capra, Lillo Brancato) who is torn between the honest, working-class values of his bus-driving father (De Niro) and the criminal, streetwise ways of his gangster mentor (Chazz Palminteri). The film makes good use of period music from classic doo-wop groups to Jimi Hendrix and Procol Harum, but any period detail the film may achieve is negated by the fact that it is clearly not shot on location on Belmont Avenue, or anywhere in the Bronx, for that matter, as any Bronxite could readily tell by the telephone poles and overhead power lines, for in this part of the real Bronx all these lines were underground. (It was actually filmed, needless to say, in Brooklyn.) As someone who similarly had to negotiate between the street and the home in the struggle to define my own young masculine identity, I desperately wanted to appreciate this film more than I did. But ultimately I was disappointed in *A Bronx Tale* for essentially the same reason that I liked *The Beast from 20,000 Fathoms*—its fidelity to a real place and time that can only be known by someone who "was there"—despite the fact that I saw them almost forty years apart. Interestingly, I impose such aesthetic demands on no other movies.

Anyone who has ever ridden in an elevated subway train or in an automobile underneath one on a sunny day knows that Stan Brakhage's *Wonder Ring* (1955), shot on the now-gone Third Avenue El, is one of the greatest of New York City films, for it captures a certain play of light and shade that was as unique to New York elevated subways as, say, luminous layered light is to the Grand Canyon. For me, Brakhage's four-minute silent 16 mm film captures a greater truth about New York than "realist" narrative movies like *The French Connection* (1971), which attempt to show the same terrain. In the Bronx, brothers George and Mike Kuchar were documenting the borough more profoundly than any Hollywood movie I was going to at the time, including *Marty*, the touchstone example of Bronx kitchen-sink naturalism. As George Kuchar described his *Mosholu Holiday* (1966), it is "a documentary-like movie about the Bronx and its hell spawn filmed in hot weather and on location. . . . A special guest appearance by Canadian TV star Bill

Ronald along with the massive presence of 'Mrs. Bronx' herself, Frances Leibowitz, and her girlfriend Iris, make this film a must-see for travel enthusiasts and horror fans" (*Filmmakers'* 147). But at that time I knew nothing about the unique charms of experimental cinema—didn't even know there was such a thing as an alternative to Hollywood. Such films would wait until later, when I graduated from high school and discovered a new world by moving into my first apartment in the Lower East Side of Greenwich Village, around the corner from the Charles Cinema on Avenue B, where Jack Smith's *Flaming Creatures* (1963) and Kenneth Anger's *Scorpio Rising* (1964) seemed to play the entire year I lived there.

Curiously, with the notable exception of *Marty*, none of the mainstream movies about the Bronx showed the pervasive presence of movie theaters in the local culture. This is strange because movies were such a part of everyday life—and not just because during the studio era people went to movies more frequently than they do today, but because theaters were ubiquitous in the Bronx. They were there, part of the street scene, mixing with the storefronts of butcher shops and bakeries, almost as common as the corner candy store; their neon marquees jostled with the electric mix of signs for the equally pervasive Chinese restaurants. They were, in short, integrated in the neighborhoods of the Bronx, and many who grew up there not only went to the movies regularly, they also had their high school graduations in them. Movie theaters were, in short, integrated into the daily rhythm of Bronx life. Indeed, there were probably more movie theaters in the Bronx than anywhere else on Earth, save Manhattan and (arrgh!) Brooklyn.

From where I lived on a small street near 170th Street between Jerome Avenue and the Grand Concourse, one could box the compass by cinemas. I could walk only a few blocks in any direction, and there was a movie theater. To the east of my apartment building was the Kent Cinema, at 190 E. 167th Street, just on the other side of the Grand Concourse; to the south on 167th Street and River Avenue was the 167th Street Theater; to the west was the aforementioned Zenith; to the north was the Surrey, near the intersection of Mount Eden and Walton Avenues, and the Jerome Theater, at Tremont and Jerome Avenues; to the northeast, The Luxor, at the crest of the hill on 170th Street near the Grand Concourse; and north by northwest (yes!) was the Mt. Eden on Mt. Eden Avenue and the Concourse. There were others, if I cast a wider net, that I went to less frequently because they were further away, including the Chester, at the east end of Tremont Avenue on Boston Road, where on a night out with my father I saw *The Beast with a Million Eyes* (1955) and he and I pretended to be scared together; the Spooner on Southern Boulevard where I saw Inoshiro Honda's *The H-Man* (*Bijo to Ekitaininingen / Beauty and the Liquidman*, 1958), the first scary movie in which I kept my eyes open and fixed on the screen from start to finish, a feat achieved through sheer power of will; the Earl Theater, on 161st Street, a few steps from Yankee Stadium, where in 1967 I went to see the exclusive Bronx engagement of Joseph Strick's adaptation of *Ulysses*—a posh affair, with special programs handed out to patrons; and the

Allerton, where for some reason, even though I was then living in upstate New York, I first saw *The Wild Bunch* in 1969 and afterward felt at once breathless and exhilarated.

Almost all these theaters were built in the late 1920s, a couple in the 1930s, and they were an indelible part of the movie experience, of "going to the movies."[3] For if their exteriors were part of the bustling cityscape, inside they were more spacious and silent than anything to be found in the real world outside. In the Bronx, apart from the famous zoo and botanical gardens, "nature" consisted mostly of small pocket parks like the one in uptown Manhattan captured so marvelously in a bravura tracking shot in *David Holzman's Diary* (1967). The cavernous quality of these theaters was crucial, because they were able to swallow me whole, to envelop me completely, giving me ample room to enter into the expansive fantasies offered on their screens. The 167th Street Theater, for example, had 1950 seats on the orchestra floor, 450 in the balcony, and 200 in the loges and boxes—about the same size as most of the other movie houses. Since by the mid-1950s, with the rapid spread of commercial television, neighborhood movie theaters were already in decline, they were hardly ever full when I went in the afternoons, so they seemed even bigger. As a kid in the Bronx, I could only imagine a place where the sidewalk ends, much less a territory where a man had the elbow room to do manly things. One stylized scene in *The Wanderers* shows the distinctive brick facades of vintage Bronx apartment buildings like canyon walls; but unlike Huck Finn, the only way I could light out for the territory was to project myself into the seemingly endless flow of westerns I saw.

My neighborhood movie theaters truly were compass points, because they helped me navigate the stormy seas of adolescence. I learned the values of postwar America through movies, a successfully positioned ideological subject. I went to the movies regularly, at least once a week, regardless of what was showing, although I tended to avoid melodramas and love stories, which seemed remote from my boyish interests.[4] I tended to go on Saturday afternoons, sometimes with friends, sometimes alone, when I would be treated to the classic program of newsreel, cartoon, coming attractions, short subject or sometimes serial, and two feature-length movies. Until I was twelve (but really until I was old enough to ignore the restriction), I had to suffer the indignity of sitting in a roped-off "children's section," often patrolled by uniformed matrons who looked like Shirley Stoler, flashlights in hand like truncheons and keeping watch, ready to pounce on us should we throw Ju-jubes at other kids in the front rows (stale ones were harder, hence better for making an impression). We had to time our rowdy activities between their patrols, like American POWs in one of the many war movies I saw.

The theaters, most of which were owned by RKO or Loew's, were organized into an exhibition hierarchy that everyone seemed to know intuitively. In the 1950s, the Ogden was regarded as being at the bottom end—in its last days, I saw the likes of *Abbott and Costello Meet the Mummy* (1955) there. The Zenith, a latecomer built in 1937 in the Art Deco style, was at the foot of a hill, in the shadows of the

Jerome Avenue El. The irony of its location in relation to its name never struck me, perhaps because the movies programmed there—like *The Beast from 20,000 Fathoms*—always seemed to me to be top-flight even though they were double features of second- and third-run films. The most prestigious theater in the neighborhood was undoubtedly the Luxor. Built in the Egyptian style in 1923, it was where I saw, among others, *Creature from the Black Lagoon* (1954), *Invasion of the Body Snatchers* (1956), and *The Incredible Shrinking Man* (1957). It was at the Luxor, too, that I saw *The Manchurian Candidate* (1962) on a very hot summer night, when the humidity outside the theater made those close-ups of Frank Sinatra's sweaty face all the more convincing. Later, as I entered puberty, I rushed to see *Nude in a White Car* at the Luxor, which by this point had seen better days. The risqué title (the film was either French or Italian), which must have been slapped on for American distribution (I can find no record of it: could I have imagined it all?), held great promise for a boy on the cusp of puberty, but unfortunately the film didn't live up to it: there was lots of footage of the convertible but almost nothing of the nude, at least that you could see. At best I was like Michel-Ange in Godard's *Les Carabiniers* (1962), craning my neck for a better view but to no avail.

Going to first-run theaters in Manhattan, where films would show before their first-run in the satellite boroughs, was reserved for special family outings, usually on New Year's Day. We would pile into the family Buick and venture south into midtown. Usually we were part of a larger caravan of kin, several cars of cousins snaking our way along the FDR Drive with all the subtlety of Charles Foster Kane's picnic parade on the beach at Xanadu. We would drive to Times Square on New Year's Day, an eerie experience recalling *The World, the Flesh and the Devil*, something no sane person would do during a weekday. Just hours earlier there had been a million partygoers jammed into these very same streets along with Guy Lombardo, as I'd seen on television. As we drove, I'd watch the streets pass by through the car window like lengthy, lugubrious tracking shots, a young boy's version of *Taxi Driver* (1976). One of the huge billboards on Times Square would always be advertising the movie we were seeing. We would go to the Broadway, the State, Radio City Music Hall, or the Capitol, the first theater to be equipped with Cinerama, and see something like *Ben-Hur* (1959) or *Exodus* (1960), movies as monumental as the theaters in which they were showing.

But it was the Paradise, located in the Bronx at 2413 Grand Concourse at 188th Street, that sealed my celluloid fate more than the lavish downtown theaters. The Paradise, also called the Loew's ("Low-ees" to Bronxites) Paradise, was one of the five Loew's "Wonder Theatres," so named because each was equipped with a Robert Morton pipe organ.[5] The Fordham Road area was the largest shopping district in the Bronx, and it had several impressive movie theaters, including the Lido, the Capri, the Valentine, the Windsor, the Grand, and the Concourse. But it was the Paradise, the exhibition chain's flagship cinema in the Bronx, that stood apart as the grandest of them all.

Located on the stately Grand Concourse near Fordham Road, the Paradise was built during the era of the great "atmospheric" movie palaces. Designed by the style's prime practitioner, John Eberson, the Paradise opened on September 7, 1929, with *The Mysterious Dr. Fu Manchu* (1929) starring Warner Oland. Like Eberson's other grandiose atmospheric theaters, the Paradise transported New Yorkers into a Baroque Italian garden decorated with marble pillars, Romanesque statues, tapestries, and bubbling fountains. Boasting 3885 seats and arguably surpassed in size in New York only by Radio City Music Hall, the Paradise had seemingly endless mezzanines, loges, and balconies. According to Michael Miller, "In the center of the lobby's north wall, beneath a statue of Winged Victory, a great fountain of Carrara marble bubbled water about a carved figure of a child on a dolphin" (Miller 8). Historians of the classic movie palaces debate about whether the Paradise had a pond with goldfish in its inner lobby, but I remember it distinctly. Outside, above the unique flat marquee with its striking sunburst pattern, a statue of Saint George slaying a dragon would animate every hour on the hour.

The Paradise's greatest and best-known feature was its spacious, arching ceiling, on which was painted an elaborately detailed mural of a night sky. This was Eberson's specialty, and apparently he designed the stars in the Paradise in the constellation of Marcus Loew's astrological birth sign, Taurus, but I don't remember that. They were just there, overwhelming, everyone's topic of discussion until the house lights went down and the show began. Some of the stars actually twinkled (or was it just my imagination?), a mural in motion—not unlike the spectacles on the screen. If the movie theaters of my youth allowed one room to fantasize, the Paradise gave the imagination free rein.

The Paradise was about a mile or so north of where I lived, which fit my personal mythology just fine. Its beckoning lights, outshining everything else around, were like the Bronx's own aurora borealis. And going north, uptown, to the aptly named Paradise was like an ascent to heaven.

The theater's stellar canopy made it the perfect venue for me to see Cecil B. DeMille's remake of *The Ten Commandments* (1956), to which my grandmother took me when I was an impressionable nine-year-old. Advertisements proclaimed: "First time anywhere at popular prices . . . See the complete intact, uncut picture exactly as it was presented on Broadway for more than 70 weeks." Prices were 40 cents for children, 75 cents afternoons except Sundays, when admission was 99 cents (Robert R). Although I had seen movies like *Shane* (1953) at the Paradise before, this time I was thunderstruck not only by the epic sweep of the movie but also by the magnificent opulence of the theater (like the monumental pyramids that Ramses constructs within the film). Eberson's masterpiece was one of those "emporiums to the illusive God of movies," and somehow I understood it to represent for better or worse what movies (at least Hollywood movies) were all about (Sharp 81). It was here that my passion for movies was born, as consuming as DeMille's Jell-O sea was for Yul Brynner and the infidel Egyptians who doubted the power of special effects and cinematic illusion. It was a kind of primal scene for me, just as it would be again four years later when I saw *G.I. Blues* (1960) at the Paradise and, a brazen thirteen, fell truly, madly, deeply in love with Juliet Prowse.

As time passed and I got older, I found myself going to theaters other than the Paradise. By the time of *Dr. Strangelove, or How I Learned to Stop Worrying and Love the Bomb* (1964), I was taking the subway downtown to films in first-run venues. I saw *2001: A Space Odyssey* (1968) during its premiere run at the Capitol in 65 mm. Super Panavision 70, an experience impossible back home (I remember having hated watching the compressed version of the Cinerama epic *How the West Was Won* [1962], which I saw shriveled and eviscerated in one of my neighborhood movie houses). By the mid-1960s I had friends with cars, and so was often going to the Whitestone Drive-In, where I could fantasize about the car culture that I'd see in teen movies set somewhere in that warm California sun. And just a few blocks down the Grand Concourse from the Paradise was the considerably more intimate and humble Ascot Theatre on 183rd Street. Built in 1935, the Ascot was possibly the only art theater in the Bronx. The posters, strangely, were always in black and white, just like the B movies at the Zenith but certainly unlike what I considered the really important movies playing down the street at the Paradise. The first film I saw at the Ascot was Ingmar Bergman's *Persona* (1966)—a difficult film by any standards and one that no one, not even John Simon, has been able to explicate fully. Afterward, certainly, I had no idea of what I'd just seen, but it was definitely not from Hollywood. In ways I couldn't as yet articulate or fully comprehend, I vaguely understood that somehow the possibilities of cinema had been shown to me. It changed my life, as when I first listened to Bob Dylan or Miles Davis. I had been expelled from the Paradise (with no apple in the Big Apple), thrust into the knowledge of art cinema ambiguity, and I could never go home again.

In 1973, when much of the Bronx, including the apartment building I grew up in and every other building on the street, had been reduced to rubble, I made a pilgrimage to the north Bronx and saw that the Paradise had met a sad fate, mercilessly bisected—twinned in industry jargon—as was happening at the time to most large downtown urban theaters across the United States that were still operating. But it seemed particularly blasphemous for the heavenly Paradise. The theater was further divided into three before finally closing, possibly as late as 1994. At least they could have named those theaters the Paradise, the Purgatory, and the Inferno, according to their location within the cavernous building, and have programmed movies thematically (art films like *Last Year at Marienbad* or *Through a Glass Darkly* in the Purgatory, horror films in the Inferno, and so on). But it was merely the bland, undignified Paradise I, II, and III, an ignominious end to a once-magnificent spot on earth.

According to one theater historian, "The 'atmospheric' was firmly rooted in a conviction that visual gimcrackery is the primary demand of the paying public and the more splendour and glitter that can be brought together to inspire an audience the better they will respond" (Sharp 74). Certainly so, and as I've only recently discovered (in fact, while researching this essay), the sumptuous interior of the Paradise was a formative fantasy shared by many. At the cinematreasures website, where people can post comments, memories, and information about old movie theaters, one writer reminisced, "I used to go to the Paradise in the 1960's. It was my refuge. I used to stare at the stars, and dream what it would be like when I was on my own. I just loved this place. I hated when they turned it into a multiplex." Another commented, "As a child in the late 40's and early 50's I went to the Paradise. The Paradise, with the moving clouds and stars was by far, one of my greatest movie experiences." Also posted is yet another shared memory that sounds remarkably like my own, with parents taking a child to see *The Ten Commandments*. The writer describe it as

> one of my formative experiences. . . . The theater was still a single screen at the time, and it was quite a spectacle to see the teeming multitudes in the orchestra level below (we were late so could only get balcony seats, but that was alright by me). The place was packed, and I have never seen a movie theater audience of that size ever again, not even for the later blockbusters. It was all spectacle, on the screen, in the great room, on the ceiling, in the monstrous lobby. I vaguely recall satyrs and maidens along balustraded grand staircases and mezzanines. (Anderson, Theatrefan, and Gm_acevedo, postings on cinematreasure.org)

Eberson wanted the paying public to be drawn by "the place of entertainment as well as in the entertainment itself," and it would seem that he succeeded with theaters like the Paradise (Eberson 106).

By 1980, with the declining fortunes of the film industry, almost every one of the movie theaters I went to as a youth was gone. The Luxor was a liquor store, the Kent a dollar store. The Zenith is now the Latino Action Pastoral Center, its marquee gone, dismantled along with the Jerome Avenue elevated subway. Ironically, while all these other theaters have either been razed or converted into convenience stores or churches, the Paradise is the only one still standing. Its interior is incomplete and the organ console is now at the fully restored Loew's Jersey in Jersey City, New Jersey. The Paradise's most recent owners began turning it into a boxing arena and concert venue but ran out of money before completing renovations. As of this writing, the fate of the Paradise remains open, lacking the narrative closure that typified the movies it showed in its glory days. Although the Bronx may not have been shown much in movies, despite being an important part of New York City, it was without doubt a place steeped in moviedom. Over the years, the Bronx may have become the far side of paradise, and the Paradise's starry sky may be dimmed at present, but it nonetheless remains lit by the memories of patrons like me who grew up there.

NOTES

1. See David Desser, "'When We See the Ocean, We Figure We're Home': From Ritual to Romance in *The Warriors*," in this volume.—Ed.

2. Doo-wop is a term used retrospectively to describe singing groups that at the time were referred to as vocal harmony R& B. Many of these groups came from Brooklyn, Queens, and Manhattan, but several from the Bronx also found modest local and even national success on the R&B charts. In addition to Dion and the Belmonts, other groups were the The Regents (responsible for the original "Barbara Ann," later covered by the Beach Boys), the Demensions [*sic*], the Halos, and the girl groups the Chiffons, the Chantels, and the Hearts.

3. Information about many of these theaters is available at kraybill.home.mindspring.com and cinematreasures.org.

4. The cultural saturation of movies in New York City was also evident on television. The city had more local stations and network affiliates than anywhere else in the country, and some programmed films heavily, including WOR's "Million Dollar Movie," which allowed viewers the luxury of seeing the same film every night for a week.

5. The other Loew's Wonder Theatres equipped with these "wonder organs," as they were known, were the Valencia in Queens, the Kings Theater in Brooklyn, the Jersey in Jersey City, and the 175th Street Theater in Manhattan.

THERE'S A PLACE FOR US
City of Characters and Spaces

"There's a Place for Us" presents essays about particular characters and spaces of filmed New York. This is the city where one meets the Godfather, Serpico, Alvy Singer, Broadway Danny Rose, or Tommy DeVito, Paul Cicero, Johnny Roastbeef, Frankie the Wop, "Johnny Boy" Civello, Teresa Ronchelli, Bill "The Butcher" Cutting, and thousands of other denizens of the world of Martin Scorsese; not to mention Donnie Brasco, "Lefty" Ruggiero, Jerry Langford, Homer Flagg, Brenda Cushman, Mama Rose Lee, Deborah Fifer, Earl Janoth, George M. Cohan, and so on. This is where one dances in the Rainbow Room, dines at The Four Seasons or Dean and DeLuca or at any of a hundred favorite spaghetti spots in the West Village; climbs the Empire State Building; speeds past the sweeping edifice of the United Nations; inhabits the tenements of Little Italy or Spanish Harlem; configures oneself, in short, in terms of the definitive and characteristic locations the city provides or the unforgettably direct, dramatic, delirious characters one meets.

This section begins with William Rothman's examination of "Woody Allen's New York," in which the author asks, if New York is Woody's kind of town, is Woody truly New York's kind of man? Central in Allen's career is his not making it in Hollywood, not being what the "God of cinema" might call a filmmaker— an issue that comes up in *Annie Hall* in a way that Rothman specifically relates to Allen's monologue at the Academy Awards in 2002. To work out Woody Allen's complex relation not only to New York but also to filmmaking in general, Rothman considers *Broadway Danny Rose* and *Annie Hall* to as well as *Manhattan*, in light of Howard Hawks's *Twentieth Century*, George Cukor's *The Philadelphia Story*, and the Emersonianism of Stanley Cavell. In the typical Allen film, writes Rothman, "New York is the place where Woody pursues happiness, but fails to find it."

Paula J. Massood's essay, "From *Mean Streets* to the *Gangs of New York*," examines urban space and ethnicity in the films of Martin Scorsese. For Massood, Scorsese "draws upon, and often revises, generic conventions to construct narratives that are at one and the same time about local and national mythologies . . . [that] masterfully connect the tribalism of New York with national narratives of isolationism, violence, and belonging. They reject the overdetermined myth of the melting pot often ascribed to the city." The analysis here centers on *Who's That Knocking at My Door*, *Mean Streets*, *GoodFellas*, and *Gangs of New York*, ultimately showing how "Scorsese's city is linked to larger national mythologies of assimilation and citizenship" and how this director is especially sensitive to the meaning, for culture and ethnicity, for personality and group affiliation, that space in the city can have.

David A. Gerstner examines the Andy Warhol who was "New-York-City urban" and "Manhattan modern." He is fascinated by Warhol's desire to be a recording device, and sees that "the frenetic swirl of unbridled capitalism in New York enabled that modern/machine experience like no other place." Warhol's persistent recording, what Peter Wollen called "storage," is contrasted with his devout commitment to empty spaces. The places of New York, for Warhol, were "blank spaces to be continuously filled *and* recorded with, for example, the performances of his Superstars and whatever other materials the city left in its wake."

Then, to conclude, my own essay is a meditation on Alfred Hitchcock's engaging outsider's view of the city, a view which in many ways resonates with my own. I focus especially on *The Wrong Man* and *North by Northwest*, noting how Hitchcock has grasped an essence of New York that is elusive to other filmmakers. For him, this place is far from generic; he visited it in his imagination before he breathed its air, and imagined himself in its prospects from a long way off. But through a meticulous devotion of attention to the smallest details of experience, he is able to render New York onscreen with a brilliance and authenticity that are pungent and enduring.

Isaac Davis (Woody Allen) possesses a crucial piece of self-knowledge at the end of *Manhattan* (Woody Allen, United Artists, 1979). Digital frame enlargement.

Woody Allen's
New York

WILLIAM ROTHMAN

Making his first and probably his last appearance at the Oscars in Hollywood in 2002, Woody Allen introduced a montage of New York films and made a plea for producers to continue filming their movies in New York after the 9/11 tragedy.

Who more fitting?

Nearly all of Woody Allen's films are set in New York City. Manhattan is the place where Woody Allen lives and works, as do the characters he plays in his films. It's the only place where we—and he—can imagine Woody thriving, or, perhaps, even surviving, at least on his own recognizance. Our sense that Woody Allen feels at home only in New York is reinforced by his character's disastrous trip to Los Angeles in *Annie Hall* (1977). It seems confirmed by *Wild Man Blues* (1997), Barbara Kopple's subtle and ultimately quite moving cinema-verité chronicle of his concert tour of Europe. Despite traveling in the company of his jazz band and his sister Letty, and with wife-to-be Soon-Yi Previn adroitly and tactfully helping him negotiate his interactions with strangers, he can't help feeling like a fish out of water. ("Hey, you've got a hell of a town here," he says in Bologna. "I know with a couple of Valium I could really learn to love it.") Only when he's onstage, playing Dixieland jazz with his friends, can he relieve his homesickness or give it satisfying expression.

So often, in his films, we see him walking, and talking, on Central Park West, Fifth Avenue, Broadway, and other bustling Manhattan streets. Invariably, in those shots, those streets look strikingly handsome. Woody Allen's Manhattan isn't a grimy urban jungle. It's the most photogenic city on earth, boasting buildings and trees that even Paris would die for. (As if we needed more proof that cameras can lie!)

New York is Woody's kind of town. But does that mean that Woody is New York's kind of man? To paraphrase his favorite Groucho Marx line, surely Woody Allen wouldn't want to live in a town that would have someone like him as its representative. If Woody Allen is a representative New Yorker, what does that say about New York?

Woody is also a native New Yorker, of course—at least if we count Brooklyn as part of New York City. The man we know as Woody Allen was born Allen Konigsberg, and it was in Brooklyn, not Manhattan, that he spent his childhood and adolescence. Brooklyn is an "outer borough" firmly within Manhattan's orbit. Until 1898, though, it was autonomous—a great city separate from, and almost equal to, New York City itself, which was already dominated by Manhattan.

In Hollywood movies of the classical era, Brooklyn retained something of its own identity, although Brooklynites were generally reduced to comic stereotypes (and, in war movies, rarely survived to the end of the film). In the real world in which Woody Allen grew up, what Brooklyn retained of its identity was a sense of separateness. Even for me, growing up in Flatbush a decade or so after Woody, "going to the city" meant crossing the river into Manhattan. Brooklyn was the place *outside* what it was *inside*.

That Woody spent his formative years in Brooklyn, not Manhattan, helps explain the doubleness of Manhattan in his films. It is the real place in which— onscreen and off—he lives his everyday life. And within Woody Allen's Manhattan there are also special places, apart from the bustle of the city, that Woody loves to seek out. One of his favorites is the pocket park off Sutton Place, in the shadow of the Queensboro Bridge—a spot so lovely that one doesn't have to be Fred Astaire—one can even be a nice Jewish boy from Brooklyn—to imagine one's romantic dreams magically coming true there. Such places, in Woody's films, seem filtered through his imagination and memory, vestiges of the romantic yearnings of that clever, scrawny boy, growing into manhood, who made forays into "the city," but lived across the river.

And yet, there he was that evening back in Los Angeles, the city New Yorkers most love to mock, speaking on behalf of New York to the countless millions around the globe for whom the Academy Awards are a sacrament, not show business as usual. Woody began his brief monologue with a joking explanation as to why he was the one whom the Hollywood powers-that-be chose to represent New York on this occasion:

> And I said, "You know, God, you can do much better than me. You know, you might want to get Martin Scorsese, or, or Mike Nichols, or Spike Lee, or Sidney Lumet. . . ." I kept naming names, you know, and um, I said, "Look, I've given you fifteen names of guys who are more talented than I am, and, and smarter and classier. . . ." And God said, "Yes, but they weren't available."

Characteristically, Woody belittles himself in this little joke, confesses his inferiority, and at the same time shows off his formidable wit and thereby asserts his superiority. If you've got it, flaunt it. But in a humble way. Is this false humility? Not really. Surely, Woody genuinely respects the directors he names. He is acknowledging that they have talents he can't match. But he is also reminding us that he has a talent they can't match—a power of wit, a kind and degree of smartness (but not class!) that this joke exemplifies. And is there a (slight? not really so slight?) edge to his joke? Why *was* he available for this gig when those other New York–based directors had previous engagements? Is he alluding to the disastrous impact on his popularity, and his prestige, of Mia Farrow's breakup with him following the disclosure of his affair with her adopted daughter? If so, is he apologizing to the public, or castigating it?

Woody is more or less implying—at least for the sake of the joke—that in God's eyes, and his own, he's not much of an artist, if he's an artist at all. Woody is far from God's—or Hollywood's—first choice for this role, but he'll do. But if that's God's attitude toward art, how classy or smart—or talented, for that matter—can God be? If Woody's joke is at his own expense, it's also at God's expense, then, and at the expense of the Hollywood establishment, the powers-that-be responsible for putting on this show and inviting him to participate in it. ("I would never want to belong to any club that would have someone like me for a member.") The joke mocks Hollywood for selling—and mocks the public for buying—the crazy idea that the Academy Awards are about art, not about money. But, again, the butt of the joke is also God, who not only rubs shoulders on an everyday basis with agents and other low-life Hollywood types but lacks the clout to sign an A-list director.

And yet, in jokingly envisioning the Cosmos as Hollywood writ large, Woody envisions God—hence Hollywood—as *human*; indeed, as something of a *mensch*. In God's presence, Woody doesn't quake or quiver. He feels free to ask God the question that has been bugging him. And God, having already been turned down by so many directors, is no doubt anxious to press his advantage with this hack whose availability bespeaks the fact that he needs this deal as much as God does. Nonetheless, God doesn't beat around the bush, as it were, but gives Woody a direct, and truthful, answer. Even as they are haggling with each other, Woody and God have a real conversation, a conversation of equals.

I like to think of God, as this joke envisions Him, as spiritually akin to Broadway Danny Rose, Woody Allen's warmest, most lovable character. Danny Rose is a talent manager whose life revolves around buying and selling, who is forever angling for a better deal, but who nonetheless never stops being a *mensch*.

Or perhaps God, in Woody's joke, is closer to Oscar Jaffe, the John Barrymore character in *Twentieth Century* (1934), who gets carried away imagining how he would stage a spectacular production of the Passion Play, complete with camels and whirling dervishes, but only if he can get them at "rock bottom prices." For all his artistic pretensions, Oscar (and John Barrymore himself, perhaps), like Danny Rose, operates in a New York world in which everything revolves around buying and selling. Oscar is no *mensch*, but at least he is true to the spirit of the New York world in which he lives, loves, and operates. Oscar's world is a marketplace far closer to an Old World bazaar than to the contemporary America of multinational corporations. *Broadway Danny Rose* (1984) envisions Danny Rose as a throwback to that world, a world that the film envisions as threatened with extinction. It is a world only a step or two removed from a *shtetl*. Hence Oscar's scorn for his nemesis Max Jacobs (Charles Levison), *né* Max Mandelbaum, who changes his name "for some mysterious reason" when he abandons New York to make it in Hollywood. Presumably, the movies Max produces after he leaves New York are, to borrow

Woody Allen's own characterization of most Hollywood movies then and now, "conceived in venality" and "aimed at the lowest common denominator."

Oscar is contemptuous of Max for moving to Hollywood—a half-century before Rob (Tony Roberts) in *Annie Hall* incurs Alvy Singer's contempt by making the same move. (Ironically, Rob calls Alvy "Max" throughout the movie.) Oscar claims that he is "closing the iron door" on Max for betraying the art of theater. Surely, though, venality and aiming at the lowest common denominator are Oscar's vices, no less than Max's. Max really earns Oscar's scorn, I take it, for abandoning the New York world that is Oscar's as well as Max's own. Oscar's New York is a world of buying and selling, not a world of art, but at least it is a human world.

By jettisoning the name "Mandelbaum" in order to make it in Hollywood, of course, Max is revealing his ambivalence about his specific identity as a Jew. (Ever since Allen Konigsberg changed his name to Woody Allen, by contrast, he has hinged his career on cashing in on his Jewishness, not on covering it up.) It is important to keep in mind, however, that the New York world which both films oppose to Hollywood is not an exclusively Jewish world. It is an inclusive world of immigrants, of children of immigrants, of outsiders of all kinds (except for African Americans, but that's another story). In *Twentieth Century*, "New York," as opposed to "Hollywood," signifies a world-within-the-world of Americans engaged in the business of making something of themselves in an America whose established culture—or established lack of culture—they find inhuman, alien, and alienating. In the person of Woody Allen, onscreen and off, that world lives on, although on borrowed time. In *Twentieth Century*, Hollywood, as personified by Max Mandelbaum/Jacobs, is in denial of its roots. But in the bulldozed-over Hollywood of the twenty-first century, few roots of any kind remain. Studios once built by immigrants have become cogs in an interlocking network of multinational corporations. And New York, too, is on its way to becoming an inhospitable place for the likes of Woody Allen, as galloping gentrification strips neighborhoods of their individual character and threatens to turn all of Manhattan into a place inhabited only by careerists who are young and very rich.

For the sake of the joke, Woody Allen's Academy Awards monologue envisions Hollywood as still doing business in a way that keeps faith with its New York roots. Hollywood is not about art, it's about business. But so is New York. Woody doesn't buy into the view, which Hollywood began promulgating so effectively in its great postwar musicals, that "There's no business like show business"—the view that entertainment may not be art, but that it's just as good or even better, and certainly more American. Woody's joke implies, to the contrary, that show business is no different from any other business. This reflects Woody Allen's own oft-stated position that entertainment may have its value, but it's a lower order of enterprise than art. In his view, Hollywood movies are not in the same league as, say, the films of Fellini and Bergman. Those are real works of art.

Although there are some that he values, Hollywood movies, unlike his beloved Dixieland jazz, do not constitute a great artistic tradition in Woody Allen's view. It's not that he believes that Hollywood movies once were great but have now become debased. They always were what they are now. Hence he feels no need to distinguish between Hollywood's past and its present when he says, in the remark we have already quoted, "Hollywood for the most part aimed at the lowest common denominator. It's conceived in venality." Hollywood has always been motivated, as he puts it, "by pandering to the public, by making a lot of money. People like Ingmar Bergman thought about life, and they had feelings, and they wanted to dramatize them and engage one in a dialogue. I felt I couldn't easily be engaged by the nonsense that came out of Hollywood."

Presumably, the rare Hollywood movies that were not "aimed at the lowest common denominator," such as *Twentieth Century*, weren't simply "nonsense." But they were still entertainment, not art, in Woody Allen's view. Hollywood movies are what one has to break away from, not emulate, if one is to be a real film artist à la Bergman and Fellini.

To be sure, Bergman and Fellini are artists who have made great films. But *Twentieth Century* is a great film, too, a significant instance of the art of film. And *Annie Hall* and *Manhattan* are great, if flawed, films as well—greater artistic achievements, in my judgment, than, say, *Interiors* (1978) or *Stardust Memories* (1980), which suffer from their maker's sense that films have to look and feel like Bergman's or Fellini's if they are to count as works of art.

Woody Allen's Achilles' heel as a film artist is his inability or unwillingness to recognize the continuity between his own concerns and those of popular American movies at their best, especially the Hollywood comedies of the 1930s and 1940s that Stanley Cavell calls "comedies of remarriage." Films like *It Happened One Night* (1934), *The Awful Truth* (1937), *His Girl Friday* (1940), *The Lady Eve* (1941), *The Philadelphia Story* (1940), and *Adam's Rib* (1949) do compose an artistic tradition fully worthy of embracing, and continuing. Woody Allen has always resisted recognizing this. Thus he finds himself in an untenable situation. He has a rare and precious talent—"genius" isn't too strong a word—for making a kind of film behind which stands a great artistic tradition that he does not recognize as such, an American tradition he resists acknowledging as his own. ("I would never want to belong to any club that would have someone like me for a member," indeed.)

Nowhere is this more painfully evident than in *The Purple Rose of Cairo* (1985). Mia Farrow plays a waitress during the Depression searching for an escape from her dreary life. After losing her job she goes to the movies in the hope of raising her spirits. Much to her surprise, the hero of the film she is viewing walks off the screen and into her life. The fatal flaw of *The Purple Rose of Cairo* is that its cheesy film-within-the-film bears absolutely no meaningful relationship to any real Hollywood films of the period or, for that matter, to *The Purple Rose of Cairo* itself. What a waste of an eloquent performance by Mia Farrow—in their relationship as director and star, if not in their offscreen lives, they unfailingly bring out the best in each other—and of an inspired premise ideal for exploring the continuities, as well as the discontinuities, between Woody Allen's own films and the remarriage comedies of the 1930s.

Twentieth Century posits an opposition between New York and Hollywood that Woody Allen takes at face value. Yet Howard Hawks's film, with its brilliant screenplay and its monumental John Barrymore performance, also overcomes or transcends that opposition and thereby paves the way for the remarriage comedies that follow it. Originally a Broadway play, *Twentieth Century* made the move from New York to Hollywood, the same move made by Max Mandelbaum but without breaking faith with the New York world that was the play's subject and the source of its power. (Fittingly, Ben Hecht, the writer whose wit is stamped on both the play and screenplay, made the transition from New York to Hollywood without selling out and without changing his name, although admittedly the name "Hecht," like "Jaffe" and "Jacobs," is not as conspicuously Jewish as "Mandelbaum." Is "Konigsberg"?)

In the film of *Twentieth Century*, Oscar Jaffe retains his Jewish name (which is matched by "Mildred Plotka," the name of the Carole Lombard character before Oscar changes it to "Lily Garland"). And the film retains Oscar's telltale resentment of Max Mandelbaum's name change. Max is played by the hawk-nosed Charles Levison, who looks Jewish, and was (although "for some mysterious reason" he is listed in the credits as "Charles Lane"). Both Oscar and Mildred Plotka/Lily Garland, however, are played by the eminently non-Jewish Barrymore and Lombard. Nothing in Barrymore's performance either affirms or denies that the character he is playing is Jewish (or, for that matter, the actor himself, who had recently played a Jewish attorney in *Counsellor at Law* [1933]—in that performance, too, he gave his character no stereotypically Jewish mannerisms—and whose own more-than-ample nose is the most prominent feature of his noble profile). By playing Oscar Jaffe not as a stereotypical Jew, but as a larger-than-life version of John Barrymore (who was himself larger than life, of course), Barrymore gives a performance that renders moot the question of the character's Jewishness. What matters isn't whether Oscar Jaffe is Jewish. What matters is that he remains faithful to and unambiguously embraces a world that *Twentieth Century* identifies with New York, and opposes the venal and pandering Hollywood personified by Max Mandelbaum. In affirming its New York roots, rather than covering them up, the film at the same time embraces its identity as a Hollywood film. It is not renouncing Hollywood. It is planting New York's flag on Hollywood soil. It is declaring that Hollywood has changed, or, perhaps more accurately, is challenging Hollywood to change, to follow its lead. The comedies of remarriage, and the whole constellation of genres aligned with them, joyfully take up that challenge.

In remarriage comedies of the 1930s and 1940s, New York is the quintessential place, at once real and mythical, where modern American men and women pursue happiness. Happiness, in these films, requires an Emersonian philosophical perspective that enables them to live every day, and every night, in a spirit of adventure. To enable these New Yorkers to achieve this new perspective on their everyday lives, there is often a point when the action shifts from New York to a place just outside the city, a Shakespearean Green World that, as Cavell delights in pointing out, a number of the films call "Connecticut" (49). In *Eternal Sunshine of the Spotless Mind* (2004), a contemporary remarriage comedy, the lovers find such a place in Montauk. In *Broadway Danny Rose*, the lovers find it in the last spot a New Yorker would think of looking, the so-called Jersey Meadows.

In virtually every other Woody Allen film, however, the Woody character fails to achieve the requisite perspective—not in any place outside New York, where he immediately starts missing New York, and not in any of those beautiful places in Manhattan that he loves to haunt (and to film). He haunts such places because he can imagine his romantic dreams coming true there. But those places also haunt him. They haunt him with memories of the unfulfilled romantic yearnings of the nice Jewish boy from Brooklyn he once was, and still is. In Woody Allen's films, these places—like Brooklyn itself, they are inside the city, but also apart from the city—have the allure of romance and magic. Evidently, though, their magic isn't strong enough to break down Woody's resistance to change: at once a reluctance to allow his romantic dreams to come true, and a reluctance to confront, to free himself from, the past. The bottom line is that in the typical Woody Allen film New York is the place where Woody pursues happiness, but fails to find it.

Annie Hall is paradigmatic. It opens with a monologue in which Alvy Singer, the Woody character, speaks directly to the camera, sorting out his thoughts about his relationship with Annie Hall (Diane Keaton). Why did they break up? Why can't they come back together, this time committed to a relationship that will be "the same, but different," as *The Awful Truth* puts it?

If Alvy loved Annie the way Dex (Cary Grant) loves Tracy (Katharine Hepburn) in *The Philadelphia Story*, he'd move heaven and earth, even at the risk of a hernia, to try to win her back. But does he really love her? How could anyone? She's so, well, ditzy. Her ditziness is charming, up to a point, and at first Woody does make efforts to preside over her education in the hope that she might be transformed into a woman capable of having conversations with him about the things that interest him. Increasingly, though, that enterprise seems hopeless, both because it becomes ever more obvious that Annie is simply none too bright, and because it also seems more and more obvious that Alvy doesn't have the imagination to see this woman differently from the way we see her. Failing to grasp the teaching of the remarriage comedies that, as Hepburn puts it in *The Philadelphia Story*, "the time to make up your mind about people is never," Alvy gives up on Annie too easily to have Cary Grant's standing.

Alvy is certain that he's smarter than Annie. But he's as much in need of an education as she is. By the standards of films like *The Philadelphia Story*, neither is prepared for a relationship worth having. They would have to change. But they resist change. That's why their breakup is inevitable. Resisting change, Alvy clings to the view that his pursuit of happiness is doomed to failure. That view dooms his relationships to failure. Yet he persists in it anyway. Woody Allen is always described—and describes himself—as neurotic. Is that what his neurosis comes to?

Annie Hall, like most Woody Allen films, is peppered with witty assertions of New York's superiority—to Los Angeles, especially (Diane Keaton's home town, the city whose only "cultural advantage" over New York, according to Alvy, is that you can turn right on a red light), but also to the Middle America that is Annie Hall's homeland. To a New Yorker, a sense of superiority comes with the territory. But to a New Yorker who is also a nice Jewish boy from Brooklyn—especially one as physically unimpressive as Woody—so does a sense of inferiority. Although Woody is formidably clever, he is also riddled with phobias. More damning, he is too fearful, and perhaps too complacent, to confront and overcome his fears. He's not only neurotic, he's cowardly. Little wonder he fails to achieve a relationship worth having! As films like *The Philadelphia Story* teach us, such a relationship requires of both parties the courage to take risks in the hope of moving in the direction of their dreams.

In such comedies, relationships worth having are conversations of equals. At the Academy Awards show, Woody Allen jokingly envisioned himself as having such a conversation with God. Having such conversations with other human beings, though, is a problem for the characters Woody plays in his films (and, perhaps, for Woody himself).

In *Annie Hall*, Woody Allen is, of course, the film's director as well as its protagonist. The man in front of the camera and the man behind the camera are one and the same. Thus when Woody speaks directly to the camera, as he does at the very opening of the film, he seems to be speaking to us, and speaking for the film. This places him in a privileged position, it would seem. This matter is complicated, however.

In that opening in which Alvy addresses the camera directly, sorting out the circumstances that led his relationship with Annie to end, his monologue, which the body of the film that follows illustrates, invites us to view him in incompatible, but intimately related, ways. Is he a patient confiding to his therapist? Or is he a stand-up comic working a room? If he is a patient, our position is superior to his. He is exposing his inadequacies; we get to analyze them and pass judgment. And yet there's hope for him; he is telling us all this because he believes it will help him to change. On the other hand, if he is a comic delivering a monologue, his is the superior position. He gets to show off his cleverness at keeping a step ahead of his audience; our role is limited to laughing or not laughing or at most kibitzing. To be sure, a shrewd comic like Woody Allen knows that the key to making us laugh is to first win us over—to motivate us to identify with him, thus root for him. Assured that the comic is one of us, we relax our guard, believing we know where we stand with him. We think we know what to expect, but he has really been setting us up for the old bait-and-switch, playing us for a sucker. He apparently has the upper hand. But as long as he keeps mining his unhappy life for gags, rather than trying to change his life, there's no hope for him.

In his address to the camera in *Annie Hall*, and by extension in the body of the film that serves to illustrate it, then, Woody oscillates unstably between asserting his superiority to us and declaring his inferiority. The only constant is that he's not our equal.

And his delivery invites another pair of interpretations as well. Woody shares with his fellow clowns-turned-directors Charlie Chaplin and Jerry Lewis a tendency to judge others, and to lecture them, as if from a position of moral or spiritual authority. The interpretation I have in mind, then, is that his monologue/narration is like a rabbi's sermon (a Reform rabbi, to be sure). After all, it offers spiritual guidance. And it has a moral, one that Woody claims the authority to state in the two jokes that bookend his monologue/narration. (The first: "Two elderly women are at a Catskill Mountains resort. And one of them says, 'The food in this place is really terrible.' And the other one says, 'Yeah, I know. And they serve such small portions.' Well, that's essentially how I feel about life. It's full of loneliness and misery and suffering and unhappiness. And . . . it's all over much too quickly." The second: "This guy goes to a psychiatrist. He says, 'Doc, my brother's crazy. He thinks he's a chicken. The doctor says, 'Why don't you turn him in?' And he says, 'I would. But I need the eggs.' Well, I guess that's now pretty much how I feel about relationships. They're totally irrational and crazy and absurd and sad. And we keep on doing it because most of us need the eggs.") Not much of a moral by the standards of remarriage comedies, or by rabbinical standards. Then again, a rabbi isn't usually constrained by the condition that his moral has to do double duty as a punch line. And the flip side of viewing Woody's monologue/narration as an address *by* a rabbi is viewing it as addressed *to* a rabbi, or directly to God, in the hope of receiving, not offering, spiritual guidance. If his search for love is crazy, how can he be cured of it?

Manhattan (1979) is the first Woody Allen film in which his character has an arc, as screenwriters call it, that tackles head-on Woody's ambivalence or duality. The film ends with Isaac Davis, the Woody character, and, I like to think, Woody Allen himself, coming into possession of a crucial piece of self-knowledge, which Tracy (Mariel Hemingway; and is it a coincidence that she shares her name with Katharine Hepburn's character in *The Philadelphia Story*?), speaking for the film, puts into words when she says to Woody that he has to accept that people change and he has to learn to trust people. Woody usually has a witty comeback for every accusation, but not this time. That he recognizes her words as the simple truth is registered in the chagrined look he gives to the camera (as great a bit of screen acting—Woody Allen is vastly underestimated as a screen actor—as Chaplin's celebrated laughter-through-tears at the end of *City Lights* [1931]).

Woody knows in his heart that what Tracy says is true. He cannot—and knows he cannot—deny what is, in effect, the Emersonian teaching of remarriage comedies. If he truly loves her, he must wish for her to further her education, to be free to change, to grow, to walk, step by step, in the direction of her dreams. In any case, his hands are tied. If she leaves for London as she promises to do, he risks losing her, but if he tries to stop her, he will certainly lose her. If he disavows this principle that he knows in his heart is true, he won't be worthy of this woman. If he embraces this principle, as she does, he will become Tracy's equal. That is, *he* will suffer change. But he is afraid to change. Changing feels to him like dying. Oy! Why did God make it so hard to be a human being?

And if Woody does change, does overcome his fear of change, will what we love about him be lost? Will he stop being funny? We too, perhaps, have to accept that people change, have to learn to trust people.

After Tracy says her piece, we are given a sustained close-up of Woody, grudgingly admitting that she is right. This rueful acknowledgment of her perspective is addressed directly to the camera. Since it is Woody behind the camera as well as in front of it, this acknowledgment is, in effect, addressed by Woody to himself, as well as to us. It is certainly not addressed to Tracy. Her response to his reaction is not shown. Is this because Woody Allen, behind the camera, is only interested in his character, not Tracy? I think not. She has said what she had to say. The rest is up to him. If he doesn't change, their conversation is over. Period. Nothing he might say or do here and now would make a difference, or call for a response from her. No apologies he might give, no promises he might make, would prove that he has really changed. Only time will tell.

And what has time told?

In *Broadway Danny Rose*, Woody Allen finds a profound solution—unfortunately, not a general solution; not one he has been able, or willing, to apply to other films—to the problem of how he might keep faith with the ending of *Manhattan* without forfeiting his unique gift for being funny. I think of *Broadway Danny Rose* as Woody Allen's one perfect film. Certainly it is one of his funniest. Not coincidentally, it is the Woody Allen film that most fully embraces the Emersonian perspective of films like *The Philadelphia Story*. Far more than *Annie Hall*, it incorporates key features of such comedies. For example, it has a Green World whose magic ultimately has efficacy; the lovers share a great adventure that they both come to recognize as the time of their lives; the man believes in the woman's capacity for change, and presides over her education; the woman undergoes a change so traumatic as to be tantamount to death and rebirth; their conversation is one that leads to reconciliation and forgiveness; and so on.

In *Broadway Danny Rose*, Woody Allen plays a character his performance invests with all the familiar Woody mannerisms, yet who is decisively different from earlier—and later—Woody characters. Danny Rose is exactly like other Woody characters, and exactly like Woody himself, it would seem, except for one crucial difference: he doesn't have a sense of humor. Danny is no less clever than Alvy Singer, say, but he is not witty. Or, rather, he doesn't use his wit, or wits, for the purpose of being funny. Like Buster Keaton in his films, Danny doesn't find people funny. Not coincidentally, we cannot doubt his earnestness and sincerity. He is a character capable, and worthy, of love—and of winning Tina, the woman incarnated so winningly by Mia Farrow.

Woody Allen can wholeheartedly wish for Danny Rose to be happy, knowing that he deserves it. He deserves it, in Woody's eyes, because he is *not* Woody. Or is it that Danny *is* Woody, but Woody magically purified of the ambivalence, the perversity, the neurosis, the fear of change, that have always made him Woody? Danny Rose is Woody Allen's most miraculous creation—a character Woody Allen loves unconditionally, even though he's a character who could not possibly be played by anyone other than Woody, the man who would never want to belong to any club that would have someone like him for a member. What makes this miracle possible?

It would not be possible apart from Woody Allen's inspired decision to forgo the superior position—it's also an inferior position, as we've argued—of narrator.

Danny Rose's story is told, not by himself, but by a group of real New York–based stand-up comics gathered in the back room of the Carnegie Delicatessen. They wile away their time by—what a brilliant framing device!—swapping Danny Rose stories (far better for their appetite than swapping versions of the Aristocrats joke). We come away feeling that these veteran New York comics (such as Corbett Monica, Jackie Gayle, Will Jordan, Milton Berle), and Woody Allen himself, would want to belong to any club that would have someone like Danny Rose for a member. Woody might even be willing to share in the fun—who would want to miss a performing parrot's rendition of "I've got to be me"?—at the most remarkable Thanksgiving dinner in the history of America.

Accepting that people change and learning to trust people are the opposite of Danny Rose's problem. His problem is that he devotes himself too unselfishly to helping his clients to change, to grow. And that he trusts not wisely, but too well. Or so it seems until the film's ending, when Danny's faith in people, although sorely tested, is rewarded. There are no guarantees that Danny and Tina will live happily ever after. Or even that they will have a future together at all. We feel sure that they will, though. Their reconciliation at the conclusion of the film is a deeply satisfying happy ending. They have broken through to a relationship worth having. Theirs will be a conversation of equals. We want them to be happy. We want them to be together. We don't want their New York to change.

And yet, of course, New York has changed. Woody Allen's New York, like Ozu's Tokyo, has moved irrevocably into the past. Woody himself has aged so much that he can no longer play the romantic lead as he did in his best, most heartfelt films. His more recent films contain some remarkable turns by younger performers. (Mira Sorvino in *Mighty Aphrodite* [1995] and Sean Penn in *Sweet and Lowdown* [1999] stand out in my mind.) However, no young actor has been able to breathe life into the kind of character that Woody used to play. In *Melinda and Melinda* (2004), for example, Will Ferrell is given lines and bits of business that cannot be performed without channeling Woody. However hard he tries to make Woody's familiar mannerisms and way with words his own, Ferrell's efforts only underscore Woody's absence. With a pretender in Woody's place, Woody Allen's New York loses its soul. You can take Woody Allen out of New York, but you can't take New York out of Woody Allen; and if you take Woody out of his films, you risk taking New York out of them, too. For a New York without a soul is an oxymoron. It is no New York at all.

Thus I find it a hopeful sign that, with his work at an impasse, Woody Allen chose to film *Match Point* (2005), which I have not yet had an opportunity to see, not in New York but in London, and that he returned to London to film *Scoop* (2006). Has he overcome, at last, his fear of change?

Before I close, allow me to interject just one last word.

Surely, in Woody Allen's view, God would have done better if he had invited Danny Rose, rather than Woody, to represent New York at the Academy Awards. Then again, God probably did make Danny an offer. But he wasn't available.

Charlie (Harvey Keitel) literally hides his relationship with Teresa (Amy Robinson) because of her difference: her epilepsy and her dreams of leaving the neighborhood, in *Mean Streets* (Martin Scorsese, Warner Bros., 1973). Digital frame enlargement.

From *Mean Streets* to the *Gangs of New York*

ETHNICITY AND URBAN SPACE IN THE
FILMS OF MARTIN SCORSESE

PAULA J. MASSOOD

*Sometimes I think the best thing would be to make
films here in New York, not to deal with Hollywood,
simply try to do things you really believe in.*

—Martin Scorsese

*Little Italy for me is in a sense a microcosm for some-
thing much, much larger.*

—Martin Scorsese

Martin Scorsese is almost as famous for being a New Yorker as he is for being a filmmaker. Along with other New York directors such as Woody Allen and Spike Lee, Scorsese maintains strong links to the city of his birth and, except for a decade-long residence on the West Coast in the 1970s, he has lived and worked constantly in New York, locating his production company, Cappa Productions, and many of his films in the city. Scorsese's career has been prolific and his films varied, ranging from documentaries to historical epics set at different points in the nineteenth and twentieth centuries. However, he has consistently turned his sights on the city's neighborhoods, especially Little Italy and Lower Manhattan, presenting detailed and often intimate portraits of their streets and people. In stories set in Little Italy's Elizabeth and Mulberry Streets, or at the Five Points' convergence of Park, Worth, and Baxter Streets, Scorsese's films explore the interconnected themes of ethnicity and the maintenance of literal and figurative borders. He draws upon, and often revises, generic conventions to construct narratives that are at one and the same time about local and national mythologies.

The majority of Scorsese's films have some relationship to the city, often providing detailed maps of particular neighborhoods. This essay focuses on a

UNIVERSITY COLLEGE Library CORK

selection of Scorsese's films that link urban space with ethnicity, such as Little Italy's Italian Americans in *Who's That Knocking at My Door* (1967) and *Mean Streets* (1973), and the Irish immigrant population of the Five Points neighborhood in Lower Manhattan in *Gangs of New York* (2002). In considering these films, along with *Goodfellas* (1991), I will discuss the ways in which Scorsese presents New York as both utopian and dystopian—a place of family, tradition, and group identity that is also limiting and insular and where any form of border crossing is often life-threatening. Moreover, the films reflexively play with generic conventions, often calling out similarities between the gangster film and the western, two genres concerned with location and the often violent expansion of turf. In this way the films, while specifically "New York" in setting and (as will be further discussed) in sound, are overwhelmingly—and self-consciously—American in theme. They masterfully connect the tribalism of New York with national narratives of isolationism, violence, and belonging. They reject the overdetermined myth of the melting pot often ascribed to the city and replace it with the boiling cauldron described by Travis Bickle in *Taxi Driver* (1976): "All the animals come out at night: whores, skunk pussies, buggers, queens, fairies, dopers, junkies, sick, venal . . . Someday a real rain will come and wash all this scum off the streets." Travis is looking at the city as an outsider with no desire to belong. In the films discussed here, point of view originates within the community and conflict revolves around the tension between individual and community desires. For this reason, *Taxi Driver* is not included in this essay.

While *Who's That Knocking at My Door, Mean Streets, Goodfellas,* and *Gangs of New York* span more than three decades in Scorsese's career, they are linked in ways that extend beyond gangs, gangsters, and turf battles in their focus on setting, story, and style. Of these films, *Who's That Knocking* and *Mean Streets* are the most closely related, belonging to what was originally planned as a trilogy. It is often said that Scorsese's films, particularly those focusing on Italian American characters, are semi-autobiographical, and this early, partially completed trilogy is most clearly connected to the director's youthful experiences in Little Italy, with many scenes shot in his family's or neighbors' apartments and buildings. In their focus on the experiences of a group of young men from the neighborhood, the films introduce the prevalent themes in Scorsese's oeuvre, which include family, morality (especially Catholicism), and fidelity to tradition (often presented as parochialism or a blind allegiance to social mores). The films, like Scorsese's earlier student shorts (1964's *It's Not Just You, Murray!*, for example), introduce certain of the director's stylistic trademarks, particularly an interest in formal experimentation (via editing, camera movement, and sound) and the self-conscious referencing of American classical cinema, European art film, and documentary filmmaking movements such as direct cinema and cinéma vérité. This last influence in particular has contributed to the association of the director's films with authenticity: the look of Scorsese's films supports the belief that they present an insider's version of events.[1]

Who's That Knocking at My Door: Mapping Little Italy

Who's That Knocking and *Mean Streets* are coming-of-age tales, which loosely focus on a group of young men from Little Italy, the district roughly located between Elizabeth and Mulberry, and Houston and Canal Streets, in lower Manhattan.[2] *Who's That Knocking* was to be the second in the planned trilogy, following *Jerusalem, Jerusalem*, an unmade film about teenage boys at a Catholic retreat. *Who's That Knocking* picks up the story once they finish school, following the experiences of J.R. (Harvey Keitel), a young man from the neighborhood, and his relationship with a woman (the "girl" [Zina Bethune]) he meets while waiting for the Staten Island Ferry. Scorsese began the film (originally titled *Bring on the Dancing Girls*) as his graduate project while he was at New York University in the mid-sixties. Over the next few years, he found more funding, enabling him to shoot additional scenes and to lengthen the film into a feature. The film went through various cuts and titles (including *I Call First* and *J.R.*) before the completed version was shown at the Chicago Film Festival in 1967.

Who's That Knocking is relatively experimental in structure. It combines conventional continuity editing with more thematic montage sequences, location shooting, moving camera (handheld and tracking shots), and a sound design that combines direct sound, voiceover, and popular music from the time (reminiscent of Kenneth Anger's use of popular music in *Scorpio Rising* [1964]).[3] The film's opening shots, crosscuts between a statue of the Virgin Mary and a mother feeding her children, introduce the themes of religion, morality, and sexuality that saturate the film (and many of Scorsese's films until, perhaps, *The Last Temptation of Christ* [1988]).[4] The film next cuts to a group of young men fighting on the street. While character loyalties are undefined so early in the film, the action is reminiscent of the neighborhood gang battles in films like *Rebel Without a Cause* (Nicholas Ray, 1955) and *West Side Story* (Robert Wise, 1961). The fight scene is shot on location with a handheld camera, and is accompanied by the sounds of "Jenny Takes a Ride," by Mitch Ryder and the Detroit Wheels, on the sound track. The combination of camerawork and sound in these opening scenes provides an important clue as to the way Scorsese uses the city space and reflexive filmmaking to encapsulate J.R.'s world, where social roles are strictly defined and the street becomes the battleground for the maintenance of group identity (Italian American against Puerto Rican, black against white, and so on). Further, the references to youth culture from a slightly earlier time period suggest the ways in which J.R. might be out of step with contemporary urban life.

Scorsese's familiarity with a variety of films and national cinemas is much in evidence in *Who's That Knocking at My Door*. Shot on location on the streets and in the apartments of Little Italy, the images and camerawork make the film resemble a documentary as much as a fiction film. Moreover, the use of direct sound for dialogue and for presenting the city's ambient noise contributes to the film's overall effect of realism because it suggests Scorsese's attempt to capture not only the sights but also the sounds of the neighborhood. Sounds often compete with one another while dialogue is layered with the noise of traffic, other voices, and music in the background, replicating Scorsese's memories of the neighborhood: "I was living in a very crowded area where music would be playing constantly from various apartments across the street, from bars and candy stores. The radio was always on; a juke box would be playing out over the street, and in the tenement areas you'd hear opera from one room, Benny Goodman from another, and rock 'n' roll from downstairs" (Thompson and Christie 28). The polyphony captures the experience of tenement living; of over-crowded apartments, thin walls, and the sense that one's personal business is always already community knowledge. These diegetic sounds, combined with the director's more self-conscious use of popular music on the sound track, present a cityscape at once immediately present (inasmuch as the location shooting and direct sound provide access to the neighborhood's streets and sounds) and highly imaginary (because the sound often provides ironic counterpoint to the images).

This play on the constructed nature of film, and therefore of urban experience, is explored by means of the figure of J.R., whose character is defined by the movies, particularly John Ford's 1956 film *The Searchers* (Friedman, *Cinema* 28). While J.R. is definitely a neighborhood boy, his knowledge of a variety of film genres indicates an imagination that has the potential at least to extend beyond Little Italy's borders. This is suggested in his attraction to the girl, whose looks, behavior, and speech all code her as being from another neighborhood (perhaps uptown) or some other place altogether. J.R.'s attention is first drawn to her as she reads a copy of *Paris Match* while waiting for the Staten Island Ferry. He initiates a conversation about John Wayne and *The Searchers*, inspired in part by the images in the magazine. J.R.'s enthusiastic discussion of the film serves as the beginning of their relationship, and his invocation of Natalie Wood's fate in that film ultimately foreshadows their own doomed romance. Like Debbie Edwards in *The Searchers*, the girl's purity is tainted by a sexual assault she endured before meeting J.R. And like Ethan Edwards's (Wayne) response to Debbie's abduction, J.R. cannot bear the thought of someone having trespassed on what he views as his property.[5]

J.R.'s relationship with the girl is meant to highlight his internal struggle with morality and sexuality, but it also suggests the limits of his world. The girl's blond hair and contemporary clothing stand in visual contrast to the gray-haired matron from the opening shots of the film, and her standard speech patterns are in aural contrast to J.R.'s more pronounced New Yorkese. Furthermore, the girl rides the Staten Island Ferry for the experience rather than as a necessity. J.R. cannot imagine taking the ferry "just for the ride." His experiential borders are too narrow for such a conceptual leap and his class pragmatism is unable to accommodate such unproductive pursuits. She is a *flâneuse* whereas he embodies the ideology of a worker (even if he doesn't have a job). For J.R. and his friends, Little Italy is home, and except for rare forays uptown to meet women or see films, they rarely stray from the familiar. As with his limited geographic outlook, J.R. has a restricted social view; he cannot consider the girl outside of strictly defined parameters, as either Madonna or whore. She eventually rejects both roles, providing a rare moment of female agency in this all-male world.

Mean Streets: Crossing Borders and Developing Identities

If *Who's That Knocking* introduced Scorsese's Little Italy to audiences, *Mean Streets* solidified its presence onscreen. The film reprises many of the themes first explored in *Who's That Knocking*, particularly questions of morality, insularity, and border crossing. Like the earlier film, *Mean Streets* focuses on a loose collection of young neighborhood men, with central attention paid to Charlie, a type of J.R. figure again played by Harvey Keitel. Like J.R., Charlie is torn between his parochialism, typified in voiceovers about redemption and his frequent acts of playing with fire, and larger ambitions to satisfy the dueling expectations of his Uncle Giovanni (Cesare Danova), a Mafia capo, and his girlfriend Teresa (Amy Robinson). Charlie's concern for redemption structures the film, from his opening voiceover, in which he intones, "You don't make up for your sins in church; you do it in the streets," to his failed attempt to escape the neighborhood in the film's concluding moments.

Unlike *Who's That Knocking*, which Scorsese made while in New York, *Mean Streets* was made while he was living in Los Angeles. The film is characterized by its Little Italy location, a setting that provides character and story substance, but it was only partially shot on location. The cast and crew spent just six days in the city shooting a few interiors, the San Gennaro street festival, and a few other exteriors (Kelly 79). This doesn't diminish the influence of setting on the narrative; however, it points to the way in which Scorsese's New York is a constructed space, inspired just as much by film history and the director's imagination as by actual landscape. The element of construction will be taken to its logical conclusion in later films, like the musical *New York, New York* (1977) and the period piece *Gangs of New York*; the first was shot mostly at MGM and at the Biltmore Hotel in Los Angeles, and the second mostly in Rome. In *Mean Streets* Scorsese re-creates the look of the area wherever he could, including shooting the narrow hallways and modest stairwells of the neighborhood's tenement buildings for a more accurate depiction of New York life (Connelly 6).

The technical experimentation of Scorsese's earlier film is developed in *Mean Streets*. In many scenes we follow (via handheld camera) Charlie and friends like Johnny Boy (Robert De Niro) as they walk through the streets of Little Italy, exchanging greetings with neighbors and friends. The location shooting integrates the characters into the space and suggests that they belong in the neighborhood. In these scenes, the sound design follows suit, with direct sound recording that captures the ambient noise of the city, including traffic, people talking, and music from unidentified diegetic sources, an effect similar to that in *Who's That Knocking*. The dialogue also continues Scorsese's use of highly stylized Italian American urban vernacular, which once again places characters in the space and provides moments of comic relief. The first scene between Charlie and Johnny Boy, for example, includes a partially improvised exchange in which Johnny Boy concocts a story involving characters with names like "Joey Clams" and "Frankie Bones" as a means of dodging responsibility for a loan repayment. The situation is serious, but the playful language of Johnny Boy's story diffuses the tension.

In addition, *Mean Streets*'s verité look and sound (which shares similarities with other low budget American films from the time, especially blaxploitation films) include many highly stylized and reflexive moments that have become Scorsese's trademark.[6] In the scene immediately preceding the discussion between Charlie and Johnny Boy, for instance, Charlie enters his friend Tony's (David Proval) bar. A slow-motion tracking shot introduces the space, and red lighting provides atmosphere as Charlie's voiceover narrates his thoughts.[7] As in *Who's That Knocking*, music is used as a counterpoint to the scene; this time it's the Rolling Stones' "Tell Me" that functions on both the diegetic (in the bar) and nondiegetic (on the sound track) registers. A similar combination of camera movement and sound will be used again in *Goodfellas* in a scene in which Henry Hill (Ray Liotta) takes his future wife, Karen (Lorraine Bracco), to the Copacabana Club in Manhattan. Just as Charlie controls the narrative at this point in *Mean Streets*, the long tracking shot that follows Henry and Karen from the street, through a service entrance, through the kitchen, and into the nightclub communicates Henry's mastery of space in the later film.

The bar scene ends with Charlie fantasizing in voiceover about Diane (Jeannie Bell), an African American stripper he's been watching. His attraction to Diane and his relationship with Teresa, Johnny Boy's epileptic cousin, directly conflict with his ambitions to succeed in Giovanni's network. More important, he projects his desires of border crossing and transgressing societal mores onto the bodies of women, just as J.R. and the girl in *Who's That Knocking* do. In both films the male characters rarely leave their neighborhood, and when they do it's for a specific purpose: J.R.'s errand to his grandmother's house in Staten Island in *Who's That Knocking* or Charlie's trip to the Village, in *Mean Streets*, to collect an outstanding payment. Women have little agency in Scorsese's films, and yet they often signify movement. In *Mean Streets* Charlie plans to meet with Diane in the

Village (away from the neighborhood), but he doesn't show up because he's too afraid of becoming involved with an African American woman, a failure fore-shadowed in the Stones' song playing in the earlier bar scene.[8] Teresa is from the boys' neighborhood and is therefore safe, but her epilepsy codes her as different, and Charlie's uncle warns him away from her for this reason. Moreover, Teresa's desire to move "uptown" and her request that he accompany her is a further sign of her difference. She envisions alternatives to the subservient role she's been assigned by family and friends. Charlie, on the other hand, cannot imagine life outside of Little Italy.

While Charlie resists Teresa's attempts to take him uptown, his relationship with her cousin Johnny Boy forces him to make a move. In an effort to save Johnny Boy from Michael, an unpaid loan shark (Richard Romanus), Charlie fer-ries Johnny Boy and Teresa out of the city. Like an earlier scene in which Charlie and his friends have difficulty navigating the few short blocks from Little Italy to Greenwich Village, in this scene Charlie cannot find his way to Greenwood Lake, his stated destination outside the city. Instead of leaving New York, the trio loses the way in Brooklyn and all three are subsequently shot at by Michael's sidekick before crashing into a hydrant on a side street. The film's concluding moments suggest that border crossing is dangerous, whether it's a literal emigration from the neighborhood or a more figurative departure from one's upbringing and tra-ditions. It cannot be forgotten that Charlie's uncle warns Charlie away from the deviance that Johnny Boy and Teresa represent.

After *Mean Streets* and *Italianamerican* (1974), a documentary about Little Italy and the immigrant experience, Scorsese spent fifteen years exploring a wide vari-ety of narratives and genres, including comedies and musicals. While many of the films, such as *Taxi Driver, New York, New York, Raging Bull* (1980), and *The King of Comedy* (1983) are set in New York, and *Raging Bull* even includes the familiar topic of Italian American life, Scorsese didn't return to the gangster genre until *Goodfellas*, his 1990 adaptation of Nicholas Pileggi's *Wise Guy: Life in a Mafia Family* (1985).[9] According to Scorsese, the film "has really nothing to do with people I knew then [the 1960s and 1970s]. It doesn't take place in Manhattan, it's only in the boroughs, so it's a very different world" (Friedman, *Cinema* 169). On the sur-face, Scorsese's claim is true; *Goodfellas* focuses on Henry Hill, a half Irish/half Sicilian mid-level "wise guy" (gangster), living in the boroughs. Yet the story is similar to the earlier films in its presentation of New York during a similar time period and its focus on characters trying to achieve success through unconven-tional means, similarities the director himself suggests: "Of course there's a direct line [from *Mean Streets* through *Raging Bull* to *Goodfellas*]. I have a couple more [of these movies] in mind, hopefully make a chronicle of a lifestyle. It's like looking at that world again from a slightly different angle; the same movie over and over again" (Strauss A8).

Goodfellas: Little Italy in the 'Burbs

Mean Streets, observes Scorsese, is about "the American Dream, according to which everybody thinks they can get rich quick, and if they can't do it by legal means, then they'll do it by illegal ones" (Thompson and Christie 47). This desire for class mobility, exemplified in Charlie's role as Giovanni's collection agent, is also a means of moving up the family hierarchy and is at odds with Charlie's more personal desires for a life with Teresa. In *Goodfellas*, Henry Hill has no such conflict, and the film charts his ascension up the Cicero family structure, from youthful errand boy in his childhood neighborhood of East New York (Brooklyn) to his adult role of trusted enforcer with a wife and kids in the relatively suburban neighborhoods of Queens and Long Island. In effect, Henry is a successful Charlie, and his geographic mobility from the city to the suburbs (out of his parent's apartment to his own house with his own family) signals his economic migration. This move reflects the historical widespread middle-class exodus from the city in the sixties and seventies (and suggests that gangsters, like other Americans, are not immune to the lure of the suburbs). This mobility is again signified by women: Henry's wife Karen is similar to the female figures from earlier Scorsese films who are outsiders by virtue of their ethnicity, class, or aspirations. A middle-class Jewish girl from Long Island, Karen represents Henry's successful climb up the social ladder.

Goodfellas continues the themes of insularity, ethnicity, and the maintenance of tradition from Scorsese's earlier films, especially in its detailed presentation of the closed world of "the family" through Henry's and Karen's voiceovers. Because the voiceovers require the audience to identify closely with the two characters, they contribute to a first-hand sense of both the appeal and the claustrophobia of the Hills' lives. Of Henry and her relations with the other members of the Cicero gang Karen observes, for example, "We were all so very close. I mean, there were never any outsiders around, absolutely never. And being together all the time made everything seem all the more normal." This insularity is further suggested by the predominance of interior settings in the film—houses, stores, diners, jails; New York's borough neighborhoods appear in *Goodfellas* but only to the extent that they suggest Henry's rising affluence. The narrative is developed through interior spaces rather than using exteriors, as in *Who's That Knocking* or *Mean Streets*. This shift may have been due to *Goodfellas*'s larger budget and studio backing, or it may be an indication of the reduced importance of the urban setting to the genre as a whole: the goodfellas commute to the city, but their lives are located in the suburbs. This revision of the gangster film became the basis of HBO's suburban gangster saga, "The Sopranos."

Henry is a master of his space, as the Copacabana scene suggests, but he remains an outsider by virtue of his birthright since, by contrast with most of the men he meets and operates with in the Mafia, he is not Italian American: no matter how much he's accepted and valued by the Family, his Irish blood prevents

NOTES

1. This is especially the case with *Mean Streets*, whose marketing stressed Scorsese's knowledge of the film's subject and setting, a "place that is his [Scorsese's], first by right of long residence, second by right of survival" (Phillips 64). Two examples of such press coverage are McCandlish Phillips's "From Little Italy to Big-Time Movies" and Guy Flatley's "He Has Often Walked 'Mean Streets.'" It is also supported on the DVD release of the film, which includes a short documentary, *Martin Scorsese: Back on the Block*, in which Scorsese identifies the actual spaces and personalities that inspired the film.

2. In the subsequent decades, the Little Italy of Scorsese's early films has shrunk, with Chinatown inching its way north from Canal Street and chic Nolita ("North of Little Italy") working its way south from Houston Street. Now, Little Italy is concentrated along Mulberry, between Canal and Spring Streets.

3. Scorsese credits Anger's use of popular music as an influence on *Who's That Knocking* (Thompson and Christie 21).

4. Much has been written about the role of religion in Scorsese's films. It is well known, for example, that Scorsese seriously considered entering the priesthood as a child and young man, and many of his early films, particularly *Who's That Knocking* and *Mean Streets*, feature characters torn between Catholic tradition and more modern morals and ambitions. This line of discussion will be pursued here only inasmuch as it contributes to themes of insularity and mobility. For more elsewhere, see Braudy.

5. The western reappears in the film when J.R. takes the girl to a screening of *Rio Bravo* (Howard Hawks, 1959). John Ford's westerns, especially *The Searchers*, play a central role in a number of Scorsese films from this time, often suggesting the "frontier" qualities of New York's urban space during the seventies. This culminates in *Taxi Driver*, and the figure of Travis Bickle who functions (albeit psychotically) in the city space in a similar manner as the western hero in a frontier town: he's there to create order out of chaos. For more on the connections between the films, see Stern 32–68 and Kolker 239–40.

6. The film has a similar look and sound as *Shaft* (Gordon Parks Sr., 1971) and *Superfly* (Gordon Parks Jr., 1972), also New York films from the time. Moreover, Scorsese was offered funding by Gene Corman, Roger's brother, with the proviso that the story be changed to fit African American characters (Thompson and Christie 39–41). Scorsese turned down the offer, but the precedent had already been set with *Shaft*, which was originally intended for a white cast.

7. There's a moment in the scene when Keitel is positioned on the same dolly as the camera and shot from behind as he makes his way to the stage. The effect maintains the distance between the character and camera while allowing the background to change. This camera set-up has become a signature shot for Spike Lee, who has maintained that *Mean Streets* and Scorsese's films in general have been pivotal in the development of his own filmmaking style.

8. Greenwich Village often functions as the gathering point for deviants from Italian American norms in Scorsese's early films. For example, in *Mean Streets* Johnny Boy picks up two Jewish women in a bar in the Village and brings them back to Tony's bar with hopes of sleeping with one of them. Later in the film, Charlie, Tony, and Johnny Boy give two gay men from the bar a ride to the Village.

9. Scorsese was initially drawn to Pileggi's nonfictional account of Hill's life because of its basis in reality. He wanted to treat it "in the spirit of documentary" and present the story in Henry's words (Keyser 197).

10. However, it was Scorsese's first large-scale project. He had already directed *The Last Temptation of Christ* in 1988 and *The Age of Innocence* in 1993. Even so, the budgets for these films were much smaller: $7 million for the former and $34 million for the latter.

---

him from truly belonging. It is this outsider status, along with fear for his life after he's arrested on a federal charge for narcotics trafficking, that enables him to turn against his former friends and compatriots in a life-threatening break with tradition. His fears are well founded: in the earlier murder of Tommy (Joe Pesci), Henry's unstable sidekick (resembling an older, more dangerous Johnny Boy), the family has already communicated that deviance can be deadly, even for those related by blood. The final scene in the film includes shots of a newly constructed and anonymous suburban neighborhood to which he has been exiled as a resident in the FBI's witness protection program, accompanied by Henry's voiceover complaining about his new life as an "average nobody." In this conclusion, Henry's life actually follows a trajectory similar to Charlie's in *Mean Streets*—both men are forced to leave the city and find their own "Greenwood Lake." Charlie fails whereas Henry succeeds but ends up drowning in suburban anonymity. Worse, Henry's new home, a model of the suburban American Dream, is a homogeneous nightmare, a place so devoid of ethnic difference that it is characterized by the use of ketchup on pasta. In this sense *Goodfellas* suggests a twist on the more dystopian themes of insularity and ethnicity in Scorsese's earlier films. The film's urban landscape is full of intense rivalries but an integral element of its allure is its diversity. Henry learns the real value of this diversity only once it's been taken away.

Gangs of New York: Taking It Back to the Streets

"The teeming tenement drama, the awesome neighborhood capos, the arcane codes of street honor, the tribal antipathies, the Catholic pageantry, even the background opposition to an unpopular war suggest the filmmaker's lived history in some alternative universe," writes J. Hoberman. While it might seem as though Hoberman is describing *Who's That Knocking at My Door*, *Mean Streets*, or even *Goodfellas*, he's actually discussing the nineteenth-century New York of Scorsese's *Gangs of New York*. In many ways, this film, set in the Five Points section of Lower Manhattan between 1846 and 1863, was a departure for the filmmaker, particularly in its enormous budget (reported to be $100 million) and even larger main set constructed on the backlots of the Cinecittà Studios in Rome.[10] In other ways, however, the film both continues and develops the interconnected themes of ethnicity and border maintenance that are prevalent throughout Scorsese's career. The director was first attracted to the project in 1970, upon reading Herbert Ashbury's *The Gangs of New York* (1928), a sensationalist account of the city's underworld. Scorsese first started thinking about an adaptation of the project shortly thereafter and by 1979, during the same time period he was making his more contemporary New York pictures, he had a completed script (by Jay Cocks).

Five Points in the mid-nineteenth century, like Little Italy in the twentieth, was a tiny neighborhood overflowing with people. *Gangs of New York* features

Amsterdam Vallon (Leonardo DiCaprio), a young man seeking to avenge the murder of his father (Liam Neeson) at the hands of William "Bill the Butcher" Cutting (Daniel Day-Lewis). A subplot involves a love story between Amsterdam and Jenny Everdeane (Cameron Diaz). While the paired stories of Amsterdam-Bill and Amsterdam-Jenny are primary plot lines, the narrative devotes just as much time to describing the area's intense gang warfare. The city space is filled with rival gangs fighting to control a small piece of Manhattan, what the filmmaker has described as "chaos, tribal chaos" (Bordewich 44). Early in the film, one character (in voiceover) introduces all the players: the Nativists, the Plug Uglies, the Bowery Boys, the Forty Thieves, and so on. The gangs are violent and their viciousness is established in the film's first half-hour, which involves a battle between the Nativists and the Dead Rabbits, filmed with hundreds of extras and virtuoso camera movement, editing, and sound. This battle has two functions in the narrative: first, it introduces the backstory through its explanation of the circumstances of Amsterdam's father's death. More importantly, it suggests that early New York's turf battles were not only struggles for control of the neighborhood but also intense ethnic rivalries between members of the city's diverse population: Irish, English, German, African, Chinese, or "Native" people of Dutch and English descent, "born right-wise to this great land," according to Bill. Like the street battle that starts *Who's That Knocking*, city space is used here to present a world in which social roles are strictly defined and borders are often violently maintained. While the film has often been described as "medieval" in look, the battle also references frontier battles from Hollywood westerns; and the Five Points set looks like a frontier town.

As in the earlier films, Scorsese's presentation of New York here draws from both the codes of realism and reflexive filmmaking techniques. While the film's massive budget for sets and costumes and its smooth camera work and polished sound design have no relationship to the director's well-known documentary interests, they suggest a concern for historical accuracy.[11] Much of the film's press, for example, was devoted to explicating the director's desire for authenticity from set to sound (including dialogue). The production crew drew visual references from Jacob Riis's photographs of the area and reflects aural influence from speech guides like *The Rogue's Lexicon*. But as the entire set was constructed in Rome, the film presents the city as Scorsese imagined it would have been, not as it was. It is a space inspired by a multiplicity of references from American history and popular culture, including the western.

Much has been made of this film's historical failings, but its lapses provide a clue to Scorsese's view of the city, which in some ways remains the same today as it was in the sixties.[12] In even more important ways, however, Scorsese's city is linked to larger national mythologies of assimilation and citizenship. The best example of this is provided by the scenes of the Draft Riots, which appear near

the end of the film and function as the narrative's culminating moment of conflict. The riots occurred in July 1863 and were the result of increasing tensions between the Republican and the Democratic Parties over the recently passed (March 1863) Conscription Act requiring that all adult white men register for military duty (black men were not considered citizens and were, therefore exempt). The Democratic Party presented the draft as an attack on the working classes, particularly the city's Irish population, because exemptions could be purchased for $300, an amount far exceeding the abilities of many of the city's work-ing population. On July 13, two days after the first lottery, rioting began and last-ing for five days.

Like many of Scorsese's cherished westerns, such as *The Searchers*, the Civil War is just below the surface of the narrative in *Gangs of New York*, structuring local and national identity. One of the film's inaccuracies is its suggestion that Bill Cutting (based on an actual figure) was killed during the riots rather than years earlier. By blurring history and fiction, Scorsese actually foregrounds the Civil War by connecting the local tribalisms between the Nativists and the Dead Rabbits to larger national issues of citizenship and belonging (already referenced in the Nativist discourse and actions). Through the film, the Nativists function, the evil foil, a reminder of the prejudices and violence of nationalism. But, historically, once the Conscription Act was enforced, New Yorkers (particularly the Irish) turned on the city's black population, lynching men, women, and children in one of the country's deadliest moments of racial violence. By acknowledging this ugly moment in American history, *Gangs of New York* reminds us that gang wars are often microcosms of larger acts of national violence; triggered by seemingly local issues, such as the control of turf, they also reveal the traumatic effects of more comprehensive social and economic policies created elsewhere. The movie's tagline, "America was born in the streets," is correct, then *Gangs of New York* (and many of Scorsese's other films) remind us that the American Dream continues to be redefined on its urban battlefields.

One of the sustaining oxymorons about New York is that it is both politically mixing people from hundreds of different nationalities and ethnicities, and radically local and insular, with one block's allegiances differing from another in ways that remain unreadable to outsiders. While recent development efforts have diluted the complexity of many of the city's traditionally closed neighborhoods (for example, gentrification in the Williamsburg and Greenpoint sections of Brooklyn, Jackson Heights in Queens, or Manhattan's Lower East Side), New York remains a fiercely tribal space, where neighborhood animosities often for generations, citizenship and belonging still depend on being "born right-wise to this great land," and turf is hotly contested. In this city, a space as innocuous as a corner can signify power, belonging, and identity. This is the New York that Scorsese captures in his films.

11. Over his career, Scorsese has directed and/or produced a number of documentary films for television or theatrical release: titles include *Italianamerican* (1974), *The Last Waltz* (1978), *A Personal Journey with Martin Scorsese Through American Movies* (1995, TV), *My Voyage to Italy* (1999), and the "Feel Like Going Home" episode of *The Blues* (2003, TV).

12. For more on the film's relationship to actual people and events from the time, see both DiGirolamo and Bordewich, along with much of the film's advance press.

The Empire State Building, secured forever as a site from a specific time and place in *Empire* (Andy Warhol, 1964). Courtesy PhotoFest New York.

Can't Take My Eyes Off of You

ANDY WARHOL RECORDS / IS NEW YORK

DAVID A. GERSTNER

The City is a Good Machine.
—Henwar Rodakiewicz

"I Want to Be a Machine"

Andy Warhol was truly modern. And urban. To be precise, Warhol was New York City urban and, more specifically, Manhattan modern. Warhol was New York's mechanical *flâneur* extraordinaire of the twentieth century since he embraced the city, art, artist, and the machine as one and the same. Warhol strolled through, looked at, and relished the prurient delights of New York. Warhol, Patrizia Lombardo succinctly notes, was the "twentieth-century prolongation of the intoxication with the metropolis" (35). Most importantly, Warhol experienced the city phenomenon through an array of mediating devices, especially the movie camera and tape recorder. His films are a tremendous document (visually and sonorously) of the great American machine, New York City.

As Henwar Rodakiewicz's epigraph to the 1939 short *The City* indicates, the city was the ideal machine for ever-productive twentieth-century America. To be sure, Warhol, like Rodakiewicz and so many other American artists, enthusiastically engaged the modernist impulses generated by mechanized urbanity and its creative energies. Throughout the twentieth century, New York was the capital for artists to galvanize and soak in the rush of modernity (see Gerstner, *Manly Arts* ch. 4). For Warhol, the (mechanical) art form that embodied his scopophilic and corporeal pleasures with the city was film. What other medium could unblinkingly record both the nonstop excesses and the trivial, but decadent, ennui that made New York, New York? Indeed, in New York something was always happening. Enticingly, New York, like the aesthetic to which Warhol aspired in his filmmaking, was simultaneously "raw and crude" while it promised the "New" and the "Now" (unlike, as we will see, the old, Eternal City, Rome) (see Warhol and Hackett 166; Warhol, *Philosophy* 157). The camera eye (certainly better, or more accurate, than the eyes with which humans are born) gave Warhol the best chance of not missing a single moment of the often-exciting, sometimes the boring, but always reliably the "raw and the crude" city.

Warhol's claim "I want to be a machine" often meant "I want to be a recording device." Mostly, Warhol wanted to be a recording device of all the scenes in New York. In Warhol's view, the city and the movies were two of the greatest contributions to modern culture: "I don't think that there is any place in the world like New York City as far as street life goes," he wrote. "Here you can see every class, every race, every sex and every kind of fashion bumping up against each other. Everyone gets to mix and mingle and you can never guess what combinations you're going to see next" (*America* 148). Given all this "mixing and mingling" and endless "combinations" taking place in the New York streets, it is no wonder he longed to be a recording machine. Even flora and fauna were records of urbanity for Andy; referring to his "Flowers" series from 1964, Paul Bergin observes that "Warhol's flowers are the flowers of the city rather than of the field" (Bergin 360). And as to records and recording, for Warhol nothing is better than *to be* a movie, because to be a movie is to be at once that which does the recording and that which is recorded. In this way, Warhol's dream to be the machine allowed him to be the scene *and* turn it into art.

Indeed, for Warhol, the machines of modernity—movies, cities, and artist—collapsed into one another. The indistinguishable dynamic among these twentieth-century phenomena was modern art itself. Warhol records this experience of merging when he states his New York Superstars' "lives became part of my movies, and of course the movies became part of their lives; they'd get so into them that pretty soon you couldn't really separate the two, you couldn't tell the difference—and sometimes neither could they" (Warhol and Hackett 180).[1] And neither could Andy. The blurring between body and machine, the loss of their distinction, was one of the perverse gifts of commodity culture in which Warhol reveled. The frenetic swirl of unbridled capitalism in New York enabled that modern/machine experience like no other place.

"Movies, Movies, and More Movies"

It is nearly impossible to read Warhol's writings or writings about Warhol without seeing the movies and New York mentioned along the way, often many times in the same breath. Though New York was the heart of his aesthetic world, he was an ardent fan of Hollywood stars and, indeed, of the machine that produced their aura. However, Warhol turned to filmmaking somewhat late in life and when he did turn to Hollywood, his homage to the industry was more perverse than honorific. He was born in 1928 in Pittsburgh, Pennsylvania. He began his creative career as a painter and commercial graphic designer. When he arrived in Manhattan in 1949, he produced artwork for book and record covers and developed very successful advertisements for women's shoes and the fashion industry in general. It was commercial art and graphic design that first made his name in the inside circles of Madison Avenue.

Although Warhol was aware of the vibrant New York art scene of the period (particularly work by the likes of Jasper Johns, Jackson Pollock, and the other Cedar Bar Abstract Expressionists), it appears he was less familiar with the queer underground filmmaking fomenting in the United States and, especially, in New York. "In the postwar 1940s and early 1940s," Roy Grundmann reminds us, "such important filmmakers as Kenneth Anger (*Fireworks* [1947]), Curtis Harrington (*Fragments of Seeking* [1946]), and James Broughton (*The Adventures of Jimmy* [1950]) brought discourses of homosexuality under their own authorial control" (Grundmann 7). Around this filmmaking milieu, queer painters, writers, and poets worked the terms of their homosexuality through the aesthetics of their chosen medium. Chief among these artists was poet-impresario Charles Henri Ford, who, according to both Warhol and himself, introduced Andy to the underground cinema scene in 1963. This was a pivotal period in which to be made aware of queer filmmaking since the police had raided screenings and confiscated queer experimental films across the country, including New York. Films such as Anger's 1963 *Scorpio Rising*, Jack Smith's 1963 *Flaming Creatures*, and Jean Genet's 1940 *Un Chant d'amour* resonated with Warhol for the aesthetic form and images they put to use (Anger's beefy and leather-clad motorcyclists from the Hells Angels; Smith's fairy-tale, Orientalist orgy; and Genet's prisoners and their homoerotic communication between cell walls). Moreover, these cinematic images made their way directly from the filmmakers' own cultural scene—both during the films' making and when they were screened. Biker boys, transvestites, fairies, junkies, ex-prisoners, and hustlers filled the lives as well as the films of Anger, Smith, and Genet. Aesthetically, Warhol followed suit since his filmed world burst with the same sort of outcasts and (as Warhol called them) "beauties."

Indeed, Warhol's quick instruction in both underground filmmaking practices and state censorship taught him how "to negotiate, in films such as *Blow Job* (1964), the oppressive conditions brought about by the repressive state apparatus's 'interest' in this form of art" (Grundmann 8). The movies were more than a representation of queer life at this particular time and in this particular place. They were queer life itself.

Warhol considered making film prior to his encounter with Ford, but 1963 was the year he bought his first movie camera and voraciously began movie making (Warhol and Hackett 24–29; Bockris 133; Gerstner "Ford Interview"). In Warhol's hands, the movie camera became an obsession; the camera was his mechanical eye that he provocatively and dilettantishly escorted through his experiences in New York. While Richard Dyer counts eighty films made by Warhol between 1963 and 1967, this number does not take into account the hundreds of "screen tests" Warhol made (Dyer, *Now* 150).[2] Warhol filmed anyone and everyone who stopped by or hung out at his Factory during this time: the first Warhol Factory in 1963 at 231 East Forty-seventh Street; the second in 1968 at 33 Union Square West; the third, in 1974 at 860 Broadway on the corner of Union Square North and Seventeenth Street. A final "Factory" that housed the Warhol-empire offices was acquired in 1982. It "stretched," according to Bockris, "an entire block from East Thirty-second to East Thirty-third Street between Madison and Fifth Avenue" (327). Andy moved into this final location in late 1984 but found the lighting poor and considered finding another place to paint. The East Thirty-second Street address had little of the glamour and social activity the first three Factories held. Bob Colacello, the editor and film reviewer of Warhol's film journal, *inter-View* (later, *Interview*), wrote, "The Factory itself became famous in the sixties as the all-night filming sessions turned into twenty-four hour parties" (Colacello 30).[3] At the Factory, while Warhol "called into question the very process of filmmaking, of what a movie was," Colacello argues, "he was also satisfying his most obsessive need to look, to watch" (29).[4] As David Denby put it, he "takes the voyeurism that is inherent in all movies and adopts it as the sole principle of his work, show-ing literally everything" (42).

From the moment he purchased his first 16mm Bolex, the movies fed Warhol's endless desire to look, to record. From 1963 to 1968, recording the goings-on in New York was at the heart of the artist's entrepreneurial movie obsession. As a young boy in Pittsburgh, Warhol loved the idea of New York, the pleasure of reading movie magazines, and going to the movies (he often dreamed of being a movie star when he was bedridden as a child [Bockris 21]). For the rest of his life, he embodied both the city and the movies and made them the center of his modern aesthetic.

"I Really Believe in Empty Spaces"

What was perhaps the best part of machine life, as Warhol articulated it, was that its ability to reproduce—record in the case of the camera and tape machine—allowed existence to be at once present and absent. That is, recording for Warhol (image, sound), as Peter Wollen argues, was "a form of storage" ("Note" 166) that efficiently preserved the object on film or tape so that the now-recorded (or "old") object could be discarded in order to create new empty space for the next new object. In this way, objects recorded on film were forever present in their original context but, at the same time, absent from that space. Because of the recording device, everything could be at once present (when projected or played back) and absent.

As with many of Warhol's philosophical claims, contradiction defined the assertion. In this case, Warhol's project wasn't so splendidly efficient. Indeed, his statement, "*I really believe in empty spaces*, although, as an artist, I make a lot of junk" (*Philosophy* 143; his emphasis) posed something of a practical dilemma. Although, as Wollen suggests, Warhol's strategy for collecting was founded in the belief that the "recording/storing apparatus should not make evaluative distinctions, and to avoid 'clutter' (the single aesthetic imperative) it should adopt a serial procedure of segmentation and ordering" ("Notes" 166), he ultimately amassed an enormous amount of uncatalogued stuff (bubble-gum wrappers, receipts, strips of film) that took up more and more space! His "serial procedure" to "avoid clutter" meant putting all his found *objets d'art* into "time capsules" that he stored in New Jersey (thereby cluttering New Jersey). "What you should do," Warhol suggests, "is get a box for a month, and drop everything in it and at the end of the month lock it up. Then date it and send it over to Jersey" (qtd in "Notes" 166). Even Warhol, at times, found his collecting theory frustrating: "I opened a Time Capsule and every time I do it's a mistake, because I drag it back and start looking through it. Like I found some film fragments in one and then you just wonder where the rest of the film is" (Hackett 577). Currently, many of the "time capsules" are held at the Andy Warhol Museum in Pittsburgh while the Museum of Modern Art holds their Warhol film collection in the town of Hamlin, Pennsylvania.

How is it possible, then, for Warhol to paradoxically insist on a love for empty space while adoring an over-cluttered New York? Perhaps removing all the collectibles from the city to New Jersey helped maintain an "out of sight, out of mind" attitude. In Warhol's logic, the brilliance of the movie camera lay precisely in its ability to record the urban debris while simultaneously making room for new, empty, and productive space. In other words, Warhol's New York places were blank spaces to be continuously filled *and* recorded with, for example, the performances of his Superstars and whatever other materials the city left in its wake. What was recorded then on film was permanently stored to make available new spaces for new productions and performances.

In this way, New York was more modern than, say, Rome. For Warhol, the "Eternal City" refused to properly store away its antiquity where it belonged in the twentieth century: on film. New York was always making room for the new. In fact, the city was (in)famous for tearing down landmark buildings to make way for crisp, sleek, and modern office and apartment towers. The most notorious demolition that triggered a vigorous landmark-preservation campaign in the city was in 1963 (the year Warhol bought his Bolex) when McKim, Mead, and White's 1910 Beaux Art Pennsylvania Station was torn down to make way for a new Madison Square Garden. New York's history, especially in relationship to architecture, has proven to be an exercise in tearing down the old to deliver the promise of the New (see for example Page). Ever the pragmatist, and since this was the way things were in modern life, Warhol's theory of empty space and film might be viewed as the surest way to facilitate landmark preservation.[5]

To Warhol's mind, the best way to preserve the "old" cultural production was to record it or put it into boxes—literally. For example, his eight-hour "time capsule" recording of the most iconic New York structure, the Empire State Building (*Empire* [1964], made just one year after the Pennsylvania Station debacle), secured forever its architectural significance as a site for, and from, a specific time and place. At any time after filming *Empire*, the Empire State Building remained available for viewing from anywhere in the world—from dusk to dawn—because it is now permanently inscribed on celluloid.

Additionally, and true to his strong work ethic, Warhol reasoned that if old buildings were razed it served the world well because people would be employed to build new buildings (Warhol's New Deal policy, sort of). Best of all, Rome (if Andy was to have his way) and the Empire State Building would never really be lost.[6] In fact, everything stored on film would be permanent and seen in its finest state, neither dusty nor decrepit. Empty and fresh space was, therefore, vital since it gave artists and everyone else a place to do things. In this way, New York on film proved ideal for Warhol's aesthetic of empty but cluttered space.

Warhol's mechanical eye also recorded more than New York architecture. His countless movies store what is quite possibly the richest document of New York City's 1960s underground movement. Warhol's movie world was one that moved constantly through the drug and sex scenes of the Factory to the beds of the art and drug colonies residing at the Chelsea Hotel on West Twenty-third Street, to the ultra-sensational downtown environments of Exploding Plastic Inevitable, the Velvet Underground, and Nico performances, and to the dance performances of Yvonne Rainer and Merce Cunningham at Judson Church near Washington Square. In his films Warhol looks incessantly at New York's fabulous and wayward (usually one and the same). Warhol's "kids"—or Superstars: Gerard Malanga, Billy Name, Ondine, Edie Sedgwick, Candy Darling, Brigid Berlin—and all those who participated in his movie world, performed for the camera their unique talents: getting a haircut, dancing, injecting drugs, sleeping, eating, reading poetry, lounging in bed, looking in the mirror, having sex, and on and on.

Prior to *The Chelsea Girls* (1966), Warhol usually shot his subjects in single takes, often using black-and-white stock, and with little or no direction. His "screen tests" generally lasted three minutes or so and were portraits of Factory visitors or his entourage who were asked to look into the camera, unflinchingly, while Warhol's kino-eye stared directly back, framing his subject in a tight close-up recalling more traditional portraits. The effects were awkward, erratic, poised, and beautiful, given Warhol's chiaroscuro lighting and the uneasy direction to sit still for three minutes.

Other films, such as *Blow Job*, also used tight framing but observed a more active performance on the part of the subject. In this film, we watch a young man's changing expression as fellatio is presumably performed *on* him; his facial performance is an action that leads to the viewer's jouissance of the moment.

Like the three-minute screen tests, no editing interrupts the action. In *Blow Job*, however, the action is allowed to play out through several reel changes, flickering, flaring, and blowing to white between each reel. As if to capture every drop of action, Warhol's mechanical eye gazes attentively for the film's entire thirty-six minutes. As Grundmann points out, the film was shot on 16 mm and originally projected at sixteen frames per second—to attenuate the action—with a playing time of forty-one minutes. Later, the film was projected at eighteen frames per second, reducing screen time to thirty-six minutes (191n1). Once the relieved young man lights his cigarette, it is easy to imagine the director calling, "Next!" in order to empty the set and make way for a subsequent performance. Here, then, is a case of a particular New York blow job (or a performance of receiving one) forever and perfectly preserved.

With the addition of sound, Warhol made short performance films that recorded his New York Superstars' expertise and talents. Although slightly more "scripted" than the screen tests (some, importantly, by Ron Tavel) in terms of directing a Superstar's talents, the chance happening and the unexpected action were more the rule than the exception. With scratchy sound track and image and uneven performances, the films remained true to Warhol's aesthetic of the "raw and crude." For example, in *Poor Little Rich Girl* and *Vinyl* (both 1965), Superstar Edie Sedgwick performs her beautiful vulnerability while, in *Vinyl*, the young and handsome Gerard Malanga, "Pope" Ondine, and Sedgwick read, dance, and perform erotic sado-masochistic pleasures in an idiosyncratic interpretation of *A Clockwork Orange* that only Warhol and his friends could conceive.

The films prior to *The Chelsea Girls* render the perverse and creative energies that are New York. New York is indeed a matrix of creative perversity, with the endless frenetic motion of the streets, the conflicted desires of its millions, and the constant sense that one stands on the threshold of new experience. Especially during the 1960s, New York was the site of corporeal and artistic experiment filtered through unabashed and, for Warhol's kids, incessant sex, intense drug use, and the sounds of the Velvet Underground and other bands mixing with the taxi horns, police sirens, and a panoply of voices gathering from around the world. By 1966, *The Chelsea Girls* dynamically uses film form and space to mechanically bundle these frenzied and heightened arenas of New York's experimental scenes where art, artist, and spectator are commingled.

A script is now provided for *The Chelsea Girls* projectionist to guide the adjustment of sound and to indicate reel changes (the original presentation of the film was purportedly less directional for the projectionist). The projectionist is thus the choreographer of this double-screen spectacle of Warhol's New York—everyone gets the chance to perform in or with a Warhol flick.[7] Like New York, the film viewers see is created on the spot, right in front of them, then moves on to other scenes. *The Chelsea Girls* is a record of the Superstars' lives, from the most banal experiences (Nico trimming her bangs) to the eruption of violence that often lurks at the surface of Warhol's interest in the banal (Ondine beating Pepper). Shot in part at the Chelsea Hotel and in locations on West Third Street, New York's radical and creative spaces from Twenty-third Street and below are not only stored on film, they are stored in such a way that evokes the frenetic energy of the city that often appears and feels abstract and figural. This is to say, the double-screen projection and its inevitable inaccuracy at each screening, the black-and-white images juxtaposed with color images that zoom in and out of focus, the audible chaos and noise of sound tracks overlapping between reels constitute an invaluable document of 1960s New York *as well as* an experiment in form that evokes the sensations of that New York. To my mind, double-screened *The Chelsea Girls* registers the excessive experience of New York that leaves one feeling simultaneously ecstatic and ill.

Poet John Giorno's nap in *Sleep* (1963; 5 hr 21 min), the sex-charged *Couch* (1964), Robert Indiana's nibbling of a mushroom in *Eat* (1964; 35 min), and the lovely dance-performance of choreographer Paul Swan in *Paul Swan* (1965; 66 min) reveal the range of New York experiences Warhol's camera documented.[8] But perhaps the film that confirmed Warhol's belief that making his movies was "pure fun" and that empty space for new performance was continuously necessary is *Space* (1965). Made in the first Factory with Superstars Sedgwick, folk singer Eric Andersen, and one of the few African American Superstars, Dorothy Dean, the film shows the Factory kids singing tunes like "Puff the Magic Dragon," undressing one another, throwing food, and getting stoned. Hilariously, Sedgwick, who has been unsuccessfully trying to memorize the "Hail Mary," attempts to perform the Catholic sign of the cross. Needless to say, Edie's exercise doesn't quite work—because of her fragile personality and, perhaps, her drug-induced state. In short, the film puts into the can an everyday experience of hanging out (drug taking, flirting, drinking, and other sorts of frolicking) at the early Factory space.

Space, as well as a handful of other films from 1965, is a bridge film between the more static portrait films and the double-screened *The Chelsea Girls*. In the same year as *Space*, Warhol experimented with video and directed the stunning double-screened portrait of Sedgwick in *Outer and Inner Space* (the film may also be shown on a single screen). Nineteen sixty-five clearly marks a transitional period that leads to a new (albeit diverse) phase in filmmaking, moving toward the narrative-driven *My Hustler* (1965, shot in the gay Manhattan resort, Fire Island) on the one hand and, on the other, *The Chelsea Girls*. In fact, experimentation is significantly awake in *Space*, where, particularly in the first reel, the camera and microphone break away from the tight framing of the earlier films. Here, Warhol roams freely through the performance area with the camera, as he observes the kids' shenanigans until, in the second reel, the camera stabilizes and focuses on the action in one area.

After Warhol was shot by Valerie Solanas in 1968, the movie camera fell out of his hands and into those of Paul Morrissey, who directed *Andy Warhol's Flesh*. Assuming the traditional New Yorker position in the film industry, Warhol became more the financial backer/producer than the director of his films. In any case, Warhol's films of New York artists, art patrons, junkies, millionaires, politicians, and movie stars doing their thing is the recorded trace that keeps city spaces both empty and productive.

Can't Take My Eyes Off of You

In *Cue's New York*, Emory Lewis writes:

> If you wish to see other variations on the theme of near-nudity, try the joints along West Third Street in Greenwich Village. Some of these are honky-tonks, so never carry large sums of money or ostentatiously display it. Some of these clubs change their names every few months. The Savannah Club specializes in interracial shows. Sometimes, a pretty young lady turns out to be a man, or vice versa. These transvestite acts turn up now and again, but they are much less frequent nowadays. Perhaps this is because the streets are filled with the "gay" ones. One landmark of the Third Sex is the Eighty-two Club, which has been confusing the public for decades at 82 East Fourth Street just off Second Avenue. (191–192)

This was Andy Warhol's New York. Indeed, his experiences with this New York scene filtered his creative and corporeal response to the world at large. But, it is the way Warhol looked at New York in the twentieth century that makes his art provocative.

Writing recently in the *New York Times*, Sylvia Plachy recalled photographing Warhol before and after Solanas fired on him in 1968. Plachy remarked that on her first photo shoot with the artist, she "took six frames and only once did he look back at me" (B2). On their second encounter, according to Plachy, the near-death experience following the Solanas shooting made him "more subdued." Nonetheless, when she was later a professional photographer cruising Studio 54 she spotted Warhol standing alone. His look at the world had apparently changed little: "He usually stood alone, with tape recorder in hand, avoiding eye contact." To not look back at or make contact with one's interlocutor may, on the one hand, reveal Warhol's shyness, aloofness. It may, on the other hand, indicate what he considered the failure of the human ocular. The refusal to look directly at the camera or human machine suggests the way Warhol realized the inadequacy of the human eye to absorb the tremendous amount of information and activity emanating from New York that, as Cue's *Leisurely Guide* tells us, had "been confusing the public for decades." I am also partial to Tony Rayns's lovely suggestion that Warhol's distance from personal or eye contact was mechanically erotic: "For

[Warhol], the *avoidance* of personal involvement and the *embrace* of neutral, non-judgmental recording technology generated exactly the kick that a shy and repressed Catholic boy needed. Masturbation was no party-game for Andy. For him, hand-jobs were as lonesome as he imagined cowboys to be" (89; emphasis in original). For Warhol it was, frankly, impossible to fully see—that is, experience—the enormity of the city as merely a human being.

This is why Warhol believed it is better to be a machine. It was better to record lived experience—sounds and images—because the machine picked up the details, the imperfections, and the beautiful contradictions of the metropolis the human eye and ear could never possibly register. For Warhol to see thoroughly it was necessary to intermingle with, and become an extension of, the machine and machine culture. As he stood alone in the current of New York, where architecture, gender, and all other sorts of "gay" repertoire mixed, the camera created combinations that surprised, then disappeared in a flash. Warhol's mechanically recorded archive assures that with a flick of the recorder's switch, the city will truly never sleep.

NOTES

I'd like to thank Charles Silver in the Film and Media Studies Center at the Museum of Modern Art for arranging my viewing of Warhol's films.

1. Rosalind E. Krauss discusses how, unlike the transcendent sublime for the body the Abstract Expressionists purportedly enabled, Warhol's bodies are "anything but left behind" in the experience of the work of art (112).

2. According to Grundmann, Warhol reportedly made about five hundred screen tests between 1963 and 1968 (4).

3. Amy Taubin's essay, "****," confirms Colacello's remarks about filming at the Factory: "Some came to see the freaks, others came to freak out. But primarily they came because the camera was always running. The camera inspired 'acting out'" (28). For further information on Warhol, visit www.warholstars.org/index.html.

4. Stephen Koch recognized Warhol's voyeuristic propensity with film: "Even more than it does most movies, voyeurism dominates all Warhol's early films and defines their aesthetic" (42).

5. Warhol's concept here echoes one of his master Marcel Duchamp's retorts about New York and its promise of the creative new: "New York itself is a work of art, a complete work of art. . . . And I believe that the idea of demolishing old buildings, old souvenirs is fine" (qtd in Tomkins 152).

6. Certainly, Warhol was aware of the Italian filmmakers such as Fellini (*La Dolce Vita* [1960]), Pasolini (*Accatone* [1961]), and De Sica (*Miracle in Milan* [U.S. rel. 1951]), whose films clearly showed a postwar "modern" Rome. The problem with these images of modern Rome, as Warhol would have considered it, was that the people and narrative got in the way of the single, unedited shot of any one building. The Coliseum, for example, may have made the ideal eight-hour companion piece to *Empire*.

7. In 1967, painter Gregory Battcock noted that although the "image differences in the various evenings in *The Chelsea Girls* are not very great," the timing by the projectionist is "beyond his control." Thus, Battcock continues, "exact and dependable repetition, an expected feature within the film medium, is very simply and immediately challenged" (354).

8. Giorno is the founder of Performance Poetry. In 1964 he organized Giorno Poetry Systems that used multi-media platforms and technologies as part of his poetry (often recorded on albums and tape). Robert Indiana is a Pop artist/painter who was inspired early on by such things as traffic signs and commercial trademarks for his work. Paul Swan was a sculptor and dancer who studied dance with a Diaghilev star, Mikhail Mordkin. He was eighty-two when Warhol shot this film.

A member of the American people: Manny (Henry Fonda), who eats here every night. *The Wrong Man* (Alfred Hitchcock, Warner Bros., 1956). Digital frame enlargement.

A Clean, Well-Lighted Place

HITCHCOCK'S NEW YORK

MURRAY POMERANCE

Some lived in it and never felt it.
—Ernest Hemingway

City of Dreams

It was in his imagination that Alfred Hitchcock first visited New York, and his was a meticulous imagination. "I . . . was completely familiar with the map of New York," he told François Truffaut. "I used to send away for train schedules—that was my hobby—and I knew many of the timetables by heart. Years before I ever came here, I could describe New York, tell you where the theaters and stores were located. When I had a conversation with Americans, they would ask, 'When were you over there last?' and I'd answer, 'I've never been there at all.' Strange, isn't it?" (Truffaut 90). If Hitchcock's was an attenuated and compacted New York, absent the Brooklyn Navy Yard and the East Village, Yorkville, the Sheep Meadow, Morningside Heights, and Herald Square, it was perhaps no more abstracted, no less idiosyncratic a New York than any New Yorker's and it had the merit of having been examined in the smallest detail, such a detail that later, many years later, when he came to represent it on film, his "drawing" could be finely rendered and accurate, as any responsible draftsman's should be. If his dream New York was cultivated rather on the bourgeois side, incorporating restaurants and theaters but not the high-end pawnshops of Forty-seventh Street or the tenements of Little Italy, it provided him with the graciously inviting cityscape that could stimulate his desire and his creativity without constraining him from proceeding further afield, as time went by, in order to represent dramatically the apartment blocks of West Eleventh Street that frame *Rear Window* (1954), the police halls and Queens residence and Queens diner that characterize *The Wrong Man* (1956), the mansions of Glen Cove and other locations that are celebrated in *North by Northwest* (1959).

When in 1937 the Hitchcock family, accompanied by his assistant, Joan Harrison, first visited America, for them America was first and foremost New York.

They arrived on board the *Queen Mary* on the twenty-second of August. Hitchcock, according to John Russell Taylor, wanted "to look the situation over for himself" (*Hitch* 148). Settling into a suite at the St. Regis Hotel on Fifty-fifth Street just east of Fifth Avenue, a place that would later become his New York "home away from home" (McGilligan 202), Hitchcock was wined, dined, and reported in a general spirit of effusiveness, wonderment, and not a little gluttony. Much cited is a tale of his dinner on August 26 at the 21 Club on West Fifty-second Street, where, infatuated with American steaks and American ice cream, he devoured three portions of each, in alternation, along with "a gulp of strong tea" and brandy (Spoto 187). He mounted the staircase to the beef locker to examine the meat firsthand afterward. He gave reporter H. Allen Smith a field day. He did a radio show. All the while, "the New York offices of the major studios were busy trying to learn who was offering what" (Spoto 189). He went off with his family to visit Saratoga Springs in company with the "debonair" John Hay "Jock" Whitney (Leff 23) and also Washington, D.C. In New York, Hitchcock was lunched by Katherine "Kay" Brown (Mrs. James Barrett, the East Coast story editor for David O. Selznick); they had already met in letters, and they liked one another on the page.

Brown's assignment from Selznick, however, wired on August 23, before Hitchcock's arrival, was pointed and urgent:

I AM DEFINITELY INTERESTED IN HITCHCOCK AS A DIRECTOR AND THINK IT MIGHT BE WISE FOR YOU TO MEET AND CHAT WITH HIM. IN PARTICULAR I WOULD LIKE TO GET A CLEAR PICTURE AS TO WHO, IF ANYONE, IS REPRESENTING HIM AND WHAT HE HAS IN MIND IN THE WAY OF SALARY.

(Behlmer 278)

She was instructed to "discover his salary demands and the status of his negotiations with MGM . . . but offer Hitchcock nothing" (Leff 23). The intense press and industry attention he was receiving, however, not to mention the family's touring plans and Hitchcock's generally buoyant enthusiasm for everything American, necessitated that the "quick-witted" Brown (Leff 23) should have him to herself for some sufficient length of casual interaction that without undue probing the Selznick queries might find ready answers: she brought the Hitchcocks to her home on Long Island for a bout of beach picnics, family coziness (Brown's daughter Laurinda and Patricia Hitchcock were contemporaries, and good playmates), and country air (McGilligan 202). They came to Amagansett, a village founded by settlers from Britain in 1630; latterly a home to New Yorkers like the Barretts who needed a place away from town, where the air was invigoratingly salty and the gardens profuse.

According to Thomas Schatz, by August 1937 Hitchcock "had been corresponding regularly with Kay Brown, and the two got along so well that Hitchcock, his wife Alma, and his co-scenarist Joan Harrison all stayed for several days in

Brown's home on Long Island. Brown had the negotiations moving but Hitchcock still was not ready to commit, although by the time he returned to England he was leaning toward Selznick" (273). Two years later, the Hitchcocks emigrated to America. There is a photograph of the three of them striding in lockstep on the deck of the *Queen Mary*. The look of optimistic ebullience on all three faces, the assured relaxation of Hitch, the prepared eagerness of Alma, the proud delirium of Patricia as they "step toward" their new lives, are all unmistakable (Cogeval 440). In wondering what soupçon of the United States could so positively have motivated not only the filmmaker but his entire family as well, that they should appear in this frame of mind, it is difficult not to estimate that the experience of New York and in particular a few days with Kay Brown in Amagansett were the balm that soothed the memory and enticed hopes for the future.

To the Englishman who had only dreamed of America, but who had dreamed in meticulous detail, the Amagansett beach, broad and white and bordered by stretches of wildly romantic dunes and lush dune grass, not to mention "wind-trimmed shad-bush, beach plum, and holly" (Rattray 81), and by patches of wild grape and bayberry, the sands dotted in the early morning by the specters of fishermen's trawls and cleansed by the Atlantic tides, would have seemed a vision of paradise by comparison with the gray, stony washes of Eastbourne or Seaford or with Brighton sands (the most accessible beaches to the Hitchcocks, who were living at Shamley Green, in Surrey). Kay Brown would likely have shown them long potato fields running off to the horizon, acrid with the smell of arsenic in early September, and would have pointed out whalers' homes from the previous century. She might well have dined them at The Hedges Inn in East Hampton or at the Montauk Island Club where they could have tasted "unsurpassed cuisine française" (*East Hampton Star*, September 2, 1937). It would be inconceivable that they did not find, lying around the Brown house, a copy of that week's *East Hampton Star*, in which Jeannette Edwards Rattray's "Looking Them Over" column featured a mention of Norman B. Geddes visiting the area and an appreciation of Cornelia Otis Skinner's new play, *Edna His Wife*. From all of this, and from sight of the summer mansions of New York's high society, such as John Van Houten's "cottage" on Further Lane or William M. Ward's "Willward Lodge" on Indian Well Hollow Highway (Kelsey 24), Hitchcock could have fathomed the magnitude and style of the American ruling class represented twenty years later by Lester Townsend and his house in Glen Cove (photographed in Old Westbury), to which Roger O. Thornhill is escorted under guard in *North by Northwest*. Hitchcock would also have captured in Amagansett a rarified sense of the earthy, long-lived, politically passionate, morally convicted, and culturally eager sensibility that was New York's birthright. Not yet a tourist industry unto themselves, the Hamptons of the late 1930s, especially the quiet village of Amagansett, exhibited in microcosm a great deal of the deep character of New York, and of America, its serious and unremitting struggle for self-improvement and self-display, its resistance to the force of nature. Like Shamley Green, where the Hitchcocks resided on "a property of great charm—and great luxury" (Spoto 128), the Hamptons showed Hitchcock a New York scene that was both lush and hypercivilized. Here he would have been able to be one of the first to make an automatic telephone call (Kelsey 156). Here, too, he could have found models for later sketching the puissante and lofty Mrs. Sutton (Alma Kruger), who would inhabit *Saboteur* in 1942 (sheltering the Nazi villain under the umbrella of her social status and wealth). On the country roads at night, especially near Montauk, he could have learned the ambience that he would replicate in *North by Northwest*, when Roger Thornhill escapes from his would-be killers in Laura Babson's Mercedes and teeters along the cliff edge of the sea.

But principally, of course, Hitchcock was able to have the conversations with Brown that would soon bring him back to America, this time as a contracted director for Selznick International, and that would initiate the adoptive affection for the United States, and particularly for New York, that he showed in so much of his mature work. The view of New York City and Long Island to which we are given access in Hitchcock's films—*Saboteur* (1942), *Spellbound* (1945), *Rope* (1949), *Rear Window* (1954), *The Wrong Man* (1956), *North by Northwest* (1959), and *Topaz* (1966)—is typically that of an eager, yet distant outsider who has gained an affection, even an addiction, for New York on the basis of visits, real and virtual, not inhabitation. Such adoptive personalities are perhaps the truest New Yorkers, in that whatever they visit they cherish and whatever they taste they remember forever. Perhaps for this reason, Hitchcock's New York tends to be a surface rather than an environment, a perspective rather than a community. What I mean to imply by this is not at all that the stories Hitchcock configured in New York lack communal engagement, or densely articulate relationships between feelingful characters: Jeff Jefferies is extremely involved as he watches his neighbors in *Rear Window*; Barry Kane is extremely involved with the blind Philip Martin, and involved, too, as he tries to catch the villain Fry on the Statue of Liberty in *Saboteur*. But New York itself, as it plays upon the screen in Hitchcock, is often a precisely drawn abstraction, a packaging, a memento, of real lived experience there rather than the kind of mundane but familiar—and thus casual—view a New Yorker would have. Hitchcock's abstraction, indeed, lies exactly in his clear and precise composition, the unrelenting significance of his detail. Hitchcock as filmmaker of New York was not only a tourist but an accomplished and attentive aficionado, even a self-declared New Yorker. What makes his filmic New York so interesting is the extent and focal quality of that attentiveness.

Topographic Characterization

Since early in his career, Hitchcock had been using the settings of his stories in a characteristic fashion, bringing them to the foreground with as much dramaturgical meaning as was afforded the protagonists who moved in them. His films thus often seem to take issue with the dictum of Affron and Affron:

> Of the two elements subject to photography, actor (or human figure) and décor (or place), it is the human figure that is privileged in film, particularly in the Hollywood sound film. The skill of the actor and the eloquence of the script focus the viewer's attention on what is said; the skill of the actor and the eloquence of the set, on what is seen. (35)

From the boardinghouse in *The Lodger* (1927), the tube car in *Blackmail* (1929), the circus in *Murder!* (1930), to the ski slopes in *The Man Who Knew Too Much* (1934) and the mountain village in *The Lady Vanishes* (1938), the scene for Hitchcock is not a background against which dramatic action is set for contrast, nor an underprivileged photographed element, but an active contributor to the business of the plot. In abstracting particular features or aspects of the setting for incorporation into the story—for example, the East Berlin Kunstmuseum in *Torn Curtain* (1966)—Hitchcock shows a sensitivity to sociological and cultural nuances of detail unmatched by that of any other filmmaker (see Pomerance 100–101), as well as a capacity for ironically manipulating the scene and the action in relation to one another (altering what Kenneth Burke called the scene : act ratio [*Grammar*]) in a manner that produces entertainment through wit, irony, and pregnant circumstantiality. Far more than Schoedsack and Cooper manage with the Empire State Building and the great ape King Kong (1933), then, Hitchcock makes scenes telling in and of themselves, so that when they are read against the drama unfolding within them a multiply layered intentionality is made evident.

While Hitchcock's New York settings are not necessarily more dramatic than others in the context of the body of his work as a whole (his use, say, of San Francisco in *Vertigo* [1958] or of Copenhagen in *Torn Curtain*), they are strikingly noteworthy when seen against other filmmakers' depictions of New York onscreen. And they are never postcard treatments, even when the subject is a scene that is widely familiar, such as, for example, the Statue of Liberty. One need but consider the oblique, even hilarious, use to which he puts this monument in *Saboteur* (1942), shooting inside the torch and then outside it in the wind as the nefarious Fry (Norman Lloyd) clings for his life and finally falls. Hitchcock is profoundly evocative, using relatively tiny morsels of characterization or architecture to invoke a broader setting that envelops and supports the action. For example, the gateman at Grand Central Station (Irving Bacon) who frowns at Gregory Peck and Ingrid Bergman in *Spellbound* (1945) precisely invokes railroad culture, the stolid old institution of Grand Central, and a worn etiquette characteristic of service employees in New York of the time. What we see as J.B. and Constance try for the train is not merely a portal through which they and other lovers must pass to gain access to a mode of transportation, but part of a grand edifice, through which the vast commuter traffic of a great metropolis shuttles in routine.

Hitchcock's observations of the city are noteworthy in their canniness. Consider that the apartment complex of *Rear Window* is constructed to represent something of a typical West Village scene, which would have been full of stylish people without vast resources. Some are in the arts: the photojournalist Jefferies who is our protagonist (James Stewart), the songwriter (Ross Bagdasarian), the dancer Miss Torso (Georgine Darcy), the sculptor (Jesslyn Fax). Some are young and unestablished: the newly married couple (Havis Davenport, Rand Harper), the sunbathing girls. Some have never had success in life: the couple with the dog (Sara Berner, Frank Cady), the Thorwalds (Raymond Burr, Irene Winston), Miss Lonelyhearts (Judith Evelyn). While there is a concentration of population such as this in any urban setting, the especially high property values in New York make for crowded conditions and a way—precisely demonstrated through the design of this film—in which people very unlike one another, except in class and expectation, might be in extremely close proximity, carrying out their independent daily routines in ironic juxtaposition. Hitchcock here gives numerous markers of precise New York location and style; for example, Lisa Fremont's (Grace Kelly) Sutton Place origins (reflected in her speech tone and experience, her class evident in her clothing and her ability to have dinner delivered from the 21 Club) and Stella the nurse's (Thelma Ritter) working-class demeanor and typical Brooklynite street savvy: these appear to be contradictory, but in the end Stella's forthrightness resolves as a tacit feature of Lisa's personality and history. One overriding characteristic of the experience of working-class New Yorkers who are not tourists (as Hitchcock actually is): they don't, for the most part, see their neighborhood world, or even have a superior point of vantage from which to see the whole city, as an aesthetic spectacle. They don't have the aerial shot, in other words (and they aren't typically among those who ascend to the top of the Empire State Building in order to procure it). In *Rear Window*, in order to provide us with a real New Yorker's perspective, Hitchcock chains us to the viewing position of a cripple whose world must be entirely presented through his rear (-facing) window. So it is that we see the action of other protagonists only in fragments, as it becomes circumstantially visible through their own rear windows; and we see Eleventh Street, our geographical "reality," only as a few inches of it become visible at the end of a short alleyway. As well as a view of the local scene known by a man in a wheelchair, then, this is a view of the world as it would be known in New York by any but the most wealthy; a limited, even tediously repeated view in which one would have to take pleasure in the smallest and most local of details. Regardless of the plot of *Rear Window*, one gains a pungent sense of what it is to live in New York merely by watching its action transpire through the limited perspective that is offered us. David Bordwell's observation that "character takes precedence over place" (Bordwell et al. 51) is thus only one basis for reading this film, a basis, indeed, that eliminates for the viewer much of the visual pleasure Hitchcock has so carefully prepared.

At one point in the film, Lisa, entranced by the chords the songwriter is trying to put together into a song, wonders aloud to Jeff what inspires a man to compose a song like that. Jeff answers that he gets his inspiration from the landlady once a month. This is certainly an accurate (and funny) comment on the class position of artists; but it answers to the composer's doggedness and perseverance, not his need to use his imagination for mundane purposes, since the same landlady is lording it over all the tenants we see. I think another motive lies in his need to escape from the singularity and predictability of his world, as symbolized by this limited view. And if he turns away from the courtyard, he sees what Jeff sees in the many instances when he turns away: his own apartment, every detail of which is noxiously familiar. And to turn away from oneself is to be faced irreconcilably with this lively—yet unalterable—courtyard. As the composer dreams up melodies, Jeff dreams up adventures, and Miss Lonelyhearts dreams up love affairs, and Mr. Thorwald dreams up a new future for himself. A few times we see Jeff's detective friend Doyle (Wendell Corey) drop in. He never exhibits the kind of fascination with the courtyard that Jeff does, that we do. He sees it instantly for what it is in real terms—a kind of dead end, and this because he doesn't have to live here.

In *Rope* (1948), the apartment dwellers set out to take a sort of exciting voyage, as they would have it; and in the finale they learn that they are to be confined to their (philosophically) limited state forever. For this confinement to seem dramatic, the apartment must first suggest exactly the fluidity and boundlessness that makes all things possible, that makes the actually determining and morally limiting spaces of the city seem to open up endlessly in a panorama of vivid Technicolor. *Rope* is the antithesis of *Rear Window*; in the first, boundless possibility is resolved as definition, constraint, loss of freedom, and paralysis; in the second, definition, constraint, loss of freedom, and paralysis are resolved as boundless possibility.

North by Northwest

In *North by Northwest*, Hitchcock uses the United Nations Secretariat on First Avenue to dwarf both the diplomat Lester Townsend (Philip Ober) and Roger Thornhill (Cary Grant), who are implicated with one another in a gruesome murder that takes place in what we are to take as the Members' Lounge. The actual building was used (without permission) for an exterior establishing shot of Thornhill pulling up in a taxicab, and then the lobby and lounge areas were re-created on a soundstage, the former as an exact duplicate of the actual lobby by Eero Saarinen, which towers as a seemingly endless interior space cut by sweeping horizontal curves. The receptionist and Thornhill are here made to seem little more than tiny pieces in an immeasurable machinery of high politics and top-level international business. While the Members' Lounge is cozier, its rear window panels opening onto the city, the large number of people in circulation in all directions of view, and the generally untidy state of conversations in progress combine to shrink Townsend's personality, when he presents himself to Thornhill, so that he is nothing more than a bureaucratic cipher. After Townsend is knifed and Thornhill caught—holding the knife—next to the body by a photographer, Thornhill is seen fleeing the building in a shot taken from the roof and looking down into the gardens that margin the entryway: he seems like an ant.

When in the company of his mother (Jessie Royce Landis) Thornhill explores Room 796 of the Plaza Hotel in search of the deliciously elusive George Kaplan, it is necessary that the premises should be sufficiently comfortable as to properly belong inside the expensive bastion of this hotel (now closed as such and to open soon as private residences, with its Palm Court and Oak Bar preserved), while at the same time appearing sufficiently nondescript as to support the anonymity of Kaplan and the haunting possibility that Thornhill and he are so alike they may reasonably be mistaken for one another: Room 796 must be an elegant example of what Deleuze called "any-space-whatever," a neutral zone for the privileged traveler. This is achieved through a meticulous reconstruction of the room by designer Robert Boyle, in shades of beige, with neutral furniture and the slightly disquieting preponderance of uncluttered space one finds in plush New York hotel rooms: an alienating space where familiar objects might otherwise be. In other sequences at the Plaza we are treated to careful reconstruction of the Oak Bar and location shots of the lobby, in order to establish the veracity of the locale, its classiness, and Thornhill's cozy familiarity. Since the story begins with Thornhill being kidnapped because he is taken to be Kaplan, it is vital to Hitchcock's deeper intent here that the mistaken identity be transparently clear to the audience as a circumstance that is unavoidable for the wealthy Thornhill—money does not buy the ability to guide unfailingly the way others perceive us—and so early on, his placement, even ensconcement, at the Plaza is crucial to the charge of his being lifted from there.

Money does, however, buy access. At the Plaza, it is the monied who hang out and it is monied folk one is likely to encounter as guests, just exactly as it is folk without money and class one is likely to encounter as employees. Meticulous casting and scripting follow from, and reflect, the setting instead of dominating it as Bordwell predicts, the dialogue and vocal tone of the chambermaid Elsie (Maudie Prickett) and the valet (James McCallion), both of whom Roger encounters in Room 796, defining them as alien to the class in which he finds himself. And as he and his mother descend in the elevator with the villains Licht (Robert Ellenstein) and Valerian (Adam Williams), the pompous silence of all the riders is a telltale description of the sort of people who would be using an elevator like this in such a place—people whose very presence at the Plaza speaks volumes. The visual and acoustic joke that Hitchcock is here able to play, as Mrs. Thornhill turns to the two kidnappers and says with utter innocence, "You gentlemen aren't *really* trying to kill my son, are you?" can have its striking (and, for Roger, mortifying) effect only where otherwise one could hear a pin drop, that is, in a closed space populated by such people as consider themselves to be above any demonstration through small talk that they notice their environment and care about their fellows—a place such as an elevator in the Plaza Hotel. (Soon, in *Requiem for a Heavyweight* [1962], Ralph Nelson would stage a matching scene with Anthony Quinn and a poodle-bearing matron in the elevator of the St. Moritz, only a few steps down Fifty-ninth Street.) If the primary joke is Mrs. Thornhill's ability to express her naiveté so blatantly, a strong overtone is that the vulgarity of Licht and Valerian's violent plans is juxtaposed brazenly against the effete decadence of the gilded elevator cage and of the socialites who conventionally travel there.

As though to suggest obliquely that this is a modern story, one that might apply to virtually anyone wandering the streets of a large city in an age when the social roots of identity and capability have been severed by occupational fragmentation, rapid social change, and the ubiquitous presence of strangers (thanks to increases in mobility of all kinds), the film opens with a kind of street ballet: a sequence of carefully staged shots taken on and around Madison Avenue as crowds of pedestrians head home after a day at work, all of these people more or less interchangeable with one another. In an elaborate rear-projection sequence, Thornhill and his secretary (Doreen Lang) ride in a taxi to the Plaza, and the route is precisely replicated from reality, with the taxi passing through Grand Army Plaza and swinging westward along Fifty-ninth Street, before swerving around in a U-turn to deposit Roger at the gilded entrance to the hotel. Through the windows as this sequence progresses we see hundreds of others, just like Roger, heading for their cocktails in the exact way that he is. Perhaps dozens of them are on the way to being kidnapped, too.

Later, to escape New York (because his picture with the dead Townsend has been printed on the front page of every major newspaper in town), Roger uses the ticket windows at Grand Central Station (filmed on location). Here we are treated to an aspect of life in New York (certainly in the 1950s, but persisting today) that charmed and intrigued Hitchcock: an employee might work in an exact job and location for such a long time that he becomes virtually a part of the setting; the New Yorkiness of the moment is typified not only by the building or location in which an event occurs but by the extent to which that location has worn off on the personality of a character who works there. The ticket seller (Ned Glass) who tries unsuccessfully to nab Roger is a model of a kind of shrewd, streetwise, and gloriously mundane working personality one might find at any ticket window in New York, behind the wheel of any taxicab, serving in any restaurant. He has worked so long selling tickets at this window that it has been transformed into *his* window, the tickets he sells there into *his* tickets; indeed, he has actually *become* the ticket agent he seems to be, rather than merely agreeing for years on end to play at being one. He is foiled not because he moves too slowly to get to his telephone to signal the police about Roger's presence (we have a shot from inside the booth showing Roger's photograph propped up next to the window), but because Roger Thornhill is also a New Yorker, a man long accustomed to reading the intent that is etched on his interlocutors' faces; he has picked up that the agent is stalling him, and has taken flight. To be sure, the long-tenured employee is a premodern character, inexorably replaced by younger people on the move who infiltrate the city and push such older types into retirement as they proceed toward temporarily occupying positions in a relentless attempt to climb.

Climbing is hardly necessary for Mr. Lester Townsend of 109 Baywood, Glen Cove. While Hitchcock's scriptwriters composed the dialogue we hear in his films, and his designers built and/or decorated the settings that are not actual locations, such as, for instance, the library and lobby of the Townsend house, they worked to his vision unrelentingly, and with this mansion he was positioning his protagonist as a man comfortably at home with the East Coast aristocracy. The exteriors of the Townsend residence were shot at Old Westbury Gardens, the John Shaffer Phipps Estate, a seventy-room mansion built in 1906 on 160 acres on Old Westbury Road, just east of Garden City. For "Townsend," who was occupied as ambassador to the United Nations, the mansion would have been an easy half-hour commute from Pennsylvania Station. And as a counterpoint to the splendor of the estate, a splendor visible as the limousine in which Roger is imprisoned moves up the drive, we find scenes set shortly afterward at the Glen Cove, Long Island, police station. Here is yet another meticulously described social scene, the courtroom of a small Long Island town most of which would have existed principally in order to cater to the needs of the millionaires living in the countryside around, such as, presumably, Townsend. The demeanor of the policemen we find there, the polished cleanliness and yet smallness of the court chamber, perfectly contradict (and thus embellish) the grand house with its vast lawns, on which we saw Leonard (Martin Landau) engaged in a solitary game of croquet.

In Hitchcock's careful architecture, each point of narrational gravity is supported and balanced by accompanying points: the mansion supported by the police station; Jeff's tiny apartment balanced and supported by a vision of the 21 Club uptown and far away, from which dinner has come; the cramped interior of Liberty's torch in the finale of *Saboteur* balanced shockingly against the overly windy, frightening exterior, where physical support is at a minimum and every step is life-threatening.

The Wrong Man

That every step is life-threatening is, of course, the great philosophical truth beneath all of Hitchcock's oeuvre. In *The Wrong Man*, a "true story," we are treated to the fateful movements of a musician, Manny Balestrero (Henry Fonda), who tries to cash an insurance policy one afternoon so that his wife, Rose (Vera Miles), may have some vital dental work done, only to be fingered by the insurance clerk as a stick-up man who attempted a robbery days before. The police track him to his house, arrest him, book him, and put him through the inexorable grindings of the justice mill (the lineup, the holding cells, the indictment, the trial) before the actual thief—due either to coincidence or heavenly grace: Hitchcock allowed us to believe either—is apprehended. In the meantime, Mrs. Balestrero collapses from nervous strain (and her too pregnant sense that in this mortal coil, true justice is lost to us) and loses her mental balance. Manny is brought to the very limit of his faith—both in God and in the American way of life. This film is shot almost entirely on location in black and white, nicely mirroring in its authenticity, grittiness, and stark beauty Alexander Mackendrick's startling exposé of the New York gossip columnist scene, *Sweet Smell of Success*, that was also shot on location in black and white and released six months later.

If the dramaturgical function of the city backgrounds in other Hitchcock New York films is to ironically emphasize and characterize the action, the function in *The Wrong Man* is to work a remorseless punition upon the body of Manny Balestrero, to utter again and again that the exercise of authority, brutality, and systematization we are witnessing is being situated for real, carried out in the framework of the real, and imprinted for real in the dramatic unfolding. It is for this reason that George Barnes's lighting—lighting is always an agency of scenic characterization—is unaccented, flat, topological rather than theatrical. We must believe in the everyday quality of the action we are seeing, in the commonsense interpretation of events that characterizes undramatized interaction. Fonda's cheekbones, pronounced by the lighting of Arthur Miller for *The Ox-Bow Incident*, of Joe MacDonald for *My Darling Clementine*, or of Winton Hoch for *Mister Roberts*, are here lit in such a way that they recede into the plane of his face, reducing his status to that of the ordinary person. This "available" lighting—it is in fact an artful construction, with artificial light added to the available light of the scene, that reads invisibly, as though only available light were being used—meshes with the authenticity of real location settings to lend strategic logic to the action and believability to the actors, and also to stimulate in the viewer the conviction that she is observing all this in what seems like an actually unfolding, not filmically constructed, New York.

Virtually all the scenes in *The Wrong Man* give precisely this quality of real engagement, thus in a way diminishing our filmgoing pleasure to the degree that we are made to lack what can clearly be discerned as an artfully concocted spectacle, but I wish to emphasize three scenes in particular. The first is a night sequence shot inside Sherman Billingsley's Stork Club, at 3 East Fifty-third Street (the present site of Paley Park). This is the sequence that runs beneath the main title, as bourgeois couples modestly shuffle along the dance floor and a small off-camera combo plays Bernard Herrmann's lazy mambo theme. The camera captures the cramped glitter of the place, a much experienced waiter gliding among the dancers with corsages, the gleaming dance floor roofed with a huge cloud of balloons, well-dressed diners at tables with double cloths finishing up late-night meals like chicken hamburger with tomato sauce, french fries, and buttered green peas (tipsontables.com). This scene shows one of

> the last vestiges of a city with a Runyonesque soul—before the post-war build-ing boom replaced a lot of the brick and brownstones with glass skyscrapers; when the language and culture of the city was still WASPy and the dominant vices were drinking and philandering. In Hitchcock's New York City films, the social strata are well defined, and viewers enter a world of power and money where everything is fashionable, expensive and recherché. (Shevey)

Shot to represent a typical evening at the Stork Club, Walter Winchell's and Bing Crosby's hangout, the club has the look of a representation, of a movie scene designed to replicate a reality: there is something a little posed and stiff about the customers, something a little contrived about the waiter's movement; and the music, coming from a band we cannot see, might be nondiegetic title music just as well as actual dance music the customers are using. Adding to the artificiality of the moment is the fact that it immediately follows a short speech by Hitchcock himself about how this film is "a *true story*—every word of it" and "different" from the "many kinds of suspense pictures" he has given audiences before: a statement delivered in the deadpan voice already familiar to watchers from his television appearances and always signaling the presence of a wit at work. So far, at any rate, this particular New York scene seems a little stilted, a little formal, a little set up for the camera. So also does the following shot seem contrived, where—after a series of gentle lap dissolves that bring about a tempo-ral progression in which many, then most, of the customers leave the club—we see the band continuing the music, but a little wearily, in a medium-long shot of the bandstand. This little artificiality immediately follows both the director's credit card and a gesture of exhaustion from a white-jacketed waiter who is fingering the bill for a table at screen right. Manny (or at least a recognizable Henry Fonda) is at left, playing his bass; a saxophonist is in the center of the screen; a man playing maracas is at right; a horn player with a muted instrument is at right rear; and in the extreme foreground is the pianist/band leader who gives a subtle signal that in a few bars they will quit. After three more bars, sum-marily, and in a matter-of-fact and businesslike way, they do.

We are looking at the musicians positioned underneath the cloud of balloons, which is now shiny and somewhat provocative. In the silence, which suddenly seems sudden, something quite strange and cinematically wonderful happens. Without the camera moving, the moment is converted from an artificial and con-trived cinematic shot to a view of actual unaffected reality: Manny turns his back to the camera, the pianist/band leader looks down, the maraca player looks over at Manny, all of these persons bluntly disregarding the fact of the shot after hav-ing, for several moments, gazed outward professionally to their dancing (and filmgoing) audience. The balloons now look like nothing so much as decoration suspended from the ceiling of a nightclub, rather than an art director's symbols of gay abandon. We cut to a waiter walking away with money from a last table, as the guests stir, then back to the bandstand, a little closer now, as the pianist puts away some music in a folder. In the next shot, Manny picks up his bass and walks out of the club (and off-camera), saying "'Night" under his breath. Outside, as he walks away between the dark shadows of a pair of patrolling cops, we have found ourselves on the late night city streets—but not the streets of noir, which are, like the film form that so often shows them off, an entirely cinematic construct. This is now a real street, patrolled by real cops.

Hitchcock has architected this opening sequence to lead us to a square commitment to urban New York realism by building upon the dissolution of a double fantasy, first the nightclub, which is no quotidian domain, and which fades gradually as the guests depart in small groups across various dissolves; and then the film frame, which typically holds and presents a vision that is special, supramundane, and which is abruptly snapped when Manny turns away in abject silence when the music is gone. We are carefully (and self-consciously) given a view of the extraordinary, and then in front of our eyes it is turned off (yet still in a way that is logical for the scenic moment), and then we find ourselves in—to my mind—the most authentic cinematic representation available of New York, which is to say, just a gaggle of workmen professionally finishing up and going home. We move, as it were, from the image of New York to the New York that subtends that image. So "true" does Manny's story become when he turns away from the camera and walks out of the club that it seems no longer a story; and, too, turning away, Fonda disappears into his character forever.

A second screen moment to which I would like to draw attention is very brief, an establishing shot taken on West 178th Street in the Bronx, on the New York side of the George Washington Bridge, as Manny and Rose proceed on a hunt for people who can give him an alibi. Here, they have come to search for a Mr. La Marca, who turns out to have died. What we need to see in order to understand the circumstances of the action is essentially this: Manny and Rose entering a tenement, optimistically mounting the stairs and knocking on flat No. 3, confronting the inhabitants—who happen to be two giggling little girls (recalling, in a way, the girls of *I Confess* [1953] and the two young women in the Albert Hall lobby in *The Man Who Knew Too Much* [1956])—and learning to their great chagrin that the target of their search will never be found. To prepare for this action, however, Hitchcock provides a stunning long shot: As Manny and Rose resolve to hunt, in a medium two-shot set on the veranda of a country lodge where they met Mr. La Marca, a slow dissolve presents us with the twin headlights of a car in the center of Manny's chest. As Manny and Rose fade, and haunting, tentative music (prefiguring the "chase" music of *Vertigo*) comes in, we see that the lights are those of a car heading toward us on a street. Soon it becomes clear that we are directly adjacent the New York end of the George Washington Bridge roadway, the flaring car lights echoed in a long line of street lamps and the long lines of lamps on the bridge. It is twilight, and somewhat foggy. The car pulls up screen center, and soon Manny and Rose emerge. A similar shot, an echo, soon follows this sequence, as, searching for a second man, Mr. Molinelli (who has also died), they draw up in front of a building on a street next to a pier where a huge steamer is docked. (An artful and considerably more artificial-looking version of this shot appears in *Marnie* [1964] and has aroused serious discussion from such critics as Robin Wood.)

Mr. La Marca, whoever he was, makes no appearance in this film and is present only as an invocation. To find out about him in a way that is intelligible to us, Manny and Rose need only proceed inside a building to his old apartment. It gives us no help in understanding Manny's situation to learn of Mr. La Marca's social circumstances—say, the neighborhood in which he lived. Why, then, are we treated to an establishing shot of the car pulling up next to the bridge, a shot, indeed, that is so magnificent to look at, so provocative, and so eerie? (Needless to say to Hitchcock aficionados, such a shot also prefigures the Fort Point sequence of *Vertigo*.) More: as the camera pans to follow Manny and Rose moving from the car to the building, the dissolve to the two of them climbing the stairway occurs before we even see them going through the apartment doorway; thus, the entry shot, central to the diegesis, is elided in favor of the establishing shot, which is entirely marginal to it.

And soon later, at the end of the Molinelli sequence, standing under a cloud of her own shadow projected by the corridor lamplight on a bare tenement wall, Rose starts to sob and lose control. This is the moment of her mental collapse. "There's no alibi! . . . It's perfect! . . . It's complete!" she cries, as Manny, turned away from the camera again and himself covered with shadow, gazes at her, mute.

It can certainly be argued that the exterior establishing shots are in place here because the insides of the two apartment buildings are so similar, so interchangeably reflective of a certain shabby working-class status; and cutting from Mr. La Marca's door to Mr. Molinelli's would seem too undifferentiated a maneuver without the exterior setup. And surely, if one setup is given, both should be. But it is also true that the two tenement interiors could have been photographed to emphasize their difference. What is more likely than mere differentiation, I think, is that multiple realities came into play for Hitchcock. In the actual account, researched for the production of the film, of the life and experience of Emmanuel Balestrero, there were actual locations of potential witnesses who could presumably have established his alibi, and part of the commitment Hitchcock had made involved presentation of those locations, or locations very much like them. And the establishing shots, especially the shot beside the George Washington Bridge, provide a remarkably concise and pungent sense of authentic New York background, background, indeed, which is so lively it becomes a part of the action.

But it is difficult not to esteem another possibility: that Hitchcock, the longtime fan of New York, who had admired it so meticulously and at such a remove, could finally place himself both physically and professionally in actual and dramatically stunning locations; to go further, in precise locations from which the workings of the city would be revealed. To be close to a pier, after all, is to be involved in shipping and the life of the docks, to come into detailed knowledge of the waterfront. And to be right next to the gargantuan structure of the bridge—that bridge any boy can find on any map of New York—to see the lamps, the railings, the traffic flowing off, is to make the most radical voyage away from studying maps at home in Leytonstone.

Finally, a mention of the sequence which for me remains after several viewings the most touching in the film. Manny, having left the Stork Club, goes into the subway, the Fifth Avenue station of the E train. It's a long stairway down, lit by a harsh light. He rides the train out to the Roosevelt Avenue/Jackson Heights station, where, emerging at street level in the Victor Moore Arcade, he enters directly into a connected coffee shop. Here, in the middle of the night, among only a scattered few other eaters, and served up by counter men who know him by name and ask about the family (prefiguring the relationship between Roger Thornhill and the lobby magazine seller at the beginning of *North by Northwest*), he sits in delicious solitude to have his toast and coffee and check out the Hialeah races in his paper.

It is here, when Manny is turned away not only from other people but also from the action of the story, that we meet him in an extraordinary bubble of reposeful solitude and selfness. He is deeply and entirely a man, only a man, a man like other men, an American man, a contemporary American man, yet a simple man, a man with talents and desires but no superhuman features, a member of the American people in every nuance of that phrase, a member of society, and therefore an innocent. It is in this utterly exact New York setting, this haven which serves the real needs of its clientele as do so many other similar havens in this giant city, that the truth of Manny is conveyed to us, so that his fall into the modernized claws of justice will all the more seem tragic and monstrous.

"I'll bring your toast over to your table," says one of the counter men after Manny has finished ordering, in a sweet and generous tone of voice. It is a statement that says everything, since without it the very delivery of the toast will announce itself, and since Manny eats here every night and knows what will happen; it is a statement that says, "I want to say something to you, I am connected to you." And the voice: that counter man's voice is the true voice of the real New Yorker, courteous, generous, knowing, competent, alive to the moment, free. That moment is a perfect moment, utterly tranquil and silent, sanctified, in the city that never sleeps.

ACKNOWLEDGMENTS

I am grateful to Jaymz Bee, Carleton Kelsey, Garrison Lutz, and Marci Vail.

WHIJPERING
EJCAPADEJ OUT
ON THE D TRAIN
City of Moves and Traps

In "Whispering Escapades Out on the D Train," we discover New York as a city of moves and traps. If modernity is characterized by new, heightened patterns of geographic and social mobility, New York is the topos in which the vehicles clash and thunder, race in all directions, head toward an uncertain and starkly desired future. At the same time, the intensity of the ethnic variation in the city's culture and the limited physical space in which so many struggling people are confined lead to confrontations, border crossings, alienations, attacks, and a general state of instability. Thus, through both passage and confinement, through both "moves" and "traps," we find an electric tension created in New York that doesn't match that of any other place on earth. The movie screen has been an ideal space for projecting this tension dramatically.

First, David Desser's analysis of *The Warriors* places it somewhere between Allen's "comic-romantic view of the city in *Annie Hall* and [John] Carpenter's nightmare imagery [in *Escape from New York*]." Desser sees this film as being a mythical reflection of Xenophon's *Anabasis*, a tale of warriors' return home after a defeat in battle, with the effect that myth replaces not only a historical but also a contemporary vision of New York; indeed, "in its use of a small group of displaced 'soldiers' making their way through hostile territory—where the 'natives' know the terrain better than they, natives defending their turf from uniformed invaders—the Warriors may recall the young U.S. soldiers in Southeast Asia." Filmmaker Walter Hill is shown in this analysis to be a descendant of Howard Hawks and Sam Peckinpah, using this film to work themes of masculinist bonding and social relations against a background image of New York as a new wilderness.

Then, David Sterritt's essay "He Cuts Heads" is a discursion on Spike Lee's New York, ranging from Lee's earliest films and *Joe's Bed-Stuy Barbershop* through *She's Gotta Have It* and *Do the Right Thing* to *Mo' Better Blues*, *Crooklyn*, and other films and culminating in *25th Hour*. In all of these, and increasingly, Sterritt finds Lee's "unique capacity for finding the political in the personal, the radical in the conservative, the timeless in the quotidian, the United States of America in the City of New York, and the transcendent soul in the earthly condition shared by black folks, white folks, and all folks."

Gwendolyn Audrey Foster's "New York Class-Passing Onscreen in the 1930s" argues that New York City, "by virtue of its anonymity, architecture, size, societal infrastructure, and mythic embrace of the American Dream (of social and economic mobility), allows—even fosters—a liminal space where the possibility for class mobility seems endless." Examining George Cukor's *Dinner at Eight*, Gregory La Cava's *My Man Godfrey*, Lloyd Bacon and Busby Berkeley's *Gold Diggers of 1933*, Edgar Selwyn's *Skyscraper Souls*, George Steven's *Swing Time*, Roy Del Ruth's *Employee's Entrance*, John G. Adolfi's *Central Park*, and W. S. Van Dyke's *Manhattan Melodrama*, the essay explores variations on the theme of class-passing, especially as it is played out against the background of New York high society. Special attention is given to the problem of social harmony, since "Americans are eager for the classes to get along. Nowhere is this truer than in New York, where, after all, the classes *must* get along. The disparity between the rich and poor is growing and ever present. The edenic myth of the city as 'the glorious jam' or the fantastic 'melting pot' seems necessary for the city to exist peacefully both in reality and in filmic diegesis." Yet at the same time, and persistently, "Depression-era films of New York left viewers with conflicting messages" of class mobility, with stars repeatedly engaging in a ritual of disrupting the class structure through class-passing while the plots show that, with social class, "anything" really cannot "happen."

Finally, Aaron Baker's analysis of Robert Rossen's *Body and Soul* examines the role of boxing and athletic heroism in the working-class Jewish population of New York, centering on the film as a reversal of the typical cinematic denial of Jewish participation in this sport. The protagonist must combat his parents' dislike of boxing as "a physically dangerous activity that is exploitative of others and controlled by criminals" in order to assert his masculinity and make money when there were few other ways to do so. New York figures in this film as the center of boxing and as a city with a huge Jewish population. Configured in the story of Charlie Davis, then, is a singular version of the American Dream, one played out against a background of assimilation, social pressure, disorder, and identity crisis. Screenwriter Abraham Polonsky's "socialist politics influenced the deviation in *Body and Soul* from Hollywood's mythology of utopian self-reliance." Pummeled by thugs because he would not take a fix, Charlie must show that in this demanding city, a working-class hero can be strong enough to both protect himself and represent his people.

Ajax's (James Remar) claim to the fearsome Baseball Furies: "I'll shove that bat up your ass and turn you into a popsicle!" *The Warriors* (Walter Hill, Paramount, 1979). Digital frame enlargement.

"When We See the Ocean, We Figure We're Home"

FROM RITUAL TO ROMANCE
IN *THE WARRIORS*

DAVID DESSER

In *Annie Hall* (1977), Woody Allen's alter ago Alvy Singer complains, "The failure of the country to get behind New York City is antisemitism. . . . Don't you see the rest of the country looks upon New York like we're left-wing, communist, Jewish, homosexual pornographers? I think of us that way sometimes and I live here!" These sentiments are very much au courant, referring to New York's fiscal crisis of 1975 (most of *Annie Hall* was shot that year) and the refusal of the Ford administration to offer the city a bailout. New Yorkers took this very hard, with the *Daily News* rendering what would become surely one of the most (in)famous headlines in all of tabloid journalism: "Ford to NY: 'DROP DEAD'" (October 30, 1975). New York's fiscal problems only fed into an image of New York as a city in decline—dangerous, dirty, and decaying. Allen himself plays with this image later in *Annie Hall* when he tells Rob (Tony Roberts) that he should leave L.A. and his insipid television show and return to New York to do real acting, like Shakespeare in the park; Rob exclaims, "Oh, I did Shakespeare in the park, Max; I got mugged. I was playing Richard II and two guys in leather jackets stole my leotard." At once disavowing the real dangers of New York by the joke about stealing a leotard yet also playing into perceptions of the city's violence, Allen does indeed fall in line with the greater national sentiments about the city. Of course, *Annie Hall* also pays glorious tribute to the city, with idealized views of the riverfront and the Fifty-ninth Street Bridge (which links Manhattan to Queens on the east side of the island), among other places turned into settings for romance and redemption.

Four years after the release of *Annie Hall*, John Carpenter returned to the image of New York as a place housing the dregs of society with his witty examination of societal attitudes toward Manhattan in *Escape from New York*. In this comic action thriller, Manhattan Island is a walled-off maximum security prison, the tunnels and bridges off the island mined, the waters surrounding it patrolled by a national police force. The multiracial, multicultural denizens of the city are indeed the wretched refuse welcomed by the Statue of Liberty. Walter Hill's *The Warriors* (1979), whose iconography and attitude clearly influenced Carpenter's serio-comic excursion into the city's persona, falls somewhere in between the comic-romantic view of the city in *Annie Hall* and Carpenter's nightmare imagery. Hill's film, controversial in its day more for the offscreen antics it inspired than for any of its actual content, represents one of the most genuinely interesting and creative takes on the city's imagined persona and its imaginary possibilities. Hill's New York City fits into a category of urban cinema isolated by Geoffrey Nowell-Smith: "Most interesting, however . . . are the films in which the city as it is acts as a conditioning factor on the fiction precisely by its recalcitrance and its inability to be subordinated to the demands of the narrative. The city becomes a protagonist, but unlike the human characters, it is not a fictional one" (104).

In adapting Sol Yurick's then little-known 1965 novel *The Warriors*, which is loosely based on *Anabasis*, as we will see shortly, Walter Hill vastly underplayed the social problem elements of the book and moved it closer to Xenophon's tale of heroic grace and adventure. In retelling this story of a band of warriors making their way through gang-infested territories and inhospitable terrain to return to their home by the sea, Hill transforms New York City into a mythic land of timeless beauty, terror, and fantasy. A breezy amalgamation of comic book art, punk aesthetics, and Hollywood-style action, *The Warriors* utilizes then-current images of New York as a city in decline—dangerous, dirty, decaying—to recast and re-imagine the city as a mythic realm of transcendent action and redemptive romance.

Anabasis

Anabasis is the most famous work of the Greek writer Xenophon, also a general and a student of Socrates. In the period between 401 B.C. and March of 399 B.C., Xenophon accompanied a large army of mercenaries hired by Cyrus the Younger to aid in his efforts to take the throne of Persia from Artaxerxes. Although Cyrus's army was victorious, Cyrus himself was killed in battle and the expedition rendered moot. Stranded deep in enemy territory, the Spartan general Clearchus and most of the other Greek generals were subsequently killed or captured by treachery. The bulk of the story concerns the ensuing return of the Greeks to their home, in which Xenophon played a leading role.

The use of *Anabasis* is pretty direct in *The Warriors*: the Spartan general Clearchus becomes the Warriors' war chief, Cleon (Dorsey Wright), similarly killed by treachery following the Warriors' attempts to join up with Cyrus (Roger Hill), here president of the Grammercy Riffs who seek to take the throne, so to speak, of New York City (Cyrus dies before accomplishing this task). The name Cleon for the war chief is also an interesting choice for the nearly contemporaneous figure in Greek history, a famed opponent of Pericles, who died in 422 B.C. (though most New Yorkers, at any rate, are more likely to know the name "Cleon" from the former New York Mets outfielder Cleon Jones—doubtless a deliberate double entendre from Walter Hill). The adaptation of ancient Greek history easily permits adaptations from Greek mythology as well. Clearly, the name Ajax for one of the Warriors' fiercest fighters needs no glossing, but one would also claim the same derivation from the Greek myths for the Baseball Furies street gang, and it would be hard not to see the all-female gang, The Lizzies, as clearly siren-like in their seduction of the Warriors on their odyssey back to Coney Island. Even the Turnbull ACs—identical bald heads poking out of the windows and door of a graffiti-covered school bus—recall the multiheaded hydra of Heraclean fame.

The mythical, rather than historical, mode is further impacted by the use of picturesque nomenclature for all the principal characters. Swan (Michael Beck) may recall Greek mythology, as well, if we allow for the memory of Zeus's incarnation in this form for his seduction of Leda, mother of Helen of Troy. The mythology of the American West(ern) is invoked by the names Cochise (David Harris) and Cowboy (Tom McKitterick), the former dressing in (stereotypical) Native American regalia, the latter sporting a hat typical of the western. Names like Snow (Brian Tyler) and Vermin (Terry Michos) further a nomenclature typical of ancient folk tales and heroic legends.

And if the mythical rather than the historical is the dominant mode in the film, so too the mythical replaces the contemporary. Real-life New York City street gangs in the 1970s certainly favored automatic weapons over fighting implements like two-by-fours, steel chains, and baseball bats or hockey sticks. Although both the Rogue leader and the Lizzies do rely on revolvers, that, too, is rather quaint in an age of .45 automatics and Uzi machine pistols. In the prominent featuring of a switchblade, first wielded by one of the Punks and later put to use by Swan in the climactic confrontation with the Rogue leader, one thinks of another mythical use of New York City: *West Side Story* (1961). In its highly theatrical staging and mythic transformation of the city, *The Warriors* might profitably be compared to the Robert Wise/Jerome Robbins transformation of the eternally popular stage musical, though lacking the Romeo-and-Juliet romanticism that makes *West Side Story* a universal, rather than strictly a cult, favorite.

The People Ride in a Hole in the Ground

Called to a conclave of street gangs, the Warriors travel from Coney Island to the Bronx to entertain an offer from Cyrus, president of the Grammercy Riffs. He has called a truce so that all of New York's major youth gangs can meet to hear his bold idea of uniting under one leader to run the city. When Cyrus is killed by the psychotic Luther, leader of the Rogues, the truce is off. Worse for the Warriors, the Riffs think that they're the ones who killed their boss. They spread the word: get the Warriors, dead or alive.

If the New York subway system is one of the city's greatest engineering achievements and a famous tourist attraction, there are little of those elements apparent in Hill's nightmare odyssey of little boys lost. A full twenty-eight of the film's ninety-two minutes take place on the city's subway trains, platforms, and stations or in the bowels of the countless miles of dark, dank tunnels that link New York's disparate boroughs (save for Staten Island, not accessible by subway). Instead of a tourist-eye view, Hill constructs and reconstructs the subway system as part of the overall mythic patterning of the film.

As it happens, the geography of the subway system, as that of the city itself, is a bit suspect in Hill's hands. It appears that the Warriors ride the D train from their home in Coney Island into Manhattan, where they must change at Fourteenth Street/Union Square. Although the D train does indeed stop at Stillwell Avenue in Coney Island, it does not stop at Fourteenth Street. In order to manage a stop at Stillwell Avenue and a change at Union Square, the Warriors should ride the N train. By the same token, the only train that stops at Dyre Avenue, the Warriors' fateful last stop in the Bronx, is the number 5 train, which one can indeed get at Union Square. However, the 5 train does not stop at Ninety-sixth Street, the scene of the colorful encounter with the Baseball Furies in Central Park on the Warriors' odyssey back to Coney Island. To manage a stop at Ninety-sixth Street, the Warriors would have had to change to the number 4 or 6 at 125th Street (which wouldn't make much sense since the 5 is an express train and would get them to Fourteenth Street/Union Square much faster than the 4 or 6). Such inaccuracies occur in films all the time. Perhaps a bit odder in the creative, but mistaken, geography of the city and its subway system is the Warrior Fox's strange comment to the Orphans that they are making their way home from a big meeting in the Bronx—when, in fact, they are still in the Bronx! Although it may be unclear how many stops the Warriors ride on the 5 train after their escape from the Turnbull ACs, the fire on the tracks that halts their journey is on an elevated (above-ground) platform. Every stop in Manhattan for the number 5 train, whose first stop is 125th Street, is below ground. Thus the Warriors have at that point not yet made their escape from the Bronx.

There is no great need to be a stickler for geographic accuracy. Complaining that Hill somehow gets his subway routes confused might make as little sense as complaining that New York City street gangs don't wear Kabuki-style makeup along with their baseball uniforms (nor do they wear baseball uniforms in the first place). For that matter, the men's room in a New York subway station is hardly large enough to contain the multi-character fight between the Warriors and the Punks. The point is, rather, that Hill utilizes a familiar New York icon, one often associated with danger and risk, and transforms it to his own narrative and pictorial needs.

The opening credit montage of New York City street gangs boarding the subway train at a variety of stations perhaps plays into the very fears regarding New York circa 1979. But the Warriors themselves find respite whenever they ride the rails. It is only when the trains stop—in the Orphans' territory, at Ninety-sixth

Street, at Union Square, even back home at Coney Island—that danger rears its troublesome head. But while the train wends its way through the dark, all is well. The Warriors' excitement on their journey up to the Bronx from Coney Island manifests itself on the subway car as they joke and jostle the entire way. They feel a moment's safety after escaping from the hydra-headed Turnbull ACs; they laughingly relax upon entering the train after easily defeating the Orphans; and on the way from Union Square to Coney Island they finally unwind—Cowboy curled up asleep, Swan and Mercy (Deborah van Valkenburgh) exhaustedly leaning against each other. It's here, too, on the post-traumatic ride back to CI, that Swan comes to terms with his feelings for Mercy, taking pride in his relationship with her as he refuses to allow her to straighten out her hair as they sit opposite the two strait-laced white couples who board the train after a late-night date. It might, for all we know, even be the white kids' prom night—something we imagine is far from the Warriors' experience. One of the white girls drops a corsage as she nervously leaves the train. Swan picks this up and gives it to Mercy who, although confused—"What's that for?"—gratefully accepts it. This is to say that the subway, which takes them on their great adventure to the Bronx and on their odyssey back to Coney Island, also provides both respite and insight, especially for Swan.

The Armies of the Night

Vietnam is everywhere in *The Warriors*, yet it is also nowhere to be found. Certainly in 1978–79 Vietnam was everywhere in the cinema, from Michael Cimino's Academy Award–winning *The Deer Hunter* (1978) and the Oscar-nominated *Coming Home* of that same year. The more modestly budgeted and received *Go Tell the Spartans* that year also not only examined Vietnam, but did so through the eyes of two lenses: the disastrous French campaign at Dien Bien Phu in 1954, which drove the French out of Indochina, and the heroic self-sacrifice of 300 Spartan soldiers at the Battle of Thermopylae in 480 B.C. *Apocalypse Now*, long in the making, finally appeared the same year as *The Warriors*. Thus Hill's return to the Greek-Persian wars (Xenophon's *Anabasis* occurred a mere eighty years after Thermopylae) might have been the occasion, in allegory at least, to examine Vietnam. Hill's mentor, Sam Peckinpah, had used both the Old West (in *The Wild Bunch* [1969]) and World War II (in *Cross of Iron* [1977]) to speak about Vietnam in thinly veiled format. Hill's consciousness of Peckinpah's *The Wild Bunch* was clearly demonstrated in *The Long Riders* (1980), though it contained somewhat less of the "end of the West" elegy than Peckinpah's film and, arguably, none of the Vietnam content. Yet Hill's own follow-up to *The Long Riders, Southern Comfort* (1981), is a clear, even obvious Vietnam allegory with its story of under-armed National Guardsmen lost in the Louisiana bayous in 1973. If I would ultimately argue that *The Warriors* loses any real opportunities to speak about Vietnam at the very height of America's first wave of post-Vietnam self-recrimination, the film nevertheless reveals a certain "Vietnamization" in its story, theme, and style.

In its use of a small group of displaced "soldiers" making their way through hostile territory—where the "natives" know the terrain better than they, natives defending their turf from uniformed invaders—the Warriors may recall the young U.S. soldiers in Southeast Asia, unfamiliar with the landscape, too young to know much better. Vermin's comment that "Coney Island must be fifty to a hundred miles from here" bespeaks a total lack of knowledge of one's geographical location, just as Swan's "We ain't never even been to the Bronx before" is indicative of their innocence and inexperience. In fact, it is a mere twenty-seven miles from the seashore of Coney Island to the tip of the Bronx.

There is a constant reference to both "army" and "soldiers." The original poster art for the film proclaimed, "These are the Armies of the Night." (The controversy surrounding the film led to a change in poster art.) On a number of occasions, gangs are linked to armies. The Orphan leader berates the Warriors, insisting, "You come armyin' down here . . . invading our territory, without even a parlay." Similarly, there is a constant refrain about being a good soldier, about soldiering on. A soldier/civilian dichotomy is invoked by the Orphan leader when he tells the Warriors that they can pass through their territory if they take off their colors (uniforms) and proceed as civilians. Instead, the Warriors, via another martial metaphor, proclaim that they will "march right through these lame fucks' territory."

The idea of "territory" also implies a martial setting, yet the vagaries and fluidity of boundaries within New York's gang culture—the Rogues drive across the city unimpeded, the Lizzies and the Punks seem to share the territory around Union Square, the Riffs make their way to Coney Island, the Warriors' territory— also recall the Vietnam War. The very character of the war itself was vastly different from the taking and retaking of territory characteristic of World War II and the Korean War. The United States never invaded or took territory in and from North Vietnam, while the Viet Cong operated throughout South Vietnam in both urban, village, and jungle regions. Terrain, then, became an undifferentiated morass through which U.S. soldiers moved at their own peril, often unable to distinguish friend from foe.

Of course, the wearing of uniforms—gang colors—does enable the Warriors to understand when they are in hostile territory. Spotting the Baseball Furies outside the Ninety-sixth Street subway station immediately informs them of danger. Similarly, when at the Fourteenth Street station Swan spies the Punk on roller skates who then meets up with his overall-wearing companions, the Warriors regroup for imminent battle. Yet the inability to distinguish friend from foe—a situation in which the foe may very likely be an attractive young woman, a common motif in Vietnam War films, for instance (Go Tell the Spartans, Apocalypse Now, Full Metal Jacket [1987])—is reproduced in The Warriors through the deceptively friendly demeanor of the Lizzies, who lure Cochise, Vermin, and Rembrandt (Marcelino Sánchez) back to their lair and soon thereafter attempt to kill them.

Similarly, Mercedes Ruehl's policewoman, luring Ajax with explicit sexual prom-
ises, leads to his capture by the NYPD. The overall sense of paranoia and lingering dread experienced by the Warriors and transferred to the audience through
Hill's skillful filmmaking is that same sense of impending doom that Francis Ford
Coppola and Michael Cimino would so magnificently capture in their 1970s
Vietnam epics and which Oliver Stone in *Platoon* (1986) and Stanley Kubrick in
Full Metal Jacket would later eerily reproduce. And some of that paranoia stems
precisely not just from the hostile terrain, the inability to distinguish enemy from
ally, but also from the way that a seemingly friendly female face may disguise an
implacable foe.

Finally, one might speak of the "Asianization" of the fighting techniques on
view in the film. Virtually all of the fighting is characterized by Asian martial arts.
Cleon's aikido toss of the first gang-banger who rushes at him followed by an
elbow strike to the second amidst the chaos that ensues from Cyrus's shooting is
strictly Asian martial arts, as are the series of kicks and elbow strikes that bring
Cleon down and, presumably, kill him. Though hardly the kung fu fighting of,
say, *Enter the Dragon* (1973), the martial arts on view in *The Warriors* belongs very
much to a wave of martial-arts inflected action scenes becoming de rigueur in the
American cinema at precisely this period. In an interview on the Special Edition
DVD of the film, Walter Hill likens the baseball-bat fight scene with the Baseball
Furies to samurai fights, while Billy Weber, one of the film's editors, recalls being
told by Hill to make the fight scenes "like Kurosawa." I have claimed in an earlier
essay ("Kung Fu Craze") that the martial arts that fitfully entered the American cin-
ema in the late 1940s and 1950s stemmed, in films like *White Heat* (1949) and *Bad
Day at Black Rock* (1955), from the first U.S. encounter with Asia via the Pacific and
Korean Wars. America's triumphant victory in World War II and its more tentative one in Korea enabled a more gradual and tranquil adoption of aspects of
Asian life and culture. But the traumatic defeat in Vietnam led to a kind of wholesale adoption of the ways of the Other, turning the enemy who had defeated us
(America) into ourselves and turning ourselves into the Other. Thus at the very
same time that Hollywood began the paroxysm of self-doubt characteristic of
The Deer Hunter, Coming Home, and *Apocalypse Now,* lower-budget films undertook
another strategy in their post-Vietnam self-examinations: having Asian martial
arts wielded by white heroes who developed those very skills in Asia, specifically
while serving in Vietnam. (See Desser "Martial Arts Film" for a detailed chronol-
ogy of the creation of a martial arts genre in Hollywood cinema and a theorization
of the specifically post-Vietnam context of this formation.) The wielding of martial arts by the Warriors, whose specific ethnicity is *not Asian,* is, I would argue,
what's at stake here. Though we do see an Asian street gang in the film's opening
credit montage of New York City street gangs—a gang whose members might
very well be Vietnamese and not Chinese, judging by their relatively slender
build—the Warriors never encounter any gang that isn't more "native" to

New York: white, black, or Puerto Rican. It is this absence of an Asian street gang that yields significance to the use of Asian martial arts—precisely absent is the very source of this presence. Thus Vietnam is both everywhere and nowhere in *The Warriors*.

Journey to the End of the Night

"Is this what we fought all night to get back to?" In Swan's rueful and bitter comment upon glimpsing the tired early-morning cityscape as he exits the subway, we see a young man who has grown. This is what the epic journey is all about: learning what is important as, on the way, you have great adventures, all leading you not only home, but to the meaning and significance of it. In this case, home is less than it was before, but that is another kind of archetypal journey: the Bildungsroman. The education novel, named for the likes of Goethe's *Wilhelm Meister's Apprenticeship* (1795), actually became an American specialty with Mark Twain's *The Adventures of Huckleberry Finn* (1884). His legacy of the coming of age of a young man in search of himself in the wide American landscape, or a similar search on foreign shores (as in the novels of Ernest Hemingway), is arguably the fundamental structure of much of mainstream American literature. The form was very much taken up by the most influential writers of mid-twentieth-century America—Saul Bellow, Philip Roth, Ralph Ellison in particular—to add a specifically ethnic and racial dimension, although the racial Other, as Leslie Fiedler so forcefully demonstrated in *Love and Death in the American Novel*, was already a fundamental component of the American boy's coming of age. The ethnic writers transformed the wilderness, the territory, the West, into the Great City: Bellow's Augie March, famously Chicago born; Roth's Wild Man of Newark; Ellison's Invisible Man in New York City itself.

Twain's legacy also includes, as Fiedler further contends, the theme of escape from a female-dominated society and the resultant homosocial relations among men: in nineteenth-century novels, among white men and men of color in the wilderness (Cooper, Twain) and on the high seas (Melville). I would argue that this mainstream American Bildungsroman is carried into the cinema through such homosocial genres as the western and the war movie, particularly as manifested in the works of Howard Hawks. Hawks's vision of the all-male group, where men live by a code of professionalism and whose integrity is threatened by the presence of women, is very much in the Twain-Melville-Hemingway mode. Manly activities such as big-game hunting (*Hatari!* [1962]), air-freight flying (*Only Angels Have Wings* [1939]), cattle driving (*Red River* [1948]), gun fighting (*Rio Bravo* [1959]), and race car driving (*Red Line 7000* [1965]) dominate his action-oriented cinema; and in film after film the hero bonds with a best friend, is a leader of men, and struggles to reconcile heterosexual needs with homosocial communities. Although all of Hawks's films by no means qualify as Bildungsromane, many do; but more importantly, he transfers the motifs of Cooper, Melville, Twain, and Hemingway to the world of the cinema in ways that influence *The Warriors* both profoundly and substantively.

The Hawksian universe is very much the world of men, with values of male camaraderie, professionalism, the centrality of work—typically dangerous work and thus the concomitant confrontation with one's mortality—and the necessary completion in love and friendship with another, particularly a woman who has the kind of masculine qualities possessed by the hero's male buddies. In addition to the entry of the woman into this all-male enclave, Hawks would often focus on the education of the young man by the older man, who trains him into the ways of the (initially) womanless world. Particularly in films like *Red River, Rio Bravo*, and *El Dorado* (1966) we find that male camaraderie and the teacher-student relationship arguably supersede more traditional romantic longings and completions. In the secondary hero, often played by an up-and-coming young star, we find the coming-of-age tale that defines the Bildungsroman. This is certainly the case in *Red River*, where the relationship between Thomas Dunson (John Wayne) and Matthew Garth (Montgomery Clift) is the primary object of interest and where Dunson's paternity over Matthew has been achieved without a woman. The wifeless man and the motherless boy bond in a way whose homosocial elements clearly verge on the homosexual—a motif made even more manifest by the inordinately close bond between Jim Deakins (Kirk Douglas) and Boone Caudill (Dewey Martin) in *The Big Sky* (1952). I would argue that this film, a big budget, action-packed variation on the Lewis and Clark Expedition through America's teeming wilderness, is Hawks's least appreciated and least discussed film precisely for the ways in which it slips from a veiled homosocial archetype into an outright homosexual one. Yet this film, as much as any other by Hawks, is the perfect paradigm of Fiedlerian ideology: men, together, on the flight from civilization, away from the apron strings of moms and wives, bonding in the wilderness; the only woman who stands between the two men is Native, her "darkness" an index precisely of her lack of civilizing qualities and thus a suitable object of attraction, there merely to establish (largely unsuccessfully) the heterosexuality of the heroes.

Hawks's homosocial legacy was carried forward in American cinema by Sam Peckinpah. His preferred genre of the western enables his cinema to achieve those qualities of the flight from women in his heroes who light out for the territory and the resultant homosocial world and worldview they embody. To Hawks's perhaps ambivalent view of the place and value of women in his action films, Peckinpah brings a sometimes more overtly misogynistic tone, certainly in films like *The Wild Bunch* and, most notoriously, *Straw Dogs* (1971). Traces of this tone appear as well in *The Getaway* (1972) and *Cross of Iron*, and perhaps in other films as well. One might say that for Peckinpah, the more anti-womanist tone is accompanied by a questioning of masculinist values as well, leading to an overall darker and more ambiguous cinema. The all-male group, which prizes professionalism (even if imperfectly achieved), male camaraderie (even if difficult to sustain), and a reveling in the existential qualities of dangerous work (even if, unlike Hawks's heroes, they meet that existential end), still characterizes his cinema. For all its darker and more cynical tone—attributable one might claim precisely to the Vietnamization of American culture to which Peckinpah was so sensitive—his cinema still belongs to that mainstream of American masculinist culture passed down from Cooper to Melville to Twain to Hemingway and on to him via Hawks.

Hill is very much the patrilineal descendent of Hawks and Peckinpah. He works exclusively in those masculinist genres that have come to be associated with Hawks and, especially, Peckinpah: the western (*The Long Riders, Geronimo: An American Legend* [1993], *Wild Bill* [1995]), the war film (*Southern Comfort*), the gangster film (*Last Man Standing* [1996]), the policier (*48 Hrs.* [1982], *Red Heat* [1988]), and the boxing film (*Hard Times* [1975], *Undisputed* [2002]). Such genres are certainly defined by the homosocial world, and Hill's cinema is even more circumscribed than either Hawks's or Peckinpah's by its all-male groups, where there are virtually no women characters in so many films (*Hard Times, Southern Comfort, Trespass* [1992], *Undisputed*) or no significant women characters in the majority of them. The specificity of the flight from women appears memorably in Hill's most commercially successful film, *48 Hrs.*, where Nick Nolte's burned-out-on-marriage Jack Cates positively avoids dealing with his put-upon wife (Annette O'Toole). Unsurprisingly, by the time of the sequel in 1990, Cates is long-divorced, with O'Toole nowhere to be found. That Hawksian ambivalence toward women and Peckinpah's misogyny reappear forcefully and memorably upon the introduction of Mercy in *The Warriors*. Upon her initial appearance, one Warrior says to another: "You know what that is, don't you." To which comes the reply, "Yeah . . . trouble!" Although Mercy will later be redeemed, it's that threat to the all-male group she immediately represents (a threat in more ways than one—to the group's safety and later the group's gendered homogeneity) that continues the homosocial tradition of American art and culture into which Hill comfortably fits. The wilderness, too, the place where a boy can be a boy—and thus maybe never become a man—in the absence of troublesome, civilizing women, predominates, whether it is the inhospitable landscapes of the Old West or the New: not for nothing does *48 Hrs.* take place in San Francisco or *Trespass* in St. Louis, traditional Gateway to the West.

The Warriors builds on the image of New York as the new wilderness that Americans were imagining, a wilderness that had overtaken formerly civilized urban centers. As early as Don Siegel's *Coogan's Bluff* in 1968 (his first collaboration with Clint Eastwood), the imagination of New York City as an extension of the western landscape is apparent. Though his film works an obvious hick-versus-city-slicker thematic, since Coogan is a modern-day Arizona cop replete with cowboy hat and western boots who is sent to New York to take a prisoner into custody, Siegel makes it apparent that despite its sophisticated surface the city is

a new frontier in need of a cowboy hero as of old. Such images of the urban frontier continue throughout the decade, culminating in *The Warriors*. Both *Dirty
Harry* (Siegel, 1971) and *Death Wish* (Michael Winner, 1974) rely on actors associated with the western (Clint Eastwood and Charles Bronson, respectively) to spin
tales of urban vigilantism that twenty years earlier would have been made in the
more obvious guise of the western. Cineastes Martin Scorsese and Paul Schrader
use John Ford's *ur*-western, *The Searchers* (1956), as a crucial intertext for *Taxi
Driver* (1976), the most powerful and controversial of the urban vigilante potboil-
ers, whose power and controversy might fairly be said to stem precisely from its
re-imagining and re-situating of the western mythos. *The Warriors* is a western,
then, in many of the same ways as are the masculinist extensions of the western
apparent in Siegel's films, for instance, but it also has a bit of Scorsese's demythol-
ogization at work.

Hill's cinema, overall, is not as rich as that of Hawks or Peckinpah. He has little
of the counterbalance to his action films that Hawks does with his equally popular and critically acclaimed romantic comedies. Even when Hawks's characters act
like children, as in *Twentieth Century* (1934), *Bringing Up Baby* (1938), or *Monkey
Business* (1952), there is something deliciously grown up about their antics and even-
tual union. And neither Peckinpah nor Hill can lay claim to the absolutely adult
coupling between Hildy Johnson (Rosalind Russell) and Walter Burns (Cary Grant)
in *His Girl Friday* (1940)—perhaps the most genuinely sophisticated film ever
made in Hollywood.

Peckinpah, too, strayed from his violent, masculinist melodramas with his more
contemplative and female-friendly works like *The Ballad of Cable Hogue* (1970) and,
perhaps, *Junior Bonner* (1972). But it is not the role and function of women that
enriches Peckinpah's cinema so much as it is the elegiac tone he manages so
beautifully in films that are, unsurprisingly then, his masterpieces: *Ride the High
Country* (1962), *The Wild Bunch*, and the director's cut of *Pat Garrett and Billy the Kid*
(1973). The end-of-the-West tone lends dignity and tragedy to the doomed all-male
relationships and the inevitable passing of the values embodied by men desperate
to hold on to them and perhaps to each other. One thinks of Dutch Angstrom's
(Ernest Borgnine) plaintive cry of "Pike!" as he falls near his dying companion,
Pike Bishop (William Holden). In his last breath this heroic outlaw, this good bad
man, thinks only of his greatest loss, not that of his life, but that of his friend.

One reason that Hill's career has been in both popular and critical decline since
1990 (thirteen films directed from 1975 to 1990; only five credited features since then
through 2005) may be that his masculinist worldview no longer obtains. Although
the decline of the western itself obviously didn't help the success of Hill's 1990s
offerings in that genre, other genres in which he works continue unabated, but
perhaps with different values attached, different characters engaged. *The Warriors*,
successful at the time of its release, has increased its critical and cult prestige and
popularity (inspiration for a videogame released in 2005; slated for a remake by

Tony Scott to be released in 2008). One reason may very well be the way it functions at one and the same time as a new-styled western, a war film, an adventure story, and a classic Bildungsroman—a true coming-of-age story that involves not only the youthful confrontation with the wide(r) world, but the young man's falling into romance with a suitable (Hawksian) woman. Aside from the oddly unclassifiable *Streets of Fire* (1984), billed as "A Rock & Roll Fable," which features both a romantic female lead (Diane Lane) and an action-oriented, Hawks-styled woman sidekick (Amy Madigan), no film of Hill's besides *The Warriors* relies so centrally on a woman to bring the hero to a new level of awareness and maturity. That Swan emerges as the primary protagonist is clear when he becomes war chief, and then when the remaining Warriors follow his lead; and when he is separated from the rest of the gang and interacts in a lengthy narrative segment exclusively with the initially ironically named Mercy.

Swan is the most introspective of the gang, the one most thoughtful about the journey—it is he who comments, as noted above, "We ain't never been to the Bronx before"—and who rises to manhood in his assumption of the role of leader. This leadership role specifically revolves around an understanding of the group's vulnerability as they make their way back home, a far cry from the macho posturing and foolish risks taken by Ajax and from his own rather gentlemanly treatment of Mercy. His threat, "Maybe we ought to pull a train on you; maybe you'd even like it," is hollow. Later, he rescues her from the police, leading to what I would claim is the key moment of Swan's introspection and to the redemption of both Mercy and himself: the journey through the subway. It is here, in the labyrinthine depths of the endless miles of subway tunnels, that Swan truly comes into manhood. With another mythic allusion, this one obviously to Theseus who defeated the Minotaur in the Labyrinths constructed by Daedalus (and is one stretching if one's mind travels to Joyce's Stephen Dedalus, hero of one of the greatest of all Bildungsromane, *A Portrait of the Artist as a Young Man*?), Hill completes Swan's transformation from gang-banger to mythic warrior and knight errant. His journey through the depth of the subway tunnel with Mercy in tow brings his first revelation as he tells her, "I don't like the way you live . . . I keep hoping I'm going to run into something a little better." But she, in essence, lives the same way he does: for the moment, a twisted carpe diem, reminding her battered hero, "I want something now. This is the life I got left!" Finally Swan acknowledges his nightmare odyssey, there in the tunnel, sweat and grime covering his face, on the run from street gangs and subway cops: "You know, you're just a part of everything that's happening tonight and it's all bad!"

But from there, it isn't all bad. The Warriors defeat the Punks in the film's longest, most exciting fight scene. On their trip back to Coney Island, Swan comes to realize the tenderness he feels for Mercy as he gives her the prom-night corsage. The panoramic view of working-class Coney Island that greets Swan, and which causes a wave of self-recrimination, leads to a further realization. It is as if in exiting the subway in the harsh light of day, the Warriors return from the realm of myth to the realm of the real. The neon-lit Wonder Wheel that magically appears from out of the dark of the film's first shot is now revealed to be an aging Ferris wheel, built in 1920, product of a bygone era of fun and fame in the now-faded amusement park for which Coney Island was once renowned. (Woody Allen's *Annie Hall*, invoked at this essay's start, reminds its audience of those very years of Coney Island's glories.) But the real Coney Island, home to immigrants, senior citizens, the lower middle class, holds nothing for the heroic Warrior, a young man ready to leave his boyhood behind: "Maybe I'll just take off," he says. And in his newfound maturity he has won his ladylove who, also having proven her mettle, is ready to take off with him. It isn't quite Huck Finn and Jim lighting out for the territory, but it certainly is the new mythic hero, a bit more down to earth as he walks across the sand of his former home.

A conversation overlooking the starkly spotlighted Ground Zero. Frank (Barry Pepper, l.) and Jacob (Philip Seymour Hoffman) in *25th Hour* (Spike Lee, 40 Acres & a Mule Filmworks, 2002). Digital frame enlargement.

He Cuts Heads

SPIKE LEE AND THE NEW YORK
EXPERIENCE

DAVID STERRITT

*You've been hoodwinked. You've been had. You've
been took. You've been led astray, led amok. You've
been bamboozled.*

—Malcolm X

The title of the movie that put Spike Lee on the cinematic map in 1983, *Joe's Bed-
Stuy Barbershop: We Cut Heads*, contains two clues to the shape of Lee's career. For
one, Lee cuts heads—not in the barbering sense but in the sense of working to
expose and excise the received ideas, regressive fantasies, and unexamined prejudices we carry around within our minds.

For the other, the only African American filmmaker to sustain a major career
in modern cinema is a New York City filmmaker to his bones. After his sopho-
more year at a southern college he returned to Brooklyn without a summer
job. "I had gotten a Super 8 camera," he recalled later, "so I spent the whole
summer just going around New York City and filming stuff. That was really when
I decided that I wanted to be a filmmaker." After making this decision, he said,
"I wanted to attempt to capture the richness of African American culture that
I can see, just standing on the corner, or looking out my window every day"
(Lindo 165).

Those corners and windows were in New York when Lee was growing up.
They were still in that city when he went to graduate school at New York
University and shot his first theatrical feature, *She's Gotta Have It*, on Brooklyn
locations in 1986. He has traveled widely for several of his "joints," but his heart
clearly lies in the city where he came of age and will probably reside forever. The
filmmaker who never slows down—few can match his prodigious output of features, documentaries, commercials, and more—feels nowhere more comfortable
than in the city that never sleeps.

Spike Starts Out

Shelton Jackson Lee, nicknamed Spike as an infant, was born far from that city—in Atlanta, Georgia, on March 20, 1957, to Jacquelyn Lee, a schoolteacher, and Bill Lee, a musician. Lee's father moved the family to the "jazz Mecca" of Chicago, then joined a migration of jazz musicians to New York in the late fifties. Settling in Brooklyn, the household lived first in Crown Heights, then in Cobble Hill—where the Lees were the first African Americans to arrive—and then in Fort Greene, a neighborhood seen by many outsiders as disreputable.

Lee graduated in 1975 from Brooklyn's own John Dewey High School, then returned to Atlanta after being accepted by Morehouse College, which his grandfather and father (a classmate of Martin Luther King Jr. there) had attended. Tuition money came from his grandmother, a graduate of Spelman College, the all-female equivalent to Morehouse's all-male campus. Lee's mother also went to Spelman, and it was in the year of her death (1977) that he started experimenting with film and shot *Last Hustle in Brooklyn*, his debut short. He graduated from Morehouse in 1979 with a degree in mass communication, and that autumn he headed for the Tisch School of the Arts at NYU, where he spent three years earning an MFA in film production. He then took an internship at Columbia Pictures in Los Angeles, but decided not to stay there because he didn't know how to drive, he "didn't have the resources [there] to make films," and he simply "wanted to come home" (Lee 32).

Lee had a mixed experience at NYU, where teachers questioned his grasp of "film grammar," and he sensed a tacit racial bias in their criticisms. "Any time a black person is in a white environment," he has said, "and they are not always happy—smiling, eating cheese [—] then [others] say he's a militant or has an attitude" (Lee 33–34). His first-year film, *The Answer* (1980), did nothing to reverse that impression. Discussing it with Nelson George, an African American critic, Lee described it as the story of "a black screenwriter hired to direct a fifty-million-dollar remake of *Birth of a Nation*. We included clips from *Birth of a Nation*. They didn't like that thing at all. How dare I denigrate the father of cinema, D. W. Griffith?" George observed that *The Answer* indicts *Birth* as a "racist" work, and Lee replied, "Yeah. No shit, Sherlock." George suggested that his film "offended" people, and Lee responded, "Yeah. I didn't care." In short, he was ready from the get-go to work against the grain of mainstream white cinema (33–34).

Lee's problems at NYU notwithstanding, he made three movies there. His thesis film was *Joe's Bed-Stuy Barbershop*, reflecting his avowed interests in "humor," in the "gangster genre," and in "the incorporation of negritude into that" (Lee 34–35). The film centers on Zachariah (Monty Ross), who takes over a barbering business after proprietor Joe (Horace Long) dies in a mob-related hit. Zach fares poorly at "head cutting" and his economic future looks grim until he meets the criminal who had set Joe up in the numbers game. The movie has strong revisionist impulses toward the black-mobster genre, especially in its attentive portraits of Zach and his wife, Ruth (Donna Bailey), a social worker.

Through them, as black film scholar Paula J. Massood notes, "the film provided some of the first sympathetic and detailed glimpses of the borough's African American faces, personalities, and communities." Massood also points out Lee's use of rap music and break dancing as indicators of the story's specific New York time and place (125). Although it is set squarely in Brooklyn—at the intersection of Flatbush Avenue and Myrtle Avenue, to be precise—it proved anything but parochial in its appeal, sharing a prize at a Swiss film festival and winning a student Merit Award from the Academy of Motion Picture Arts and Sciences.

He's Gotta Have It

Brooklyn has not always been as friendly to Lee as the filmmaker has been to the borough. He has spoken candidly about the problems he encountered shooting *She's Gotta Have It* there in 1986, and he has expressed displeasure with aspects of the movie itself. "I remember," he said later, "we were shootin' in [a] loft in the middle of the summer—it musta been a hundred and four degrees. . . . We only shot for twelve days, but every night . . . I had to think about tryin' to go out and raise money for the very next day." As for the finished product, "the acting was bad. . . . I didn't really know how to direct" (Mitchell 46–47).

Be this as it may, *She's Gotta Have It* marked Lee's emergence as an independent filmmaker of enormous promise, and consolidated the viability of 40 Acres & a Mule Filmworks, Inc., his Brooklyn-based production company. It also linked Lee with what Massood calls a "Brooklyn chronotope," working a variation on theorist Mikhail Bakhtin's term for a unified construction of narrative time and space. Before we see any characters we see the Brooklyn Bridge, then the Brooklyn building where the heroine lives. Manhattan plays a bit part—an Elsewhere that only one of the film's dramatis personae finds appealing.

The woman who's "gotta have it" is Nola (Tracy Camilla Johns), whose active sex life signals a refusal of double-standard morality. Speaking directly to the audience—in a self-reflexive maneuver that would become a Lee trademark—she says she wants to "clear [her] name," not of hypersexuality but of imputations that her occasional breaking of lovers' hearts is somehow less excusable than similar behavior by a man would be.

There are three men in Nola's life, and sometimes in her bed. One is Jamie (Tommy Redmond Hicks), who introduces himself in another of the direct-address shots that Lee calls "confessions": "I believe that there is only one person . . . in this world that is meant to be . . . your lifelong companion." Jamie thinks this makes him a sentimental sweetheart, but novelist Terry McMillan calls him the kind of man who "would try to put the clamps on you after you fucked him real good and . . . would orchestrate and plan out your entire life" (24).

The second man Nola currently dates, Greer (John Canada Terrell), is a model with a surplus of self-regard. His confession confirms this: "I'm the best thing that ever happened to Nola. . . . It was I who made her a better person." As egotistical as this sounds, it's his later sentences that make him a bona-fide Lee villain. "If she would have only listened to me and moved out of Brooklyn," says the Manhattan dweller, "we would be together this very day. It's not civilized over there."

Lee himself plays Mars, the third boyfriend. At first Mars thought Nola was "freaky-deaky," he confesses; but after having "def" sex with her, he decided that "all men wants freaks, we just don't want 'em for a wife." This crisply illustrates yet another kind of male hubris.

The movie strikingly integrates its story with the sights, sounds, folkways, and mores that would surround a young Brooklynite in the mid-eighties. Depicting a "black urbanscape . . . different from any other African-American space screened thus far," as Massood writes, the film replaces such iconic locations as Manhattan's fabled Apollo Theater and 125th Street bustle with Brooklyn shots of "identifiable subway stops, the Fulton Mall, the Promenade along the East River, and Fort Greene Park," all filmed on location (126, 129). The result is a Brooklyn movie par excellence, making up in authenticity what it lacks in budget and polish.

Wake Up!

Lee then left his beloved borough for the South, locating the dark 1988 musical comedy *School Daze* at fictional Mission College, a black institution where "Uplift the Race" is the motto, sexual machismo is everywhere, and prejudice runs rampant between lighter-skinned and darker-skinned students. As great as the difference in location is between this southern-set movie and Lee's more frequent New York pictures, there are clear continuities of psychology and theme. *School Daze* does not resolve the racial and sexual issues it raises, ending with a student (Larry Fishburne) saying "Wake up!" to the other characters and the audience. Lee's next movie, *Do the Right Thing* (1989), also rejects the pretense of "solving" knotty problems. And the very first words we hear, spoken by the disc jockey Mister Señor Love Daddy (Samuel L. Jackson), are "Wake up!"

Do the Right Thing tells an emphatically New York story in a rhetorically Aristotelian form. Place: the Bedford-Stuyvesant neighborhood. Time: the hottest day of the year. Action: the growth of race-based animosities centering on Sal's Famous Pizzaria [*sic*], owned and operated by an Italian American family. A young black man called Buggin' Out (Giancarlo Esposito) tries to organize a protest against Sal (Danny Aiello) for not hanging pictures of African American celebrities on the Italian-only "Wall of Fame" that decorates the pizza joint. Various tensions cluster around this, culminating when rap fan Radio Raheem (Bill Nunn) plays his ever-present boombox too loudly in Sal's place of business. Sal unleashes a racist tirade against Raheem, a policeman arrives and kills Raheem with a chokehold, and a "trustworthy" black guy (the delivery man Mookie, played by Lee himself) responds by hollering "Hate!" and throwing a trashcan through Sal's window, sparking a riot.

Do the Right Thing concludes with a series of dialectical moments that are the film's most fascinating component. After infuriated African Americans destroy

Sal's pizzeria in the wake of Raheem's death, the black man who escalated this violence, Mookie, has a partial reconciliation with Sal, surprisingly complex in its emotional dynamics. Then two quotations appear: one from Martin Luther King Jr., saying violence is always self-defeating, and another from Malcolm X, saying violence in self-defense may be necessary and commonsensical. Finally we see a photograph of these leaders embracing each other, suggesting that their philosophical differences were skin deep compared with their shared commitment to African American equality. These images and words do not inform us what the "right thing" is supposed to be. Instead they open the door to thought and dialogue.

The dialectics of *Do the Right Thing* are not limited to its ending. Its music, for instance, echoes three kinds of consciousness in the Bed-Stuy personality mix (Johnson). Rap songs represent the street folks. Romantic string tunes evoke middlebrow culture. Jazz, soul, and pop carve out an eclectic ground between, conjuring up the whole history of African American entertainment. (Dialectics again: the radio host's recitation of legendary black entertainment names is an oral-culture counterpoint to the photos on Sal's wall of fame.) The film's visual style does similar things, as when Lee chooses sharp *cuts* to separate shots of Sal and Raheem during their disastrous fight—suggesting the cultural gulf that divides them—but uses quick-swinging *pans* to depict Raheem's crank-up-the-volume boombox contest with a Hispanic man, suggesting that these two inhabit the same psychological world even if they express themselves through competition and contrast.

For me (see Sterritt *"Do the Right Thing"*), this film recalls the distinction drawn by social philosopher Paul Goodman between two kinds of violence. In Goodman's view, "natural" violence is rooted in human nature and erupts spontaneously out of deep-seated drives—the violence of parents defending their children against physical attack, for instance. By contrast, "unnatural" violence is stirred up artificially, as when a government incites frenzy against a country that poses no immediate threat (Goodman, "Natural Violence" 26–27). In this sense, the destruction of white-owned property in *Do the Right Thing* seems altogether "natural" to me. Physically, it's true to past experience in real urban ghettos. Psychologically, it's true to the imperfections of human nature when challenged by both short-term provocation and long-term urban poverty.

Discussion of *Do the Right Thing* as a New York movie must consider the attacks on Lee's portrait of Bed-Stuy as a "Sesame Street" version of ghetto life, too clean and orderly to be believed. One example comes from *Time* critic Richard Corliss, who used the "Sesame Street" comparison and added later, "All we know for certain is that *Do the Right Thing* is not naturalistic. Golden sunset hues swath the street at 10 in the morning. The color scheme is chicly coordinated. . . . At first the dilemmas are predictably pastel too" (62). I think this criticism has its own tinge of racism, though. On any given day in even the "worst" neighborhoods, most folks are just living their lives, not slogging about in dirt, drugs, and crime.

It's true that ingrained poverty has taken a mental toll on many of Lee's characters: check out the three guys who sit forever on the corner, commenting on the action like a Greek Chorus with a four-letter vocabulary. Still, the situation speaks for itself, and there's no reason for Lee to exaggerate things with hackneyed views of inner-city misery. Lee has energetically vented his exasperation with the black neighborhoods cooked up by Hollywood movies. "If this film were done by a white filmmaker," he told me, "it would have been all dark. There would've been no loud colors. It would have been raining every day, and in complete despair—with no humor but [with] rapists, crack addicts, drug dealers, pregnant teen-age mothers throwing their babies out of windows." That, he said, is "white people's idea of black ghettos" (Sterritt "Hotly Debated New Film").

Do the Right Thing has also been accused of downplaying Bed-Stuy's growing diversity, focusing on black-white conflict at the expense of, for example, the neighborhood's Asian American population. I don't take this point too seriously, since black-white conflict is a mighty substantial subject in itself; and other tensions are certainly noted, especially via the Korean store owners across from Sal's eatery. They prompt an especially poignant and provocative moment, when one of the street-corner slackers wonders why Asian Americans are reaching economic stability so quickly in New York while African Americans so often seem stalled in poverty. Once again, Lee articulates the conundrum without claiming he can solve it.

Steeped in New York politics, *Do the Right Thing* is dedicated to African Americans killed in then-recent incidents of "alleged" police brutality, and Lee hoped it would influence the 1989 mayoral election. (Thanks to the film or not, black candidate David Dinkins did defeat white candidate Edward I. Koch, the incumbent.) The film also appears to reference the case of Michael Griffith, a black man whose death by beating, after he left an Italian American pizzeria in the Howard Beach section of Brooklyn's neighboring borough, Queens, sparked a "day of rage" protest. This surely gave Lee ideas for *Do the Right Thing*, even if he did locate his version of the atrocity in the borough he knows best.

Another allusion to New York politics is a view of the words "Tawana told the truth" scrawled in huge graffiti letters. This refers to Tawana Brawley, who in 1987 accused six white lawmen of abducting and abusing her. (One of her defenders was the Rev. Al Sharpton, amusingly mentioned in the film's screenplay.) Brawley's legal case against the men failed when a grand jury decided she had concocted the story (and supporting evidence) to mask her own malingering. Lee's reference to the "truth" of her claim goes far beyond his own opinion on the matter, however, suggesting that Brawley's story—*even if false*—reflects deep truths about the justified fears of an African American community within a white-dominated urban purview.

Accordingly, such in-the-moment references do not "date" the film. On the contrary, Lee feels its incendiary elements (which some commentators wrongly expected would cause violence in movie theaters) reflect not only outrage over specific injustices but also a "complete frustration with the judicial system" felt by the black community. One day after the film's premiere at the Cannes Film Festival, Lee told me, "A black man was . . . strangled to death . . . in New York City, in a police precinct. . . . This film is not science fiction. All this stuff is happening" ("Hotly Debated").

Urban Ills

Lee's next film, the 1990 drama *Mo' Better Blues*, also proved controversial. The protagonist is Bleek (Denzel Washington), a black jazz musician who is involved in romance with more than one woman and involved in business with a manager, Giant (Lee), who has grave gambling problems. Some critics felt the portrayals of two Jewish nightclub proprietors were steeped in antisemitic stereotypes. Lee's defenses of the Moe and Josh Flatbush scenes (featuring John Turturro and Nicholas Turturro) have emphasized their satirical intent and, less persuasively, viewers' longtime tolerance of African American stereotypes in Hollywood films. I find this argument shaky because, to put it bluntly, two mass-media wrongs don't make a sociocultural right. *Mo' Better Blues* remains a noteworthy New York movie, however, evoking minor-chord and major-chord moods with equal sensitivity. The latter are most moving at the story's end, an idealized vision of black family life that anticipates the emotionally similar *Crooklyn* (1994).

By this time Lee's more contentious critics were becoming ever more exercised over what they perceived as a willful insistence on muting the drugs, crime, and other ills that were (and are) a part of inner-city New York existence. Having made his point that such matters should not be mandatory in films about African American urban life, Lee made *Jungle Fever* (1991), which directly takes on the New York City drug scene. Wesley Snipes plays Flipper, a black architectural designer living in Harlem with his wife and child. He falls for Angie (Annabella Sciorra), an Italian American office temp who lives in Bensonhurst, a Queens neighborhood not celebrated for racial tolerance. (In an interesting touch, Lee named Angie's family the Tuccis, after a white Cobble Hill household that was friendly to him as a child.)

As used in the film, the phrase "jungle fever" refers to interracial lust, leading many moviegoers to think of the Flipper-Angie romance as the story's primary business, with crack-cocaine abuse a mere subplot. In fact, though, Lee was passionate about the drug-related scenes, which center on Flipper's addicted brother Gator, played by Samuel L. Jackson, who won a Cannes acting award. Gator spends his time smoking crack with his girlfriend; badgering Flipper and their mother (Ruby Dee) for money; and alienating their father (Ossie Davis), a clergyman with a checkered past. Flipper eventually enters a Manhattan drug den—the enormous Taj Mahal, a virtual cosmos of crack—to track Gator down. In the climax, Gator is slain by their father during a confrontation recalling the 1984 killing of rock singer Marvin Gaye, also a cocaine abuser, by his father, also a minister. The film's finale reiterates its seriousness about drugs: Flipper and his little girl are approached by a crack-addicted prostitute, whereupon he clutches his daughter close and screams *"No!"* as the camera zooms frantically toward his outraged, horrified face.

Along with its gaze at the urban drug world, the most memorable New York angle of *Jungle Fever* is the clear-eyed contrast it draws between Harlem, pictured as a neighborhood affording security and dignity to its middle-class residents, and Bensonhurst, seen as a haven for attitudes that are reactionary at best (e.g., the Old World habits that burden the father of Angie's fiancé) and terrifying at worst (e.g., the bigotry that brings a beating on Angie when her family finds out her lover is a black man). The neighborhood portraits in *Jungle Fever* are stylized (albeit less than the ones in *Do the Right Thing*) but no less revealing for that.

Lee directed his long-dreamed-of biopic *Malcolm X* in 1992, following its hero from Boston to Mecca to Queens, among other places, including the Audubon Ballroom in Harlem, where the leader was assassinated on February 21, 1965. Returning to a smaller scale, Lee directed the intimate *Crooklyn* in 1994 from a screenplay he wrote with two of his siblings. It shows a little girl named Troy (Zelda Harris) growing up in Brooklyn during the early seventies, and again Lee depicts his favorite borough in affectionate terms, despite the persistent money problems faced by Troy's parents, a jazz musician (Delroy Lindo) and a teacher (Alfre Woodard).

One message of *Crooklyn* is that being a spirited child in a Brooklyn apartment offers a spiritual freedom that more than compensates for the shortage of physical space. Lee underscores this by shooting the non-Brooklyn episodes—when Troy spends a summer in the South with pious, persnickety relatives—through an anamorphic (wide-screen) camera lens that is not converted to its normal aspect ratio for projection. This creates cramped, contorted images that evoke the psychological strangulation Troy feels in the South despite the relative increase in fresh air and elbow room. For her, as for Lee in this most autobiographical of his films, Brooklyn is best. Period.

Clocking

Clockers, a 1995 drama based on Richard Price's novel, stands with Lee's most important New York City films. In their screenplay, Lee and Price transformed the narrative by focusing less on its white policeman, Rocco (Harvey Keitel), and more on a young black man, Strike (Mekhi Phifer), who agrees to kill a drug dealer's enemy as a step toward escaping his bottom-rung work as a "clocker," or low-grade crack dealer. Strike's brother Victor (Isaiah Washington) gets arrested for the murder despite his straight-arrow reputation, but Rocco thinks Strike is the culprit. Rocco turns out to be wrong, and the screenplay implicitly explains Victor's violence through a sort of "black rage" theory, contending that the pressures of being a well-behaved black man in a badly behaved urban environment caused Victor to suffer a buildup of antisocial impulses that couldn't be contained indefinitely.

Massood's discussion of *Clockers* (188–205) notes Lee's wish to move beyond cinema's fashionable "hood" format, which he disparagingly called the "black gangster, hip-hop shoot-'em-up . . . drug genre." She also points out the film's architectonics, observing that much of it takes place in the courtyard of a Brooklyn housing project that constitutes "a carceral city, where the surrounding buildings act as sentries . . . guarding the boundaries." To support this she cites critic Amy Taubin's description of the clockers' dealing area, a raised platform in the plaza, as "both stage and prison," evoking a version of Jeremy Bentham's "panopticon" penal complex that philosopher Michel Foucault uses as a metaphor for modernity's practice of encouraging people to police their own behaviors by making every external point a locus of possible surveillance.

While these are valuable ideas, the setting of *Clockers* does not strike me as quite so "carceral" a place. We are introduced to the Nelson Mandela housing project—ambiguously named, since Mandela represents both interminable imprisonment and ultimate empowerment—in a shot whose strong visual symmetry suggests the project's entrapping qualities and, at the same time, a sense of solidity and security that may be comforting for the solid citizens who live alongside the law breakers. A number of Lee's films open by ushering viewers into a New York neighborhood, and while *Clockers* does so more ambivalently than, say, *Do the Right Thing* or *Crooklyn*, it nonetheless implies that we are entering civilized terrain, however precarious that civilization may sometimes seem. The project's buildings do have a hint of the observation tower about them, and the clockers are aware of their visibility to residents and police. Yet the buildings are people's homes, after all, and if their main usefulness were for spying, the criminals would have no hope of getting away with anything. We are in a "bad" section of Brooklyn, but we *are* in Brooklyn, and for Lee that's a positive thing.

Massood also links Strike's love of model trains (even though he's never traveled on any train but the subway) with the history of African American migrations and the sociocultural baggage (dreams of utopian cities, the heyday of the Pullman porter, etc.) carried by this history. Strike's romanticizing of railroads does relate to such matters, and I would only add that the film's conclusion (with Strike speeding away from Brooklyn on a passenger train) anticipates the ending of Lee's later *25th Hour* (2002), which also uses New York City as the launching point for a mythically tinged journey toward a different corner of the American scene.

Coney Island and the Bronx

Lee's two releases of 1996 were *Girl 6*, about commercial phone sex—written by Suzan-Lori Parks, it was his first movie penned entirely by someone else—and *Get on the Bus*, about men heading for Minister Louis Farrakhan's so-called Million Man March in 1995. He made the documentary *4 Little Girls* in 1997, about the Alabama church bombing that killed four children in 1963. But he returned to New York for his next two theatrical features, *He Got Game* and *Summer of Sam*, released in 1998 and 1999, respectively.

He Got Game centers on a black high school basketball star, symbolically named Jesus Shuttlesworth (Ray Allen), who is being courted by college teams with offers of big money, wild sex, and often both. Jesus wants to make the decision that's morally and pragmatically right for him. Yet almost everyone is pressuring him to sign with one school or another—including his estranged father (Denzel Washington), who is in prison for the (inadvertent) killing of his wife (and Jesus' mother) during a quarrel, and who is promised early parole if Jesus signs with a particular state college. Brooklyn is the tale's main setting, and we are taken to a neighborhood Lee hasn't explored before: Coney Island, home of the legendary fun park and, in recent decades, of a large African American population. In a stirring allegorical trope, Lee uses the park's soaring yet shabby amusement rides as subtle signifiers of the inherently tainted nature attaching to mere worldliness in all its forms. Seen in the background of shots centering on other matters, they evoke both the bygone promise of a city where anything once seemed possible—where the laws of gravity themselves were subject to phantasmatic defiance for the price of a roller-coaster ticket—and the decadence that the progression of inexorable time and the metamorphoses of material tastes have allowed to fester. Lee doesn't hammer any of this home, preferring to let his understated mise-en-scène speak for itself, which it does to bittersweet effect. Also noteworthy is Lee's use of an Aaron Copland score, which works brilliantly as accompaniment to ballgames and other scenes. Its status as emblematically all-American (and authentically Brooklynite) music points again to Lee's sense of New York as the nexus of a potentially great, if deeply flawed, nation.

Summer of Sam probes the Bronx much as *Jungle Fever* explored Bensonhurst, seeing it as exotic terrain that is as psychologically distant from Bedford-Stuyvesant and Cobble Hill as it is geographically nearby. Lee's first film to focus primarily on white (Italian American) characters, it takes place in 1977, when serial killer David Berkowitz, the self-dubbed Son of Sam, was terrorizing New Yorkers with his deadly .44 caliber exploits. (In a deliciously New York maneuver, Lee had journalist Jimmy Breslin—to whom Berkowitz had sent letters in his campaign to taunt the police—appear as himself in the film.) The central character is Vinny (John Leguizamo), whose marriage is threatened by his desires for raw, lowdown sex which he refuses to satisfy with his wife, since this would shatter his conception of her as a properly pure spouse. Vinny's tough-guy friends are bent on tracking down the serial killer to assert control over their turf, dampen the police presence that Berkowitz's crimes have brought to the community, and engage in vigilante violence for its own exciting sake. In addition, Berkowitz has shot two people near a place where Vinny enjoyed steamy intercourse with his wife's cousin, making him afraid the killer (who has a penchant for slaughtering couples making out in cars) may now come after him. Another key character is Vinny's close friend Richie (Adrien Brody), a natural-born outsider who dresses in exaggerated punk-style gear. Richie becomes the prime suspect when the neighborhood crew tries to pin down Son of Sam's identity and terminate him with extreme prejudice. (The real Son of Sam lived in Yonkers, it turns out, making him not a true New Yorker but a mere suburbanite.)

From the start of his career, Lee has presented himself as an outspoken artist who never hesitates to take uncompromising stances. "I have always been an instigator," he told me ("Hotly Debated"). Yet there is a flip side to this position that has received little critical comment: Lee has a touch of the social worker in him, reflected in the cautionary subtexts that pepper his work. It's no accident, for example, that Bleek's father fulminates in *Mo' Better Blues* about unwed black teenagers constantly having babies, and that his friend mentions using condoms when he has sex; and of course *Jungle Fever* and *Clockers* take staunch anti-drug positions. In short, Lee clearly feels a need to nudge the African American community toward what he considers safer and saner behaviors. No movie illustrates this more vividly than *Summer of Sam*, which extends the hot-as-hell pressure that plagues Bed-Stuy in *Do the Right Thing* to a much broader swath of the city, including a visit to Plato's Retreat, the Manhattan sex club that drew huge attention during the seventies before AIDS and a more generally repressive American climate closed the doors of such enterprises with a resounding slam. Despite the movie's title, Son of Sam himself is a minor character, functioning mostly as a berserk metaphor for Lee's view of the seventies as a period of amoral excess—a time so anarchic that goofballs like Vinny and his pals aren't far off in thinking they can do whatever they want and walk away with clean consciences. Lee's moralizing is prominent in other films as well, including his 2002 documentary *Jim Brown: All American*, which devotes its first half to Brown's athletic success, its second half to Brown's movie-acting career and to ethical lapses that tarnished his reputation, not least (one can infer) in Lee's own eyes. Beneath his radical exterior, Lee harbors some surprisingly conservative attitudes—making his oeuvre all the more complex, rewarding to ponder, and impossible to pigeonhole.

A Guided Tour of American Racism

After directing *The Original Kings of Comedy*, a 2000 performance documentary, Lee returned the same year to New York for *Bamboozled*, a deeply serious satire. Damon Wayans plays a black television executive named Pierre who is ordered by his white boss to come up with a fresh, audience-grabbing idea. Angry with TV's general disdain for the black community, Pierre takes revenge by designing a show (in cahoots with Sloan, his secretary [Jada Pinkett-Smith]) so outrageously offensive that Americans in general, and his colleagues in particular, may be forced to rethink their unexamined bigotry. The result is *Mantan: The New Millennium Minstrel Show*, so hyperbolically racist that its black actors have to darken their faces another shade (using that old standby, burnt cork) in order to revive the shameful minstrel-show tradition, complete with Sambos shuffling in a watermelon patch to music by the Alabama Porch Monkeys.

In a twist recalling *The Producers* (1968), the show is a walloping hit, eliciting howls of glee from its hopelessly unreflective bourgeois viewers. A subplot focuses on members of a black-power rap group called Mau Mau, who explode with rage over the show (and their own failure to win a spot on it). Eventually they take violent action, killing its star in a live internet event. This brings a police reprisal that results in the death of Sloan's brother (a Mau Mau member) and Pierre's demise at Sloan's hands.

This is grim stuff, but not as grim as the long montage sequence that ends the film: a guided tour through racist imagery manufactured, circulated, and savored by generations of white American society. This imagery ranges from caricatured "coon" artifacts to movie and TV clips that reflect (and have crucially shaped) the country's racial unconscious. The sequence proves the culpability of mainstream culture in spiritual and psychological genocide, inflicted on minority citizens by hegemonic media shot through with greed, complacency, and irresponsibility. *Bamboozled* is a New York movie that speaks to racism everywhere.

Destiny, Annihilation, Hope

Bamboozled fared poorly at the box office, even by Lee's modest standards, and he spent all of 2001 and some of 2002 on shorts and documentaries. He then returned to theaters with *25th Hour*, adapted by David Benioff from his novel. Another white-centered film, it tells the story of Monty (Edward Norton), a young New Yorker spending his last night with friends (a schoolteacher, two Wall Street businessmen) and family (his father, James [Brian Cox], who is a Queens bar owner) before starting a seven-year prison stretch for drug dealing. The movie also shows Monty's relationship with his African American girlfriend, who may have betrayed him to the cops, and his anxieties over a wasted past and a perhaps horrific future.

25th Hour takes its characters through many New York City locations, one of which stands out: Ground Zero, the site of the obliterated World Trade Center. Hollywood remains jittery about representing this tragic place, but Lee employs it to devastating effect, beginning with the opening credits, accompanied by somber Terence Blanchard music and solemn views of the two light-shafts that memorialized September 11, 2001, in its aftermath. The gravity of this film's intentions is thereby established at the outset.

The story of Monty and the theme of 9/11 are most fully integrated during two indelible scenes. In one, Monty stands before a mirror and reflects on all the people he could blame for the rotten turn his life has taken. They include "nigger" gangs and "towel-head" taxi drivers—the Others now teeming in a city once filled with white immigrants like his father—plus Osama bin Laden and his terrorist ilk. Seen from behind as his body slumps into a stooped posture reflecting his humiliation, Monty excoriates them all in a stream-of-consciousness monologue (fleshed out by mercilessly harsh imagery) before admitting that his guilt stems from his own actions and his fate rests on his own shoulders. This sequence recalls Lee's use of direct address in *Do the Right Thing*, when he interrupts the story for a string of racial epithets spewed into the camera by characters wrenched from their expected places in the movie's chronotope. The device has even more impact in *25th Hour*, due to the excellence of its execution and to Lee's courageousness in unmasking the prejudices—some of which (bin Laden) may have justification!—that are embedded in American culture, in world history, and (one suspects the filmmaker is acknowledging) in Lee himself.

Equally powerful is the scene where Monty's businessman friends converse in an apartment overlooking the starkly spotlighted Ground Zero site, which is relentlessly visible as the dialogue unfolds in a single bravura shot. Their discussion of Monty is unsparing, touching on everything from the potential he once held to the question of whether he will kill himself rather than suffer in prison. In sum, they are discussing a blasted, annihilated life alongside a blasted, annihilated place. Eventually the camera moves slowly toward the window behind them, recalling the stunning single-take scene in *Do the Right Thing* when Sal talks with his son Pino in front of a window looking out on their Bed-Stuy street. Lee thus etches the ineluctable, inescapable nature of the individual and societal catastrophes with which this film so bravely grapples.

The conclusion of *25th Hour* is arguably the finest achievement in Lee's career to date. Monty climbs into his father's car for the fateful drive to prison, and James unexpectedly offers to turn west and keep on driving, bringing his son to some distant destination where he can start a new, anonymous life. Bruised from a beating he took during his long anticipatory night, the exhausted Monty dozes as his father's monologue spins on. The screen fills with James's fantasy, envisioning a utopia untainted by bygone errors and pregnant with the possibilities America offers for the free, unfettered spirit. Past mistakes recede, races commingle in domestic harmony, and new generations build ways of living untarnished by the wrong decisions of their forebears.

The film's final shot reveals this daydream's phantasmal quality, showing the car heading north from New York City toward the Ossining prison's implacable gates. New York may not hold the spiritual and psychological riches James has imagined. But the city that never sleeps—and it is such a city, as Monty knows from firsthand experience—is, for Lee, the best possible place to start realizing that those riches might possibly exist. *25th Hour* is a quintessential expression of Lee's unique capacity for finding the political in the personal, the radical in the conservative, the timeless in the quotidian, the United States of America in the City of New York, and the transcendent soul in the earthly condition shared by black folks, white folks, and all folks.

Race, family, and the positives and negatives of city life are Lee's enduring themes. While he usually probes them in New York terms, he is also concerned with his country as a whole—a vast, variegated presence of which his chosen city is a microcosm and a synecdoche. All of American society has been hoodwinked, took, had, and led astray, to borrow Malcolm X's words. Lee's artistic mission is to unbamboozle us at last.

Ginger Rogers and Fred Astaire cut loose in *Swing Time* (George Stevens, RKO, 1936).
Set by Van Nest Polglase. Digital frame enlargement.

New York Class-Passing Onscreen in the 1930s

GWENDOLYN AUDREY FOSTER

Trottoirs throng'd—vehicles—Broadway—the
   women—the shops and shows, . . .
A million people—manners free and superb—open
   voices—hospitality—the most courageous and
   friendly young men; . . .
The beautiful city, the city of hurried and sparkling
   waters! the city of spires and masts!
The city nested in bays! my city!
                              —Walt Whitman, "Mannahatta"

To invoke the plethora of historic and iconic images of New York City—Grand Central Station, the Brooklyn Bridge, the Statue of Liberty, the Washington Square Arch, the modern skyscraper, and the hordes of people who gather at Bryant Park outside the New York Public Library, shop on Park Avenue, shuffle off to work on the massive public transit system, or dance and mingle at any one of the city's famous night clubs—is to invoke the metaphor of social mobility. Arguably, there is no city more firmly established as a fantasy space, a liminal space, where social mobility, both upward and downward, is ever present in the images and lore and the promise of its myths and sayings. The promise of social mobility is as firmly embedded in the architecture of New York City as in the films set there.

New York City, by virtue of its anonymity, architecture, size, societal infra-structure, and mythic embrace of the American Dream (of social and economic mobility), allows—even fosters—a liminal space where the possibility for class mobility seems endless. Films of the 1930s, in particular, with their embrace of change, consumption, modernity, and individualism, offer zones where anything can happen in terms of class. The Art Deco New York City of the filmic liminal space of the thirties, especially in the era of the economic Great Depression, offers a zone of class mobility where characters routinely make and remake themselves, in a way passing in terms of class, across socioeconomic borders. "Class-passing" is a frequently used trope in films of the thirties, especially those set in New York. These films offer a zone of liminality, for, as Kathleen Rowe notes, liminality allows "society to carve out spaces of times that exist on the edge of normal activities and that are marked by contradiction and ambiguity . . . allowing society to comment on itself through experimentation and play" (8).

The city not only allows, but actively encourages, the performance of "class-passing" in myriad ways that are displayed in such city films as George Cukor's *Dinner at Eight* (1933), Gregory La Cava's *My Man Godfrey* (1936), Edmund Goulding's *Grand Hotel* (1932), Lloyd Bacon and Busby Berkeley's *42nd Street* (1933), Edgar Selwyn's *Skyscraper Souls* (1932), Mervyn LeRoy's *Three on a Match* (1932), Roy Del Ruth's *Employees' Entrance* (1933), and Robert Florey's *The House on 56th Street* (1933). The climate of the modern city is architecturally tied to the cultur-ally specific norm of class-passing New York style, as individuals climb the ladder (or take the Art Deco elevator) to success. Indeed, success in these films is defined as class-passing. In upwardly mobile New York City narratives, class mobility appears to be the "American way." Nothing pleases film audiences more than wit-nessing (and thus co-producing) the spectacle of an actor who successfully punc-tures the walls of socioeconomic privilege. This is particularly true of the film comedies and dramas of the 1930s; films that revel in actors who class-pass upward (Jean Harlow in *Dinner at Eight*) and downward (when William Powell pretends to be a bum in *My Man Godfrey*).

Filmmakers and audiences rely on the trope of class-passing and mutability in the cinema to define "class," and police its borders from the Bowery flophouse to the elegant Fifth Avenue penthouse. One could argue that class is the Other that is rarely spoken of, at least directly, yet it is the subject—the Othered subject— most often sung about and practiced in *42nd Street*, and spoofed in *My Man Godfrey* and *Grand Hotel*. Class-passing is at the heart of the city and its visual representa-tions in such "working world" films as *Skyscraper Souls* and *Employee's Entrance*. Class-passing is thus exposed in these films (and others like them) as a perform-ance, not unlike the construction of gender, whiteness, and sexuality. My essay examines class-passing as it is performed, othered, celebrated, and punished in the New York City films of the 1930s. Why and how do audiences and stars repeatedly engage in the ritual of disrupting the class system with co-produced images of class-passing in New York City? How is class-passing inscribed visually through clothes, architecture, possessions, and other trappings of prestige, and in performances through language, gesture, and speech? How is New York City inscribed as a backdrop for class mobility in films of the 1930s?

My Man Godfrey Serves Dinner at Eight

New York City is zoned as the liminal space where anything can happen in *My Man Godfrey,* a screwball comedy with a strong social message. The plot, for those unfamiliar with this celluloid gem, is quite simple. Two spoiled Park Avenue socialites pick up a "forgotten man" from the city dump, a Hooverville located at the foot of the Brooklyn Bridge. Although the film is a light comedy, there was nothing funny about the plight of those who were reduced to standing on bread-lines during the Depression in New York. There were breadlines throughout the city, with hundreds of thousands of men and women waiting for food. First in line were members of the working class; as the Depression got worse, they were joined by professionals and managers thrown out of work by the financial down-turn. Tens of thousands of people lived in the streets, in Central Park, and in shanty towns, often called Hoovervilles as an ironic tribute to the failed presidency of Herbert Hoover. By 1931, millions were out of work. Though the federal govern-ment ignored the problem, Governor Franklin Roosevelt was among the first to respond with a large-scale relief program. One of the main problems was to get the public, especially the wealthy, to support some type of relief effort. Many films, including *My Man Godfrey*, were public platforms that espoused social change and economic relief.

Godfrey Smith (William Powell), the "forgotten man," is coldly used as a game prize in a scavenger hunt. Irene Bullock (Carole Lombard) decides to bring home this "bum" to her Park Avenue family, where she hires him as a butler. Unbeknownst to her, Godfrey Smith is not actually a "forgotten man," but a wealthy socialite named Godfrey Parke of the Boston social set. The relative anonymity of New York City provides a space in which Godfrey class-passes downward. He is looking for meaning in life, himself an admitted former "spoiled brat." The time he spends working as a butler in the Bullock household provides him with the ability to really look at his class privilege anew, and by the end of the film he not only saves the Bullocks from financial ruin but becomes an entirely new man. He single-handedly turns the city dump into a swanky, co-operatively owned nightclub called, appropriately, The Dump, putting to work many of the men with whom he spent time in the same ruin when he class-passed as a "forgotten man." Passing himself off as a lower-class person, or at least an out-of-work "bum," Godfrey finds that the "only difference between a derelict and a man is a job." His transfor-mation from lost rich brat to a performer of social responsibility eclipses the for-mulaic plot points of the screwball romance: Irene meets Godfrey, the two fall in love, much hilarity ensues because of their supposed class difference, Godfrey's class-passing is exposed, and the two are married.

Importantly, *My Man Godfrey* really has two endings. The formula ending, of course, is a marriage bringing together the lovestruck, but what's striking about this ending is its obligatory nature. The film actually ends before the actual wed-ding, robbing the spectator of the wedding scene. Instead, Irene steamrolls God-frey into marriage, in a way undermining the significance of marriage, especially where she utters the last line, "Stand still, Godfrey. It'll be over in a minute." The credits rise immediately, making a mockery of the institution of marriage while at the same time barely serving it up to the patient audience. The subtext is that there really is no class difference between the couple, so perhaps the marriage is not so transgressive after all. What is transgressive, however, is the ending before this ending, where Godfrey unveils his New Deal-inspired nightclub, The Dump. Standing in his large office, Godfrey has a huge picture window behind him where the audience can clearly see the Brooklyn Bridge, here used as a signifier of promise of social mobility and the promise of a job. New Deal politics, social responsibility toward the poor, and activist governmental policies are embraced by Godfrey as much as they are emblematized in the important symbol of the Brooklyn Bridge. Keeping in mind that the city suffered so terribly during the Great Depression, and was even the epicenter of its starting point (the crash of Wall Street in 1929), Depression-era films set in New York used a shorthand to speak to audiences about the economy and to invoke fantasies and realities about the dire need to address the economy and the "forgotten men" and women of the streets of New York.

While some critics accuse Gregory La Cava of not fully delivering social satire in My Man Godfrey, the film preaches to the upper classes (and the government) that they must be responsible to their fellow man. Christopher Beach finds it problematic that Godfrey uses "a utopian entrepreneurial solution to economic hardships . . . without resorting to New Deal methods of social engineering" (48). For Beach, the film is not closely enough tethered to New Deal politics, but I think this reading is far too literal. Godfrey, after all, is a class-passer who is taught to use his wealth not to ridicule the poor, but to take responsibility for them. This was one of the main tenets behind the New Deal and, after all, the New Deal was born in New York. As Ric Burns and James Sanders argue in New York: An Illustrated History:

> To a remarkable degree the New Deal had been born in New York, constructed on the streets of Manhattan and in the state house at Albany during the first decades of the twentieth century. Now, in the hour of the country's greatest need, the city's progressive political culture would be carried to the corridors of Washington and be given dramatic expression on the national stage.
>
> In retrospect, the extraordinary revolution in national government that would make it possible for New York to do so would represent perhaps the single greatest accomplishment in the city's history, as well as the single biggest sea change in American government since the early days of the republic. (423)

Despite Beach's reservations about the political nature of the film, he does credit My Man Godfrey for its social commentary, pointing to scenes that captured the large schism between the wealthy and the underemployed:

> The scenes at the beginning of the film—especially the juxtaposed scenes that take place at the dump and the Waldorf-Ritz ballroom—suggest the

potential for strong social comment. At the ballroom, for example, we see elegantly dressed men and women carrying and dragging various discarded objects for the scavenger hunt. With the appearance of Godfrey as one of these unwanted objects, the scene captures better than any other in Depression-era comedy both the insane gap between rich and poor and the utter lack of social consciousness displayed by the wealthy few. (48)

Beyond mere social commentary, though, class-passing is used in this film in order to address audiences of all classes and invite them to walk in the shoes of Godfrey the class-passer, thus performing as class-passers themselves. Audiences could identify in myriad complex ways with Godfrey and Irene across boundaries of gender and class. Audiences could explore what it might be like to be spoiled and rich while they simultaneously enjoyed laughing at and scorning the ridiculed upper classes. The film invites multiple spectatorial viewpoints, places of spectatorial class-passing, from the point of view of Irene, who gushes and falls helplessly in love with Godfrey, to that of her maid; or, they could identify with Godfrey as both a member of the lower underprivileged classes and a wealthy man since they experience him in both guises. It is this spectatorial site of multiplicity that is invoked in New York films, and New York itself. The sneaky thing about *My Man Godfrey* is that it uses the romantic comedy genre to preach to the audience and the world without ever seeming to preach. The endless possibilities invoked in the symbol of the Brooklyn Bridge are equaled by endless spectatorial viewpoints, both in the film and in the city itself.

Viewing the world from the top of a skyscraper is certainly a pleasure associated with New York City, but it is also a reminder that the massive hordes of people below are equal as human beings whether or not they are rich bankers or homeless people. *Skyscraper Souls* (1932) uses the vantage point of the skyscraper to tell the story of a businessman who is hell-bent on building a towering monument. Here the skyscraper is directly linked to the pleasure of social mobility. David Dwight (Warren William) is not stopped when he is told his plans for a skyscraper are out of bounds. He builds his skyscraper by the end of the film and celebrates his success with the statement, "It goes halfway to hell, and right up to heaven, and it's beautiful!" Along the way, however, Dwight goes from being a successful lawyer to an unscrupulous, insanely driven banker. His transformation allows for some interesting commentary on his class mobility. When he was a lawyer, he was a decent man, but as a businessman, he turns into a double-dealing hypocrite. He pays for his skyscraper with his soul.

William plays a similar role in *Employees' Entrance* (1933), that of Kurt Anderson, the big boss at a major department store. He seduces the innocent Madeline (Loretta Young) at a drunken office party. The shocking behavior of the ruthless businessman is on trial in *Employees' Entrance*. As if William's date rape of a young woman employee were not bad enough, William plays businessman Anderson as a monster who is completely unmoved when an employee jumps out of a window to his death after Anderson fires him. Informed of his employee's suicide, he coldly remarks, "When a man outlives his usefulness, he ought to jump out a window." Several films of the period were set in department stores, since these provided a convenient location for couples of different classes to meet. Toward the beginning of *Employees' Entrance*, Madeline is a penniless woman, hungry and walking the streets of New York. On the city street, just as she is about to shoplift something to eat, she meets Anderson and he gives her a job at his department store, despite the Depression. Madeline's social mobility from beggar to worker is complicated by the fact that she is Kurt Anderson's employee, but she is not romantically interested in him while he is clearly interested in her. Instead, she falls for Martin West (Wallace Ford), who is about equal to her in social class. Anderson forbids his workers to marry, asking for their full allegiance to the workplace, but Madeline and Martin marry secretly. Anderson then develops a strong relationship with Martin. This Pre-Code film exposed workplace sexual harassment as much as it did the difficulties of holding down a job during the Depression in New York. Anderson tries to break up Madeline and Martin's marriage but fails. Their romance and future safe, the narrative returns to Anderson, who continues to run his department store with ruthlessness. William made a career out of playing the ruthless tycoon who would do anything for money and power; however, beneath the surface his class origins often show. He is often really a low-down gangster in the clothing of the upper class. He is a new-style businessman, representative of new money, thus not fully capable of class mobility, except for the matter of money.

Nineteen thirties' films set in New York City made a very deliberate distinction between genteel old-schooled businessmen and new-style businessmen. That difference involves class. *Dinner at Eight* (1933) allowed for a space to contrast old-money and new-money types. Wallace Beery plays a crass mining tycoon named Packard. Packard is contrasted with Jordan (Lionel Barrymore), an old-moneyed (classed) gentleman with a shipping line who is nearly undone by changing market techniques and by Packard. Class-passing enters the scenario when Packard's wife, a lower-class floozy (Jean Harlow), wishes to pass into the classier circles of society. By the end of the film, Harlow saves Barrymore by insisting that her husband not ruin him. Along the way, many of the jokes are at the expense of Harlow's character. Her class status shows in her speech, dress, and behavior, despite her best efforts. Harlow and Beery's characters are unsuccessful at class-passing but are nevertheless portrayed with loving sympathy. Their inability to fully class-pass, despite their wealth, demonstrates that class is in some ways impossible to attain. Nevertheless, in *Dinner at Eight* audiences were allowed to participate and identify with both classes, suggesting that somehow, in the end, class is less important than decent behavior and intentions. Christopher Beach accurately pinpoints the "ideological contradictions" found in 1930s films and attributes them to the growth of the consumer culture in America:

> Motion pictures, along with other consumer products and institutions such as the radio, the automobile, the photo-newsmagazine, installment buying, and the self-service supermarket, became central features of American life, changing both patterns of consumption and the social relations affected by such patterns. These changes helped to create a society that was more dependent on the "commodity spectacle" than ever before. While class discrepancies—measured in strictly economic terms—may have been greater during the 1930s than in preceding decades, the fact of an increasingly consumerist ethos paradoxically produced interests that brought the various classes closer together. (50)

Manhattan Melodrama

New York is the backdrop for *Manhattan Melodrama* (1934), a strange film that includes the ideological contradictions displayed in films such as *Grand Hotel*. This odd mix of male melodrama and gangster film starred Clark Gable as gangster "Blackie" Gallagher and William Powell as upstanding lawyer and politician Jim Wade. In order to foist the two men of different classes into a brotherhood of sorts, the narrative begins with the two men as boys who are orphaned by the famous New York ferry accident, the *General Slocum* disaster, in which a ferry in New York's harbor out for an afternoon picnic caught fire in June 1904, sinking and killing almost everyone on board. We meet the two boys a bit later when it becomes clear that the young Blackie, played by Mickey Rooney, is destined by class to be a bad kid. He cuts school and shoots craps while young Jim (Jimmy Butler) studies to become a lawyer.

Myrna Loy enters the picture as Eleanor, the girlfriend of Blackie (now a gangster played by Gable). Despite their class differences, Jim and Blackie have held onto their friendship over the years. Cross-class problems arise when Jim becomes a crusading New York district attorney who ends up having to prosecute his best friend and send him to the electric chair for murder. In the meantime, Eleanor leaves Blackie for Jim, largely because Jim promises the things associated with the upper class—marriage, children, and an upstanding lifestyle. Interestingly enough, she clearly loves Blackie as much as she loves Jim. Similarly, Jim and Blackie love one another despite class obstacles. The clearly utopic space of *Manhattan Melodrama* allows for both cross-class romance and cross-class allegiances.

The politics of class become truly bizarre, though, when Blackie talks Jim (now governor-elect) out of giving him a reprieve from the electric chair. Why would Blackie throw his life away? According to the narrative it is merely because Jim "has class." At several points in the film Blackie looks at Jim, almost romantically, and comments on Jim's "classiness." Gable plays one of the most sympathetic murderers known to melodrama. Blackie gives up his life as much to honor his friend, Jim, the governor-elect, as to impress Eleanor. His obsession with pleasing and impressing those of the upper class goes beyond mere posturing. He dies as if he is meant to die, as if this is the "natural" thing for a gangster of his class. The film is quite disturbing in its embrace of a defeatist message toward class mobility. Blackie can never really have class as he goes to the electric chair and dies willingly. The film alludes to the kinds of choices men could make in their lives, especially in New York. One boy chooses the easy lower-class path, making his money the "wrong" way, while the other boy builds his life as a lawyer, district attorney, and finally governor of New York. Clearly, the film favors the upper-class profession of lawyer as a choice, undermining the fact that class is not just a personal choice but a result of many factors such as environment, family, and so on. Jim allows his friend to die in the electric chair, but because he is morally guilty he publicly humiliates himself and resigns as governor. He has found out that Blackie murdered someone because he was a political opponent of Jim, and he admits this to the public as he turns in his public resignation. The film ends with Myrna Loy and William Powell class-free but ready to make a fresh start, a space with which Depression-era New Yorkers probably identified. This Big Apple film is famous because it is the film that the legendary gangster John Dillinger snuck into (in Chicago) on July 22, 1934, only to be gunned down by police after the picture concluded. How ironic that Dillinger died because of his infatuation with Myrna Loy, an actress who simply dripped of class. In the narrative of *Manhattan Melodrama*, Blackie dies at least partially because of his infatuation with Loy's character.

Lower-class characters frequently sacrifice themselves for "classier" characters in many 1930s films. This disturbing phenomenon is closely related to that of African Americans giving up their lives for white characters in so many American films. The romantic and melodramatic parallels between Dillinger and Blackie prove that, even compared to films with outrageously contrived plots, truth really is stranger than fiction. But *Manhattan Melodrama* is nevertheless a paean to the greatness of New York in terms of its ability to open spaces for intra-class contact and inter-class love, and other forms of relationships.

Dancing Up in *Swing Time*

Just about everything exciting or meaningful in 1930s New York class-passing films takes place in New York's Art Deco apartments, swanky New York nightclubs, in brownstones, on stairs and in elevators, and in the unbelievably luxurious Art Deco apartment sets such as those designed by Cedric Gibbons at MGM. His style, clean lines, high ceilings, art modern furnishings, magisterial lighting, and silk and brocade upholstery punctuated by lines and arrows (usually vertical in nature) correspond with the dream of upward mobility as it is exemplified in such films as *The Single Standard* (1929), starring Greta Garbo.

Another popularly used set is of course the nightclub. A fine example of this usage can be found in *Swing Time* (1936), a Fred Astaire/Ginger Rogers musical set in the elegant Silver Sandal and in the Club Raymond, decorated by New York designer John Harkrider, who also designed the nightclub sets for *My Man Godfrey*. The Silver Sandal was named after the actual New York club The Silver Slipper, a world-renowned nightclub on West Forty-eighth Street that had reigned as one of New York's finest until it closed in 1932. The Club Raymond, decorated predominantly in white, was itself inspired by the Rainbow Room at Rockefeller Center. With tables that seated up to three hundred, a quilted ceiling and studio re-creation of a panoramic overview of New York at night, the "Club Raymond" set was indeed "swell." In an effort to further emphasize upward mobility in a rather concrete metaphorical sense, the Club Raymond included a "sleek cylindrical glass elevator from which guests alighted after their sixty-odd-story journey up from terra firma" (Mandelbaum and Myers 105).

The cross-class romance in *Swing Time*'s New York is between John "Lucky" Garnett (Fred Astaire), a gambler and dancer engaged to Margaret Watson (Betty Furness). Lucky shows up late for his wedding and is confronted by his would-be father-in-law, Judge Watson (Landers Stevens), who challenges him to earn $25,000 to prove he is not just a layabout and thus "earn" the hand of his daughter. In the meantime, Lucky naturally falls for Penny Carole (Ginger Rogers) and the fun comes in watching him try *not* to earn the $25,000. *Swing Time* is one of the most magical of the Astaire/Rogers films, with musical numbers that address class and employment issues, such as "Pick Yourself Up." Other classic musical numbers such as "Waltz in Swing Time," "A Fine Romance," and "Never Gonna Dance" take place in the utopic spaces offered by New York nightclubs that, depicted onscreen, offered Depression-era audiences endless hope and aspiration for better times. Scenes set in such places, as much as they reveled in the romance of consumption and nubile young bodies, significantly did the cultural work of bringing the "right" couple, the man and woman of the same class, together happily. After all, Astaire was "Never Gonna Dance," according to the song, unless he could be with Rogers. Howard Mandelbaum and Eric Myers accurately describe the New York nightclub setting for this song in their beautiful volume, *Screen Deco*:

> The redecorated Silver Sandal, the most stunning of the three *Swing Time* nightclubs, was saved for last.
>
>   A glittering dream world of black and silver, it enhanced Fred and Ginger's "fine romance." Two huge staircases converged in a semi-circle to form the club's entrance. Guests descended the staircases alongside curving tiers of tables, each table bearing a silver tablecloth and a softly glowing Saturn lamp.

At the bottom of the staircases was the spacious dance floor with its design pattern of concentric diamonds in black and gray. Underneath the miracu-lously unsupported platform where the staircases met was the round, white bandstand, placed above a foreshortened view of midtown skyscrapers inlaid on the floor. All of this was set against huge windows revealing a star-strewn night sky, which added a shimmering undulation to Fred and Ginger's "Never Gonna Dance." (105)

The shimmering bodies of Astaire and Rogers perform a courtship duet that transcends class as much as it revels in it. As Lucy Fischer observes in *Designing Women: Cinema, Art Deco and the Female Form*, "In both *Top Hat* and *Swing Time*, the characters played by Astaire and Rogers are rather middle-class individuals who manage to circulate almost entirely within the realm of the upper crust, a social stratum associated with the glamorous Style Moderne" (125). Not only do Astaire and Rogers mingle with the elite but they are dressed for the part in chic tuxedo and stunning gown designed to conform to the horizontal lines of the set and to metaphorically lift them in class status. Thus, class mobility permeates the dancing body, the clothing, the songs, and the sets as much as, if not more than, the actual plot of *Swing Time* does. That New York is the backdrop for the nightclubs of *Swing Time* is important to note, for the city has somehow always stood for an equality that transcends actual class and actual economic circumstance.

This utopic liminal space, where economic realities are displaced by phantas-mal projections of class harmony, is not newly formed in the thirties' musical. Walt Whitman, for one, celebrated a similarly fashioned liminal space in New York in his *Leaves of Grass*. As Ric Burns and James Sanders write, Whitman's poetry celebrated New York as a glorious respite from the mundane:

Walking the same streets as other New Yorkers, Whitman glimpsed a new kind of city being born—a great democratic vista that as yet only he could see. Where some saw a crowd of alien strangers, he saw an endless river of people, each pursuing his or her own destiny. Where some saw the clash of races, classes, religions, and nationalities, he saw a *daily sharing*, and reveled in the dissonant chorus of New Yorkers, calling it "the glorious jam." Where some saw tumult and unrest, he felt the thrilling excitement of city life, and the rising of a new kind of culture, based on curiosity, fantasy, and desire. (103–04)

New York is my hometown, and I must admit that I harbor similar edenic fan-tasies about it. I was moved to tears recently when, watching the nightly news, I saw footage of New Yorkers marching together to protest the Republican National Convention (held in New York in 2004). What moved me was seeing hordes of people of every different persuasion and every race, ethnicity, class, and age walking together peacefully demonstrating in the face of an incumbent administration that used the city as a backdrop for political purposes because it was the site of the World Trade Center bombings of September 11, 2001. The utopic display of such a mix of real people was perhaps for me as moving as the fantasy musicals must have been for some Depression-era audiences eager for a visual display that offered promise for change, a promise that seemed, even in its phantasmal projection of fantasy, to be more real than such empty platitudes as "prosperity is just around the corner" (a popular Depression-era saying that La Cava neatly mocks in *My Man Godfrey* by having Godfrey say, "I just wonder, *what* corner!").

Troubles' End

Americans are eager for the classes to get along. Nowhere is this truer than in New York, where, after all, the classes *must* get along. The disparity between the rich and poor is growing and ever present. The edenic myth of the city as "the glorious jam" or the fantastic "melting pot" seems necessary for the city to exist peacefully both in reality and in filmic diegesis. Not unlike the movies of the 1930s, Walt Whitman sought to project a vision of "what a modern democratic metropolis could be. Embracing the entire human landscape of New York, Whitman hoped to show his fellow citizens what brought them together, rather than what drove them apart" (Burns and Sanders 103). Along with the myth of class transcendence came untruths about the Depression in films of the 1930s. As Ted Sennett writes, "It was not uncommon for films of the period to insist that things were improving. *Stand Up and Cheer* (1934) actually proclaimed the end of the Depression" (70). In times of dystopic realities, utopic fantasies reign supreme. In *Stand Up and Cheer*, Ginger Rogers actually proclaims, "The long lost dollar has come back to the fold." Her outright false proclamation is met with a display of perhaps hundreds of chorus girls wearing oversized coins and performing an elaborate Busby Berkeley production number in celebration of money.

The song "We're in the Money" similarly features Ginger Rogers in a skimpy coin-dotted costume in *Gold Diggers of 1933*, one of many films centered around the lives and fantasies of actors on Broadway. This New York fantasy featured three poverty-stricken dancers who become involved with an upper-class Bostonian, J. Lawrence Bradford (Warren William), and his younger brother Robert (Dick Powell), who passes himself off as poor songwriter Brad Roberts. This element of class-passing becomes an important plot point when Brad's identity is revealed. First, however, we meet our underclassed female characters: warm-hearted tough cookie Carol King (Joan Blondell), Trixie (Aline MacMahon), a sharp-tongued gold digger, and Polly Parker (Ruby Keeler), the dull, safe love object of Brad. The out-of-work showgirls are thrilled to hear that a Broadway show is going into production. Brad, posing as an average Joe, lends the producer enough money to get the show going. Although the film is directed by Mervyn LeRoy,

Busby Berkeley choreographed the famous production numbers, including the "Forgotten Man" number, a curious plea for forgotten men, unemployed war veterans who stood on breadlines and lived in the streets of New York. In this sequence, Joan Blondell is dressed as a prostitute. She talk-sings the lyrics, bitterly condemning society for deserting her man after sending him off to war. African American singer Etta Moten actually sings the number as the camera pans across the desolate faces of the suffering women. In a politically transgressive moment, the men in uniform emerge as men in a breadline after marching in a ticker-tape parade. Then they emphatically walk toward the camera, with war-torn expressions accusing the audience as the song continues, an amazing finish for a film that began with "We're in the Money." *Gold Diggers of 1933* allowed for a liminal space where the cultural work of dealing with the Depression could be accomplished by enacting utopic fantasies in conjunction with dystopic realities, the real and the false on one stage.

The shabby apartment the women share in this film, the way they get along with nothing and complain of constant hunger, not to mention their use of lower-class idiomatic expressions, add humanism to the dehumanized spectacles that emerge from the fantasies of Busby Berkeley. These anti-humanistic fantasies turn women into objects in the famous "Shadow Waltz" production number in which identical looking peroxide blondes play neon violins in a vast white set. The girls, like the violins, are arranged in various kaleidoscopic patterns. At the close of the number, they all form one giant violin. In between musical numbers, the central couple becomes romantically entwined. Polly, the "good" girl (who is emphatically not a gold digger), falls for a man she thinks is as poor as she is, but finds out he is actually the wealthy Robert Bradford. Predictably, the two get past their class differences and the film culminates in their promise of connubial bliss; however, what we the audience remember most is the "Remember My Forgotten Man" number. Like so many films, *Gold Diggers of 1933* has an ending that seems forced, tacked on, and obligatory, very much in keeping with the ending of *My Man Godfrey*. Sure, the couple gets together, but what stands out—"The Forgotten Man"—has nothing to do with the central couple and everything to do with class in New York in the thirties. These films contain contradictory messages, but we must ask if the resolution, often tacked on and obligatory, erases everything else we have seen in the film. I think it does not. Utopian celebration is *not* necessarily at odds with radical sociopolitical messages, especially in films set in New York.

One way to deal with the hard realities of Depression-era New Yorkers was to romanticize unemployment. *Central Park* (1932), a curious little program picture directed by John G. Adolfi, positively romanticizes the starving, unemployed central couple, Dot (Joan Blondell) and Rick (Wallace Ford). Set entirely in Central Park and shot on location, *Central Park* constructs the famous city landmark as another liminal space where anything can happen. It is an edenic paradise, where the homeless fall in love and people from all walks of life manage to live together in harmony.

The swelling orchestral music of the Vitaphone Orchestra, led by Leo F. Forbstein, starts even before the credits of *Central Park*, pulling the viewer into romantic union with the visual elements of the film. The credits roll over an awkward aerial shot of the city. This bird's-eye shot careens toward Central Park as the music swells. When the story begins, it introduces us to the incongruities that make the park itself famous. First we glimpse barnyard animals, roosters, and ducks. As we realize we are at the zoo, the camera makes a sly joke by panning upward to the buildings at the edge of the park at the top of Manhattan. A bum yawns as he wakes on a park bench and watches as a farmhand leads cattle across the street in the middle of Central Park. This incongruous meeting of animals usually associated with the country and skyscrapers and taxis associated with urban life acts as a metaphor for the central characters who are Midwesterners a bit lost in the big city.

But before we meet the central couple, Adolfi finds time to further romanticize the class harmony of the park. The romantic music continues as we see a series of shots that look as if they belong in a documentary, such is their realism. First, a sailor and a young woman are shown sleeping in a small boat at the edge of a beautiful lake in the park. Clearly, they have spent the night together in a sexual liaison. We cut to a wealthy man in a top hat and tails walking his poodle. Next, a couple of lower-class boxers perform a workout. Then, a wealthy woman rides comfortably in a horse-driven cart and some wealthy equestrians are out for a ride in the park. Finally, we come to an "ethnic type," probably Italian, perhaps an unemployed opera singer, who stands next to a park bench as he sings the scales and treats us to a bit of opera. Has he been sleeping on the park bench? It is impossible to know. His clothes are fairly well kept. He has a hat lying on the bench. No matter how poor, the unemployed in 1930s movies always make an attempt at dressing well. The men always wear hats. At the worst, they may be unshaven. They are never referred to as "street people," "bag ladies," or even "homeless." They are down on their luck, but not responsible for an economy that failed the country. It is simply impossible to imagine a more recent film that treats people (now termed homeless) so sympathetically as noble and even romantic types, with the possible exception of *Down and Out in Beverly Hills* (1986), itself a remake of a Depression-era French film, *Boudu Saved from Drowning* (Jean Renoir, 1932).

The romanticization of poverty and joblessness continues in the scene in which Dot and Rick "meet cute" in the tradition of romantic comedy. As the camera goes in for a tight shot of some hotdogs cooking on a grill at a vendor's stand in the middle of Central Park, we realize as viewers that food is out of reach to many people during the Depression. Sure enough, on one side of the hotdog stand we find Rick, literally licking his lips as he stares at the food cooking on the grill. He looks across to the opposite window and sees Dot, a beautiful blonde who is similarly starving as she eyes the hotdogs optimistically. Their eyes meet and their love is sutured together by a shared starvation for food. The hotdog vendor is clearly annoyed by their behavior. As he tries to shoo them away, some kids playing ball nearby accidentally break one of his windows. A scuffle ensues and as the vendor accuses Rick, Dot manages to steal a few precious hot-dogs. Her theft is offscreen, perhaps to soften the act, but in a world where people are starving her clever act of thievery is celebrated in the next romantic scene.

Rick finds Dot sitting on a little footbridge, the perfect setting for a romantic tryst. The desperation of starvation and the act of theft are morally smoothed over by the romantic music and the utterly frank yet tender remarks between the couple. Ford and Blondell make poverty, homelessness, and thievery positively romantic. Dot, scarfing down a hotdog on the footbridge, motions to Rick to join her and gives him some food. "First meal I've had in days," says he. Dot responds, "I'm not exactly overfed myself," as Rick looks at her very thin body. Despite the cavalier attitude toward hunger, starvation was no laughing matter in the 1930s. In 1931, ninety-five people died of starvation in New York.

Dot asks Rick where he lives. Maintaining some sense of middle-class deco-rum, he responds as if he actually has an address: "Behind that tool shed, on a bench." Dot also has been living in the park. "We are all members of the same club," she says. They quickly turn to the question of employment. "Working?" Dot asks Rick. "Does anybody work in this town?" he responds. Forbstein's roman-tic score continues, even as they discuss the harsh realities of poverty. Dot shows Rick the holes in the bottom of her shoes, worn thin from walking around the city looking for a job. Her witty repartee is delivered in a manner that only Blondell could manage. "They are worn so thin I could stand on a dime and tell you if it was heads or tails." She might be a country girl from the Midwest but she has clearly picked up the realism at the core of New York humor. When they break off from their romantic rendezvous, Dot quips, "Till we eat again." As it turns out, she came to the city to work on Broadway with stars in her eyes like so many young men and women, dreaming of fame and the lights of the stage. But, she explains, "The nearest I ever got to it was being an usher on the balcony at the Roxy." Rick, too, has theatrical ambitions. He was in the rodeo in Arizona.

These small town kids get involved with a group of thugs led by Nick (Harold Huber, who frequently played thugs, gangsters, and low-life characters in films of the thirties). Nick recognizes Dot from a bogus Broadway audition and he picks her up at the edge of Central Park by posing as a New York detective "with his boys." He gets Dot involved as a dupe in a robbery scheme involving the theft of a large amount of money that is meant to be distributed to the unemployed of New York. She is asked to pretend to be a wealthy socialite who will open the trunk of money and officially donate it in the name of the wealthy donors. Her class-passing is very near successful because she is dressed for the part. Meanwhile, she doesn't really know that she is involved in a crime. Rick comes to her rescue, though, breaking into the elegant restaurant in the center of Central Park.

He runs after Nick and his men as they flee into the park with the money. A kind-hearted policeman (Guy Kibbee) is killed in the shootout. Both Nick and Dot are under suspicion and held at the police precinct. They manage to sweet-talk the head detective into letting them go, so long as they promise to stay together. The film ends with the same, almost neorealist, series of images of people from different classes coexisting in Central Park.

But *Central Park* is interesting for what is left out of the plot as much as for what is included. We are left with a couple who are still unemployed, still homeless, but deeply in love. Homelessness, unemployment, and all that goes with living on a park bench are made to seem positively romantic and sweet. Once again, class issues are made safe and even irrelevant. Central Park is portrayed as an edenic universe where class does not matter at all. It is surprising, then, that with all its documentary flavor, *Central Park* has less of a political agenda for social reform than a fantasy film such as the musical *Gold Diggers of 1933*, or even the screwball comedy *My Man Godfrey*. The poor are constructed as noble and decent. Goodness trumps class and arguably becomes a form of class itself. After all, even if they must steal to eat, Dot and Rick are decent swell kids. They are morally superior to the rich, spoiled Bullock family of *My Man Godfrey*. Like Blackie of *Manhattan Melodrama*, Dot and Rick emblematize poverty and lower classedness as a form of goodness only present in the poor underclass. This is a dangerous message that shows up in quite a few Depression-era films. It's not dangerous in that it celebrates the decency of the common folk of New York, but it is dangerous to romanticize poverty and lower-classedness.

Depression-era films of New York left viewers with conflicting messages, particularly to do with class issues and issues centering on unemployment and poverty. Nevertheless, they did manage to address these issues in ways that incorporated New York City as a backdrop and a character in their stories. Though these films didn't always offer political solutions, they did provide spaces to directly address the gap between the rich and the poor, the gap between classes, and the physical spaces between the flophouse and the penthouse. The architecture of the city as the films show it, its spires, its upwardly reaching skyscrapers, its bridges, its parks, and its penthouses, continue to beckon to the masses, offering both the crushing realities and the outrageous fantasies of social mobility. Class-passing New York films of the 1930s worked to provide a fantasy of class harmony, in a city that prides itself on its ability to contain people of difference, while offering endless opportunity for social mobility. While not always able to deliver on that promise, New York stands—onscreen and off—as a tribute to it.

"What are ya gonna do, kill me? Everybody dies." Charlie Davis (John Garfield, l.) with Roberts (Lloyd Goff) in *Body and Soul* (Robert Rossen, Enterprise, 1947). Digital frame enlargement.

Midtown Jewish Masculinity
in *Body and Soul*

AARON BAKER

From the 1890s until the Second World War, Jews played an important role in American prizefighting. Although first-generation parents considered it "antithetical to their religious teachings and cultural traditions," boxing had a strong appeal to impoverished second-generation Jewish-American youth, as a way to make money and to measure up to a physical notion of masculinity prominent in other urban communities (Riess, "Tough Jews" 60). As young Jewish men found success in the ring, tolerance for boxing increased somewhat among older Jews, who began to accept its role in "combatting anti-Semitism and negative stereotypes." By 1928 there were more Jewish than Italian or Irish contenders, and in 1934 half of the eight divisions of professional boxing had Jewish champions (Riess 75, 73).

Besides their achievements as prizefighters, Jewish Americans have also been prominent in the cultural representation of boxing. Clifford Odets's 1937 play *Golden Boy* dramatizes the struggles of a young boxer with the choice of individual achievement as a prizefighter or an emphasis on family and community in the culture of his immigrant father. A decade later, Budd Schulberg published his novel *The Harder They Fall* (1947), which tells the story of a fighter exploited by the mob. Such criminal exploitation in prizefighting is also the central theme of Art Cohn's screenplay for *The Set-Up* (1949) and Irving Shulman's script for *Champ for a Day* (1953). In 1949, Kirk Douglas starred in *Champion*, a noir melodrama, written by Carl Foreman and produced by Stanley Kramer, about the moral costs of success in the ring, and Shulman adapted his novel *The Square Ring* for the 1952 film *The Ring* about an L.A. boxer battling discrimination.

But as much as these stories successfully represent boxing as an allegory of working-class life, they also avoid acknowledgment of the proud tradition of Jewish prizefighters. Odets wrote the title role in *Golden Boy* with Jewish actor John Garfield in mind, yet the boxer protagonist in the play is Italian American. Odets's play limits the onstage presentation of ring violence in accordance with Aristotelian dramatic convention, but also as an expression of distaste for blood sport. Jewish pugilism was slighted again when Warner Bros. refused to loan Garfield to Columbia for its 1939 screen adaptation of the Odets play, the role going instead to William Holden, an actor so Anglo that he couldn't convey even the generic urban ethnicity favored by the melting pot ideology of so much American film and television. Garfield got his chance to play a fighter in a Warner Bros. film, *They Made Me a Criminal*, released that same year. Yet even here the experience of his character demonstrates the dangers of the prizefighting rather than its glories, as he is falsely accused of murder by his manager. The only positive image of boxing that *They Made Me a Criminal* offers comes in its last scene, when the Garfield character wins a bout to support a school for delinquent boys who are headed for the undisciplined life he has led. Even after the Second World War, prizefight stories told by American Jews still locate the sport's masculine physicality in other ethnicities. Schulberg's 1947 novel focuses on a boxing world by that time dominated by African Americans and Latinos like the book's fighter, Toro Molina. Carl Foreman's Oscar-winning script for *Champion* also avoids Jewish success in the ring, adapting instead a Ring Lardner story about an Irish fighter named Kelly. Art Cohn's script for *The Set-Up* is about a fighter named Thompson, and the boxers in Schulman's novel and screenplays are also Anglo-American or Latino.

One exception to this cultural denial of Jewish achievement in prizefighting is *Body and Soul* (1947), which represents both sides of the intergenerational debate. Set in New York City during the Depression, *Body and Soul* offers the experience of its main character, Charlie Davis (John Garfield), a young fighter from a Jewish family, as justification for parental dislike of boxing, seeing it as a physically dangerous activity that is exploitative of others and controlled by criminals. Yet *Body and Soul* also validates Charlie's desire to put forward a strong, assertive masculinity and earn a living at a time when there were few other opportunities. By tempering the individualism of Charlie's identity with the responsibilities implied by the older generation's critique of boxing, *Body and Soul* attempts to define an American hero for working-class Jews.

As the American city with the largest Jewish population, and as the center of the boxing business, New York figures prominently in *Body and Soul*. Irving Howe notes that by 1910 there were over one million Jews in New York, and that even well after World War II, "only in New York City is there a significant divergence from the overall trend of American Jews to move into the middle class" (611). In *Body and Soul*, New York is therefore an important locale not only because of its large Jewish community but also due to the working-class segment of its population, for whom boxing had particular significance. Garfield, who also produced the film, and screenwriter Abraham Polonsky had a very personal investment in the place of the film and the community it represents: both, like Charlie Davis, were from the Lower East Side of Manhattan. However, in contrast to Polonsky's, Garfield's, and Howe's insistence on the continuation of a Jewish working class in New York, Hasia Diner asserts that, at about the time that *Body and Soul* was made, the Lower East Side signified for Jews, within a context created by "the triumph of American Liberalism," "the opening up of suburban communities and professional opportunities" (19). According to Diner, because of such assimilation the Lower East Side changed from "a particular neighborhood where many Jews lived" to a symbol of "the Jewish experience in America" (19). In its "warren of crowded, dirty mean streets" Jews had recreated the European culture of the "Old World." Yet it was also a place their children left through "the American dream of mobility" (20).

Body and Soul begins with Charlie waking from a nightmare the evening before a title fight. He has had a long and lucrative reign as middleweight champ, but he is haunted now by shame and guilt from his complicity with Roberts (Lloyd Goff), an exploitative promoter and gambler. Roberts has taken more than a fair share of the profits from past bouts and has also persuaded Charlie to throw the upcoming fight. Worst of all for Charlie's conscience, Roberts has been responsible for the deaths of two of the champ's friends when they protested earlier dirty deals: his first manager, Shorty Polaski (Joseph Pevney), and Ben Chaplin (Canada Lee), the former titleholder.

After waking from his nightmare, Charlie drives to see his mother (Anne Revere) and former fiancée Peg Born (Lilli Palmer), both of whom are estranged from the fighter because of his selfish choices. The ensuing scene in the mother's cramped Lower East Side apartment, with noir shadow, brings out the exploitation and violence that still cling to Charlie. A single bulb over the table in the center of the room lights the mother's kitchen, allowing darkness around the edges of the image to encroach on them as Charlie tells her of his torment. Peg returns from shopping, sees Charlie, and runs into an adjoining bedroom, turning off the light so that when he enters and tries to embrace her, we see them surrounded by shadow and framed tightly by a window (Rainsberger 216).

Along with such noir compositions symbolizing the greed and violence that encroach on Charlie and his family, *Body and Soul* also relies heavily on Polonsky's dialogue. In several interviews Polonsky claimed that he succeeded during the making of *Body and Soul* in preventing director Robert Rossen from changing his dialogue or the story itself. Polonsky also commented that when he wrote for the movies, his intention was to create language that could "play an equal role with the actor and the visual image" (Cook and Lovell 41). He succeeds in *Body and Soul* when, after the failed reconciliation with his mother and Peg, we next see Charlie in his dressing room before the climactic title fight. Roberts enters, hears the champ angrily boast that he plans to win, and responds: "What's wrong, Charlie? The books are all balanced. The bets are in. You bet your purse against yourself. You gotta be business-like, Charlie. . . . Everything is addition or subtraction, the rest is conversation." With lines like these, Polonsky makes the point that "criminality can be businesslike," offering us what Thom Andersen called "a critique of capitalism in the guise of an expose of crime" (186–87). The Roberts character combines criminality and the traits of a successful businessman, as if to suggest the potential for the two to overlap. His lock on access to title fights allows him to demand half of Charlie's earnings (the traditional manager's share is one-third), and like a company store he consolidates his control over the fighter's services by advancing money that he calls "a little on account." Roberts's name, conservative suits, and public avoidance of sex also make him look and act less like a gangster than like the stereotype of a repressed WASP businessman.

Polonsky's characterization of Roberts draws on a real life figure, James Norris, who was prominent in the prizefight business at the time *Body and Soul* was made. A wealthy businessman, Norris set up the International Boxing Club (IBC) that ran Madison Square Garden, the arena then located at Fiftieth Street and Eighth Avenue in midtown Manhattan and known as "the Mecca of boxing." In the late 1940s, Norris "controlled almost 90% of all championship fights," staging them at the Garden with the help of Organized Crime figures such as Frankie Carbo, who used strong-arm tactics to gain the cooperation of fighters and their managers (Sammons 96, 179). Boxing historian Jeffrey Sammons describes the state of professional boxing under Norris and the IBC as "stable" and profitable for the television networks and advertisers (165). Roberts's respectable appearance in *Body and Soul* draws on the real-life model of Norris, who demonstrated that in professional boxing crime and business did overlap.

Consistent with Polonsky's literary aspirations, Roberts's colloquial directness articulates the motives behind the character's "legitimate" exterior, making clear his intention to manipulate fighters to maximize his profits and strong-arm anyone who gets in the way. Roberts's language not only directly communicates his motives, it also reveals his own proletarian origins. Like Garfield's character for much of the film, Roberts exemplifies a hardboiled response to disadvantage as he pursues success by any means possible, even the ruthless destruction of others like himself. Such a self-interested reaction to class barriers has been endemic to prizefighting throughout its history. Joyce Carol Oates describes this working-class cannibalism when she writes that "boxers fight one another because the legitimate objects of their anger are not accessible to them. . . . You fight what's nearest, . . . what's ready to fight you. And, if you can, you do it for money" (63). *Body and Soul* uses Roberts's betrayal of his working-class origins and his influence on Charlie to illuminate the ultimate goal in prizefighting and in the recipe for success frequently offered to those at the bottom: do what you gotta do to move up, and leave your people behind. That's exactly the notion of achievement that Charlie's mother objects to when she first hears of his choice to fight: "Did you hurt the other boy good, Champion?" she asks her son. While Polonsky wants to celebrate the toughness and charisma of the Jewish prizefighter in *Body and Soul*, he also shows how masculinity defined through assertions of superiority over others undermines the egalitarian politics valued by family and community.

Along with its colloquial dialogue and allegorical use of shadow, *Body and Soul* also employs a realistic visual style. Cinematographer James Wong Howe filmed the climactic fight scene using a hand-held camera to convey the brutality of Charlie's experience and its impact on his moral choice. Having been a boxer himself, Howe felt that the conventional way of shooting prizefights, with a camera on a "big bulky dolly in the ring which can't move around and can only go up and down and sideways," couldn't convey the experience of a fighter. He therefore rented two lightweight Eyemo cameras and put on roller skates to film the fight. Using a smaller camera allowed him to move in closer to Charlie when he gets hit and then quickly turn to show what the fighter saw—"nothing but hot light flashing down"—before cutting back to Garfield's face. Howe told the grip pushing him around the ring not to worry about distance because he wanted the image to be out of focus at times to suggest the grogginess of a fighter who has been hit (Rainsberger 217–18).

The visual style used in the climactic fight contributes to our identification with Charlie's decision to reject the fix and hold onto his title and pride. Roberts had promised him a fifteen-round decision with the challenger Marlowe (Artie Dorrell) winning on points. In return for holding back, Charlie was to receive a big payday and avoid the physical and emotional pain of being knocked out. Yet after seeing how Roberts had welshed on the same promise to Ben when Charlie took the title and almost killed the African American champ, we are not surprised in the thirteenth round when the gambler gives the signal for Marlowe to go for the knockout. Howe's hand-held camera falls to the mat with Charlie when Marlowe knocks him down twice, and we see in close-up the confusion on the champ's face. Along with the bumpy, out-of-focus shots, this close-up conveys in a visceral way Charlie's pain and bewilderment so that it makes sense when he decides to throw away the money and risk his life by winning the fight.

I have indulged in this analysis of *Body and Soul*'s combination of Polonsky's street poetry and Howe's noir/realist camerawork to illustrate how the film presents its critique of the capitalist myth of self-reliance. I want to emphasize also, however, that Charlie's identity as a Jew plays an essential role in the alternative ethos offered by the film. While he warns of the danger in essentializing about Jewish identity, Stephen Whitfield acknowledges the strong traditional association between Judaism and communitarian politics like those endorsed in *Body and Soul*. Amongst the several explanations that he offers for this association, most resonant for *Body and Soul* is the affinity Whitfield points out between concern with "the destiny of the Jewish people" and ideas of "egalitarianism and collectivism pivotal to socialist doctrine" (*American Space* 118). Whitfield also notes that radicalism as an ideology fits the strong intellectual emphasis in Jewish culture. Polonsky, who had been a college professor, union organizer, and attorney before working in Hollywood until he was blacklisted in 1952, was a strong adherent to both collectivist and intellectual tendencies.

Polonsky's socialist politics influenced the deviation in *Body and Soul* from Hollywood's mythology of utopian self-reliance. Even on the rare occasions when Hollywood films represent barriers of social difference, the standard response emphasizes the heroism of a determined individual who rises above such obstacles. The boxing film was a better fit for Polonsky's politics and Garfield's working-class star persona because it tended toward a more contextualized view of identity than in most Hollywood movies, and allowed invocation of the history of tough Jewish masculinity in prizefighting. Lester Friedman notes that in the years after the Second World War, Israel's militant self-assertion resonated with those Diaspora Jews who "felt humiliated by the revelations of Jewish passivity in the face of Nazi atrocities" (100). Daniel Boyarin takes the position that Zionism has been as much "a cure for the disease of Jewish gendering as a solution to economic and political problems of the Jewish people" (277). Zionism's response to the question of Jewish masculinity therefore endorsed what Boyarin calls "the new muscle Jews" (277). Likewise, the violent physicality of Garfield's prizefighter gives material force to the film's critique of capitalism, but also responds to concerns about Jewish masculinity, to what Friedman calls "the nagging belief that Jews were . . . perpetual victims who would prefer to be murdered rather than defend themselves" (108).

Body and Soul's use of the Jewish boxing tradition to address this concern with masculinity becomes most evident in a scene before the climactic title fight (presumably at Madison Square Garden, although probably to block legal repercussions the venue is not named) when the Holocaust is invoked directly. As middleweight champion, Charlie has become a hero, especially for Jewish males in his neighborhood like the grocer, Shimen (Shimen Ruskin), who tells him: "Over in Europe the Nazis are killing people like us, just because of our religion. But here, Charlie Davis is champeen. So you'll win . . . and we are proud."

Typical of the few texts that refer to the Holocaust in the first decades after the war, *Body and Soul* does not represent the Shoah directly, but instead invokes it to dramatize the importance of standing up to other instances of injustice—in this case racism as well as class disadvantage (Whitfield, *Search* 175).[1] In this sense, the film appears to be liberal on the issue of racism in America, certainly a hot topic as veterans of the war were being reintegrated socially. Charlie develops a close relationship with Ben, the African American ex-champ, and feels tremendous guilt when he does not stand up for him against Roberts. Michael Rogin questions the film's position on race, however, by asserting that Charlie's view of Ben is compromised by his own self-conception as white—and therefore as superior to the African American fighter—manifested in how the film "conditions Jewish/black solidarity on Jew knocking out black" (216).

The contradiction between Rogin's reading of Charlie as built upon the unjustified superiority central to whiteness and the class solidarity between the black and Jewish fighters parallels how Polonsky underestimated the difficulty of portraying tough masculinity as a form of real-world protection for the Jewish community. Richard Dyer argues that whiteness and masculinism share the assumption of superiority defined in relation to a racialized or feminized Other (*White* 30).[2] While Ben is Charlie's racial counterpoint, his feminized Other is his father, who fits what Boyarin calls "the Eastern European ideal of a gentle, timid, and studious male" (2). Physically small and wearing glasses, the elder Davis (Art Smith) is self-deprecating, and, consistent with the politics of gender in *Body and Soul*, respectful of his son's ambition for a more forceful masculinity. Even after Charlie insults his father by loudly proclaiming to his mother that "I don't want to end up like Pop," Davis senior gives his son ten dollars to buy boxing equipment.

Despite this incongruity between a preferred masculinity represented by Garfield's character and the film's endorsement of working-class unity, Polonsky still tries to use Charlie's principled stand in the climactic fight to fit the different interests together. Charlie's "individual redemption" represents a victory for Polonsky, who disagreed with director Robert Rossen's idea that Davis should be killed by Roberts for not throwing the fight. Robert Sklar argues that the screen-writer's choice of a more upbeat ending undercut the social critique of the film by linking it with "the hundreds, if not thousands, of Hollywood movies [that] depict society's problems being solved by individuals triumphing over evil men" (186). Yet when asked if his conclusion compromised what *Body and Soul* says about class, Polonsky responded: "The film had a happy ending only in the sense that instead of selling out, [Charlie] doesn't" (Server 89).

While his decision to win allowed Charlie to follow his mother's advice to "fight for something, not for money," in another sense it ironically compromised the film's insistence on responsibility to others. Even though we do not see Charlie die as Rossen wanted, the last shot of the film following the fight shows him walking with Peg to his mother's apartment on the Lower East Side, having chosen the unity of community yet still surrounded by the dark shadows that have threatened him and his family throughout the film. At the visual level, where Polonsky and even Garfield probably had less input, director Rossen got the ending he wanted after all.

Nonetheless, considering his political ideology, it is a testament to Polonsky's skill as a writer and his determination to make movies that he ever got the chance. Because of his work during World War II for the Office of Strategic Services, the FBI labeled him a "dangerous" filmmaker and wiretapped his phone conversations. FBI Chief J. Edgar Hoover, who feared civil rights activity as much as communism, was also concerned by Polonsky's agitation against restricted-covenant housing that prevented residential integration in Los Angeles (Buhle and Wagner 10, 12).

Polonsky's belief in the political potential of the boxing film is demonstrated by how, before his successful pitch of what would become *Body and Soul*, he had been working for six months at Paramount on a biopic about Barney Ross, Jewish war veteran and former champ in three weight classes (Buhle and Wagner 110, 109). In two essays he wrote in 1945 for a journal edited at UCLA entitled

Hollywood Quarterly, Polonsky complained that "writing for the movies is writing under censorship," but he also endorsed the possibility of putting "enough concrete experience into the mold to make imagination live" (qtd in Buhle and Wagner 105). Such interest in placing "concrete experience" within Hollywood narrative may have drawn Polonsky to the boxing film. Like most sports films, movies about prizefighting must present a certain realism, about the social and economic complexities of the sport, in order to appeal to viewers knowledgeable about boxing. Such verisimilitude often complicates the utopian simplicity of Hollywood narrative by bringing with it the historical complexity of sports in the real world, especially when drawing on the experience of actual athletes. Polonsky certainly knew that any film about Barney Ross would inevitably have raised issues of social identity foreign to most Hollywood stories, but that was probably part of what interested him about writing a screenplay about the boxer's life (on the conventions of the boxing film, see Grindon, Baker).

The debate between Abraham Polonsky and Robert Rossen about how to end *Body and Soul* might be best understood within this context of using but also subverting Hollywood forms. While Rossen saw Charlie Davis surviving a choice to renege on the deal with Roberts as implausible, Polonsky was more interested in how the upbeat ending typical of Hollywood filmmaking could be used to endorse an ideal of working-class heroism. Polonsky later commented that it would be "crazy" for left-wing filmmakers to conclude their movies "by killing off the proletariat" (Buhle and Wagner 116).[3]

Real-Life Case Study: John Garfield's Streetboy Honor

The star of *Body and Soul,* John Garfield, shared with Polonsky an interest in combining working-class physicality with left-wing politics. Polonsky commented that while Garfield "felt inadequate as an intellectual," he also possessed an admirable versatility: "as an actor Garfield was total, and he could play an intellectual with the same vigor and astonishing rapport as a cab driver" (Buhle and Wagner 131). In *Body and Soul* Polonsky and Rossen gave Garfield a good opportunity to demonstrate such range, arming his character and the others around him with dialogue and narrative situations that raised issues of class and ethnicity, yet that also had the energy and violence to allow Garfield to showcase his forceful physicality.

The tough decisions that John Garfield made in the last four years of his life after *Body and Soul* parallel those confronted by the boxer he plays in the film. Like Charlie Davis, Garfield (born Jules Garfinkel in New York in 1913) had a troubled adolescence until a caring high school principal steered him away from delinquency and into acting. Garfield's first break came with the Group Theater in the mid-1930s, followed by seven years at Warner Bros., where he became typecast as what David Thompson calls "a social outsider" (277). Robert Sklar states that Warner Bros. signed Garfield with the intention of making him another

Jimmy Cagney: a fast-talking, wisecracking urban tough guy; Cagney was getting older and was increasingly resistant to the studio's attempts to put him in mug roles. Sklar explains that Warner Bros.' interest in Garfield was motivated by its desire to maintain Cagney's "particular social symbolism from the early 1930s: the uncanny rapport with the young rootless working-class city boys," and even more importantly, "the studio's special relation with the New York crowds, . . . the important revenues produced at the Strand and other New York theaters" (88–89).

Garfield's success in his first role, as rebellious but attractive Mickey Borden in a Michael Curtiz melodrama, *Four Daughters* (1938), allowed him to escape Cagney's shadow and define his own star image as street tough yet vulnerable and sexy—and therefore appealing to both male and female viewers. His second big role for Warner Bros., in a boxing film entitled *They Made Me a Criminal* (1939), brought together these two traits. Garfield plays a prizefighter named Johnny who is framed for a murder in New York and goes on the lam to an Arizona date farm, which is a reform school for a group of downtown delinquents (the Dead End Kids), and for Johnny as well, as he becomes a positive role model for the boys and falls in love. Garfield quickly chafed at the roles Warner Bros. typecast him in, so when his studio contract ran out in 1946, he chose to set up a company independent of the studio, Roberts Productions, a bold move that along with his choice of roles—in movies such as *Gentleman's Agreement* (1947), *Body and Soul*, and Polonsky's first film as a director, *Force of Evil* (1948)—reinforced his rebel image.[4] Once Cold War hysteria hit Hollywood, such a reputation brought on the political harassment that contributed to his death.

Not only did *They Made Me a Criminal* help establish Garfield's star appeal, it also is one of a group of classic era films, including *Winner Take All* (1932), *Kid Galahad* (1937), *Golden Boy* (1939), and *City for Conquest* (1940), about New York prizefighting. As the center of the fight business New York was a natural setting for these stories, and Warner Bros., known for stories about the working-class ethnics who populated the sport, was the right studio for most of these boxing pictures. Oddly enough, such fight films all adopted a populist ideology that vilified New York as a dangerous place full of "shysters and sharpies, the monopolists, and rich society snobs who have caused the Depression. . . . Rural areas in these films, on the other hand, recalled the country's agricultural past, its traditional values of self-help, its rugged individualism, yet also its good-neighborliness" (Baker 109). As a result of this fear of the city, all these films show the protagonist as rehabilitated, set straight, or healed somehow by his escape either from New York altogether (*Winner Take All, They Made Me a Criminal, Kid Galahad*) or at least to an ethnic neighborhood with old-country values (*Golden Boy, City for Conquest*).

As a more politically sophisticated film, *Body and Soul* avoids such a simplistic fear of New York and instead points more directly to the economic and criminal realities of boxing as the problem. For example, as we have seen, the Roberts character who owns the main venue for big fights was based on the real-life owner of Madison Square Garden, James Norris. Just as historically accurate is how the movie shows Roberts's tactics as consistent with a real-world pattern whereby, as "championship matches at the Garden . . . became social affairs that drew a glittering audience" and big profits, organized crime arrived with strong-arm tactics: intimidating fighters and managers to ensure the most lucrative match-ups and thrown fights (Riess, *City Games* 177–79). Jeffrey Sammons calls *Body and Soul* "a fictional yet representative account of prizefighting," and notes that Charles Johnson, the president of the Boxing Managers Guild of New York, complained about its "aspersions" (145).

Although Polonsky clearly wanted to reaffirm the link between Judaism and radical politics in *Body and Soul*, when the film came out in the fall of 1947, it was exactly that association that Jewish studio heads—Louis B. Mayer at MGM and Jack Warner at Warner Bros.—sought to avoid. Neal Gabler describes how Mississippi congressman John Rankin, a major force in reestablishing the House Un-American Activities Committee in the mid-1940s, "mainly distinguished himself by insisting on the links between Judaism and communism" (355). According to Gabler, antisemitism of this sort was characteristic of HUAC; he quotes a committee investigator warning a Columbia University professor in 1946 to "tell your Jewish friends that the Jews in Germany stuck their necks out too far[,] and Hitler took care of them and the same thing will happen here unless they watch their steps" (354–55). Many Jewish executives in Hollywood, including Jack Warner and Louis B. Mayer, were as strongly anticommunist as HUAC, but they were also concerned about how the association of Jews with subversive politics and the general antisemitism on the committee might harm them. When HUAC issued its initial set of subpoenas calling movie industry people to testify in 1947, ten of the nineteen people identified as "unfriendly witnesses" were Jews.[5]

In Gabler's view, Jewish Hollywood studio heads sacrificed those under investigation "to save themselves from the wrath of anti-Semites" (374). However, Jon Lewis offers an alternative explanation. He sees the decision to side with HUAC, which cleared the way for "indictments, incarcerations and an industry-wide blacklist," as motivated not simply by fear of antisemitism from the committee but also by pressure from investors in New York—the Wall Street brokerage houses and other financial institutions that bankrolled Hollywood (7). Lewis states that the disruption of labor organizing in Hollywood, declining box office receipts, and the problems created by the federal government's antitrust action against the industry all moved New York to reorganize the film business on a more efficient corporate model. In Lewis's view, HUAC was one part of that strategy; it functioned to get rid of rebellious talent, stars like Garfield, who supported a 1945 strike at Warner Bros. that involved "the use of tear gas and high-powered water hoses on picketing strikers" and who made the kind of social-problem films like *Body and Soul* that were viewed as bad for foreign box office (23).[6]

As tough as Garfield appeared to be onscreen, he could not fight his way out of the power relations in which he found himself. When a newspaper story quoted a former FBI agent as testifying that Garfield had acted as a "drawing card" to increase membership in communist organizations, scripts stopped coming in (Swindell 229–30). Even after Garfield appeared before HUAC in 1951, he was unable to clear himself. *Variety* reported that members of the committee were dissatisfied with Garfield's denials of past association with communists and asked the FBI to check his testimony against Bureau records.

Besides being unable to clear himself to get the kind of roles he had done in the past, Garfield was also ostracized by his left-wing friends for agreeing to testify. His marriage, weakened by relationships with other women, broke up over his decision in May 1952 to write a tell-all article for *Look* magazine entitled "I Was a Sucker for a Left Hook," in which he admitted being "a dupe of the communists." The strain of his testimony, divorce, lost friends, a career threatened, and the resulting insomnia all contributed to Garfield's death from a heart attack in May 1952 at the age of thirty-nine. Biographer Larry Swindell says that Garfield's death resembled that of several other left-wing movie people, including Canada Lee from *Body and Soul*, who died "shortly after they were ground to pieces by HUAC" (263).

There is a scene in *Body and Soul* in which Peg expresses her fears that if Charlie remains in business with Roberts, he will wind up like Ben: badly injured from too much punishment in the ring and unable to make the best decisions for himself and those around him because of money owed. She tells Charlie to get out while he can. The heroism that Polonsky attempted to instill in Charlie was about trying to prove Peg's fears wrong, showing that the working-class hero could be tough enough, man enough—like the Jewish champions of the ring—to protect himself and still represent his people. Ironically for the actor who played Charlie, Peg's premonition about the inability of individualized masculinity to shoulder such a burden alone turned out to be all too true. Even Polonsky acknowledged this in a 1962 interview. When asked if Garfield's blacklisting accelerated his early death, Polonsky responded: "Yes. He defended his street-boy's honor and they killed him for it" (Sarris 147).

NOTES

1. DVD and videotape copies of *Body and Soul* that I purchased in 2001 lack Shimen's reference to the Holocaust found in an earlier video copy of the film that I have. I can only speculate on why these lines were cut. Perhaps someone involved with its transfer to video and DVD, unaware of the need at the time to displace direct statements about the Holocaust into other issues, found the historical reference irrelevant to the story and edited it out. Another explanation might be that a decision was made that *Body and Soul* would have broader appeal with less emphasis on Charlie's Jewishness.

2. Dyer refers to this affinity when he states that "white women do not have the same relation to power as white men. . . . The archetypal role of white women has been to foster individualism in white men while denying it to themselves" (*White* 30).

3. I quote here not Polonsky's exact words but a summary of what he said as written by
Buhle and Wagner.

4. The name of the crooked promoter character in *Body and Soul* was an inside joke play-
ing on the name of Garfield's business partner, Bob Roberts, with whom the actor set up
Roberts Productions in 1946. Roberts worked with Garfield on only three films, *Body and
Soul, Force of Evil* (1949), and *He Ran All the Way* (1951), as he was named by actor Martin
Berkeley in HUAC testimony and blacklisted.

5. One of those called to testify, screenwriter Ring Lardner Jr., commented, "There was
considerable feeling that this was a force in which anti-Semitism played a strong part"
(Gabler 366).

6. Even though Sklar calls *Body and Soul* "as close to a work of the left as any produced to
that time in Hollywood," and Thom Andersen categorizes it as the first example of a cycle he
calls "film gris," so named for a "psychological and social realism" that conveys the "drabness
and greyness" that we associate with communism (183), *Body and Soul* was nonetheless a
significant box office success. It opened on November 9, 1947, and in less than two months
earned $3.25 million dollars, placing it twenty-eighth on the *Variety* box office list for the year.

∫TAYIN' ALIVE
City of Danger and Adjustment

In "Stayin' Alive," we find essays approaching New York as a city of danger and adjustment. From Sol Nazerman to Tony Manero and Spider-Man; from Linda Seton to Francine Evans and Margot Tenenbaum, the characters we meet in New York films are subject to extremes of threat and transform themselves in prodigious adjustments of philosophy and lifestyle. The New York drama is therefore typically mythic in proportion, the City appearing to augment the experience of those who inhabit it until it is iconic and representative in the extreme. The intensified anxiety lived out by Meg Altman in *Panic Room*, for example, reflects upon the extremes of personality and characterization we find in the films of Sidney Lumet: the jury room stresses of *12 Angry Men* or the fearful strains tearing the protagonist apart psychologically in *The Pawnbroker*. To position any domestic drama in New York—*Six Degrees of Separation*, for example, or *Birth*—is to turn up the heat, confine the antagonisms, and produce a desperate need for change. So it is that there is not only something exciting and extreme about New York films, but also, very often, something optimistic and progressive. This is the place where the past is converted into the future. These are the players who exemplify our condition, but also sharply emphasize it.

To begin, Pamela Grace's analysis of Sidney Lumet reveals this filmmaker to be repeatedly, almost obsessively, concerned with issues of community, morality, corruption, and order in a substantial number of New York films ranging from *12 Angry Men* and *Bye Bye Braverman* to *Night Falls on Manhattan* and the forthcoming *Find Me Guilty*. She gives a detailed analysis of four films in particular, *12 Angry Men*, *The Pawnbroker*, *Serpico*, and *Q & A*, with a view to revealing Lumet's cinematic approaches to the problem of truth and evil. A single, claustrophobic set is used for almost all of the first film, in order to bring the opposing moral viewpoints of diverse New Yorkers into sharp abutment. In *The Pawnbroker*, a technique of flash frame editing allows for introduction of horrifying memories of the concentration camps that can be juxtaposed with the protagonist's present-day horrors of experience in and around his shop in Harlem. In *Q & A*—one of a number of films Lumet has made to focus on the issue of police corruption and public order—a staggeringly powerful central performance gains power by its mise-en-scène against other typical New York characterizations.

Next, Joe McElhaney gives a meticulous analysis of Roman Polanski's *Rosemary's Baby*, where the decaying and cramped apartment setting adds to a feeling of nauseating confinement and disorientation. In general, Polanski follows Ira Levin's novel in referring to "city landmarks and stores, restaurants, and theaters, the kinds of details that repeatedly display the author's intimate knowledge of the city"—this posing an interesting challenge to the non–New Yorker filmmaker who wished to be faithful to the novel and authentic in his way of setting it onscreen. McElhaney shows how this film is not only a powerful portrait of New York City and the kinds of tensions one finds there, but a portrait seen through the eyes of "Polanski's distinctly Eastern European sensibility," one which is in many ways as foreign to New York as is Rosemary's. A particularly intriguing reference in McElhaney's analysis is to the New York theatrical world, reflected in many ways in the film. Finally, *Rosemary's Baby* "becomes a film that raises questions about the relationship between the individual and the collective in terms of the history of urban space—and of New York City in particular—but at the same time a film that firmly answers none of its own questions."

Elisabeth Weis and Randy Thom explore the problem of aural intrusion in New York apartments, concentrating on the use of sound in *Rosemary's Baby* and *Rear Window* in their essay "The City That Never Shuts Up." For many, the New York experience is one of apartment living, in which hearing often takes precedence over seeing. The metropolitan environment described by Georg Simmel, one in which people catch sight of strangers they cannot hear, is thus often overcome by a strange new spatial organization in which the city acts to bring people closer together—often people who are not seeking proximity. Weis and Thom ask in particular how city streets and neighbors are characterized for apartment dwellers by what they can hear. Is there, they wonder, a "distinctive New York sound for films that are actually shot in New York as well as situated there"? Comparing *Rosemary's Baby* and *Rear Window* against Woody Allen's *Manhattan*, which presents a hygienic New York, and the films of Martin Scorsese and Spike Lee, that focus on particular ethnic neighborhoods, Weis and Thom note how both "define the city as neither dangerous nor exciting, as we might expect from popular representations of New York," and proceed to meticulous analysis of the soundscapes as related to the plots of the two films, with particular attention to the use of *scourse* music—active source music that replaces underscoring.

Then, Steven Alan Carr's "Wretched Refuse: Watching New York Ethnic Slum Films in the Aftermath of 9/11" begins by postulating that although New York is archetypal as a metropolis, still "the archetype is really no more than a series of fragmented images that could stand in for any city: the filthy and crowded tenement room, the corner bar at 3 A.M., the deserted back alley, or the bustling, haphazard open-air market." Following from Jacob Riis's *How the Other Half Lives*, Carr produces a systematic examination of "New York as the object of a White Anglo-Saxon Protestant gaze transfixed in horror upon what it perceives as the invading immigrant hordes," very specifically in terms of two key films, produced by Samuel Goldwyn, *Street Scene* and *Dead End*. In these films the tenement and the slum neighborhood that was home to numerous immigrants at the turn of the twentieth century are seen as breeding grounds for problematic, often antisocial behavior, yet one recurring trope is the cinematic erasure of the body of the immigrant from these films. This erasure, its global consequences, and its historic development in film to the present day, Carr links to the globalization "at war with itself" that Baudrillard sees as fundamental to understanding the problem of 9/11. "When the towers collapsed, so too did the idea of inventing and inverting urban space from old world ghetto to a new world global financial center."

And finally, Wheeler Winston Dixon's "Night World: New York as Noir Universe" argues that "New York at night is more nocturnal than any other place onscreen." Focusing on the mutability of character and moment in noir films, this essays considers in depth Hobart Henley's *Night World*, Wallace Fox's *Bowery at Midnight*, Phil Karlson's *Scandal Sheet*, Henry Levin's *Night Editor*, H. Bruce Humberstone's *I Wake Up Screaming*, Anthony Mann's *Side Street*, and Mark Robson's *The Seventh Victim* to localize the noir New York as a "zone of promise and change, which is nevertheless fraught with genuine peril . . . the place where we wish for escape."

Captain "Mike" Brennan, NYPD (Nick Nolte), reaches under the skirt of Sylvester, known as Sophia (Brian Neill), twisting his genitals as he tries to extort information in *Q & A* (Sidney Lumet, Odyssey/Regency Enterprises, 1990). Digital frame enlargement.

City of Nightmares

THE NEW YORK OF SIDNEY LUMET

PAMELA GRACE

Sidney Lumet's New York is a city of multiple ethnicities, sympathetic oddballs, idealists, criminals, and many, many cops. Lumet's films examine the city's neighborhoods and institutions, with special interest devoted to the justice system. As of the beginning of 2006, Lumet has directed forty-two feature films, a large percentage of them set in New York City. Between 1948 and the present, he has also directed and produced several television programs, many of which also take place in New York.

Lumet moved to New York with his parents a few years after his birth in Philadelphia in 1924. He grew up in a Jewish neighborhood in the Lower East Side, where his father, Baruch Lumet, worked in Yiddish theater and radio before going on to English-language roles on Broadway and television. The young Sidney began his theatrical career at the age of four, appearing in the Yiddish theater and then on Yiddish-language radio. He first appeared on Broadway in an English-language role when he was eleven.

Lumet's education and work were also centered in New York. Just before joining the army, he studied dramatic literature at Columbia University for one semester. After the war, he taught acting, began directing for television, and eventually became a celebrated film director. Success did not lure Lumet to Hollywood. When asked why he spent virtually his entire life in New York, he responded, "It's a great city . . . There's almost no choice. I almost can't imagine living anyplace else" (Goldberg 158). Asked what New York has given to his movies, he said, "It's capable of telling any kind of story, from the most lyrical and romantic to the most desolate and alone. Just within the city itself, New York has any atmosphere you could ever imagine to tell a story" (Kaufman 174).

Lumet's films express an intense love of the city and its people—and outrage at injustice and inhumanity. His New York films cover a wide range of themes. *12 Angry Men* (1957) looks at the workings of an ethnically mixed jury; *The Pawnbroker* (1964) explores the silent suffering of a Holocaust survivor, the damage caused by his loss of empathy, and his painful return to human emotions and a sense of community; *Bye Bye Braverman* (1968) is a comedy about a group of

Jewish friends going to a funeral in Brooklyn; *The Anderson Tapes* (1971) depicts a heist in a New York apartment building; *Dog Day Afternoon* (1975) re-creates a bizarre Brooklyn bank hold-up when a man tried to steal money to pay for his male lover's sex change operation; and *Serpico* (1973), *Prince of the City* (1981), *Q & A* (1990), *A Stranger among Us* (1992), and *Night Falls on Manhattan* (1997) look, in different ways, at the work—and corruption—of the police department.

This essay discusses two early films, *12 Angry Men* and *The Pawnbroker*, and then compares the representations of New York in two films about the NYPD, *Serpico* and *Q & A*.

A Love Song to New York: *12 Angry Men*

Lumet's first feature film emphatically announces its New York City location. A slow, smooth tilt, flowing upward like an admiring visitor's gaze, takes us up a massive set of stone steps, up the granite columns of a Roman revival building, to a cornice bearing a quotation from George Washington: "The true administration of justice is the firmest pillar of good government." The location is 60 Centre Street, the New York State Supreme Courthouse. The opening shot poses a question: can we, as New Yorkers, or as Americans, live up to the ideal emblazoned in this quotation? The pillars supporting the engraved words seem to add to the question. As seen from below, the Corinthian columns do not appear powerful or intimidating. Instead, they look delicate, graceful, a little too tall for their width, slightly vulnerable. The joints connecting the vertical sections of the pillars are visible, revealing the places where the columns would come apart if the building were destroyed. We can imagine the pieces lying on the ground, looking like the ruins of an ancient temple.

The film's first cut takes us to a high position inside the building. The smoothness of the transition gives the feeling that an omniscient camera has effortlessly glided through the thick stone wall, arriving indoors, where it will show us the workings of the justice system. The camera-narrator takes us along a corridor, around a corner, past a group of people who seem to be jurors and lawyers, to a door marked "228." After a pause, we enter a room where a tired judge is giving final instructions to a jury. Twelve men retire to a side room and, as they leave, we have two views of the defendant. From behind and slightly to the side, we see a thin boy who looks like a schoolchild sitting at a classroom desk. From the front, we look into the eyes of a frightened youth waiting to hear whether or not he will be sentenced to the electric chair for knifing his father to death. The boy's face dissolves into an image of the jury room, and the opening credits appear on the screen.

The rest of the film, except for a few moments at the end when the jurors leave the courthouse, will take place in the small jury room. Here Lumet gathers a cross-section of the city's light-skinned, middle-class, male population. Here, also, the director begins his multi-film cinematic study of New York and its residents, his piercing but sympathetic analysis of the city's angry bigots, corrupt police-men, ordinary citizens, and courageous idealists.

12 Angry Men was written by Reginald Rose, based on his teleplay, which had aired on CBS in 1954. One of Lumet's enrichments of the original text is a subtle, constant sense of location. The cramped room in which the jury members are locked has only one escape, and that is merely visual. A single wall is lined with a series of windows, which look out on downtown New York. As the jurors file into the room, hanging up coats, making small talk, and gradually taking their seats, one man walks directly to a window, lights a cigarette, and gazes out. This man, Juror No. 8 (Henry Fonda), who will be identified at the very end of the film as Davis, remains at the window until required to take his place at the table. At one point, another man casually joins No. 8 at the window, asking if what he sees is the Woolworth Building and commenting that, in all his years in New York, he has never gone inside. As the man speaks, the camera, stationed further from the window than the two jurors, declines to follow the dialogue, withholding the view of one of the city's most beautiful old buildings. Throughout the film, the beauty of the city's skyline will remain hidden, yet almost visible, just beyond our immediate view of a few nearby buildings.

Juror 8, we soon learn, is an architect. Perhaps his profession explains why he seems to turn to the cityscape for comfort and inspiration as he struggles with a life-or-death decision. His pattern of gazing out the window as he considers the boy's fate seems to connect the decision-making in the small room with the ongoing life of the surrounding city.

The jurors are faced with what one of the men, speaking for nearly the entire group, calls "an open and shut case." A man was found dead in his apartment, and the murder weapon, an elaborately carved knife, was left at the scene. During a six-day trial, the neighbor who lives directly below the victim swore that the man and his son were quarrelling, and that the son said, "I'm going to kill you." He further stated that he heard the body hit the floor and saw the son run-ning down the stairs and out of the building. A woman who lives across the street swore that she saw the murder through the windows of a passing elevated train. A shopkeeper states that he sold the carved knife to the boy and has never seen another like it. The boy pleaded not guilty, saying he was at the movies at the time of the murder. However, he could not remember what picture he saw, and he was not observed by anyone at the theater.

The jurors agree to take an initial vote to determine where everyone stands. Some people are eager to leave, hoping a decision can be reached in a few minutes. In the first round, Juror 8 casts the one not-guilty vote, angering nearly the entire group. One of the most hostile jurors loudly grumbles, "There's always one."

Juror 8 explains that he has no idea whether the boy is guilty or not, but feels the group owes the youth a few words. He briefly describes the boy's life, a life like that of thousands of New York's disadvantaged youths: he grew up in a slum;

his mother died when he was nine; he spent a few years in an orphanage when his father was in jail; and whenever his father was out of jail, he suffered daily beatings.

The idea that a child of the slums is "owed" a few words enrages one of the jurors, and the battle begins. Prejudices emerge. One juror states that you can't trust "them": they're born liars. An old man takes offense, saying, "Only an ignorant man would believe a thing like that." A stockbroker, speaking in a calm, neutral tone, says, "It's simply a fact that children from slum backgrounds are potential menaces to society." Another juror vehemently agrees, rephrasing the broker's statement in blunter language: "Brother, you can say that again! The kids who crawl out of these places are real trash."

This is an all-male jury, an unusual gathering even in the 1950s. In addition to Juror 8, the group includes a retiree (Joseph Sweeney), an owner of a messenger service (Lee J. Cobb), a house painter (Edward Binns), a marmalade salesman (Jack Warden), an owner of several parking garages (Ed Begley), an immigrant watchmaker (George Voskovec), an advertising executive (Robert Webber), a stockbroker (E. G. Marshall), a neatly attired man who has lived most of his life in a ghetto (Jack Klugman), a blue-collar worker, who describes his job as carrying out the orders of his boss (John Fiedler), and the jury foreman, whose occupation is not identified (Martin Balsam).

Over the course of a day (an hour and a half of screen time), Juror 8 gently raises questions about the evidence. How could the downstairs neighbor, an old man with a limp, get from his bedroom to the apartment door in time to see the boy running? How could he hear the argument and the falling body if the noisy el train was passing, as the woman claimed it was? Could the woman clearly see the murder as she awoke during the night, probably not wearing her glasses? Is the knife really one of a kind? Juror 8 dramatically produces an identical knife, bought in the boy's neighborhood the night before.

One by one, the jurors swing over to join Number 8. The first is the old man, whose astute observations help undermine the "proofs" of the boy's guilt. A gum-chewing, impatient juror, frustrated at the possibility of missing the baseball game that night, changes his vote for no good reason and is chastised by another for his lack of seriousness. He then decides to vote not guilty because he feels there is reasonable doubt. One angry juror goes on a rampage about "them," shocking the rest of the group with his rage and irrationality. One after another, the men leave the table, turning away from the enraged juror and his way of thinking. At the end, the most hostile juror, who wants to "lock those kids up before they cause trouble" and is ready to "pull the switch" of the electric chair, tears up a photo of his estranged son, collapses in sudden self-understanding, and mumbles "not guilty."

Throughout the long discussion, the camera roams around the room, circling the table, exploring the space, closing in on individual jurors, or selecting small groups to focus on. Significantly, Lumet's camera seems as trapped as the jurors themselves. It encounters a blank wall across from the windows, a restrictive barrier with no pictures, no view of the outside, and only a locked door with a bailiff on duty on the other side. We see a wall at the end of the room, which has two doors, marked "Men" and "Women." The camera occasionally follows jurors into the men's washroom, but remains outside the women's room, noting an absence.

After the twelfth not-guilty vote, a touching moment occurs, suggesting the possibility of understanding and generosity within the diverse city of New York. The angry father, who has just torn up his son's picture, sits alone as most of the other men walk out. Juror 8, whose opinions consistently opposed those of the angry man, gently brings him his coat and helps him into it, and the two men leave the room together. The kind of gentleness and understanding that we witness between the two jurors—a connection between a highly educated left-leaning man and a minimally educated right-wing person from a working-class background—can and does occur in New York at times. Lumet implies that it must, if we are not to be a balkanized city, where different communities based on class or ethnic background cannot communicate with each other.

City of Imported Traumas: New York in *The Pawnbroker*

In *12 Angry Men*, Lumet asked whether it is possible for a randomly selected group of white male New Yorkers to produce a fair verdict for a young man from an unidentified poor minority background. The answer was a very cautious yes: with luck, one or more committed, patient citizens can bring out the best in a group that includes hostile, ignorant, indifferent, and thoughtless people. The story, which focuses largely on the transforming effects of the deliberations on the jurors, is told from the perspective of the middle class; the disadvantaged defendant never speaks.

The Pawnbroker is centered in the kind of neighborhood the earlier film's silent defendant might have lived in. The story takes place at ground level, not in a room overlooking the city. The location is Harlem; most of the action occurs at 116th Street and Park Avenue, an area dominated by the shadows and deafening rattle of an elevated train. The residents are predominantly African American and Latino, but the neighborhood also includes a number of whites.

In contrast to *12 Angry Men*, which withheld images of the street life and personal traumas that affected the boy accused of killing his father, *The Pawnbroker* insistently portrays the day-to-day experiences of its protagonist, Sol Nazerman (Rod Steiger). More significantly, the film repeatedly interrupts the ongoing story with intrusive flashes of past events, many of which are shown so briefly that they are at first indecipherable. The viewer is subjected to the involuntary memories that gradually burst into the consciousness of the pawnbroker Nazerman, a Holocaust survivor whose wife and children were killed in a concentration camp. In one sense, *The Pawnbroker* begins where *12 Angry Men* left off. In addressing questions about self-knowledge and social responsibility in relation to civic life in the multi-ethnic and economically mixed metropolis of New York, *The Pawnbroker* delves deeply into the mind of one traumatized man. The film sympathizes with Nazerman because of his horrific suffering and yet demands that he regain his humanity enough to understand his own actions and empathize with the suffering of others.

The Pawnbroker draws some parallels between the catastrophic harm inflicted by the Holocaust and the damage caused by a lifetime of deprivation and injustice in a New York ghetto. Lumet has been accused of equating the two and thus denying the unique horror of the Holocaust. *The Pawnbroker* has also been criticized for its use of Christian symbolism and has been condemned for having a Christian character, whose first name is Jesus, die in an attempt to save the life of the Jewish protagonist. Other criticisms focus on the use of an antisemitic stereotype, a Shylock-like pawnbroker—a modern-day usurer widely hated in poor neighborhoods—and the portrayal of African Americans victimizing their own neighbors. The portrait of blacks victimizing blacks has been seen as doubly offensive: an insult to African Americans and a suggestion, by analogy, that some Jews during the Holocaust assented to the persecution of their own people. When it was first released, the film was condemned by the Catholic Church for its brief nude scenes. Defenders of *The Pawnbroker* argue that Lumet takes on religious and ethnic stereotypes in order to examine and undermine them (see Blake, Boyer, Cunningham, Desser and Friedman, and Rosen 77–117). Most critics shower the film with praise for its courageous exploration of difficult material, its expressionistic imagery, and its innovative editing. *The Pawnbroker* also deserves praise for analyzing an important aspect of life in New York: the traumas that haunt many residents of this city of immigrants and the way these traumas affect people's individual lives and their sense of social responsibility.

The film's premise is that lack of self-knowledge can lead to lack of empathy, which can lead to cruelty and criminal behavior. *The Pawnbroker* examines an extreme case: a Holocaust survivor who deals with his devastating experiences by sealing himself off from all human feeling. Nazerman states that he does not believe in God, art, newspapers, politics, or philosophy—only money. He treats everyone he encounters with coldness and indifference and blinds himself to the fact that some of his income is derived from prostitution, which he calls "filth and horror." Nazerman's suffering is hidden in plain sight: his history is written on his arm, but is indecipherable to many of his fellow New Yorkers, particularly to those who have been deprived of a meaningful education. When the pawnbroker's assistant, Jesus Ortiz (Jaime Sánchez), sees numbers tattooed on the underside of his employer's forearm, he naively asks if they are the mark of "some kind of secret society," and wonders what he would need to do to join. Jesus and his devoted mother do, in a sense, join the society of sufferers at the end of the film, when the young man is shot and killed. Ortiz's heroism is the final event that pulls Nazerman out of his spiritual prison.

Before the credits appear, there are two contrasting family portraits. The first sequence is idyllic: a child's hands reach for, and fail to catch, a butterfly. As the beautiful creature flies away, we see a little girl and then the little boy whose hands first appeared. The children seem to be enjoying the pursuit of the butterfly with little concern about actually catching it. The camera pulls back, and we see a radiant young woman and an old couple relaxing at a picnic, smiling at the children. The old man, presumably the grandfather, wears a yarmulke. The woman joyously calls out to her husband, but in this silent, dream-like sequence, all we hear is the music on the sound track. The camera pans and we see a young Nazerman. He holds out his arms, his children run to him, and he picks them up and playfully swings them around. But suddenly the little boy seems to see something offscreen. His facial expression turns to terror.

Giving us no view of what the boy saw, the film abruptly cuts to an aerial shot of a row of identical houses crowded next to each other along the Long Island Expressway. Fences separate each small backyard from the next and telephone poles protrude from the ground, holding wires that crisscross the area. The camera zooms in on one yard, where an older man (Nazerman again) lies lethargically on a lawn chair. A former professor, he now lives with, and supports, his sister-in-law, her husband, and their two children. The daughter, in her early twenties, carries a loud radio, longs to buy modern Swedish furniture, and torments her brother for drawing pictures of nudes, which she calls "pornography." In a moment that painfully recalls the earlier scene of the butterfly hunt, the sister chases her brother around the fenced-in yard and viciously tears a picture out of his hands. "What happens to the time?" says the mother to Nazerman. "Twenty-five years! Twenty-five years next Thursday. . . . My poor sister Ruth was beautiful like a picture." As she speaks, there are brief flashbacks to the young woman in the picnic scene. The mother quickly gets to her purpose—trying to persuade Sol to finance a family trip to Europe, mentioning the charms of the Old World, its culture and atmosphere. Sol responds, "It's rather a stink if I remember."

The two family scenes contrast a romantic image of life in pre-Holocaust Europe with a depiction of a degraded life in a New York suburb. Or do they? The "stink" Nazerman mentions was clearly already developing in Germany at the time of the picnic, since even the little boy knew enough to be terrified of the Nazis. The idyllic scene seems to refer to a time when the family was already surrounded by a danger that the young father may have chosen to underestimate. Does Nazerman's memory of the picnic involve self-blame about his own judgment? Is it an image of what might have been as much as what actually was? The film indicates only that the picnic represents Nazerman's irreparable loss, a loss experienced by millions of Jews, many of whom live in the haven that opened its streets to these wretched masses, New York.

As the titles appear, we see Nazerman driving into Manhattan. He enters Harlem, the film's third and most important location, and we see indications of

poverty everywhere: trash-strewn vacant lots, apparently unemployed men standing on street corners, and dark shadows cast by the el train. Yet in the middle of
this deprived neighborhood, Lumet also shows hope. Some people sweep their
steps, others sell vegetables, and some seem to be on their way to work. Jesus is
seen leaving for his day at the pawnshop. The energetic young man aspires to success and assimilation (the second, a goal some would question). He tries to teach
his mother English and lovingly promises her that there will be "no more stealing, no more numbers . . . strictly legit."

The pawnshop displays Harlem's desperation and humanity, as people go in
and out, exchanging their possessions for small amounts of cash. A nervous
white man brings in an oratory award; a kind black woman pawns a set of candlesticks, but becomes so concerned about Nazerman's depressive withdrawal
that she forgets her ticket and her two dollars; a self-taught elderly black man
wants to talk with the former professor about Herbert Spencer and Socrates, but
the pawnbroker coldly brushes him aside.

Nazerman is equally rude to the man who controls his business and provides
the income with which he supports his relatives and two other Holocaust
survivors—the local crime boss, Rodriguez (Brock Peters), who is a powerful,
intelligent, and very rich black man in control of brothels and other illegal busi-
nesses. In Edward Lewis Wallant's novel, on which the film is based (see
Cunningham), the crime boss is a Sicilian American named Murillo. Lumet's
changing the ethnicity of this character is one of the most significant departures
from the original text. The director, knowing he would be criticized for portraying a black "heavy," stated that he wanted to avoid the condescending cliché of
all-good black characters depicted as helpless victims (Lumet 13). This black
strongman serves a number of purposes: he represents intra-group violence and
the human tendency to identify with the oppressor. Rodriguez wears a white silk
jacket, lives in an expensive all-white apartment, has a white right-hand man and
a submissive white boyfriend, and clearly enjoys having a white former professor
launder his money for him. Unlike Nazerman, who chooses not to know the
source of his income, and unlike the pawnbroker's relatives in Queens, who
adopt a bland, materialistic American way of life, "forgetting" that Europe is
associated with anything other than Old World culture, Rodriguez is keenly self-
aware. When Nazerman comes to him, shocked to discover the source of the
money he lives on, Rodriguez correctly accuses his underling of self-imposed
blindness. The film's narrative associates Nazerman's inability to see the suffering
around him, and his own role in perpetuating it, with the pawnbroker's absorption in his own excruciating misery. To exemplify this ongoing misery,
Nazerman's pawnshop is designed as a maze of wire enclosures that cast shadows in every direction, seeming to trap the shopkeeper in a cage of his own making. The film's project is to bear witness to Nazerman's gradual escape from

psychic cages and frozen time. The movie traces the man's slow, painful reentry into the world of the living, his rebirth as a New Yorker.

Nazerman's reawakening occurs, against his will, as a result of a series of involuntary memories that are triggered by images and sounds in his environment. The memories are represented by sudden, intrusive intercuts, sometimes referred to as flash frames, flash cuts, or shock cuts. In the early 1960s, when the film was in production, American movies had well established conventions for representing memories. A character gazed off into space or said "I remember when," there was a dissolve, and the earlier scene was shown. Although European directors, such as Alain Renais with *Hiroshima mon amour* (1959) and *Last Year at Marienbad* (1961), had developed other methods of depicting past events that remain alive in the present, their innovations had not made their way into mainstream American film. Lumet credits his innovations in *The Pawnbroker* to his earlier television experience, not to European art films. His editor, Ralph Rosenblum, describes the process of experimentation:

> How long should an initial flash last in order to suggest the percolation of memory? Eight frames, a third of a second, seemed (incredibly) to linger too long. But four frames were impossible to read. Would viewers become irritated by cuts they couldn't make out, or would they experience just the sense of anticipation we wanted?
>
> (Rosenblum and Karen 153)

The first flashes—the most comprehensible and most palatable—are the images of Nazerman's wife, brought on by the sister-in-law's reference to Ruth during the pre-title sequence. The flash cuts will become more and more disturbing as the film continues and Nazerman's most painful repressed memories emerge. At the end of his work day, the pawnbroker takes a last look at his calendar and then walks toward his car. As he dejectedly strolls along the street, we hear the sound of a dog barking. Nazerman seems to glance in the direction of the dog and, as he does, there is a virtually imperceptible flash cut to a man in a Nazi uniform running with a German shepherd. Nazerman continues walking, and there is another cut to the Nazi, this time from a closer angle, and then another (see Boyer for a discussion of the exact length of many of the flashes). The pawnbroker is now shown in close-up, looking directly at something that appears in a following point-of-view shot: a group of youths on the other side of a tall wire mesh fence, beating a boy. The boy, a black teenager, runs to the fence, jumps up, and grabs the wires as the dog continues barking. Then his hands, seen in close-up, begin to slip downward. A sudden cut takes us from this horrifying nocturnal scene to a daytime image of a concentration camp inmate desperately gripping a wire fence, the barbs a few inches above his head. A prolonged flashback, accompanied by the sounds of the barking dog, shows the man slip, fall, and run, desperately calling out "Tessie." He grips the fence again and eventually becomes trapped by the dog's teeth. Brief shots within the flashback show Nazerman, head shaved and a Star of David on his prisoner's uniform, watching the events in agonized horror. Two other prisoners also watch, clearly concerned, but responding far less than Nazerman. A return to the beating in Harlem, inter-cut with two more flashes to the concentration camp, shows the pawnbroker reaching his car as an apparently middle-class black couple walk by the fence close to the beating, paying no attention to the violence. Two more flashes of the prisoner on the fence will appear later when Nazerman visits Tessie (Marketa Kimbrell), the widow of the man caught by the dog—a woman with whom the pawnbroker has a lifeless affair.

Lumet's tour de force is a great cinematic expression of the universality of human cruelty, suffering, and indifference. The sequence finds similarities between the gang beating of a single youth in a poor New York neighborhood and the institutional brutality carried out by the Nazis, but does not imply that the two situations are equal. The images of violence simply ricochet back and forth, each reinforcing the horror of the other. The sequence shows Nazerman's inability to respond to an immediate situation because he is overwhelmed by the memory of an earlier horror. Day-to-day violence in New York, for the pawnbroker, is not nearly as real as the traumas of the past. Nazerman is so affected by his intrusive memory that he almost loses contact with the present; he nearly runs over a pedestrian.

Another sequence of flash cuts is set off by a young, pregnant woman's attempt to pawn her engagement ring, which Nazerman immediately recognizes as glass. Looking in the direction of the girl's ring, Nazerman sees not the young woman's hand, but a pair of hands held against a wire fence. After two more extremely brief flashes of the hands, the flashback becomes a slow pan across a row of hands held against the wire. On the other side of the fence, a helmeted head moves horizontally as a hand reaches over the wire, removing all the rings from the emaciated hands. As with the previous set of flashes, a connection is made between two painful situations with no suggestion that they are equal. The pregnant girl's betrayal by her lover is simply one instance of lying and cruelty, a reminder, to Nazerman, of the systematic violation of truth and human decency that was carried out on a massive, almost unimaginable scale by the Nazis.

The memory flashes become more personal and more disturbing to Nazerman. His assistant's girlfriend (Thelma Oliver), wanting to make extra money for the young couple, offers the pawnbroker a "private session." She undresses, saying, "I'll show you how pretty I am . . . Look . . . Look." During the exchange, Nazerman learns that the girl is a prostitute working for Rodriguez, and is shocked to discover the source of some of his income. The girl continues, "It don't cost you nothin' to look." Nazerman has flashes of himself as a prisoner, face to face with a Nazi guard. The images that force themselves on him are now accompanied by screams, rain, and a taunting voice that says, "Willst du was sehen?" ("Do you want to see something?") The Nazi guard drags the young Nazerman to a door, uses the prisoner's head to break the glass, and makes him watch as his wife is forced to serve as a concentration camp prostitute. This sequence induces a new response in the pawnbroker. Instead of roughly throwing the girl out, as one might expect, Nazerman gently covers her with her coat, hands her an amount of money that surprises her, and allows her to leave, holding his fist to his face and letting out a roar of pain and outrage. For the first time, he seems to make a conscious connection between the humiliation and suffering of a fellow New Yorker and that of his own family. Nazerman is beginning to face the fact that in being complicit with the victimizing Rodriguez, he is himself a victimizer as well as a victim.

The most horrifying memory flashes occur on the subway, after Nazerman has rejected the overtures of a well-meaning woman. The pawnbroker makes eye contact with a thin older man who could be Jewish. Feeling uncomfortable, he leaves his seat, but finds himself looking into the eyes of an older Latino man. Nazerman moves again, but begins having flashes of another train, a cattle car crowded with Jews being transported to an extermination camp. To escape the intrusive memories, he runs to another subway car, but when he looks up he sees an even more disturbing scene, a boxcar that is tightly packed with Jews, who are even more disheveled and desperate than the people in the previous flash. The memory-camera finds a little boy sliding off his father's shoulders as Nazerman's wife, Ruth, calls out, "Sol! Sol, he's falling!" As Alan Rosen points out, the intensity of this memory is indicated by two stylistic departures from the previous flashes: the words are in English, and the triggering present-time scene—the New York subway car—is eerily silent (98). Closer shots show Nazerman struggling to hold onto his son in a cattle car so crowded with people that no one can bend over. Another shot shows the child lying on the floor, surrounded by numerous feet, probably about to be trampled to death. A cut returns us to the New York subway, where Nazerman staggers out of the train. He has two flashes of his son, one showing the child playing at the picnic and the other with him nearly dead on the floor of the cattle car. The subway pulls away and Nazerman reflexively reaches out his hand as if attempting to stop the disappearance of the little boy.

The involuntary recollection, the painful release of another repressed memory, has a further humanizing effect on Nazerman. As he reaches the pawnshop, he encounters Jesus at the locked gate. The boy, who considers himself Nazerman's student and looks upon the older man as a father figure, asks with genuine concern if Nazerman is all right. Rather than rebuffing him, as he had done several times in the past, Nazerman lightly touches the youth's jacket and his face. However, he cannot sustain such tenderness and soon turns on Ortiz again.

The final series of memory images circles back to the film's opening sequence. Significantly, this flashback does not intrude abruptly. It is introduced by means of standard flashback conventions, indicating that the memory is voluntary.

A customer brings in a framed butterfly collection, a number of carefully preserved winged insects under glass, which Nazerman looks at. A slow dissolve overlaps the butterfly collection with the film's opening shot: the boy's hands trying to catch a butterfly. There is a brief replay of the picnic scene, now in normal time and with frightening, ominous music. This repetition includes the shocking image that the family sees: three Nazis arriving with guns. Before Nazerman can respond to his memory, there is a cut to three petty gangsters entering the shop to rob the safe. Nazerman's assistant is collaborating with them.

Jesus Ortiz, who has become increasingly attached to his employer, is also tempted by quick money. After being brushed off by Nazerman somewhat earlier, he agreed to work with the three thieves on the condition that there would be no guns, no shooting, no harm done to his boss. However, during the hold-up one of the young men (who is white) pulls out a gun and threatens the pawnbroker. Ortiz rushes in, throws himself at the gunman, and is shot. He crawls to the street, where Nazerman, shaken and horrified, looks down and sees the boy lying on the ground as he saw his own son lying on the floor of the boxcar in the memory flash. This time there is no crowding, and the pawnbroker bends down. He holds Ortiz's head in his hands, and the dying boy apologizes for the robbery: "I said no shootin.' I said no to hurt you." Finally, Nazerman can no longer escape his own pain. He opens his mouth to cry out, but no sound emerges. He stares at his bloody hands and staggers into the pawnshop, where he sits on his chair behind the counter. Directly in front of him is the receipt spike, standing about eight inches tall, topped with a sharp point. Nazerman is flooded with images of the people he has hurt over the last few days: the pregnant girl with the fake engagement ring, the old man who simply wanted to talk, the woman with the candlesticks, a young man with an oratory award, a woman who tried to befriend him, his part-time lover Tessie, and Jesus. He pushes his left hand down on the spike, piercing his palm with the object that held the records of his insulting small loans to the desperate.

The pawnbroker's extraordinary gesture, which is original to the film, invites numerous interpretations. In an interview, Lumet associates the stigmata-like piercing with other Christian aspects of the story—the name Nazerman, "which is so close to Nazareth," the young boy's sacrifice, and the fact that Jesus Ortiz is "in love with a whore"—but provides no explanation for his inclusion of the gesture (Rapf 183). The incident has been criticized—understandably—for associating Nazerman with sacrificial and redemptive concepts of Christianity. However, if the hand piercing is seen as a reference to death on a cross, it could also recall the crucifixion of thousands of Jews, one of whom was Jesus of Nazareth, by the Romans, and the slaughter of Jews, in the twentieth century, by equally cruel means.

Nazerman's self-inflicted wound hangs in the air as an image that carries a number of religious associations. More important than any of these, however, is the simple fact that Nazerman has punished himself for his insensitivity to others; he has forced himself to feel physical pain, which shatters his psychic numbness; and he has expressed solidarity with the racially and religiously mixed group of New Yorkers who have surrounded him for years. The pawnbroker seems to be moving toward regaining his humanity.

As Quincy Jones's jazz score fills the sound track, eliminating any possible sentimentality, Nazerman walks out of his shop, past the three balls identifying his profession, and onto the sidewalk. He stares again at his blood-stained hands, leaves his gates unlocked, and walks down a New York street with no particular destination in mind.

"Who Can Trust a Cop That Don't Take Money?": The NYPD in *Serpico* and *Q & A*

For all its concentration on morality, order and chaos, and social responsibility, *The Pawnbroker* was concerned with internalized traumas and their effects on behavior and did not engage in an examination of the police. At the end of the film, when Jesus Ortiz is shot, the police arrive promptly, do their job gently and efficiently, and drive away. In other films, however, Lumet focuses intensively on the police institution, police procedure, and the relationship between police officers and moral obligation, and typically the cops do not get off lightly. Is New York a city where we can trust the police to protect the people and follow the law? Or is the only trust, in relation to the NYPD, the agreement among officers to cover up each others' crimes? Lumet traces his absorption with this issue to his childhood on the Lower East Side, where injustice was part of daily life. When asked why he made several films about cops, lawyers, and hoods in New York, he answered, with characteristic honesty:

> In truth, I don't know. I know one generalized sociological answer, which is if a justice system isn't working, a democracy can't work. OK, but that's intellectual. Clearly, the question makes total sense because I keep coming to it again and again and again. There's something in that whole life that draws me in.
>
> (Goldberg 159)

Even in *12 Angry Men* there is a brief reference to police brutality. Juror 8 states that the accused teenager claimed the police threw him down a flight of stairs. The claim is never discussed, since there were no witnesses to corroborate the boy's version of events. Lumet's interest in police violence is put on hold; it emerges in later films.

Serpico and *Q & A* are both close analyses of the NYPD. Each film is centered around a prototypical Lumet hero: an innocent "little guy" taking on a huge corrupt system. Ironically, *Serpico*, which is closely based on real events, has a relatively optimistic ending, whereas the later movie, based on a novel, ends in pessimism. In each film, a young, idealistic hero—a cop (Al Pacino) in *Serpico* and a new assistant district attorney and former cop (Timothy Hutton) in *Q & A*—turns to a trusted older man for guidance. Serpico's courageous and extremely dangerous attempts to bring about change within the police department are constantly stonewalled, even when he goes to the mayor's office. However, when he eventually approaches the *New York Times*, supported by another officer and an Inspector, the end result is the creation of the Knapp Commission, a massive outside investigation of police corruption ordered by the mayor of New York. Even though Serpico is shot and seriously injured, and is last seen sitting alone with his dog on a New York dock waiting for a ship to take him out of the country, we know that the historic cop and the hero of the movie brought about significant change in New York's police system. In *Q & A*, on the other hand, the findings of the young assistant D.A. lead his mentor, at the end of the film, to conclude, "It's too big. We'll bury it," a conclusion that the young man accepts. The film ends with the implication that corruption is a permanent part of the NYPD.

Both portraits of New York and its police department ring true. As Lumet has said, the city "can be so many things" (Goldberg 158). Both films also reflect the spirit of the Left in their respective eras of production. In 1973, public outrage at the Vietnam War was taking effect, and the Watergate investigation, sparked by a night guard's call to the local Washington, D.C., police department, was on its way to forcing the resignation of President Richard Nixon. By 1990, after eight years of the conservative Ronald Reagan administration and the election of another Republican, George Bush, the Left was discouraged and the country seemed more interested in money than integrity in government.

New York is a city where "real life," media events, and fiction movies constantly interpenetrate. New Yorkers encounter famous film stars on the streets and in theaters and restaurants; we watch directors, actors, and technicians shoot movies in our neighborhoods; and we witness live events that we later watch on national television. When Lumet's *Serpico* was released in 1973, most New Yorkers, and many other Americans, were familiar with the real Frank Serpico. We had followed newspaper and television coverage of the courageous cop's testimony before the Knapp Commission, and many of us had read Peter Maas's best seller, *Serpico*, which filled us in on the details.

Now, more than thirty years later, Frank Serpico is still a household name in New York. As depicted in the film, Serpico was shot in the face during a drug raid after testifying. It is widely believed that his fellow officers set up the incident, sending Serpico into danger, standing back themselves, and not calling for help immediately after the shooting. Serpico spent a decade in Europe hiding, recovering, and studying, and then quietly returned to the United States in the eighties, living in an undisclosed location in the countryside. In 1997, after two highly publicized cases of police misconduct in New York—the brutal torture of Abner Louima in the men's room of a police station and the shooting of Amadou

Diallo—Serpico made public appearances demanding independent investigations. He continues to speak out, criticizing the Patriot Act, police brutality, and corruption in Washington.

Lumet's Serpico is often unrealistic and occasionally self-pitying, but never less than virtuous. When first seen onscreen, his face bears a striking resemblance to renaissance images of the crucified Jesus: the face is young, handsome, bearded, surrounded by disheveled long dark hair, and covered with blood.

After an initial flash forward to the wounded Serpico, Lumet's film takes us to the young man's graduation from the New York Police Academy and his gradual introduction to police corruption. The police misconduct that Serpico discovers begins with free lunches in exchange for leniency on double parking and then quickly progresses to careless investigations, brutalization of suspects, cozy deals with drug barons, violent shakedowns of gamblers who fall behind in their monthly payments to the police, and finally to an intricate network of payoffs and cover-ups that involves all levels of the police force and even retired cops. One killing is mentioned but not shown: a cop proudly tells Serpico that the police extorted $120,000 from a drug dealer and then shot him.

The portrait of corruption in the NYPD that emerged in the Knapp Commission hearings and the Lumet film may have shocked the city and the nation in the 1970s, but it is benign compared to the violence depicted in *Q & A*. Here, there is no slow progression from petty crime to high-level corruption. In the opening scene, a sadistic cop, Captain Lt. Mike Brennan (Nick Nolte), shoots an unarmed Latino man at point blank, puts a gun into the dead victim's hand, and roughly drags two men over to the body as witnesses. A few minutes later, we see Brennan regaling an admiring group of officers with tales of his exploits: throwing a "guinea cock-sucker" out a window, forcing the man to use his own feces to give fingerprints, and roughing up some "niggers." Forced to investigate it, the chief of the Homicide Bureau of the District Attorney's office, Kevin Quinn (Patrick O'Neal), considers the shooting a "cut and dry" case of self-defense: the Latino drug dealer is "vermin" and Brennan is one of the city's finest cops. Quinn assigns the case to a young, inexperienced assistant D.A., Aloysius "Al" Reilly (Hutton), the son of a highly respected policeman who died in the line of duty.

Over the course of the film, we learn that Quinn has a history of violence, racism, and antisemitism, and that Brennan is his hit man. The mob, politicians, the D.A.'s office, and the police are all involved in a complex net of deals, double deals, and several murders. There are only two honest cops in the film: a black officer whom Brennan calls "the whitest nigger I ever knew" (Charles S. Dutton) and a Puerto Rican (Luis Guzmán). At the end of the film, the courageous black policeman, shot by Brennan, is struggling for his life, and the Puerto Rican, having killed Brennan in a shootout inside the police station, is expected to move to the suburbs. The young D.A.'s wise and honest confidant, a man who spent thirty years in the D.A.'s office himself, knows that the evidence that could convict

Quinn has been destroyed. It's best, he tells the young Reilly, to just bury the whole thing. "How about all those bodies?" the devastated Reilly asks. "A bunch of fags and spics" in the drug trade, the older man says, deliberately using language that reflects the thinking of many New Yorkers. "It's just a normal Saturday night in the city. Most people will feel good riddance." Besides, he adds, "You can't afford this. I can't. And, God knows, the Department can't." The innocent Reilly, it turns out, is not entirely untainted himself. He failed to report a partner, from his police days, who took bribes. And his posthumously decorated father, whose pension supports Reilly's mother, also accepted small amounts of dirty money.

Q & A's story is dark, and the film's lighting and images are equally bleak and disturbing. Many scenes occur at night, when the background seems pitch black and the lit areas have the eerie glow of headlights or colored traffic lights. The character who dominates the screen is Brennan, an oversized man often shot from low angles to emphasize his threatening bulk. Conveying violence in every subtle movement of his body, Nolte's Brennan seems to embody all that is frightening about New York. When not murdering someone, he is often threatening or spying on one of his victims. His homophobic attraction-repulsion response to gays and transvestites makes him especially dangerous to them. On one occasion, in public, he reaches under the skirt of a transvestite streetwalker and grabs the man's penis and testicles, twisting them as he demands information. Another time, he unzips his fly, orders a gay man in a flimsy bathrobe to turn around, and then strangles the man to death. Brennan is the nightmare of every New Yorker who is not straight and white, and the shame of the entire city. Q & A realistically allows him to go unpunished. At his death, the police department announces the demise of a heroic cop who had a nervous breakdown.

The film ends with a scene that feels as if it is tacked on to give a slightly upbeat note. Lumet takes us far away from New York, to a Caribbean island where Reilly has tracked down the woman he loves. He sits next to her on a beach, declares his everlasting devotion, and promises to wait as long as necessary if she thinks she will ever take him back. In following a straight couple to a tropical island, focusing on a romantic relationship, and leaving the city behind with its racism, homophobia, and violence, the film seems to give up on New York. In voiceover as he boards a boat, Reilly says that he knows he has to fight back, he just doesn't know where to start: "Maybe I just gotta start with myself." He wants to get beyond his own involuntary racism which, years ago, led him to look shocked when he met his lover's black father. Reilly's personal goal is noble; it is in keeping with ideas about the significance of unconscious biases, which Lumet conveyed in The Pawnbroker. However, at the end of Q & A, it functions as a distraction from the pressing issues that the film depicts.

The tone of these films progresses from relatively optimistic to very pessimistic. In 2001, Lumet returned to a location only a few doors away from the courthouse setting of 12 Angry Men to make the television series "100 Centre

Street." In 2006, shortly before turning eighty-two, he released a new film dealing with old concerns—crime and the court. *Find Me Guilty*, set in New York and Bayonne, New Jersey, focuses on the story of mobster Jackie DiNorscio (Vin Diesel), who represented himself in his twenty-one-month trial for drug dealing. Over time, Sidney Lumet has chosen material that digs more and more deeply into the corruption of his favorite city, but he has never lost his love of New York or his fascination with it.

A New York real estate coup of monumental proportions: the real building (The Dakota) that is the fictional home to the Woodhouses and the Castevets in *Rosemary's Baby* (Roman Polanski, William Castle Productions, 1968). Digital frame enlargement.

Urban Irrational

ROSEMARY'S BABY, POLANSKI,
NEW YORK

JOE McELHANEY

Dream Space and Broom Closet

Near the end of *Rosemary's Baby* (1968), a terrified and extremely pregnant Rosemary Woodhouse (Mia Farrow) is on the run from her obstetrician, Dr. Sapirstein (Ralph Bellamy), and her elderly New York City neighbors, Minnie and Roman Castevet (Ruth Gordon and Sidney Blackmer). She believes that these people are witches who want to take possession of her as-yet-unborn child for some kind of evil sacrifice and that her husband, Guy (John Cassavetes), is complicit with them. She seeks refuge with Dr. Hill (Charles Grodin), her obstetrician prior to Sapirstein, and Hill promises to admit Rosemary into Mount Sinai Hospital. She is so relieved at Hill's graciousness in this matter (a false graciousness, it turns out, as he will immediately betray her) that she tells Hill she will take whatever space that Mount Sinai can offer her: "Anything they've got. Even a broom closet would be fine."

While referring in this instance to a hospital room, Rosemary's desperate cry is one that evokes the longing of so many New Yorkers (and, indeed, many residents of overpopulated, bursting-at-the-seams cities, from London to San Francisco to Tokyo) living and moving about in an urban environment of overwhelming size but continually facing the prospect of cramped home quarters. Within these worlds, one is willing to accept any interior space provided it allows for a roof over the head. Rosemary's ecstasy over the possibility of taking shelter in this manner stands in contrast to her attitude at the beginning of the film, as she and Guy are first shown what she believes will be a dream residence for the two young marrieds: a spacious, rent-controlled apartment on Manhattan's Upper West Side. This apartment consists of four rooms in a historical building given the fictional name The Bramford but which in its exterior is clearly identifiable as the legendary Dakota, constructed in 1884 and one of the first major apartment buildings in New York City.[1] What the middle-class Rosemary and Guy walk into is, as any New Yorker would immediately recognize, a real estate coup of monumental proportions, one that can immediately inspire envy if not outright resentment from many residents of the city. However, this vast apartment, this dream space, quickly becomes for Rosemary a site of nightmare, one of enclosure and oppression in which finally a hospital broom closet, by contrast, seems more appealing if not more spacious.

The treatment of New York City space in *Rosemary's Baby*, especially its interiors, is central to this essay and situated in relation to two connecting issues. The first is the film's relationship to New York City history, both the immediate historical moment in which the film was made and the larger history of the city itself, particularly in terms of the late nineteenth and early twentieth centuries. The second is the film's representation of New York as filtered through the sensibility of its director, Roman Polanski. And here a paradox immediately presents itself. Directing his first Hollywood film on American soil, Polanski does not self-consciously attempt to transform the project into an American version of the type of European art film with which his reputation was initially established. *Rosemary's Baby* is a film in which, as Polanski has often claimed, he submitted himself to a process of scrupulously faithful adaptation, in this case that of a best-selling novel by Ira Levin. As anyone familiar with Polanski's body of work surely recognizes, however, the final result is not one in which the European auteur becomes the Hollywood director-for-hire, turning out a genre product (although as a genre film *Rosemary's Baby* certainly does not disappoint). Instead, we have a film in which the auteur uncannily recognizes his own preoccupations through another text, a strategy Polanski will repeat in varying ways throughout much of his later career. Hence there is no need to transform and alter a novel that simply confirms Polanski's own concerns. As we see, however, Polanski's fidelity in this matter was not as total as has sometimes been claimed, and the alterations and deletions to Levin's novel are often as interesting as what was retained.

In the most significant change from Levin's novel, Polanski transformed the ending, not so much its dramatic content as its tone and style. In Levin's novel, Rosemary is told by Sapirstein and her husband that her baby died not long after its birth. She does not believe this and, hearing the sound of a baby crying in the Castevet apartment next door, surreptitiously enters that apartment through a closet that connects the two apartments. She eventually comes across the Castevets and all of their friends gathered around her baby, who is not only alive but whose father, in reality, is not Guy but Satan himself. Polanski has stated that, as an agnostic, he simply could not unconditionally accept Levin's ending since "the whole idea conflicted with my rational view of the world." Consequently, in the second half of the film up to this moment, the possibility that the Castevets are satanic worshippers with evil designs on her unborn child is nothing more than the paranoid delusions of Rosemary's pre-partum hysteria: "That is why a thread of deliberate ambiguity runs throughout the film" (Polanski, *Roman* 265). The film's final sequence neither confirms nor denies this possibility but instead suggests that what we are observing may be simply a dream of Rosemary's, the last in a series of dreams we see her having over the course of the film. If this is the case, though, we never see her wake; and the style of this final dream sequence is not quite of the same order as the earlier ones, which are much more clearly separated out from the main sections of the narrative. In not releasing his spectators at the end of *Rosemary's Baby*, Polanski creates a film in which everything is marked by an indeterminacy, caught between two positions explicitly stated at different points by Rosemary herself: "There are no witches. Not really"; and: "There *are* plots against people, aren't there?" A question the film implicitly raises but never firmly answers is: Which of these two positions is the rational one?

Levin was a native of New York and his novel is filled with constant references to city landmarks and stores, restaurants, and theaters, the kinds of details that repeatedly display the author's intimate knowledge of the city. Polanski, of course, was not a native New Yorker and, to my knowledge, never lived there. The general outline of his life story has been told repeatedly: a native of Kraków, Polanski's childhood was dominated by the Nazi occupation of Poland during the Second World War. His mother was exterminated in a concentration camp and his father and sister were sent to the camps as well, although both managed to survive. Polanski himself escaped Kraków before his inevitable deportation and lived in hiding, most often with Roman Catholic families, in the Polish countryside. After the war, he eventually came to study film at the Polish Film School at Lodz. It was there that he learned, among other things, the value of a certain rigorous craftsmanship in filmmaking. It is also this kind of film school training that allowed Polanski (temporarily, as it would turn out) to adapt himself to Hollywood and to a production system that likewise places strong value on craftsmanship. The Polanski legend, however, is one in which the director surpasses Hollywood in his command of technique, becoming a craftsman who knows more than his casts and crews about putting a film together. He becomes yet another European autocrat in Hollywood, precisely controlling every formal aspect of his films in a manner that often rubs against the more relaxed collaborative and union-dominated Hollywood method. On the set of *Rosemary's Baby* he repeatedly clashed with Cassavetes, arguably the central American director of this period in forging a new kind of filmmaking style that shatters the model of craftsmanship to which Polanski's cinema is so beholden. Cassavetes's 1961 debut film *Shadows* could not offer a more diametrically opposed view of New York than *Rosemary's Baby*, with its improvised, hand-held and grainy, 16 mm look and with the actors seemingly determining the movements and placements of the camera.

But Polanski is no less "personal" a filmmaker than Cassavetes. In spite of the manner in which much of Polanski's cinema owes a debt to genre and to the sensibility of the writers whose work he adapts or with whom he collaborates, his cinema has often been seen to continually rework and displace elements of his traumatic childhood onto the situations depicted in his films. Moreover, it is a cinema in which the formal manipulation of elements is of the highest order, as he displays an absolute shot-by-shot control over narrative material that nevertheless repeatedly returns to the topics of violence, fear, and the irrational. Polanski's famous fanaticism for detail in terms of mise-en-scène is central to the experience of *Rosemary's Baby*, a film in which almost every detail within the image carries potential meaning but in which rigorous form masks and controls something that may be fundamentally beyond control.

I am not suggesting that *Rosemary's Baby* should be seen as some kind of allegory about the Holocaust. In fact, Polanski did not use a line of dialogue from the book in which one of Rosemary's friends, distraught over her appalling physical appearance at the hands of Sapirstein, compares her to a concentration camp victim. Nevertheless, the treatment of New York in the film is one that is often informed by an experience of urban space shaped by that traumatic historical moment. Rosemary is part of a long line of Polanski characters who are fugitives or exiles from their own cultures, hiding out in broom closets until the inevitable knock on the door arrives. Urban space in Polanski, be it New York, Los Angeles, London, Paris, or Warsaw, becomes something that defies anonymity: no matter how one attempts to hide, one can always be found. In this manner, *Rosemary's Baby* is very specifically about New York but also about the general concept and experience of urban space in relation to the twentieth century.

In certain respects, however, *Rosemary's Baby* is a typical Hollywood film emerging after the official end of the traditional studio system in the early 1960s and just before the emergence of the much-sentimentalized New Hollywood of the 1970s. Only its exteriors were shot on location, over a period of two weeks. All of the interiors were done on the Paramount lot in California, over the much longer period of twelve weeks, a common practice for the handling of locations on many Hollywood films, particularly beginning in the 1950s. The interior apartment spaces were built to scale by production designer Richard Sylbert, and Polanski's fastidiousness in terms of detail clearly manifests itself throughout the film in the miraculous sense of verisimilitude for the rendering of these interiors. "The real star of the picture," Polanski would later write, "would be the New York apartment where Rosemary and Guy go to live" (*Roman* 267). Furthermore, the presence of Old Hollywood is given almost continuous flesh-and-blood presence through the brilliant casting of the supporting players, many of whom were famous character actors from the heyday of the traditional studio system: Ruth Gordon and Sidney Blackmer, Ralph Bellamy, Elisha Cook Jr. as Micklas, and Patsy Kelly as Laura-Louise. Rosemary herself is played by an actress whose parents were important figures out of Hollywood's past: the director John Farrow and the actress Maureen O'Sullivan, while Farrow herself was married to Frank Sinatra at the time shooting on the film began. (He divorced her during the shoot.)

If, among other things, *Rosemary's Baby* is a film about New York City as seen through the eyes of Polanski's distinctly Eastern European sensibility, it also has as its female protagonist someone else who looks at New York from the position of an outsider. If one is to read the film literally as one in which, as Rosemary cries out when she is being raped by Satan, "This is no dream. This is really happening," then Rosemary as the victim of collective evil forces is fairly clear. But the film also suggests another possibility. Rosemary is from Omaha, and while Omaha is not a small town the name itself evokes a certain kind of midwestern provincialism. (In the novel, Minnie is from Oklahoma, a detail eliminated in the film.) What happens to the ever-so-slightly lapsed Catholic Rosemary is the type of literal horror story that confirms the most paranoid fears of small-town Christian America in relation to New York—that it is a dirty and decadent city filled with non-Christians, a breeding ground for evil, and a place in which young, innocent females are ultimately compromised if not destroyed: George Loane Tucker's extraordinary 1913 melodrama *Traffic in Souls*, in which innocent young women arrive in New York City only to be quickly sold into "white slavery," is one of the cinema's classic early examples of this attitude. But Polanski's decision to allow "a thread of deliberate ambiguity" to run through *Rosemary's Baby* allows the film to operate on at least two levels in its depiction of New York: as a film that confirms these essentially reactionary attitudes about New York, or as an elaborate parody of these same attitudes, since we view much of New York's alleged horror through the possibly paranoid provincialism of Rosemary, placing the film among the most darkly humorous of all screen comedies. Visually, the film works on both these levels. The highly restricted focalization of the narrative through Rosemary's point of view, the use of wide-angle shooting, the unusually tight framing of the actors in the foregrounds of shots, and the frequent use of a hand-held camera create an enclosed, paranoid environment.[2] But much of the film takes place in bright sunlight and is designed in vivid primary colors, a style that would be more appropriate for a formulaic New York comedy like *Barefoot in the Park*, released by Paramount a year earlier and starring Polanski's original choice for the role of Guy, Robert Redford.

If *Rosemary's Baby* is among the most memorable of all New York City films, it is also one in which very little of the city itself is actually shown. Polanski displays no wide-eyed tourist's wonder toward Manhattan. Even when the camera is taken to the streets, his tendency is to shoot very close to the actors, often with a hand-held camera, so that some of the city's more famous locations (Radio City Music Hall, Tiffany's, the 21 Club) have to be glimpsed behind or around the actors as they walk. The one major exception here is the spectacular opening shot, which begins as a very simple right-to-left panning movement across the skyline as viewed from some type of rooftop expanse on the Upper West Side. As the camera begins its languid pan, a slow reverse zoom, at first almost imperceptible, also begins revealing Central Park situated between the east and west sides of Manhattan. Again almost imperceptibly, the camera begins to descend through a slow tilt down to a group of Upper West Side apartment buildings, the descent briefly making an almost C-shaped form, tilting down even further as the zoom more forcefully continues to reverse until we find ourselves looking at the outside front of the Dakota from a steep, overhead perspective as two tiny human figures are seen entering the front door of the building—Rosemary and Guy, as we discover in the next shot. In its continuously shifting and unstable perspective and its marginalization of the human figure, this shot (in its comparatively modest way) evokes the atmosphere of the work of structural filmmakers of the period, such as Ernie Gehr and Michael Snow, in whose films the space of New York interiors and exteriors occasionally assumes central roles: the loft of Snow's 1967 *Wavelength* or the New York street shot from a ground-floor window of Gehr's 1971 *Still*.

Furthermore, the opening shot itself prepares us for many of the concerns of the film to follow: the contrast between old and new, past and present, as the more modern buildings we see at the beginning of the shot begin to give way to the gothic, nineteenth-century look of the buildings that come into view as the shot develops; the contrast between the urban and the natural, in this case the controlled natural setting of Central Park sprouting up in the midst of the Manhattan skyline; and the increasing sense of unease, at once seductive and terrifying, produced by the camera as it evolves from a slow pan (already slightly "off" since the movement is right to left rather than the more "normal" left to right) into the reverse zoom precariously balanced from an improbably high and decidedly authorial angle. Does the camera at the end of this shot represent God watching Guy and Rosemary as they enter The Bramford? Does it represent the Devil? Or does it signify nothing more than what it already clearly is, a detached and agnostic camera viewing the inevitable from an extreme and dispassionate point of view?

Luxury Apartment and Tenement Flat

For horrific experiences like Rosemary's to take place essentially within the confines of her apartment house taps into a late-nineteenth-century site of anxiety about the very nature of urban life: the tenement flat. In Vincente Minnelli's *Meet Me in St. Louis* (1944), set in 1903, the middle-class Smith family reacts with horror at the prospect of moving to New York, where only "rich people live in houses" and everyone else lives in "flats, hundreds of flats all in one building." The construction of apartment buildings in New York in the late nineteenth century marked the beginning of the haute bourgeoisie living in a shared or collective space, removing the stigma of the flat or tenement. Spaces like The Dakota offered the luxury and spaciousness of a private home but within the more convenient framework of the large, urban building with numerous modern conveniences. By the time of *Rosemary's Baby*, however, these once-luxurious spaces often found themselves cut up into much smaller units, and this is the case with the Woodhouse and Castevet apartments (see Sanders 204–06). A once-grand space now divided into something smaller obviously connotes a faded grandeur and becomes an awkward cross between the quiet privacy and luxury of the turn-of-the-century apartment and the noisy chaos of the early-twentieth-century tenement. The Castevets are not simply neighbors but are, as Guy puts it, "across the wall." This wall, through which Rosemary and Guy can clearly hear Minnie and Roman talking, allows them unwitting eavesdropping while also creating a sense of enclosure and claustrophobia. Even in a large apartment like the Woodhouse's, there is no firm sense of privacy. While the apartment building neighbors in a later Polanski film, the Kafkaesque *The Tenant* (1976), set in Paris, are portrayed as consistently hostile, oppressive, and quite literally destructive toward a protagonist (played by Polanski himself) who eventually goes insane and jumps out his window, Rosemary's neighbors achieve similar results through a much more insidious transparency. In either case, the vision we have of urban and apartment living in Polanski is one in which the collective assumes a wholly negative cast. Moreover, the needs of the collective invariably assume precedence over the needs of the individual, who may attempt to flee but must finally either be destroyed by the collective (as in *The Tenant*) or acquiesce and become, however reluctantly, a member of the forces of her own oppression. Rosemary finally chooses the latter, if only within a dream.

While shot in 1968, *Rosemary's Baby* is set in the very recent past: 1965–66. Essentially we are dealing with an interim period in American history not long after the end of the glamorous "Camelot" years of the Kennedy administration (two of Rosemary's dreams involve the Kennedys) and just before the major social and political upheavals of the last part of the decade. Within the context of New York history, this likewise places the film within a crucial moment of transition from the relatively benign years of Mayor Robert F. Wagner Jr. to the more tumultuous administration of John Lindsay. The final years of Wagner's third administration had already begun to show signs of a New York evolving toward the image that would come to predominate during Lindsay's administration and over the next three decades, that of a crime- and drug-ridden urban jungle utterly lacking in a sense of community, one in which chaos and confusion seemed to be the order of the day: Jules Feiffer's 1967 play *Little Murders*, adapted into a film in 1971, captures this attitude perfectly. Moreover, New York became a city in the midst of a major economic crisis, one in which urban decay was everywhere visible. Polanski makes no direct reference to any of these political and social changes but instead allows for a general cultural attitude about the city to seep into the look and feel of his film. During roughly the same period (1963–66), Pennsylvania Station, a masterpiece of early-twentieth-century architecture, was in the process of being torn down, and there was an increased melancholia as well as anger about the destruction of the city's historical landmarks in favor of sterile and modern "improvements" epitomized by the work of Robert Moses over the preceding three decades. Historical apartment buildings like the fictional Bramford were often being threatened by this vision of an ever newer New York. At one point in Levin's novel, Guy makes a passing reference to the closing of the 1965 Broadway musical *Skyscraper*, in which the female protagonist, played by Julie

Harris, unsuccessfully fights to preserve her brownstone against the onslaught of urban development. As in *Rosemary's Baby*, that play's narrative is dotted with the female character's dreams. What the film shows us in The Bramford is not the carefully preserved and maintained fortress world of the actual Dakota, with its celebrity-filled co-operative tenants—Leonard Bernstein lived there; John Lennon died on the sidewalk outside, on his way home—but a building in a state of ruin, populated entirely (so far as the film shows us) by elderly people. The wide-angle close-ups of Minnie, in particular, emphasize her heavily lined and wrinkled face, caked with grotesque make-up, an embodied extension of the rotting old Bramford and rotting old New York.

The one major historical event of 1965–66 cited by the film is the pope's visit to Yankee Stadium, which is shown on the television in Rosemary and Guy's apartment and also discussed during a dinner the Woodhouses have with Minnie and Roman. Roman's atheistic dismissal of the pope extends to a blanket dismissal of religion in general. For Roman, they are "all show biz."[3] *Rosemary's Baby* is a film in which the presence of the New York theatrical scene looms very large even though we actually see nothing of it. There are no visits to the theater, not even a glimpse of Times Square.[4] While Levin's novel is filled with references to the immediate theatrical world of New York in 1965–66 (Levin is a playwright as well as a novelist), Polanski significantly pares down much of this while still retaining the novel's theatrical thrust. When Rosemary keeps staring at a young woman named Theresa in the laundry room at The Bramford, it is because she mistakes her for a famous actress. Guy is a struggling actor, although all we see of his acting is in a TV commercial for a motorcycle. Above his head in bed is a copy of *The Theatre of Revolt*, Robert Brustein's analysis of modern playwrights who were intent upon attacking the values of their respective audiences. And when Rosemary attempts to rest in the midst of her menstrual cycle, she settles in with a copy of Sammy Davis Jr.'s autobiography, *Yes, I Can* (a recently published and best-selling memoir by one of Farrow's husband's closest associates). The strongest contemporary theater citations are of the two plays Guy has appeared in, John Osborne's *Luther* (significantly, a play about Martin Luther and the Protestant Reformation) and Ronald Alexander's innocuous and now largely forgotten comedy, *Nobody Loves an Albatross*.

But the most vivid sense of the New York theatrical world emerges through discussions initiated by Roman, who claims to have been the son of a turn-of-the-century Broadway producer who worked with such figures as Forbes-Robertson, Modjeska, and Minnie Fiske. These names evoke an almost forgotten and dusty New York theater world (Guy has never even heard of Forbes-Robertson), one which was at its height during the period when buildings like The Bramford were being constructed. New York theater becomes part of this repressed history of the city. But since it is associated with Roman by way of his father (who, we later discover, was probably not a theatrical producer but a man named Adrian Marcato, accused of being a witch), a linkage between theater and the devil is also established, forming part of the puritanical fabric underpinning Rosemary's hysteria. In a supremely ironic coincidence (which has its source in Levin's novel), the possible head of a satanic cult in *Rosemary's Baby* shares a combination of—and variation on—Polanski's and Cassavetes's names: Roman Castevet. Roman plays Mephistopheles to Guy's Faust, weaving tales of New York theatrical history to him while also flattering him: he claims to have seen Guy in *Luther*, remembering a gesture Guy performed. Roman implicitly seduces Guy into betraying his wife for the sake of the Devil and his followers in exchange for Guy having a major career. Indeed, most of the elderly actors in the supporting cast had illustrious stage careers, especially Gordon, Blackmer, and Bellamy, and they approach their roles with a highly theatrical relish. Maurice Evans, who portrays Rosemary's friend Hutch, likewise had a major stage career but by 1968 he would have been best known to American audiences for his occasional appearances as the father of the witch Samantha on the TV sitcom "Bewitched," a show that domesticated and suburbanized American witches. These actors turn the material into something at once deadly serious (given the intensity with which they devote themselves to it) and borderline camp, as though the entire exercise is a theatrical and playful lark, perhaps not all that far from "Bewitched" itself.

The Old and the New

When Rosemary and Guy first visit The Bramford, they pause as they walk down a hallway toward their future apartment to look at a section of the floor where there are missing tiles. What we see where the tiles are absent is not a concrete or wooden floor but a kind of soil which seems to be emerging, as though the natural world is beginning to reclaim this building, returning it to the mire from which it originally sprang. As soon as Rosemary and Guy move into their apartment, they immediately begin painting things yellow and white in an attempt to open up the space with bright colors. But this is also just as clearly an attempt to repress and paint over the past, to remove traces of the old woman who had lived there for so many years, a Mrs. Gardenia, who grew herbs and lived amongst clutter and darkness. While a central aspect of the myth of New York has been that it is an urban space perpetually driven toward destroying the old in order to make way for the new, a city for the young rather than the old, the fight for the preservation of its architectural past has also been part of its more recent history. (It is Jacqueline Kennedy, appearing briefly in one of Rosemary's dreams, who will later become the central figure in the preservation of Grand Central Station.) Nevertheless, this necessary preservation of the past also embalms it as a museum-like spectacle: the past cleaned up for contemporary consumption. By contrast, the New York we see in *Rosemary's Baby* is neither urban utopia nor urban nightmare but closer to a surrealist vision of a city in which the repressed continually rises to the surface of things, a city of off-kilter details. It is Rosemary who is most privy to noticing these details: the pictures that have been removed by the Castevets in their apartment, leaving only dusty outlines where the frames had once been; the Castevets' dinner service with plates that do not fully match; or the dirty, stain-marked area in Mrs. Gardenia's apartment where her secretary desk had once been positioned before she moved it to block the closet connecting her apartment with that of the Castevets. Does Rosemary succeed in noticing such details because she possesses unusually acute insight, far more than her husband? Or is such insight far too refined and delicate, too vulnerable to lapsing into paranoid hysteria? When Rosemary is about to go into labor and is being sedated by Sapirstein, she screams that she wants to be taken to Doctors' Hospital, where everything is "clean and sterile." For Polanski, however, the unsterile Bramford is fascinating precisely because its age is visible and because, like the human body, it is inextricably connected to soil and decay.

This decay is not a simple dead end but is often connected to a concept of the natural. The film often presents us with visions of controlled Nature: Central Park, the fountain in the foyer of The Bramford designed in the shape of flowers, the flower-printed wallpaper in the Woodhouse apartment, and so on. The very name Rosemary Woodhouse ties our heroine to the natural and the domestic (wood house), to flowers (rose), and to plant life (rosemary), while Mary, of course, ironically allows her to assume the function of the mother of the satanic child for the next millennium. The latter part of the sixties saw a significant rise in concepts of the "natural" in everything from food to childbirth. To be tied to nature was to be connected to a youthful life force, often explicitly pro-environmental, antiwar, and anti-establishment. Farrow's own persona during this period often drew upon the icon of the flower child: a featurette promoting the film showed her painting flowers on her trailer at Paramount alongside words like "Peace" and "Love." But in *Rosemary's Baby* the natural itself is most significantly aligned not with Rosemary, her husband, or any of her young friends but with the Castevets and their elderly circle of acquaintances. It is Minnie who has an herbarium in her apartment (her gardening skill inherited from Mrs. Gardenia) and it is Minnie's thick, milky, herb-infested concoctions that are chosen by Sapirstein over modern vitamin tablets for the pregnant Rosemary.

This emphasis on plant life connects with one of the paradoxes of New York City, an urban environment of concrete, steel, and metal but one in which the natural world keeps manifesting itself. This is visible not only in parks but also in the trees and bushes that spring up out of sidewalks, and in the obsession of so many New Yorkers with growing flowers and plants in their apartments (to say nothing of the millions of pets living throughout the city), as though they want to maintain some kind of fundamental connection to the natural world otherwise repressed by the city. The ironic contrast between these old people and their hippie-like, lovingly tended natural environments and their pierced ears allows them to seem at once nurturing *and* connected to the satanic.[5] The charm necklace Rosemary wears, a gift from the Castevets, is filled with what Minnie and

Roman claim is "tannis" root, the bitter odor of which Hutch more properly identifies as coming from a fungus or mold. In this manner, the film is close to F. W. Murnau's *Nosferatu* (1922) in which the monstrous is repeatedly aligned with the outdoors, with plant life, insects, and animals rather than with the lifeless horror of "the undead" of so many other treatments of the vampire. *Rosemary's Baby* is a film about New York City in which the camera is repeatedly positioned not up, toward the sky, in an attempt to encompass the wondrous modernity of the tall buildings, but down, toward the ground, to the bottom or origin of things.

If one despairing side of urban living is to be surrounded by cold and indifferent people inhabiting the same building but with whom one has not the slightest personal contact, the Castavets and their acquaintances are the nightmarish other side to apartment living: the overly friendly and intrusive neighbors, always ringing your doorbell, impulsively visiting, sifting through your mail, or asking you for favors. "We get friendly with an old couple like that," Guy warns Rosemary early in the film, "and we'll never get rid of them." To get friendly with an "old couple" becomes rather too much like having snooping parents or grandparents right next door, the very kind of family situation one moves to a city like New York to get away from. Reading the film within the perspective of Rosemary's middle American, small-town paranoia, the Castevets and their circle of acquaintances assume a function straight out of the world of European fairy tales in which "innocents" (Snow White or Hansel and Gretel, for example) are lured to their doom by deceptively kind, elderly people who are ultimately out for young blood; The Bramford becomes a variation on the gothic horror mansion. (Hutch tells Guy and Rosemary early in the film about the notorious Trench Sisters, who had resided in The Bramford and who cooked and ate children.)

But strictly within an American context, the status of the Castevets as real-life witches allows one to situate them in relation to two major moments in American history: the Salem witch hunts of the seventeenth century and the so-called "witch hunts" against real or imagined communists in the 1950s. Arthur Miller's play *The Crucible*, written in 1953 and revived on Broadway in 1964, is the most notable attempt to link these two historical moments. While Miller's play is written from a politically liberal and philosophically rational position in which the anti-witchcraft hysteria is condemned and in which witchcraft itself is a fictional product of this hysteria, Polanski's film never settles so assuredly on a moral position. Rosemary may simply be an inheritor of a Puritanical tradition of hysteria, terrified of what is in the end absolutely nothing. Or all of her instincts may be correct and the evil she perceives around her is very real. Adrian Marcato was, we are told, attacked by a mob outside of The Bramford for his alleged activities as a witch. Whether this action was justified or whether, in fact, Marcato was falsely accused of witchcraft is something the film never clarifies.

However strong the 1960s context is for the film, traces of the cultural attitudes of the previous decade are also present in muted form. On the bookshelf above Guy's side of the bed is a copy of William Whyte's classic 1956 study of postwar conformism, *The Organization Man*, in itself a study of a certain type of modern-day Faustian man who sells his soul for the collective good of his corporation; later in the film, when Guy takes Rosemary's book on witchcraft away from her, he places it on top of Kinsey's two-volume study of male and female sexuality. Marshall Berman has written of the general mood of paranoia that dominated New York during the 1950s, a sensibility in which the communist witch hunts were inextricably linked with betrayal and quite often a betrayal from those closest to us: family and once-dear friends. Berman writes of Julius and Ethel Rosenberg and "their homely plainness; they looked like everybody's parents." It is this ordinariness which suggests that "any ordinary nice folks, even your nearest and dearest, could turn out to be agents of alien powers" (Berman, "Lonely Crowd" 539).[6] Levin makes the possible linkage between Rosemary's instincts and the communist witch hunts explicit when Guy refers to Rosemary's accusations as being a "McCarthy-type smear campaign" (Levin 228). But this line, like the line comparing Rosemary to a concentration camp victim, is not heard in the film. In general, Polanski's strategy is to mute some of the more overt ethnic, racial, and political elements of the novel. For example, only in the novel is Sapirstein's ethnicity noted, as when Roman explains to Rosemary that the man is a Jew "with all the sensitivity of his much-tormented race" (Levin 140). His betrayal of Rosemary, real or imagined on her part, taps into a deeply antisemitic and folkloric fear of Jews as Satanic abductors and murderers of children. In the film, Sapirstein's Jewishness is implied but never stated. Did Polanski remove this kind of dialogue because he wished to avoid an overly facile analogy between the story content of his film and the Holocaust and McCarthy periods? Or did he remove them simply to allow such analogies to emerge without having the issue explicitly forced upon the viewer?

Such ambiguities and unresolved questions on the part of the film create a dispersed political and historical allegory. The colorful and theatrical eccentricity of the Castevets and their group at once confirms and negates accusations that their outgoing behavior is a mask for something possibly evil, allowing the Castevet circle to function as both scapegoats and aggressors. Rosemary herself functions as the victim of collective terror and betrayal, one who within twentieth-century history has assumed a most vivid enactment through fascism and the Holocaust. But she also represents the very forces of fear, paranoia, and hysteria that so often give rise to these reactionary and totalitarian ideologies. For *Rosemary's Baby* to place this story material within New York City would carry a particularly charged weight under any circumstances. But, as I have argued throughout this essay, Polanski's intervention as a European auteur with a strong visual and dramatic style, indeed a style arguably informed by his specific experience of historical upheaval and trauma, causes *Rosemary's Baby* to assume an even more powerful resonance. It becomes a film that raises questions about the relationship between the individual and the collective in terms of the history of urban space—and of New York City in particular—but at the same time a film that firmly answers none of its own questions.

The last shot of the film returns us to the opening: the extreme high-angle image of The Dakota-as-Bramford in which we see two tiny figures once again entering the building. Another young couple arriving in New York to replace Guy and Rosemary? Or Guy and Rosemary again, caught in a perpetual loop, doomed to repeat this history and this experience of New York City forever?

NOTES

1. Ira Levin's source novel explicitly cites The Dakota as another apartment building in New York City. In a conversation in the second chapter between Rosemary, Guy, and Rosemary's elderly friend Hutch, Hutch attempts to convince the couple to look for an apartment in another historical building rather than move into the cursed Bramford: "Go to the Dakota or the Osborne if you're dead set on nineteenth-century splendor." Rosemary responds that The Dakota is a co-op and that the Osborne is being demolished (Levin 29).

2. The film's cinematographer, William Fraker, has stated that about 40 percent of the film was shot with a hand-held camera and that all of it used either an 18 mm or a 25 mm lens in order to heighten this sense of enclosure (see Schaefer and Salvato 138).

3. John Guare's 1971 play *House of Blue Leaves* uses the pope's visit to Yankee Stadium as a backdrop for a story about a group of New York characters who are obsessed with theater, show business, and celebrity.

4. In the novel, Rosemary and a friend attend the off-Broadway musical *The Fantasticks*, which has a major function in the development of the plot in the second half. There are production stills of Mia Farrow walking out of the Greenwich Village theater where *The Fantasticks* was being performed, but the sequence itself was cut. All that is left of this detail is Rosemary telling Dr. Hill that she saw *The Fantasticks*.

5. A year after the film was released, the Manson family would, alas, all too horrifyingly unite the hippie / flower child icon with a self-proclaimed element of satanic violence; and all this far too close to Polanski.

6. One should also note that after the war Polanski lived another type of political repression, the postwar Soviet version of communism practiced in Poland. Polanski has often stated that, largely as a consequence of this, he has little faith in the concept of the group or collective.

In the West Village: a composer affecting the actions of several characters while his director keeps time. Alfred Hitchcock (l.) and Ross Bagdasarian in *Rear Window* (Alfred Hitchcock, Paramount, 1954). Digital frame enlargement.

The City That Never Shuts Up

AURAL INTRUSION IN NEW YORK
APARTMENT FILMS

ELISABETH WEIS

RANDY THOM

When most people refer to New York City, the borough that they imagine—and which stands for New York—is Manhattan. Even residents of New York's "outer boroughs" call Manhattan "the City." Whatever their neighborhoods, most Manhattanites share the experience of dwelling in apartments, a lifestyle that almost always includes being subjected to excessive noise from both the neighbors and the streets. (The most frequent complaint to New York cops is about noise, not crime.) How do New York films convey the sonic experience of apartment dwellers? And how are the city streets and the neighbors characterized by what we hear?

This essay takes as its focus two classic Manhattan apartment thrillers: Alfred Hitchcock's *Rear Window* (1954) and Roman Polanski's *Rosemary's Baby* (1968). These films were selected because they set up a tension between the isolation of the protagonist in an apartment and the impingement of the outside world. To choose two films in which the protagonist almost never leaves the claustrophobic apartment means that particular importance can be attributed to whatever sounds we do hear from the outside. The invasion of sounds from beyond the apartment can be called *aural intrusion*.

To be clear: as was common in the 1950s and 1960s, the interiors of both films were shot on Hollywood soundstages. The sets of both meticulously duplicated typical New York living spaces. *Rear Window*, set in Greenwich Village, has no street shots at all; its exterior sounds were entirely constructed during postproduction (after the shooting stopped), whereas the exteriors of *Rosemary's Baby* were filmed on location, and much of the production sound seems to have been retained.

To contextualize these two films, we might ask whether there is a distinctive New York sound for films that are actually shot in New York as well as situated there. The first thing to observe is that New York films are frequently dialogue-driven. They are typically smaller-scale independent films about people talking to and listening to each other. And on the sound track, if the characters aren't likely to hear a sound, neither will the audience. The relatively few stretches without dialogue are likely to be underscored by music that bridges one scene with another or that accompanies the characters as they stroll through the streets. One extreme case in point would be the comic oeuvre of Woody Allen, who as a director exhibits little interest in the aesthetic possibilities of sound, for at least three reasons. First, dialogue comedy rarely uses sound as part of its expressive palette. Secondly, Allen's characters are too self-absorbed to notice much beyond themselves. And thirdly, Allen's Manhattan (especially in his *Manhattan* [1979]) is a hygienic city. Even though New York is almost a character in his films, it is an idealization, not a representation of reality. It is Gershwin that smoothly and nostalgically occupies the background, not angry honking that would convey the city's aggression and energy.

At the other extreme are the films of Spike Lee and Martin Scorsese, who often focus on the ethnic neighborhoods that define their characters. But even their neighborhood films are more dialogue-driven than most big studio films made in Hollywood, which are characteristically packed with action rather than talk. And those Hollywood spectacles are accompanied by very dense sound effects tracks. (Sound effects are all sounds other than dialogue or music. They include conspicuous noises and ambient sound, the unnoticed atmospheric sound that defines a space.)[1] While the Hollywood aesthetic provides literally more bang for the buck, its sound tracks are at the same time cleaner, in accordance with an emphasis on "seamless" production values (which disguise the evidence of their production). New York sound tracks are likely to be grittier. Veteran sound editor Frank Warner described his concept for the ambient sound of *Taxi Driver* (1976) by calling it "dirty" (34). Warner was referring not just to the seedy neighborhoods being shown but to an aesthetic. During location shooting, the microphone picks up stray noises that can be either retained or smoothed out later by sound editors. Some directors, especially New York directors, fall in love with those bumps and squeaks and do not want the imperfections cleaned up. The result is a quasi-documentary sound aesthetic. This sense of reality is heightened by another distinction between the coasts: New York directors tend to ask for more "air"—more atmosphere or space between the character and the microphone, so that the audience is more aware of the city's ambient noise.[2]

Not surprisingly, then, the ambient sound of *Rosemary's Baby* is considerably grittier than that of *Rear Window*. But both films define the city as neither dangerous nor exciting, as we might expect from popular representations of New York. Even the occasional siren we hear does not depict the city as life-threatening; instead, the sense of menace is transferred and attributed to whatever image we are watching at the time. It is a signal to beware of that person, thing, or action. Generally, the street sounds—mainly traffic noise, children playing, and low boat whistles—are soothing and benign, in part because the world beyond the precincts of the apartment represents normality and even the possibility of rescue, once the apartment becomes a prison for its protagonist. It is the neighbors nearby who supply potential menace.

Rear Window and *Rosemary's Baby* share a set-up that exploits the possibilities for aural intrusion. Both have protagonists who spend most of the time holed up in their apartment and neighbors who may or may not present a threat. Both films are presented almost entirely from the protagonist's point of view so that we are inclined to identify with the experience of that protagonist. However, both films also question the audience's perceptions. That is, they raise the question of whether what we see and hear is "real" or represents the misguided subjective perceptions of the protagonist. We ask ourselves whether the negative reading of the neighbors' behavior is accurate or whether the protagonist is misinterpreting events. Both films manipulate us to careen back and forth between those two interpretations. Because images are more "concrete" than sounds, their referents being more immediately identifiable, in the cinema we trust more in what we see than in what we hear.

The directors of these two films had a keen awareness of the expressive potential of sound. Hitchcock's aural style is as essential and distinctive as his visual style. He did not leave the sonic decisions to be worked out by editors; he meticulously planned the relations between image and sound, with sound adding to, rather than simply duplicating, what the visuals conveyed.[3] Polanski's training at the great Polish film academy at Lodz rendered him fully versed in all technical aspects of filmmaking, including sound. He told one interviewer, "I know most of the sound effects I will want as I'm shooting. Later, in editing, others suggest themselves through the images." When asked if he worked with the same sound expert from film to film, Polanski replied, "I'm the expert" (Polanski, Interview 148).

Rosemary's Baby

Polanski's European films have much more stylized sound tracks than his later films. It is fascinating to observe how, starting with *Rosemary's Baby*, his first American film, Polanski found ways to use sound creatively while working within the American preference for less intrusive style. He did this while also balancing the film's subtle shifts between two normally incompatible aesthetics and genres: one fantastic and the other quasi-realistic.

Rosemary Woodhouse (Mia Farrow) is a young woman who moves with her husband Guy (John Cassavetes) into The Bramford, a storied old Manhattan apartment building. Rosemary gradually suspects that her adjacent neighbors— the crude and aggressively solicitous Minnie (Ruth Gordon) and her more genteel husband, Roman Castevet (Sidney Blackmer)—head a satanic cult and have colluded with her own husband to have her impregnated by the devil.

It is to a great extent Polanski's manipulation of sound that in turn enables him to deftly manipulate the audience as we alternate between agreeing with

Rosemary that there really is a plot against her baby or thinking that Rosemary is paranoid. If Rosemary's version is true, then we have to accept the existence of Satanist witches. As has often been noted, Rosemary and the audience are forced to choose between "not believing what appears to be real or believing what cannot be real" (Houston and Kinder 17).

The film presents the story entirely from the heroine's perspective. Says Polanski: "There is no scene in the film which could not be seen by Rosemary. It's very subjective" (Interview DVD). So it is interesting that in hardly any scenes do sounds have the distortion or exaggeration we have come to expect in psychological horror films. But there is a subtler way of making sounds subjective: through selection. No film includes all the sounds that would realistically be heard by a character in a given space; the audience would be overwhelmed. Instead the filmmakers select a few sounds for us to hear. And even some of those sounds, if meant to situate us in a new space, will soon fade down or out. The effect is pretty much the equivalent of what we do as hearers in real life. For instance, in a crowded restaurant we first notice the noise but eventually focus our attention on the person with whom we are speaking and mentally filter out the rest. The filmmakers have to do this for us. That said, however, there is still plenty of room for manipulation. Whereas we generally notice most things visualized in a frame, we rarely notice most sounds (in life or in film). As a result, film sounds can be manipulated with more leeway than images and still be perceived as realistic.

Rosemary's Baby keeps distortion to a minimum in order to ground the fantastic story in a realistic setting, to provide a sense of normality. Houston and Kinder identified the "heightening of the realistic" as the basic strategy of the film. "This concern with the nature of reality is expressed in the film's style, tone, imagery and structure. Visually, it presents a highly complex and textured surface which is usually linked to realism or naturalism. The environments are crowded with objects, colours, textures. But on examination, these details arouse conflicting responses to what is being perceived" (17). The authors offer as an example "unusual camera angles which heighten reality by close-up focusing on single objects, yet at the same time distorting that reality through the angle . . . creating the grotesque by distorting the realistic" (18). Perhaps the best aural equivalent of that style would be the extreme reverberation we usually hear when Rosemary confronts the Castevets at either her doorway or theirs. In reality, pre–World War II apartment corridors do feature very reverberant spaces. But heard on film, that kind of sonic reality would seem unrealistic; filmmakers would normally hold back on the echo. In *Rosemary's Baby*, the pronounced reverberation in the hallway suggests the threat Rosemary feels each time she confronts her neighbors. And its placement at the threshold of their apartments conveys Rosemary's feeling that her home is being invaded.

Defining Minnie as intrusive constitutes one of the major tropes of the film, and it is sound that conveys most of her pushiness. Minnie is introduced as a strident voice through aural intrusion. Rosemary twice hears her voice through an adjacent apartment wall before meeting her. Polanski further defines Minnie by the charm bracelet that she wears throughout. No diegetic mention is made of it, but its jangling in her scenes is an aural extension of her irritating aggressiveness. (Diegetic sound can be heard by a film's characters, as opposed to sound that is not part of that story world.) In the scene just after Rosemary learns that her friend Hutch (Maurice Evans) is in a coma, the sound of Minnie's voice before we see her enter the frame conveys aurally her imposition on Rosemary's intensely private moment. Minnie then blows a whistle to hail a cab.

Unlike the noises produced by Rosemary's neighbors, most of the sounds from the street are soothing. The morning after her rape/impregnation, Rosemary opens the bedroom window as if to seek relief from outside. The fresh air and gentle traffic sounds help dispel the sense of entrapment. When we do hear sirens from outside during the movie, it is to alert the audience to danger. For instance, the very elongated wail of a siren precedes the moment when Rosemary, after learning she is pregnant, puts back on a tainted charm necklace that Minnie had given her to control her.

It might be useful here to introduce the distinction Michel Chion makes between active and passive offscreen sound. Active sounds draw our attention to identifiable single sources and arouse our curiosity. By contrast, passive offscreen sound is mostly ambient sound, which "creates an atmosphere that envelops and stabilizes the image, without in any way inspiring us to look elsewhere or to anticipate seeing its source" (*Audio-Vision* 85). In *Rosemary's Baby*, references to children occur in both passive and active modes. While there is relatively little street noise heard when we are inside the Woodhouse apartment, on occasion the outside sound includes children playing. Normally these background sounds would not be noticed, but, of course, in this film any references to children are loaded. Filmmakers often allude to children visually or aurally to suggest vulnerability. Here, the sound of children suggests Rosemary's fears for her unborn baby. We hear children playing outside when Rosemary's doctor tells her she is pregnant. That allusion to children is reinforced by the return of the lullaby we heard in the titles (although this time in a version that does not include the woman vocalizer).

The sounds of playing children remain passive. But one sound becomes more and more active because it recurs unusually often: an unspecified neighboring pianist practicing "Für Elise." This Beethoven bagatelle, often learned by children for piano lessons, is at the same time a reference to the unborn child and an indication of normality in an apartment building to which Hutch has attributed a ghastly history involving witchcraft and infant slaughter. The piece is such a cliché that at first we pay no attention to it, but its recurrence six times forces us to notice it (and perhaps to recall how irritating the piece can be when repeated ad nauseam).

Whereas there is no diegetic mention of the piano music, the sound of a baby crying becomes a subject of character attention. Late in the film, Rosemary suffers what she is told is a miscarriage. Recovering, she thinks she hears a baby crying. She turns off the air conditioning the better to listen, but the witch who is guarding her turns it back on, cutting her off from sounds beyond the bedroom. However, Rosemary trusts what she has heard. She enters the Castevet apartment through the connecting closet that joins her home to theirs and discovers her baby, which we never see. (Polanski never lets us look inside the cradle, but there is a brief superimposition of diabolical eyes over a shot of Rosemary's reaction.) When she has to decide whether to accept the baby it emits a persistent wail—a sound that is perfectly realistic but that heightens the horror in this scene. The coven's surrogate mother exacerbates the infant's discomfort by rocking it too violently. Encouraged by Roman Castevet, Rosemary rocks the cradle with instinctive maternal gentleness and calms the baby; its cries die down to a contented gurgling. The shrill neediness of the original cries makes the audience identify with Rosemary's need to comfort the baby, and the cooing assures us that she has made the right choice. The gurgling is followed directly by the title lullaby while the camera reverses the film's opening approach toward the building by moving away from The Bramford and out to the streets. Immediately after subjecting us to his most horrific scene, Polanski provides the apparent comfort of the lullaby and the withdrawal from the building. As in the opening titles, there are no sounds of the city, just the music. But this time we recognize that the voice we hear is Mia Farrow's. And we also realize that the orchestration and the singing are altogether too saccharine—perhaps an indication of Rosemary's hyper-innocence. Moreover, by starting and ending the film with "Rosemary's" voice, Polanski offers the possibility that all the sound we have heard is subjective, that throughout the film we have been inside the head of a delusional character.

Polanski does adopt one horror sound convention: aural intrusion during quiet moments to provide tension. When Rosemary first visits the basement laundry room, a loud, unexplained crash prompts her to say that the space makes her nervous. Several times Rosemary hears chanting through her wall as she lies in bed. She hears the chanting when she is in a limbic state—when we do not know whether she is dreaming or awake. Before the impregnation scene, which blurs the boundary between nightmare and actual events, Polanski blends real and dreamed events by synchronizing Minnie's voice (heard from the other side of the bedroom wall) to the lips of an angry nun and images from Rosemary's childhood Catholic school. Polanski also uses the sound of a clock ticking to bridge the waking and sleeping worlds. Some films use conspicuous ticking to suggest time exigencies or a heartbeat. Here the heartbeat could also be that of the unborn baby. A ticking clock paradoxically suggests quietness. Here it also adds tension, as does a second metronomic motif: the overloud sound of water dripping from a leaky faucet in the Woodhouse kitchen.

The breaching of boundaries carries over into the film's use of music. Two prevailing styles of music—soothing and horrific—usually accompany the mood swings of the film. Parallel to the soothing street sounds from outside, which suggest reassurance and normality, are the gentle lullaby motif as well as an easy-listening, soft jazz record that comforts Rosemary.[4] The record is identified initially as source music when we watch Rosemary place it on her record player in anticipation of a quiet evening alone at home. It functions more like underscoring (background music not heard by the film's characters) when heard on the night she plans to conceive, and during a kitchen scene with her girlfriends. There is also upbeat light jazz underscoring when Rosemary ventures outdoors to meet Hutch. But that jazz is replaced by conventional dissonant horror music when she learns that Hutch is in a coma. We hear horror music whenever Rosemary is most terrorized, as when she feels excruciating pain, whenever she makes a discovery that reinforces her fears, when she is raped, and when she tries to escape her tormentors.

For the most part the distinctions between soothing and horror music are completely clear, and they help manipulate the audience's shifts between believing in the satanic plot or not. However, just as the impregnation is visually ambiguous—one of the most memorable lines of the film is Rosemary saying, "This is no dream; this is really happening!"—so is its sound. During Rosemary's nightmare experience we hear traditional eerie underscoring (its uncanny use of wind instruments and alternation of minor third chords make it both spooky and sensuous). The underscoring would be nothing worth mentioning except for the remarkable fact that one of the characters in Rosemary's dream refers to it! A Jacqueline Kennedy look-alike (Patricia Ann Conway) tells Rosemary, "Sorry if the music bothers you; let me know and I'll have it stopped." The musical shift from underscoring, which is by definition passive, as the audience ideally should not notice it, to active source music has been called "scourse music" by some industry professionals. Often scourse music, like the jazz heard in the Woodhouse apartment, goes unnoticed. But occasionally its use is foregrounded, as in the impregnation scene. Scourse music can then challenge us to adjust our perceptions; noticing the shift can distance us emotionally by reminding us of the work of the filmmakers. But in this case, the scene is so nightmarish and the nightmare so real that the ambiguity merely heightens the unsettling effect of the scene. Polanski has said he intended the film's interpretation to remain ambiguous (Interview DVD). With his sound he has it both ways. The sound track, like our interpretation, alternates between quasi-documentary and horror conventions, and when it slips between them the ambiguity further disconcerts the audience.

Strong arguments have been made to support a psychological interpretation, based on references to Rosemary's Catholic guilt about her sexuality and her regression to infantile behavior. In this reading, the witches are paranoid projections of a fearful first-time mother (see esp. Wexman 63–69). However, most viewers eventually accept the interpretation that her baby is the son of Satan.

Because of the apocalyptic and fantastic nature of *Rosemary's Baby*, we feel obliged to choose one interpretation over another. By contrast, it is possible in *Rear Window* that the protagonist is projecting his own fears onto everything he sees *and* that the protagonist is right in deducing that his neighbor is a murderer.

Rear Window

In *Rear Window* James Stewart plays L. B. Jefferies (aka Jeff), a photojournalist confined to his apartment with a cast on his leg. Whereas Rosemary is self-absorbed with the new life inside her, Jeff spends most of his time looking outward, specifically at a courtyard full of windows, each containing a mini-drama that is mostly seen but not heard.

Jeff eventually deduces that one of his neighbors, a salesman named Thorwald (Raymond Burr), has murdered his wife. It takes him quite a while to persuade his girlfriend, Lisa (Grace Kelly), his visiting nurse (Thelma Ritter), and a cop friend (Wendell Corey) that he is right. But the fact that Thorwald is a murderer does not negate the fact that Jeff has been spying obsessively on his neighbors, to the point of escalating his voyeurism from bare eyes to binoculars, then to the telephoto lens of his camera.

Indeed, the crime story of *Rear Window* is less interesting than its portrayal of Jeff's neuroses. Jeff, who as a photographer is a professional voyeur, is much more interested in looking at his neighbors than in looking inward—metaphorically at his own behavior or literally at his lovely girlfriend. Jeff is capable of seeing and appreciating Lisa only when she stands in a window across the courtyard like the other objects of his voyeurism.

Jeff's assumption that Thorwald has killed his "nagging" wife derives from his own fear of marriage. Jeff says if he had a wife she would have to accompany him abroad under primitive conditions; as an invalid, Mrs. Thorwald represents the extreme of being tied down at home. Among the other neighbors, Jeff notices only those who seem to reinforce his prejudices—including two newly-weds whose affection soon deteriorates (Rand Harper, Havis Davenport) and a woman he names Miss Lonelyhearts (Judith Evelyn), whose desperate failure to find a man nearly leads her to suicide. Similarly, the film's sound, though seemingly realistic, is subjective in its selectivity: Jeff looks at and hears whatever he needs to notice. As Chion has observed, "Hitchcock opens and closes freely the noises from the courtyard depending on his needs. . . . Sometimes this is to attract the attention of James Stewart (and the spectator) to the exterior; some-times, to the contrary, it is to 'close' the dramatic space on the little theater of the living room and on the intimate domesticity of Lisa and Jeff" (115).

Jeff's voyeurism is an outward manifestation of his unwillingness to be engaged (with the community, rather than watch it from a distance) or to get engaged (with Lisa).[5] Like many Hitchcock protagonists, he thinks he is self-sufficient, but he is actually emotionally stunted and incapable of a mature relationship. His apartment, like Rosemary's, is a metaphor for his isolation. Jeff acknowledges his need for other people only when he yells out the window for help in the penultimate scene, when Thorwald is advancing upon him. As in *Rosemary's Baby*, the protagonist's home is invaded. Rosemary finally cannot keep her neighbors from stealing her baby. In *Rear Window*, Thorwald eventually comes to Jeff's apartment and tries to kill him—by pushing him out the window into the courtyard, where he finally joins the community he had been watching from a safe distance. Like Polanski, Hitchcock makes extensive use of aural intrusion to breach the boundaries between apartments, and the sounds from beyond the apartment bring both danger and help.

In this film the sonic situation is considerably more complex than in *Rosemary's Baby*. Jeff is ensconced during a heat wave by his window, from which he and we can see a courtyard with apartment windows on three sides and a narrow alleyway leading to a street. As in *Rosemary's Baby*, noises from the street beyond the courtyard include benign traffic sounds, low boat horns at night, and children's games. (However, occasionally truck noise "underscores" an emotionally tense moment within Jeff's apartment, and it is not random that a loud siren accompanies a scene where the Thorwalds fight.) We usually hear voices clearly only from within Jeff's apartment; the pantomimes in the neighbors' windows are often accompanied by music that emanates from the courtyard or the street. One reason that the sound is so rich in this film is the almost constant separation between sound and image, with each commenting on the other. Jeff's discussions with his visitors as they watch and talk about his neighbors often apply equally well to his own situation. Conversely, the music coming from outside often comments on the neighbors and on Jeff.

The specific New York City neighborhood being depicted is the Greenwich Village of artists. Prominently featured neighbors include a dancer, a sculptress, and a composer. But on another level the courtyard neighbors are a microcosm of society—of the people Jeff needs to join in order to become a fully functional person. Jeff needs to be able to connect with others directly, not just through a lens from a safe distance. At one point in the film, a woman whose dog has just been strangled screams at all the residents of the courtyard about the need for the community to care about one another. Her peroration and Jeff's fall out the window are the two occasions when most of the neighbors attend to the same event. Usually, the neighbors' isolation from one another is emphasized by their separated pantomimes in the individual windows. However, the one thing that everyone facing the courtyard shares is sound.

Hitchcock generally treats the sound effects and the music in opposite ways. The sound effects usually relate to Jeff's attention. Exterior noise levels are raised when Jeff is interested in what is going on outside and die out almost completely when he is intensely involved with Lisa.[6] If Jeff is looking at one particular window, we can sometimes hear a sound or two from it. Jeff's escalation from watching with bare eye to binoculars to telephoto lens is paralleled not only visually by an escalation from long shot to medium shot to close-up, but also acoustically with his (and our) improved ability to hear sounds, even though that makes no physical sense. Nevertheless, the audience so identifies with Jeff that the sound levels seem to stay within realistic parameters. This phenomenon whereby aural point of view corresponds with visual point of view suggests why it is not really possible to draw lines between what is realistic and what is subjective, why the two are not mutually exclusive.

One of Hitchcock's nice sonic touches is his treatment of the neighbors' voices when Jeff is watching a particular window without a lens. The composer Stephen Sondheim, who wrote a contemporary review of the film, observed: "Hitchcock makes sure the dialogue from across the court is audible but indistinct. The sounds are calculated to tease the listener in the way any barely overheard conversation does, and is very knowingly controlled" (168). The muffled dialogue (actually, we do hear a few words here and there) works in at least three ways: it becomes part of the courtyard atmosphere; its nonspecificity makes it universal (for instance, the Thorwalds' arguments could apply to any bickering couple); and it makes us strain to listen—thereby making the film audience aware that we are guilty of sharing not only Jeff's voyeurism but also its aural equivalent, eavesdropping.

The big exception to the general principle of seeming realism is Thorwald's approach to Jeff's apartment, where the footsteps are long, slow, loud, reverberant—in other words, exaggerated as in a horror movie. The distortion makes sense at this point. Jeff is in the dark and in danger, so he is more sensitive to sound. Jeff's private space is being invaded. It is suddenly no longer a place of protection but one of vulnerability. Over the course of the film, the sounds intruding from outside have progressed from a sense of random noises at the start of the film to a concentration on the neighbor who physically intrudes on his space. Whereas subjectivity has looked and sounded realistic up to this point, now reality looks and sounds distorted. It takes an expressionistic technique paradoxically to convey the intrusion of reality on Jeff. (Wood 106 and Weis 119 argue that Thorwald's approach represents reality invading Jeff's psyche.) The sound/image relationships have by now been reversed. Previously Jeff had seen but not heard Thorwald; now he hears but cannot see him. Visual point of view is also reversed. As Jeff flashes camera bulbs to fend off Thorwald's approach, we experience the blinding through Thorwald's eyes.

If the sound effects and exterior voices correspond more or less with Jeff's perception until the climax, the music rarely does. There is rarely diegetic mention of the source music. Instead it often functions to make ironic comments on both the exterior action and on Jeff's behavior in ways that he does not notice. Nonvocalized pieces with lyrics that nevertheless would have been known in the 1950s include Harry Warren and Jack Brooks's "That's Amore" (heard when the newlyweds arrive home) and Rodgers and Hart's "Lover" ("when you're near me"), both of which also apply to various relationships we are watching. The most telling commentary comes from a Jimmy Van Heusen song whose lyrics are so important that we hear them clearly. The first line—"To see you is to love you, and I see you everywhere"—raises the central issue of Jeff's biased perception, especially Jeff's interpretation of every neighbor's situation as a projection of his commitment phobia. The song also applies to Miss Lonelyhearts, who plays this recording as part of a ritual she enacts with an imaginary dinner guest, for whom she has prepared a candle-lit place setting. When she raises a wine glass to toast her "guest," Jeff raises his glass, unwitnessed, in response (even though Lisa is visiting). The lyrics also forecast how Jeff will finally fall in love with Lisa by watching across the courtyard.

Hitchcock uses scourse music considerably more than Polanski. In *Rosemary's Baby* the elimination of the distinction between source music and underscoring furthers the film's major ploy of making it difficult for the audience to tell what is real and what is imagined or dreamed. In *Rear Window* scourse music works in part to break down the distinction between characters and audience; it adds to the self-conscious, or reflexive, nature of the film.[7] Reflexive films remind the audience that we are watching by drawing attention to the artifice of their construction. In Hitchcock's films the act of voyeurism is always reflexive. It is about the naughty pleasure of viewing films as much as it is about a diegetic character. The presence in *Rear Window* of Miss Torso (Georgine Darcy), a half-dressed dancer whose warm-ups are meant for us to watch along with Jeff, reminds us of the more salacious aspects of voyeurism. As a photographer, Jeff is analogous to a filmmaker. But he is also analogous to the movie viewer who sits in the dark separated safely from the action on the screen. This analogy is not an invention of film scholars; Hitchcock asked the set designer that the windows across the courtyard be shaped to correspond exactly with the dimensions of movie screens (Curtis 28).

The music slips quite subtly between underscoring and source music. For instance, it is hard to notice the shifts from Franz Waxman's opening jazz score to the rumba to which Miss Torso does ballet exercises to Leonard Bernstein's *Fancy Free*. But the music is acknowledged as diegetic when the dancer's music disturbs the neighboring composer (Ross Bagdasarian) trying to come up with a melody at his piano. Soon its function shifts back to underscoring as a slower tempo conveys the relief Jeff gets when he scratches an itch under his cast.

The most overtly reflexive music, however, is that song being written by the composer. Hitchcock told François Truffaut, "I wanted to show how a popular song is composed by gradually developing it through the film until, in the final scene, it is played on a recording with a full orchestral accompaniment."[8] We watch in stages as the composer works on the main theme at a piano, has a setback and tears up the music sheets, rehearses the piece with a small combo, and, in the film's epilogue, plays a recording of it for Miss Lonelyhearts. The progress of its composition becomes analogous to the bumpy relationship of Lisa and Jeff. Lisa stops to admire the music every time it is played, and it is a source of contention between the couple. Lisa asks Jeff, "Where does a man get inspiration to write a song like that?" Jeff answers, "He gets it from the landlady once a month," whereas Lisa wishes that she could be "creative like the composer." This is one of several suggestions that the piece's composition is parallel to the creation of any work of art, including the film we are watching. Indeed, the couple's opposing interpretations about the composer's motive mirror Hitchcock's ambivalence about whether his own films were commercial or artistic. Hitchcock's cameo appearance also encourages us to think of the composer as a surrogate for the filmmaker. He is seen winding a clock (i.e., keeping time) in the composer's apartment. Not only does the creation of the music parallel the unrolling of the film but the composer, like the director, affects the actions of several characters. He rehearses the piece at just the right instant to enthrall Miss Lonelyhearts: hearing it stops her at the last moment from attempting suicide. At the same time, the music endangers Lisa because she pauses to admire it while in Thorwald's apartment. Thus the song unites the idea of romance and danger, a favorite Hitchcockian linkage. It is when Lisa risks her life to find evidence supporting Jeff's theory that he falls in love with her.

Lisa as much as articulates the double nature of the song as both score and source music when she says, "It's almost as if it's being written especially for us." The tune functions most obviously as a piece written for Hitchcock rather than by the diegetic composer during the coda-like ending of the film, when the composer plays it in the final version, a recording for male vocalist and full orchestra. Only then do we learn of a contrivance so absurd that the song calls attention to its own artifice. The lyrics are kept muffled at first, with the result that we can better hear lines of dialogue coming from various apartments (each of which resolves its mini-drama) as the camera pans away from the composer and over the courtyard. We finally hear the song's last word and presumably its title— "Lisa"—precisely when the camera ends on Grace Kelly's Lisa, who is not listening. Thus the music assumes the role of underscoring as the film, the song, and the various relationships in this apartment and in the courtyard are all resolved at the same time and on the same note. When the music level swells way up at the end, the song no longer functions as aural intrusion but as *Rear Window*'s title music. Because the song had been introduced as composed in 1950s Greenwich Village, probably the country's densest neighborhood of artists, it defines a New York City that is a source of creativity, which provides beauty and redemption for its otherwise isolated inhabitants. And the beneficiaries include not just Jeff's community but the moviegoers sitting in the dark.

NOTES

1. Perhaps the more realistic and small-scale aesthetic of so many New York films is one reason why New York movies remained monaural in the 1950s much longer than those

produced in Los Angeles, which adopted multi-channel sound formats that paralleled the visual spectacle of widescreen and epic films of that epoch.

2. Glen Marullo, a location mixer (sound recordist) who has worked on both coasts, says his colleagues refer to the Los Angeles sound as "dry" and the more inclusive New York sound as "wet." Personal interview.

3. See Weis.

4. Actually, the lullaby's orchestration varies during the film to provide subtle shifts in mood, and at one point the lullaby is subsumed by the horror music.

5. "Jeff's voyeurism goes hand in hand with an absorbing fear of mature sexuality" (Stam and Pearson 198).

6. On the other hand, street sound levels are often raised while Jeff is asleep.

7. The most extensive analysis of *Rear Window*'s reflexivity can be found in Stam and Pearson.

8. Truffaut 160. Hitchcock considered Waxman's song as unworthy of its role. He told Truffaut, "I was a little disappointed at the lack of a structure in the title song. I had a motion picture songwriter when I should have chosen a popular songwriter" (135).

The tenement as "breeding ground" seen with a naturalist flourish: an immigrant adjusting undergarments while talking to a neighbor in a window above, in *Street Scene* (King Vidor, FeaturePro Inc./Samuel Goldwyn Company, 1931). Digital frame enlargement.

Wretched Refuse

WATCHING NEW YORK ETHNIC SLUM
FILMS IN THE AFTERMATH OF 9/11

STEVEN ALAN CARR

Within American popular culture, the image of the city traditionally has expressed the displaced fears and desires of a society undergoing rapid economic and demographic transformations. The image of the city is as central to muckraking journalism, social realism in literature and art, much of early American photojournalism, and such film genres as the screwball comedy, the crime film, the social problem film, and film noir as it is to the larger themes—alienation, the failure of the American Dream, protest—evoked by these forms. New York City is arguably the archetypal metropolis, but for the emotions inspired by the urban image, the archetype is really no more than a series of fragmented images that could stand in for any city: the filthy and crowded tenement room, the corner bar at 3 A.M., the deserted back alley, or the bustling, haphazard open-air market. Such images aggregate to express the deep-seated yearnings and misgivings of a culture in the throes of radical shifts taking place during the nineteenth and twentieth centuries: from rural to urban; from a decentered agrarian economy to a relatively centralized system of urban consumers, commodities, and consumers as commodities; from a cohesive, White Anglo-Saxon Protestant national identity to a melting pot of immigrant ethnic diversity. The ethnic slum, in particular, has served as useful shorthand for expressing concerns over the unbridled shifts taking place over the past 150 years. A metonym for both the city itself and the social problems that plague it, the cinematic slum eventually lost its power to galvanize audiences once those audiences moved in droves to the suburbs.

While as a real city—however one might define its urbanity—New York might not be particularly distinctive, as the basis and inspiration for the *cinematic city* it is of the greatest importance. New York is the site of transference for the fears and desires of a culture in the throes of massive social shifts. As the site of transference, New York inspires ambivalence in much the same manner that, as Freud observes, some patients come to emotionally identify with a psychoanalyst in ways that they identified earlier with a parental authority figure. As an American ideal, New York is the setting for Horatio Alger dime novels, whose rags-to-riches accounts, brandished to recent immigrants, offered a seductive formula for success. With the right proportions of luck, stamina, stalwartness, virtuousness, and resourcefulness, anyone in America, no matter how poor, could pull himself or herself up by the bootstraps. Immigrants and ghettos are key to understanding the importance of New York as a city, or more precisely, the importance of ambivalent and even divergent national attitudes that transfer national fears and desires onto New York.

The same city that provides the setting for Alger-like successes also hosted the filth and degradation of tenements and ghettos where immigrants lived. The influential twin to Alger's *Ragged Dick* series of dime novels, Jacob Riis's *How the Other Half Lives* (1890) reveals the importance of New York as the object of a White Anglo-Saxon Protestant gaze transfixed in horror upon what it perceives as the invading immigrant hordes. Riis's text and photographs beautifully fuse two attitudes—horror at the living conditions created by the rise of the city and horror at the immigrants who live there. So beautiful is this fusion that it at once makes natural and normal the seemingly implacable WASP gaze, a gaze that apparently has no need to distinguish the human beings it objectifies from the surroundings it deplores. Take, for example, the chapter devoted to what Riis, a police reporter for the *New York Sun*, calls "Jewtown." Riis's sympathy for the Jew and his money plays like pity typically reserved for a monster in a horror film:

> Thrift is the watchword of Jewtown, as of its people the world over. It is at once its strength and its fatal weakness, its cardinal virtue and its foul disgrace. Become an overmastering passion with these people who come here in droves from Eastern Europe to escape persecution, from which freedom could be bought only with gold, it has enslaved them in bondage worse than that from which they fled. Money is their God. Life itself is of little value compared with even the leanest bank account. (*Other Half,* 86)

Quoting from the report of the Eastern Dispensary, a charitable organization providing free medical care to the poor, Riis observes that the document "told the whole story," as it observes that the diseases suffered by those in Jewtown "are not due to intemperance or immorality, but to ignorance, want of suitable food, and the foul air in which they live and work" (88).

Although little discussion has acknowledged it, a historical arc joins these early images of the Lower East Side—or Jewtown, as Riis prefers to call it—to the surge in nationalistic victim culture that rose in the aftermath of 9/11. Just as the post–World War II demographic shifts and social mobility moved families out of the city and neutralized widespread concern over the ghetto and slum as breeding ground, the response to the terrorist attacks of 9/11 neutralized concern over the implosion of the urban downtown by collapsing the distinction between urban and suburban spaces. The collapse of the Twin Towers quickly became a convenient shorthand for an imagined collapse in so-called spirituality, traditional values, hyper-nationalist patriotism, and perhaps even the simplistic egoism and quaint arrogance of what these monuments had come to represent: arguably, a naive faith in technology, capitalism, and unilateral globalism. Hardly exclusive to its physical locale in New York, the sight of the towers collapsing became a site of shared national mourning and identity formation around victimhood, which consequently served as the pretext for ongoing military actions in Afghanistan and Iraq and a wholesale dismantling of civil liberties and constitutional safeguards for foreign nationals as well as for U.S. citizens.

In placing Hollywood's image of the urban ethnic slum in relation—and perhaps in opposition—to the more familiar images of 9/11, this essay tries to accomplish two basic goals. First and foremost, it separates "a city that never sleeps" from the image of a city that is never far from our dreams. Walter Lippmann famously calls this dreaming "the pictures in our heads" (*Public Opinion*), and we still haven't awakened fully to its possibilities. The separation affords a clearer view of the pictures emerging from a broader historical continuum expressing the fears and desires of those living within and beyond the geographic borders of New York City proper. While the link between the images of 9/11 and the subsequent belligerent jingoism it inspired arguably requires little imagination, the connection between the images of 9/11 and the depiction of the slum in two screen adaptations of popular dramatic plays—*Street Scene* (1931) and *Dead End* (1937)—seems a bit more tenuous. Imagine that the representation of the city in these films has the same power to "reach out of the past to cripple, incapacitate, or strike down the living" that Richard Slotkin observed in American literature when studying this country's adherence to the "myth of the frontier." Just as the myth of America as a "wide-open land of unlimited opportunity for the strong, ambitious, self-reliant individual to thrust himself to the top . . . blinded us to the consequences of industrial and urban revolutions" (Slotkin 5), the twin to the structuring metaphor of the frontier, the myth of the city as a cramped, stifling, breeding ground for antisocial and even pathological behavior, has blinded us to the additional consequences of suburban revolutions, the rise of transnationalism, and the forces of globalization.

Street Scene and *Dead End*, part of the Hollywood social problem genre popular throughout the 1930s and 1940s, helped strengthen this familiar image of the city for an even wider audience. Both films depict the harsh, crowded, and animalistic conditions of New York tenement buildings, and both offer a solution to the problem of crowding and filth: escape from the city. A series of vignettes portraying the uneasy co-existence between New York's various immigrant groups, the minimal plot of *Street Scene*, directed by King Vidor and adapted by Elmer Rice from his Pulitzer Prize–winning play, revolves around a romance between the Irish Rose Maurrant (Sylvia Sidney) and the Jewish Sam Kaplan (William Collier Jr.); the marital infidelity of Rose's mother Anna (Estelle Taylor); and the threatening, violent, and eventually murderous rage that ultimately drives Rose's father, Frank (David Landau), to murder his wife.

Thematically and stylistically similar to *Street Scene*, *Dead End* is a more intricately plotted drama that draws upon familiar motifs of the gangster genre, yet self-consciously engages social issues such as the gap between the poor and wealthy classes. Directed by William Wyler, *Dead End* has been justly celebrated for its elaborate recreation of the Lower East Side on a studio sound stage. Adapting the stage play by Sidney Kingsley, Lillian Hellman, a playwright herself, had to work within the recently imposed restrictions of the Production Code Administration. When gangster Hugh "Baby Face" Martin (Humphrey Bogart) returns to his old neighborhood and the breeding ground for his behavior, it sets into motion a plan to kidnap the nephew of a prominent judge whose elegant apartment towers over the squalor of the slum. Meanwhile, Martin's boyhood friend Dave Connell (Joel McCrea) is torn between two romantic relationships: one with a wealthy kept woman (Wendy Barrie), the other with Drina (Sylvia Sidney), an idealistic garment worker involved in union organizing. Also in keeping with the Production Code, the film elides—though it strongly suggests—that Baby Face Martin's one-time girlfriend (Claire Trevor) is now a prostitute suffering from the beginning stages of syphilis. The film is also notable in introducing the Dead End Kids (Huntz Hall, Billy Halop, Leo Gorcey, Bobby Jordan, Gabriel Dell, and Bernard Punsly), an ensemble of young actors who later starred in subsequent films and even their own series. While these later films domesticated the Kids' anti-social tendencies, *Dead End* brilliantly links the menacing and psychologically unstable Baby Face Martin to the uproarious pranks of the Dead End Kids. The film argues that what begins with boys forced to use the street as their playground ends in the criminal and menacing behavior of gangsters like Baby Face.

Just Saying "Shit": Naturalism and Social Thought

The city, of course, had a physical dimension of being cramped, stifling, and breeding various behaviors. The power of myth, however, rests not in its ability to fabricate but in its ability to shape and reinforce perceptions so that they may conform to, or resist, varying and competing ideologies. Here, one can read specific films like *Street Scene* and *Dead End* as symptomatic of a larger ideological arc within American culture. The ideological symptoms that these films represent provide an index of American attitudes and perceptions of the city—and, by extension, of the blandishment of a suburban existence. Ultimately, though, the films represent more than just the ideological underpinning for massive shifts from urban to suburban population centers. They comprise a larger system of myth-making that shapes consciousness, perception, and blindness to consequences.

The myth of the city is formed from a flexible and sophisticated process in which ideas emerge, morph, submerge, and re-emerge. The city-myth is its own form of ideological assimilation, absorbing oppositional social protest and domesticating it for assimilated middle-class audiences; razing whole ethnic neighborhoods to make way for the forces of global capital; and, eventually with 9/11, taking down global capital in what Jean Baudrillard calls "a triumphant globalization at war with itself" (14).

As part of the larger, ongoing arc from urbanization to globalization, the city-myth extends back, at least in its modern formulation, to the rise of late-nineteenth- and early-twentieth-century literary naturalism. Naturalism depicts human behavior as animalistic; the link intends to startle apathy and attack poverty and social injustice, making the assumption that human beings are driven to animal behavior by their living conditions. It was a way of confronting middle- and upper-class audiences by dispensing with stylistic sugar coating and rubbing the noses of these audiences in the filth and degradation of poverty and the brutal living conditions of the lower classes. In its broadest terms, naturalism emerged, at least in its American context, as an artistic response to sweeping social changes taking place at the end of the nineteenth century, in particular the rise of the city (Giles). Ratner observes that naturalism depicts individuals as "trapped in their biology or in the toils of economic and social determinism" (169). But naturalism, once and still easily dismissed as an outdated—and ill-advised—crude blend of racism, Social Darwinism, Social Realism, and psychology, has more recently undergone a reappraisal. One can view the determinism inherent in the naturalistic worldview not so much as rationalizing the status quo of harsh conditions and making them seem normal, but as a pointed and challenging response to the false hope, alienation, and vapid consumerism offered by modernity's indiscriminate celebration of individualism, freedom, and social mobility.

In France, for example, where naturalism had a much more delineated cultural history than in the United States, naturalist author Emile Zola implored a younger generation of more genteel Symbolist writers to just "say shit to the century" and all of its so-called progress (Kleeblatt). "Just say shit" offered up frankness as a weapon against decorous disregard for the truth of human suffering and social injustice. To "just say shit" epitomized what naturalism represented as an artistic style: an attempt to deflate the willful blindness of progress and prosperity with a pointed and magnified attention to the details of what human suffering was like when trapped within circumstances beyond one's control. Shit could signify a chain of other signifiers: human excrement; vile, animal-like living conditions; a basic function of all human bodies; a reminder of what makes humans animals. In addition to its frankness, shit could also signify waste and excess. Described in profuse detail, it could rub one's nose in the less pleasant and comfortable aspects of human existence. But most of all, at least in the context of Zola's message, saying shit meant a politicized provocation to authority, apathy, and the convenient societal self-deceptions camouflaged as decorum. *Street Scene* and *Dead End*, critically acclaimed Samuel Goldwyn film adaptations of two stage plays (the first written and directed on Broadway by Elmer Rice, with Beulah Bondi; the second written and directed by Sidney Kingsley, with a cast including Sidney Lumet), draw upon this sensibility to heighten our awareness of tenement life in New York, and demand our close scrutiny of immigrant living conditions.

As in any civil society, one must negotiate the complexities of both shit and shifts amid the swirling flows of imagery and discourse. As modern American society underwent profound shifts throughout the 1920s and 1930s, the ethnic immigrant often served as an acute focal point of representation. The representation of the ethnic immigrant provides a safe surrogate to express concern over modernity, displacing such concerns away from the diffuse but deeply felt structures of lived experience and onto the visible, squalid bodies of marginalized ethnic Others. The image of the ethnic immigrant represents not just the Other but the position from which one sees this Other. This position operates in constant flux, subject to ongoing ideological negotiation. Thus, while naturalism could inflect *Street Scene* and *Dead End*, their naturalist inflections could serve different ends from Zola's initial project. If Zola intended to say shit to progress and modernity, both Goldwyn-produced films were saying shit to the ghetto for its incompatibility with progress, modernity, and being American. While naturalism used graphic imagery to rail against social conditions brought about by progress, opposition to naturalism re-contextualized this imagery. Renegotiating the meaning of filth and excess, subsequent appropriations of the naturalist style subtly altered the visceral signifiers of poverty from indicting to affirming the status quo of social relations. Now, people came to be disparaged for failing to conform to that newly esteemed status quo.

Emphasis upon spectacle allowed naturalism to resonate with a discourse on photography. Both naturalism and popular photography posited a scientific, objective stance from which to conduct observation. In establishing the position of an unseen, dispassionate, and detached observer, both objectivities arguably shared the same ideological blind spot. Any framing—literary or visual, and no matter how avowedly objective—exerts its own highly selective subjectivity. The scientific veneer of this objectivity in naturalism played out as a confrontation between the observer and the selected, sordid, and magnified details of the observed. Confounding aesthetic expectations of the time, naturalism substituted science for melodrama, creating an emotional catharsis through the shock value of spectacle. Popular photography—the countless postcards, stereoscopes, and even early film—achieves a similar end, paralleling the emergence of modern incarceration and the Panopticon, an architectural design articulated by Jeremy Bentham. The layout of this modern prison affords an ideal position from which a supervisor may survey deviant bodies. The Panopticon arranges these bodies into individual cells, illuminated with backlight and encircling a central guard tower. While photography does not of necessity imprison in a literal sense, it does parallel the function of arranging "spatial unities that make it possible to see constantly and recognize immediately" yet at the same time see subjects who do not see back. Under this arrangement, the Other is "the object of information, never a subject of communication" (Foucault 200).

Naturalism and Immigration Discourse

Both naturalism and photography remained uniquely suited to the discourse on immigration to the United States, and the fascination of this discourse with the immigrant body as foreign Other. Needless to say, New York is a central punctum in late-eighteenth- and early-nineteenth-century immigration movements, and films about immigrant life in New York, such as *Street Scene* and *Dead End*, intensively illuminate the naturalist depiction of the urban ethnic immigrant. Coinciding with the emergence of scientific racism during the late nineteenth and early twentieth centuries, anti-immigration arguments expressed concern over what an incoming flood of foreigners would do to the essential character of the nation. Yet annual figures for immigration between 1881 and 1910—the greatest in this country's history—never accounted for more than one to two percent of the entire U.S. population. In fact, after a devastating economic depression in 1897, immigration had dropped from 790,000 in 1882 to below 230,000 in 1898. Of course, annual immigration continued to rise in successive years, reaching 1.3 million by 1907. Even this figure, however, never amounted to more than a few percent of the total population (Joseph 174). Nevertheless, many believed an immigrant flood was washing over the land, bringing with it a torrent of socially undesirable consequences.

With the rise of race science in the nineteenth century, many viewed immigrants as racially inferior to people of Anglo-Saxon heritage. Others—including President Woodrow Wilson—feared that the so-called hyphenated American would bring Old World animosities to a New World melting pot. Riis's *How the Other Half Lives* furthered concern over immigrants and the ghettos in which they resided. Riis argued that the living conditions of the tenements bred disease—in terms of both individual health and social vice. The book's photographs sought to depict the tenement dwellers in a matter-of-fact, objective, and perhaps even scientific style. Riis's book led to widespread social reforms in housing and education. It also established a seemingly detached way of discussing and looking at immigrants that nevertheless betrayed fascination, disgust, and empathy for these lower-class subjects.

The powerful convergence of immigration, photography, and the flexibility of naturalism created a compelling stance from which to view the city and convey a uniquely American city-myth. Unflinchingly realistic and exhaustively researched, stage productions of *Street Scene* (1929) and *Dead End* (1935) borrowed extensively from naturalism to expose the negative effects of the ghetto environment. In Elmer Rice's autobiography, one sees the underpinnings of a naturalist sensibility and its concern for how environment determines behavior when he explains the conception for *Street Scene*:

> The house was much more than a background; it was an integral part of the play. It might almost be said that it *was* the play. I had been strongly influenced by the work of the seventeenth-century French painter Claude Lorrain, in most of whose pictures there was a dominant architectural unit, usually ornate and romanticized; in the foreground were groups of figures, seen always in relation to the pervasive structure. . . . Though it was a far cry from the idyllic classical painting of Claude to a realistic play about modern New York, I was excited by the concept of a large number of diverse individuals whose behavior and relationships were largely conditioned by their accidental common occupancy of a looming architectural pile. (Rice 237)

Furthermore, the intensity of detailed observation plays a central function in both works. Early scenes in both *Street Scene* and *Dead End* show an elderly woman taking food away from a baby. In a dramatic moment from *Dead End*, one of the characters goes to visit her lover, a starving artist. She runs out of the apartment building, however, after recoiling at the sight of a cockroach. Frequent allusions to animal and insect imagery in depicting tenement life provided more than just a backdrop to suggest various taboos. This imagery reinforces the message that the ghetto is a breeding ground for anti-social behavior. In *Street Scene*, an adulterous affair triggers violent domestic abuse. In *Dead End*, a gangster returns to the neighborhood where his juvenile delinquency began and his early life of crime was bred. A band of juvenile delinquents in the latter play parallels the gangster's own boyhood. Indeed, an added subtitle to the 1940s re-release of the film emphasized *Dead End* as "The Cradle of Crime."

This detailed observation of tenement life and its stark contrast to urban prosperity insisted on the power of social conditioning to influence the individual. Shortly following the triumphant debut of *Dead End*, Sidney Kingsley wrote a piece for the *New York Times* in which he defended the new approach of a "theatre unshackled by formula" by implicitly invoking the setting for his new play:

> Here is the river, a brown river mucky with refuse and offal and variegated filth, swirling scum an inch thick. Little boys, a strange race of hairy apes, splash about in this filth. To the left, arching the river, is Queensboro Bridge, spired, delicate, weblike in its stone and concrete, which it plants like giant uncouth feet on the earth. In its hop, skip, jump over the river it has planted one such foot on that island called, ironically, Welfare. Down this chute it

drops broken men and women, destined to the hospital, the insane asylum and the prison. (2)

Both *Street Scene* and *Dead End* received critical and popular accolades. Rice won the 1929 Pulitzer Prize for Drama, and Kingsley's play enjoyed almost seven hundred performances. The popularity of both plays appears to capitalize upon different images of the immigrant. *Street Scene* makes much of how various ethnic groups remain crowded together, mistrustful and barely tolerant of one another. Part ethnic comedy, part assimilation tragedy, and part inter-ethnic romance, *Street Scene* emphasizes the value of assimilation. The first half of the play treats ethnic differences comically, with Jews, Italians, Germans, Norwegians, and Irish broadly displaying their respective cultural traits. A romance between Rose Maurrant and Sam Kaplan alludes to another phenomenally popular play of the day, *Abie's Irish Rose*. The cross-ethnic romance articulates the assimilationist ideal, in which the next generation will cast off the Old World ways of the parents to better integrate with society. By comparison, *Dead End* elides ethnicity even though Kingsley sets the drama on New York's Lower East Side. Without overt ethnic attribution, the play much more self-consciously addresses the ghetto as both breeding ground and social problem. However, Kingsley's play does allude to some vestiges of ethnicity. For example, the sympathetic character of Drina is both a garment worker and a labor activist, two occupations closely associated with Jews throughout the thirties.

The arc from overt depiction of ethnicity to the self-conscious social problem film parallels a shifting discourse on immigration. In 1924, Congress passed the Johnson-Reed Immigration Act, which established a quota system that limited immigration to no more than two percent of any one nationality residing in the United States in 1890. Once Congress effectively terminated immigration to the United States, the discourse began to shift from one that fretted over ethnic difference to one that asserted a cohesive national identity. A naturalist style could remain consistent with both overt depictions of ethnicity and a more streamlined depiction of the ghetto as social problem. In both *Street Scene* and *Dead End*, the ghetto determines human behavior. The way in which the ghetto determines behavior differs in the two films: harboring Old World hatreds in *Street Scene*, and in *Dead End* standing in marked contrast to the encroaching gentrification of high-rise apartments built along the river by the wealthy.

Naturalism and 9/11

Film adaptations of these stage productions could heighten their incipient realism, yet such potential remained bounded by a series of cultural and institutional constraints upon the motion picture industry. Produced at a time of remarkable cultural ferment within U.S. culture, both films promised radical critiques of American society. Both *Street Scene* and *Dead End*, for example, feature characters who espouse anti-capitalist rhetoric. Such dialogue resonates with the efforts of the Popular Front, a leftist attempt of the early to mid-1930s to articulate a Marxist perspective through popular culture. At the same time, however, the statements of *Dead End*'s Drina and Abe Kaplan (Max Montor), the elderly patriarch of *Street Scene*, remain subordinate to other narrative functions. Drina emerges as a love interest of the play, while the film version of *Street Scene* emphasizes comic aspects of Abe's thick, guttural accent.

In certain other respects, *Street Scene* remains a franker attempt to depict the ghetto than *Dead End*. *Street Scene* predates the strict enforcement of the Production Code in 1934. In response to a threatened boycott by the Catholic Church, the film industry created a self-regulatory censorship arm. Among other things, the Code forbade sympathetic depictions of adultery, a key element of the narrative of *Street Scene*. In 1937, *Dead End* could escape some Code strictures through cinematic gestures: it is when she moves into a harsh shaft of light that both the spectator and Baby Face Martin discover his ex-girlfriend has become a diseased prostitute. Of the two films, at least in spirit *Dead End*'s narrative hews more closely to the Code, turning its crippled-artist hero into a struggling architect. Such alterations operated consistently with the Code precepts of presenting "correct standards of life" and not engendering "sympathy" for the violation of what the code referred to as "natural law." Similarly, it is after his own mother disowns Baby Face Martin that police officers can safely unload their rounds into the gangster.

Visually, naturalist tendencies link both films in powerful ways. Both films share many of the production personnel responsible for their respective looks, unsurprisingly since independent producer Samuel Goldwyn made both films. Sylvia Sidney stars in both films, although in *Street Scene* she plays Irish love interest Rose Maurrant while in *Dead End* she plays a character whose ethnicity must be read in terms of her politics and her occupation. Richard Day designed elaborate sets for both films, which earned a great deal of applause for their realism. Gregg Toland, the cinematographer for *Dead End*, studied extensively under *Street Scene*'s cinematographer, George Barnes. As adaptations of stage plays, both films construct a kind of naturalist panopticon to look at the ghetto and tenements. Each film begins with a similar establishing shot of Manhattan. In both films, there follows a montage of successive dissolves, in which the camera tracks downward, locating the street of key narrative focus. This macroscopic to microscopic trope remains consistent with the scientific veneer of naturalism. The trope suggests the possibility of surveillance, in which the one who sees can obtain an ideal position without being seen.

The cinematography—particularly the camera angles—extends this trope. Both films include one extreme, low-angle shot of a tenement building. In *Dead End*, motivation for this point-of-view shot remains unclear. In *Street Scene*, however, a nearly identical angle and framing occurs, but includes the body of an immigrant with her back to the camera. In a naturalist flourish, the shot depicts the immigrant obviously adjusting sweaty undergarments as she talks to her neighbor in a window above. The neighbor in the window clearly does not see this take place; only the audience does. From its ideal vantage point, the audience can survey this animal-like behavior of the immigrant body. In keeping with the Production Code strictures of good taste, the low-angle shot in *Dead End* effectively erases the body and movement of the immigrant from its view. Yet it leaves the construction of the viewing position in place. A way of looking thus triumphs over what one sees. Just as one could use the characteristics of naturalism to espouse an anti-naturalist position, one could also deploy naturalist flourishes in such a way that did not challenge power, but rather reinforced its ideology.

Neither *Street Scene* nor *Dead End* functions in a particularly unique manner in condemning the ghetto. In *What Makes Sammy Run?* (1941), author Budd Schulberg answers the eponymous question about the amorality of Sammy Glick—the novel's central character—by having the book's narrator return to "the breeding ground for the predatory germ that thrived in Sammy's blood, leaving him one of the most severe cases of the epidemic."

As I have argued in *Hollywood and Anti-Semitism*, *What Makes Sammy Run?* does not demonize Glick for the sake of demonizing Jews, as much as it demonizes the Jewish Glick to convey a critique of the American Dream. The book's narrator, Al Mannheim, is particularly hostile to Glick's immigrant background. He thinks of

Sammy Glick rocking in his cradle of hate, malnutrition, prejudice, suspicions, amorality, the anarchy of the poor; I thought of him as a mangy little puppy in a dog-eat-dog world. I was modulating my hate for Sammy Glick from the personal to the societal. I no longer even hated Rivington Street but the idea of Rivington Street, all Rivington Streets of all nationalities allowed to pile up in cities like gigantic dung heaps smelling up the world, ambitions growing out of filth and crawling away like worms.

At a time when many Jews placed nationality above ethnicity, the highest form of assimilation would be to renounce one's ethnic roots. Schulberg's vision of this renunciation, seen through Mannheim, greatly values the assimilation process. Not only does Mannheim deny ethnic identity as compatible with Americanism; Schulberg appropriates antisemitic imagery to show how ethnic identity provides the breeding ground for all that is at odds with the American Dream.

Few discourses operate in a completely stable fashion. In this context, the appropriation and sublimation of a naturalist style in the representation of immigrant bodies is noteworthy. What once meant to challenge power eventually functions as surveillance meant to disempower. What once could just "say shit" to the century eventually came to mean a faith in progress and modernity at odds with the Old World ways of the ghetto and, by extension, one's immigrant heritage. The World Trade Center became the ultimate manifestation of this logic, as this 1960s urban renewal project condemned the neighborhood, ending decades of skirmishes between city leaders and the largely ethnic communities and markets that thrived there.

In a remarkably lucid essay following September 11, Jean Baudrillard observes that the attack on the World Trade Center represented not a war between the West and Islam, but a "triumphant globalization at war with itself." According to Baudrillard, globalization remains just as responsible for terrorism as it does for erecting the once monumental towers. "When the world has been so thoroughly monopolized," he notes, "when power has been so formidably consolidated by the technocratic machine and the dogma of capitalism, what means of turning the tables remains beside terrorism?" (14).

In the West and particularly in the United States, most discussions of globalization tend to locate its effects as a recent phenomenon. While the phenomenon of globalization has achieved great momentum in the past decade, the belief in its recent emergence is a luxury held by the centers of cultural and economic power that for centuries have colonized, slaughtered, and exploited indigenous peoples across the globe. Despite conventional wisdom, the destruction of the World Trade Center represents not an alleged Islamic hatred for the West but, as Baudrillard describes, the very process of globalization itself. The platitudes of U.S. foreign policy notwithstanding, no one explanation can ever fully render this complex set of circumstances. However, one can better understand the new globalism by taking a closer look at its assumptions, and how these assumptions are the culmination of a much older, more extensive, and multifaceted process spanning hundreds if not thousands of years.

In the past century, globalization has arguably achieved an accelerated momentum, in large part due to significant shifts in political, economic, and cultural life. The vicissitudes of the World Trade Center are part of a larger narrative involving the rise and fall of an American assimilationist fantasy set against the backdrop of the city-myth. And this assimilationist city-myth is apotheosized in the image of New York, particularly as it is treated in films like *Street Scene* and *Dead End*. Built atop the remnants of turn-of-the-century ethnic immigrant urban neighborhoods and haphazard patchworks of ethnic markets, urban revitalization projects such as the Twin Towers realized the Horatio Alger-like success of a melting-pot America by erasing the ethnic urban identities that once occupied its ground-level foundation. The erasure was hardly accidental. Obliterating the ghetto, urban revitalization dreamed of replacing Old World squalor with a sleek architectural monument to a burgeoning internationalism, modernity, technocracy, and global capital. When the towers collapsed, so too did the idea of inventing and inverting urban space from old world ghetto to a new world global financial center. If moving out of the tenement and into the suburbs turned out to be an unrecognized American Nightmare that allowed revitalization finally to crush urban ethnic immigrant neighborhoods beneath the massive shining skyscrapers of progress and modernity, 9/11 delivered a startling awakening into the harsh light of a new global era.

Another kind of monster: Mark Chapman (Broderick Crawford, l.), editor of a cheap tabloid in the inescapable terrain of noir, in *Scandal Sheet* (Phil Karlson, Edward Small Productions/Columbia, 1952). Collection Wheeler Winston Dixon.

Night World

NEW YORK AS A NOIR UNIVERSE

WHEELER WINSTON DIXON

The night holds promise and the night holds danger. If we view the domain of the night as a zone in which our inhibitions are loosened, we can also see it as a place without rules, where restrictions are relaxed, where people can pass us by, unnoticed in the dark. In cinema, the night can serve as a visual metaphor for gaiety and abandon, or despair and resignation. But above all, the night in film functions as a literal and figurative zone of darkness, a place that must be illuminated so that we can see. In all "night/city" films, the darkness surrounds the characters within the narrative, threatening to engulf them at any moment. The frame's blackness seeps into the faces of the protagonists in these doomed films, etching their features with fear and apprehension. In musicals and screwball comedies, the night functions as an arena of social release, a world where laughter and gaiety are unceasing. But in films that belong to night and the city as a central theme, it is despair and violence that dominate the screen. Indeed, the true domain of the noir is night, just as the inescapable terrain of the noir is the city. Rural noirs, such as Nicholas Ray's *On Dangerous Ground* (1952) and Delmer Daves's *The Red House* (1947), are few and far between.

New York at night is more nocturnal than any other place onscreen. The deserted streets become invitations to danger and violence; the depopulated spaces of the night are the mirror image of the bustling metropolis in the daytime. New York has a hold on our imagination because it is so compact, so violent, so energetic, so full of possibilities, a place where neighborhoods change from one street to the next and strangers can become intimate friends or deadly enemies on the slightest of whims. New York at night is the ultimate domain of the unreal; it is the phantom zone of eternal play and perpetual unease. Mutability is the key characteristic of New York at night, a realm transformed by the absence of illumination. Anything is possible, nothing is forbidden, all of it is just steps away from your door. The city opens its arms to you: arms of the night, and of darkness.

Before the Disneyfication of Times Square, the grind house movie theaters on Forty-second Street stayed open all night, running double and triple bills for audiences who refused to return to their apartments. The Stork Club, Sherman Billingsley's private domain, hosted such luminaries as Walter Winchell and Ed Sullivan, who reported daily on the gossip of the Great White Way. On Fifty-second Street, the jazz clubs that defined the Bop Era presented the likes of Charlie Parker, Duke Ellington, and Dizzy Gillespie, while down in Greenwich Village poets and artists gathered at the Cafe Cino, the Cafe Reggio, and other nightspots to hear the latest in cool jazz. Horn and Hardart's cafeteria chain stayed open all night, offering a cup of coffee and a hamburger to hungry denizens of Broadway. The subway, too, ran all night, and the "A" train could get you from Forty-second Street to Harlem in a matter of minutes. Newspaper stands, all-night delis, cut-rate novelty stores, Nedick's fast-food chain, Walgreen's drugstores that sold everything from toothpaste to fly swatters: everything was open, and in these spots everything was for sale.

Manhattan at night remains a world of its own, though time has passed and many long-time institutions have closed. Really, they've just moved to a new location. The city never really sleeps; it's one of the only cities in the nation to have a "night mayor," whose job it is to stay up all night in case something really major happens. And, of course, the DJs and talk show hosts, offering chat, twenty-four-hour news, and round-the-clock music, fill the airwaves with information and entertainment designed to get you through the night, so that you can last until the dawn. Unlike almost every other city in the United States, Manhattan, just eight miles long and two and a half miles wide, crams millions of people into one gigantic, ever unfolding tapestry of desire and danger. At night, this is a world at once ephemeral and real, where dreams play out in the silhouettes of electric lights and flashing neon signs, a zone of perpetual excitement, promise, and mutability. It is a domain that answers only to its own peculiar laws, and promises something for everyone, if the price is right.

Bereft of Hope: *Night World* and *Bowery at Midnight*

My essay takes its name from Hobart Henley's 1932 film *Night World*, a sharp little fifty-eight-minute thriller that takes place entirely within the boundaries of a Prohibition-era nightclub. Although it was created before the major postwar noir cycle (roughly between 1945 and 1955), *Night World*, along with a number of pre-Code 1930s films, embraces the aesthetics of noir both in visual stylization and in philosophical outlook. *Night World* features a truly amazing cast—including Lew Ayres, Mae Clark, Boris Karloff, Hedda Hopper, George Raft, Louise Beavers, Jack La Rue, and numerous others—in a hardboiled story involving murder, blackmail, gambling, and illicit liquor. But this is just one of the many films that treat the city at night as a separate realm, a zone of timelessness and pleasure, in which destinies are changed and alliances forged or broken within the span of a few hours: Wallace Fox's *Bowery at Midnight* (1942), Phil Karlson's *Scandal Sheet* (1952), Henry Levin's *Night Editor* (1946), H. Bruce Humberstone's *I Wake Up*

Screaming (1941), and many others. These films depict the city as a vast Metropolis of dreams, entangled lives, and intermingled desires, a world that is, in Otto Friedrich's memorable phrase, a "city of nets."

In *Night World*, Happy MacDonald (Boris Karloff) owns a Prohibition-era nightclub, where his wife, known only as "Mrs. Mac" (Dorothy Revier), is a cashier. Unbeknownst to Happy, his wife is having an affair with Klauss (Russell Hopton), who works as the club's choreographer. Happy is an atypical role for Karloff: a smooth operator who runs his club with a mixture of persuasion, violence, and unctuous charm. Yet it reminds us of the considerable range Karloff was capable of before he became hopelessly typecast and performed almost solely in horror films. The entire film takes place during one evening; matters reach a crisis when Happy and his wife are killed by some disgruntled bootleggers, while the club's star attraction, Ruth Taylor (Mae Clark), falls in love with Michael Rand (Lew Ayres), a young man about town whose alcohol consumption is getting out of hand.

At the end of the film life goes on, irrespective of the various deaths, plot twists, and changed fortunes in which the film delights. A symbol of New York itself, the nightclub is a scene at which people arrive and from which they depart without explanations, in a constant traffic of possibilities, hopes, despairs, and confusions, to become a part of the nocturnal fabric of the urban world. *Night World* shows us New York City during the height of the Depression, a sort of miniature *Grand Hotel* where lives intersect in a series of surprising and often violent incidents. Patterned after the numerous speakeasies that dominated New York nightlife in the late 1920s and early 1930s, including Texas Guinan's famous watering hole, *Night World* could exist only in the neon glow of the New York night world, where gangsters and socialites rub elbows, imbibing bootlegged liquor, paying off cops, shoring up with extra drinks at "last call," anything to keep the day from dawning and throwing them back into the merciless marketplace. The characters here are the denizens of New York who really don't exist during the day; they come out only at night, and their entire lives are constructed around illegal, alcoholic recreation. *Night World* is emblematic, then, of the underground trade in booze and narcotics that ruled the Depression era New York nightlife, where anything could be had for a price, if you knew the right door to knock on.

A different view of New York at night is depicted in veteran director Wallace Fox's bleak morality tale, *Bowery at Midnight* (1942), in which Béla Lugosi plays a triple role: a kindly academic, an equally munificent soup kitchen operator, and the leader of a ruthless gang of sociopathic criminals. As Professor Brenner, a criminology professor at an unnamed Manhattan community college, Lugosi is a popular and innovative teacher (who nevertheless pays too much attention to his female students). In the role of his secret alter ego, Karl Wagner, Lugosi runs the ironically named Friendly Mission, where he recruits members for his gang.

Judy Malvern (Wanda McKay), convinced that Karl Wagner is a crusading social reformer, works at the Friendly Mission as an assistant.

So complete is Brenner's duplicity that even his own wife (Anna Hope) is unaware of his double life. If to the community at large he is a model educator, and in his alter ego he is the charitable benefactor of the less fortunate on New York City's Lower East Side, behind both of these personae the real man is a ruthless killer, a sadistic martinet, and a human monster who delights in torture and murder. When Wagner has one of his criminal associates bumped off, the man is buried in the cellar by his stuttering aide, Doc Brooks (Lew Kelly), a disgraced physician who mysteriously brings the corpses back to life as zombies to do Doc's bidding, but without Wagner's knowledge. As Wagner becomes bolder in his exploits, he enlists the aid of psychopathic triggerman Frankie Mills (Tom Neal) to murder all who oppose him, even the supposedly faithful members of his own gang. Naturally, the police have no inkling that any of this is happening and, in a neat, class-conscious touch, become involved only when one of Professor Brenner's star students, Richard Dennison (John Archer), accidentally stumbles into the Friendly Mission and discovers Brenner's dual identity as Wagner. Fearing discovery, Wagner has the youth murdered in cold blood and then turns the corpse over to Doc Brooks, who soon converts it into yet another "undead" assistant.

Eventually, after more violence (and a strong subtext of dictatorial hypersurveillance, in which Wagner spies on his gang members through the then-experimental medium of television), the police crash in on the mission and uncover Brenner/Wagner's illicit operation. At the film's climax, Doc Brooks's zombies attack Brenner/Wagner and literally tear him to pieces, as the surviving cast members look on with satisfaction. The message in *Bowery at Midnight* is that in the New York night all is surface, and nothing is to be trusted. Everyone, and everything, is a front. Both the professor and the soup kitchen operator are fronts for the real Wagner/Brenner, a conscienceless criminal mastermind for whom all others are merely instruments to be used at will. The city here is relentlessly instrumental and feelingless, then, brutal, deceptive, and aggressively hungry.

Bowery at Midnight was produced by Monogram Pictures, one of the very cheapest of the Hollywood "Poverty Row" studios, and was shot in five days for less than $50,000. It is a cheap and shoddy production in every respect, with a bizarre, even preposterous, plot and threadbare production values. And yet, one must ask, why would the studio pursue a film so easy to dismiss? What better way, however, to present a cheap and rotten urban universe than in an equally cheap and rotten film? *Bowery at Midnight* seeks no higher moral plane, and refuses to pass judgment on any of its protagonists, reveling in a New York where principle always lingers in the shadow of profit. In the end, Brenner/Wagner is ripped up by his own rapacious greed and ambition, rather than by police procedure. Indeed, *Bowery at Midnight* seems to suggest that monsters like Brenner/Wagner may continue to exist in society as long as they successfully camouflage their activities and pay lip service to existing social conventions. Nothing is as it seems, and all educators and benefactors are suspect. Who knows what anyone's true motives are?

Bowery at Midnight is a vision of New York at its bleakest, a locus of collapsed dreams rather than the zone of limitless possibility pictured in early-twentieth-century immigration narratives. The New York we see in *Bowery at Midnight* is rundown, decrepit, bereft of hope, a city that reeks of failure: for example, the soup kitchen used by Lugosi's character as a front for his criminal operations is dingy and unsavory; the police hover continuously at the edges of the narrative, but never intrude until the film's final moments. *Bowery at Midnight* depicts a city ruled by crime, in which all endeavors are suspect, and average citizens are merely victims. There is nothing of the glitz and glamour of the great metropolis here, but rather an unrelenting vision of New York City as hell, a place from which there is no escape.

City Monsters: *Scandal Sheet, The Whistler,* **and** *Night Editor*

Broderick Crawford, as Mark Chapman, editor of a cheap New York tabloid, the *Express*, is yet another kind of monster. Based on the novel *The Dark Page* by noir director Samuel Fuller, Phil Karlson's *Scandal Sheet is* a bleak, violent thriller cranked out at Columbia Pictures during the final years of the reign of Harry Cohn, Columbia's legendarily vitriolic boss. Chapman is ruthless in his quest to boost circulation for the *Express*, no matter how low he has to stoop, no matter whom he has to step on or what cheap tactics he has to employ. His protégé, Steve McCleary (John Derek), is equally corrupt, posing as a police inspector at the start of the film with his equally hardboiled photographer, Biddle (Harry Morgan), in order to get graphic photographs of a murder scene before the real police arrive and chase them off. Julie Allison (Donna Reed) is a holdover on the newspaper from an earlier, more sedate regime. She despises Mark Chapman and his tactics but needs a job, so she puts up with the increasingly yellow tint of the paper's coverage. Even the *Express*'s board of directors are alarmed at the sensationalistic tone of the paper, but in a violently charged meeting Mark persuasively argues that only violence and brutality sell papers to the public and that he has no time for journalistic integrity or ethics.

Indeed, Mark, played by Crawford in his typically blunt, brutal manner, routinely refers to his readers as "slobs" and "idiots," and thinks nothing of cooking up cheap stunts to further boost circulation. One such stunt is a Lonely Hearts ball, where pathetic singles are thrown together in a cheap, garish spectacle and promised second-rate home appliances if they marry immediately and give the *Express* complete rights to their life stories. Attending this ball, Mark hustles the proceedings along but fails to notice when one Charlotte Grant (Rosemary DeCamp) recognizes him, and for good reason: under the name Grant, decades ago, he had married her, then walked out, changing his identity and building himself up at the *Express*. Recognizing that he has been discovered, Mark arranges a clandestine meeting with her in her apartment, in which he offers a payoff in return for her silence. But Charlotte is understandably vindictive and the two get into a shouting match. In a moment of anger, Mark pushes Charlotte away from him. To his horror, she falls against a wall and hits her head on a gas pipe connection. The blow is enough to kill her. Desperate to avoid detection, Mark cleans up the crime scene, and then makes Charlotte's death look like an accident; she fell and hit her head while taking a shower.

But when Steve McCleary investigates the next day, he recognizes that this was no accident; it was deliberate murder. Here, in a curious twist, even though Mark knows himself to be the killer, he is unable to resist playing up the murder in a series of sensational front-page stories, written by McCleary, that tighten the noose around his own neck. When a veteran ex-*Express* reporter, Charlie Barnes (Henry O'Neill), now a hopeless alcoholic, discovers evidence leading to Chapman's identity as the murderer, no one believes him. No one, that is, except Mark, who tracks Charlie down and kills him in one of the seedier parts of town. But despite all Mark's evasive tactics, Steve and Julie eventually track down the link between Mark Chapman and his former self, Grant, specifically in the person of Judge Hacker (Griff Barnett), who originally married Mark and Charlotte. Exposed, Mark pulls a gun on Steve and Julie, and then dictates the story of his capture and arrest as his last act as a newspaperman. Then, pretending to shoot at some police who have arrived to arrest him, Mark allows himself to be cut down in a hail of bullets in his office, just as the circulation of the *Express* reaches an all-time high (as we see by a meter, prominently displayed on the wall of Mark's office, that continually monitors the paper's circulation throughout the film). Had he lived, Mark would have been eligible for a hefty salary boost, and a financial interest in the *Express*. Now, his is just another disposable headline, another circulation grabber. Like all the other grist for his narcissistic mill, he's a sensation today, forgotten tomorrow.

Many things make *Scandal Sheet* a remarkable film. The combination of Fuller as scenarist and Karlson as director "clicks" immediately; a former newspaperman, Fuller had an intimate working knowledge of how the tabloids operated on a daily basis. As Mark, Broderick Crawford was just coming off an Academy Award–winning performance in Robert Rossen's *All the King's Men* (1949) as Willie Stark, a thinly disguised version of megalomaniacal Louisiana governor and senator Huey P. Long. Crawford's Chapman is overweight, constantly heading for a drink or a cigarette, and consumed by a relentless desire to crush his competitors, a human monster who feeds on life's miseries and disasters. The very young John Derek is suitably feral and sharp as Mark's protégé Steve, while Henry O'Neill's Charlie is a pathetic loser who can't forget that he was an ace newspaper reporter before the booze took hold. Photographed by the gifted Burnett Guffey in newsreel black and white, *Scandal Sheet* is a cynical and vicious exposé of legendary big-city tabloids such as the *New York Graphic*, the *New York Mirror*, and other newspapers that dealt in tragedy for profit, playing up the cheapest, most sensationalistic angle to attract the lowest common denominator reader. Immersed in a world of unrelenting sordidness and all-encompassing greed, the characters in *Scandal Sheet* rush headlong toward their destiny, as night and the city close in on them. The newspaper business has never seemed so rotten, so thoroughly without any redeeming values as here. The film presents life as living hell, from which the only possible escape is death.

Scandal Sheet is the ultimate tabloid movie; in the world of Mark Chapman, if it bleeds, it leads. The tabloids ruled New York in the 1930s, with only the *New York Times* and the *Herald Tribune* as some sort of counterbalance; the *New York Daily News* still bills itself as "New York's picture newspaper." The tabloids relentlessly focus on the city itself as fodder for all major stories; international headlines intrude only when they are truly cataclysmic. The world of the New York tabloids is one of murder, scandal, divorce, and instantly disposable tragedy; the *Mirror*, in particular, and the *Graphic* would always go for the lowest possible common denominator in their coverage, with splashy layouts and lurid copy. Not for nothing does Chapman refer to his readers as "slobs" throughout the film; the tabloids depicted in *Scandal Sheet* offer the readers of New York City a nightmare vision of the city, ruled by violence, darkness, and corruption.

At a taut eighty-two minutes, *Scandal Sheet* was nevertheless an A-film, due to Crawford's stature as a box office attraction. The films of the *Whistler* series, however, were in the "B" category, shorter, more quickly and loosely made, and intended to fill out a double feature. In the *Whistler* series, a group of films now forgotten by all but the most avid noir buffs but nevertheless superbly entertaining, a mysterious and omniscient figure, seen only as a shadow, and known only as "the Whistler," would introduce each story with a menacing voiceover, and then return throughout the film to comment on the greed, duplicity, or brutality of the film's protagonists. Indeed, the Whistler can be seen as the ultimate noir protagonist; he is only a shadow. We never see his face.

In the *Whistler* films, the plot and characters changed with each new entry; only the star of the series, Richard Dix (in a variety of heroic or villainous roles), and the sardonic voice and shadow of the *Whistler* remained constant. In the first series entry, William Castle's *The Whistler* (1944), Dix plays a despondent figure who hires a hit man to kill him; when he tries to call the arrangement off, it's too late. In Castle's *Mark of the Whistler* (1944), Dix impersonates a missing man to gain access to the man's trust fund; in Lew Landers's *The Power of the Whistler* (1945), Dix is a homicidal killer stricken with amnesia. The series totaled eight films, each with an unexpected denouement, until the final entry in 1948. Unavailable on VHS or DVD, the *Whistler* films pop up on cable from time to time, and remain some of the most effective and unsettling noirs of the 1940s, films that incidentally gave William Castle an early chance to hone his considerable talents as a director of suspense films.

With the *Whistler* series such a resounding success, Columbia hoped for another successful series. Henry Levin's *Night Editor*, based on the then-popular "twist ending" radio mystery program of the same name, centers on a newspaper office for most of its brief sixty-eight-minute running time and was a commercial success, although oddly it never gave rise to a series. As with *The Whistler*, the central character of the radio series *Night Editor*, and of this one film, is Crane Stewart (Charles D. Brown), the night editor of a major New York tabloid, who spins macabre tales to his cronies in the wee hours of the morning. *Night Editor* begins with a superb series of establishing shots, in which Johnny (Coulter Irwin), a reporter, staggers into the offices of the sensational New York tabloid where he works. It's three in the morning; the cleaners are scrubbing the floors; the temperature is close to 100 degrees. Johnny collapses at his desk, refusing to speak to anyone, which surprises all of his colleagues, except for Crane Stewart, who, as in the *Whistler* series, seems to know the hidden motives behind everyone's actions.

As if in response to Johnny's entrance, Crane unfolds the tale of good cop Tony Cochrane (William Gargan), and his much too understanding wife, Martha (Jeff Donnell), who become enmeshed in murder because of Tony's infidelity. Tony's quiet home life is too boring, and he begins dating rich, sadistic socialite Jill Merrill (Janis Carter), attracted to her because of her good looks, her money, and her absolutely amoral stance on affairs of the heart. All that holds Tony and Jill together is lust, but that's enough; even when Tony tries to break it off during one of their late-night rendezvous, the sheer physicality of Jill's presence overwhelms him, and soon they are locked in a torrid embrace.

This night, however, will be different. As Jill and Tony passionately kiss, Tony suddenly sees another car drive up. A man gets out, and a young woman tries to follow him, but the man abruptly and violently clubs her to death with a tire iron. Instinctively grabbing his flashlight, Tony gets a good look at the killer, Douglas Loring (Frank Wilcox), the respected president of a local bank. Tony tries to catch Loring, but Jill stops him. How will he explain his presence at the murder scene, on a lonely road at night, to his wife and son, who think he's working late? For that matter, how will he explain it to his moralistic superiors, especially the perennially suspicious Ole Strom (Paul E. Burns)?

As Loring runs away, leaving the battered and dead body of the young woman behind in the abandoned car, Tony at last breaks free of Jill's embrace and walks over to inspect the murder scene. When Jill tries to follow him, Tony tells her to stay back; "It's too horrible." To Tony's shock and horror, this only serves to excite Jill's lust. "I want to see! I want to see!" she screams, as Tony, sickened by her sexual arousal as a result of the young girl's murder, pushes Jill back in the car and drives her home. Jill, too, is cheating on a spouse, the rich but elderly Benjamin Merrill (Roy Gordon). Tony tells Jill that this is the end of their relationship. The murder has shocked him back to his senses. But what will he do about it? Jill is threatening to tell his "little wifey" everything.

The balance of *Night Editor* has an almost Dostoyevskian flavor. Tony interviews Loring, knowing him to be the murderer but unable to approach his superiors: Loring knows he was at the scene of the crime, and so, complicit in covering it up, he risks losing his job and marriage. Soon, Tony is behaving more like the killer than Loring; he covers up the tire tracks of his car at the scene, deliberately erasing them with his feet, and disposes of the tires on his car to avoid detection by the police. Loring, meanwhile, continues at the bank as a respected member of society. Only a typically unexpected turn of events exposes Loring's guilt and frees Tony from the domination of Jill Merrill, restoring him to his wife and son.

As Tony's tale unfolds in flashback, we return at regular intervals to the newsroom at night, where Crane Stewart's hardened cronies hang on his every word, eager for him to continue his tale. This frame story has a twist ending itself, in which the narrative of Tony fuses with that of Johnny, the reporter who staggered into the building at the beginning of the film. Throughout the night editor's soliloquy, Johnny has been slumped at his desk, seemingly lost in his own thoughts. But as the editor concludes the Tony story, we discover that in some curious fashion it has been a warning to Johnny, who is himself engaged in an adulterous relationship. Realizing that he has been given a chance to repair the damage to his own life before things culminate in a potential disaster, Johnny rushes out of the building to make amends with his wife. The night editor gets up from his desk and opens the windows. Dawn is breaking over the city.

This little-known allegorical tale, scripted by Hal Burdick, Scott Littleton, and Hal Smith, is perhaps one of the bleakest noirs of the late 1940s, and yet it serves as a prelude for moral instruction, a peculiar task for a noir. Shot in suitably drab black and white by Burnett Guffey and Philip Tannura, one of the great noir cinematographers of the 1940s, *Night Editor* is a strange, melancholic ode to destiny and the caprices of fate, in which the city at night serves as the backdrop for a sordid tale of infidelity, murder, and deception. As in *Scandal Sheet*, Douglas Loring, the murderer, is identified immediately. Just as we know that Mark Chapman is guilty of the murder of his estranged wife, we know that Douglas Loring has viciously murdered a young woman in her car to cover up his own adulterous affair. In both cases, the murderer is allowed to hide in plain sight, and the suspense derives from wondering how, and when, the killer's guilt will be exposed to society. With a melancholic musical score by Mario Castelnuovo-Tedesco, which effortlessly evokes the crushing heat of late summer in nighttime Manhattan, *Night Editor* is a forgotten noir in which the star of the film is really the city itself and the deserted newspaper building where only a skeleton crew holds down the city desk. As with *The Whistler*, the omniscience of the night editor is never in doubt;

indeed, he knows many more tales of life in the shadows of the city. It's unfortunate that *Night Editor* remains the single film based on the popular radio series; in mood, pacing, and atmosphere, the film is a taut and engaging production.

Night Editor could be set only in Manhattan after hours, when the temperature soars in the August heat so that even the pavement sizzles well after the sun has gone down. Set, as is *Scandal Sheet*, firmly in the tabloid universe, *Night Editor* parades before the viewer a seemingly endless series of broken down reporters, unreliable stoolies, drunken copy editors, and, above it all, the unseen public who consume the stories that the tabloid puts out. But *Night Editor* speaks of the secrets of New York City, not the stories that made it to the front page or even the second section. These are stories that are "spiked," deliberately suppressed, and the eponymous title character of *Night Editor* functions not only as the supervisor of the graveyard shift but also as the arbiter of what makes tomorrow's paper, what is news, and what is not. The world presented in *Night Editor* is one of secrets that the public will never know. These are stories that newspapermen (in this all-male universe) keep to themselves, the secrets of New York City at night, a city of a thousand shadows.

City Dreams: *I Wake Up Screaming* and *Side Street*

H. Bruce Humberstone's *I Wake Up Screaming* (also known as *Hot Spot*, the working title during the film's shooting) is another tale of big-city dreams shattered by the realities of daily existence. Vicky Lynn (Carole Landis) is a hash-slinger in a Times Square restaurant when fight promoter Frankie Christopher (Victor Mature) and his show business pals, ham actor Robin Ray (Alan Mowbray, perfectly cast) and gossip columnist Larry Evans (Allyn Joslyn), decide, almost on a whim, to promote her as a rising star: *Pygmalion* in Manhattan. Vicky is all too willing to go along for the ride, although her sister, Jill (Betty Grable), remains suspicious. Why should Frankie and his friends take such an interest in Vicky? What are their true motives?

Vicky's career moves ahead smoothly—perhaps too smoothly. She soon decides to move to Hollywood for a screen contract, abandoning Frankie, Robin, and Larry. But at this point things go terribly wrong. Vicky's brutally murdered body is found in her apartment, and obsessive homicide detective Ed Cornell (Laird Cregar) steps in to solve the case. Ed is sure that Frankie is the killer, or so it seems. He grills Frankie relentlessly, and slowly but surely builds up a compelling chain of circumstantial evidence to convict the promoter.

But in a neat twist, mild-mannered bellhop Harry Williams (perennial fall guy Elisha Cook Jr.) is revealed as the murderer, a fact that Cornell has known from the beginning of the investigation. Ed Cornell's jealousy of Frankie's relationship with Vicky has driven him to frame Frankie for the murder. With Frankie cleared, Jill and Frankie can begin a married life together. Frankie, it seems, never had any feelings for Vicky, viewing her only as an investment to promote, not as a romantic partner. Thus, Cornell's jealousy has been completely misplaced. In the final moments of the film, Frankie discovers that Cornell has created a shrine to Vicky in his apartment, complete with photographs, newspaper clippings, and a makeshift "altar" to her memory. But Frankie was never a competitor; the real problem is that, weighing in at nearly 300 pounds, Ed Cornell never had a chance with Vicky at all.

I Wake Up Screaming abounds in ironies that extend beyond the framework of the film's narrative. Laird Cregar, the obsessed detective, was in reality one of Hollywood's first open homosexuals, and his immense bulk at first prevented him from working in film at all, until he found his niche as a screen psychopath. *I Wake Up Screaming* was his breakthrough film, but he would live only three years longer, dying in 1944 at the age of twenty-eight as the result of a crash diet and abuse of amphetamines in a futile bid to remake himself as a matinee idol for John Brahm's *Hangover Square*, released posthumously in 1945 (Katz 303–04). Carole Landis, the ambitious Vicky, was equally ill-starred in real life, rarely rising above B-films. After a tempestuous relationship with actor Rex Harrison, who was then married to actress Lilli Palmer, Landis committed suicide with an overdose of sleeping pills on July 6, 1948 (Katz 781).

Of all the principals, only Victor Mature emerged relatively unscathed from the making of the film. Mature continued to work in film and television until the early 1980s, and played his last role in the appropriately gaudy spear and sandal spectacle *Samson and Delilah* (1984), in the cameo role of Manoah. That in the 1949 version of *Samson and Delilah* Mature had played the role of Samson proves that in cinema as in life, you can't escape your past. Betty Grable decided she was out of her depth in dramatic roles, and returned to cheesecake vehicles and light musical comedies, though she acquits herself quite admirably here.

With all the films discussed in this essay, appearance is everything. *I Wake Up Screaming's* vision of New York at night is handily reconstructed on the Twentieth Century Fox back lot, with the aid of rear projection and a few garish sets. Ed Cornell seems forbidding because he *is* forbidding; his sheer size, coupled with his patronizing yet doggedly determined speech patterns, marks him as a man on a trajectory toward death. Victor Mature was cast for his beefcake potential, just as Betty Grable trafficked in cheesecake; to capitalize on this, *I Wake Up Screaming* contains an utterly gratuitous scene in which Frankie and Jill go to an indoor swimming pool, The Lido Plunge, the better to show off their perfectly proportioned bodies in skintight swimsuits. Vicky is foredoomed from the film's outset, because of both her ambition and her desire to "class pass" above her waitressing milieu; throughout, Cyril J. Mockridge's extradiegetic music cues signal impending disaster.

As with many noirs, lighting in *I Wake Up Screaming* is noticeable more by its absence than by its presence. During Frankie's initial interrogation by the police, we can see only his face and the harsh light that shines on it. The policemen, especially Ed Cornell, remain in darkness. They belong in the dark. When Cornell first emerges into the light in the police station, his sheer physical presence terrifies Jill, who recognizes him as a "peeping Tom" who has been hanging around the restaurant where Vicky worked. Steve Fisher's trashy source novel has given Humberstone and his cast a world devoid of light, hope, or any promise of the future, and *I Wake Up Screaming* exists in a zone where all is a perpetual nightmare, from which one can never awake.

Anthony Mann's brutal *Side Street* (1950) depicts thirty-six harrowing hours in the life of Joe Norson (Farley Granger), a lowly clerk who steals $30,000 so that his wife Ellen (Cathy O'Donnell) won't have to depend on the charity ward at Bellevue when she gives birth to their baby. Norson wants only a fraction of the money, of course, and stashes most of it with a "friend" in a bar. But when he returns to claim the cash, both his "friend" and the money have vanished. A truly amazing list of character actors weaves through this atypically seedy MGM film, including James Crary as the duplicitous conman George Garsell, Charles McGraw as hardboiled cop Stan Simon, Adele Jergens as washed-up chanteuse Lucille "Lucky" Colner, and the slatternly Minerva Urecal as Garsell's "I take 'em as they come" landlady. Shot by George Ruttenberg in boldly dynamic compositions (a man about to be killed rushes toward the camera, only to have his head blown off when he is inches from the lens; depth of focus and sharply angled shots pick up the city at its most treacherous), *Side Street* is a classic Anthony Mann noir, from a director who worked his way up through Republic Studios (*Strange Impersonation* [1945]), to Eagle-Lion (*T-Men* and *Raw Deal* [both 1948]), and finally to the majors—in short, a man who knew what it was to have nothing and then to be offered at least a foothold in a world of cinematic substance. But Anthony Mann would never forget or escape his past. A director locked in an unceasing struggle with his origins, with the lure of the dark and dangerous, Mann's best films belong solely to the night.

The night holds the secrets of our greatest crimes. The night gives free rein to those who would disrupt our lives, who view us merely as pawns in a larger game that they play for profit or merely sadistic pleasure. Money, youth, power, love, the safety of a locked front door, the police—nothing will prevent your life from being disrupted by denizens of the night, people you don't even know, driven by compulsions even they don't understand.

Toward the end of his long career, the novelist Robert Bloch wrote a screenplay entitled *Night World*, based on his novel of the same name. The screenplay was never produced, and depicted a generic city terrorized by a killer without motive. While researching another project in the early 1980s, I contacted Bloch on the phone and asked him what had become of the screenplay, and why it was never produced. "It's the only screenplay I ever wrote on spec [speculation]," Bloch replied. "It didn't have a home, but it was a story I just wanted to tell. Who knows what goes on in the city at night?" the author of *Psycho* asked me rhetorically. "It's a whole different world, where the things you can count on during the day no longer exist. Things happen there that you don't expect. It's a world of its own." There was a pervasive feeling in that scenario that the night world is out there waiting for us, promising mystery and escape, holding the dark secret of the unexpected. Every twelve hours, we are enveloped in darkness. And with each new cycle of night, our world is transformed again.

Eternal Night: *The Sleeping City* and *The Seventh Victim*

George Sherman's *The Sleeping City* (1950) is a deeply disturbing film noir, set at Bellevue Hospital and shot on location in New York. Dr. Robert Anderson (Alex Nicol) is a young intern deeply involved in the narcotics racket, as a result of his indebtedness to loan shark Pop Ware (Richard Taba), yet another noir false father figure. When Pop gets his hooks into young doctors by loaning them money he takes his payback in the form of narcotics, which the interns get by withholding them from patients who really need them after surgery and substituting a placebo instead. The opening scenes of *The Sleeping City* are unremittingly downbeat and surprisingly vicious. A young intern, fed up with stealing drugs for Pop Ware, has an acute attack of conscience and is about to inform the police of the racket. When the intern takes a break from his shift, Pop trails him to a desolate city park and shoots him at point blank range, literally sticking the gun right into the intern's face before pulling the trigger.

The doctors and nurses who work at the hospital have long since abandoned any illusions about caring for their patients. Rather, they are seen as "depressed and neurotic individuals, bitter and desperate people with little chance for a good future" (Silver and Ward 259). If they can make a bit of money on the side selling drugs, why not? The nurses' and doctors' disregard for their patients' pain is absolute; throughout the film, we see the sick on hospital gurneys waiting in hallways for treatment that never comes. The appropriately bleak cinematography by William Muller, coupled with Bernard Herzbrun and Emrich Nicholson's shabby sets, suggests that Bellevue is a place where only the damned and the doomed may apply for treatment, one step away from the concentration camp "hospitals" provided by the Nazis.

The film's location shooting adds to this effect of verisimilitude, but when Sherman screened the finished film for hospital and local government officials they were predictably horrified. As Silver and Ward point out, "The film's producers, Universal-International [finally] agreed to appease New York City Mayor O'Dwyer's opposition to *The Sleeping City* by inserting a prologue, spoken by Richard Conte, that the film's story does not describe any particular U.S. city" (259). In a sense, this dilution claims, *The Sleeping City* does not belong just to New York City; it is any big city, any nighttime hospital shift in America, where greed, weakness, and mendacity overpower the human instinct to help those in pain and suffering. Yet no filmic city at night has the power, the menace, the promise, or the intoxication of New York.

Here, the desolation of the alley is celebrated over the grandeur of the main boulevard. Here, it is always about to be night, always a place where danger is a real and tangible possibility. And when the lights go out, what then? The true world of night and the city is one in which the viewer is irretrievably lost, never to be found. The films can be noirs, or horror films, crime thrillers, or happy stories in which the protagonists don't get what they deserve. These films are now part of our shared cinematic consciousness, films to be screened at 3 A.M. on "The Late Show," films that document the zone between corporeal existence and absolute decay. The films exist to be run, and rerun, and repeated ceaselessly until they become a form of oblivion—the endless repetition of night. Watching these films at night, we are already a part of them, a part, indeed, of New York itself, because we inhabit the same world of darkness, absence, and exquisitely jazzy loneliness that is the domain of the night there.

Oblivion reaches out to touch us. We look out the window, and there is the night. We look at the television—the night has become endless. Looping back upon itself, this night will never end, never release us. This night will last forever. The night covers up a multitude of sins, hides the identities of those who don't wish to be discovered, prevents justice from being meted out, and swallows up the innocent. There is no safe place in the city at night, even in one's apartment. The locks can be forced, the door opened ever so slightly, and there is the person you never thought you'd have to face. But now you have to, because you belong to the night.

Manhattan is, in many ways, the *ur*-city of night. It is the metropolis that commands our cinematic imagination, which speaks most directly to our social fears and aspirations. Unlike Los Angeles, a sprawling neon wilderness of endless freeways and interchanges, Manhattan is compact, set out in a simple grid, easy to encompass. Perhaps a good place to end this essay is with a consideration of Mark Robson's *The Seventh Victim* (1943), one of the series of superb gothic films produced by Val Lewton for RKO in the early 1940s. Set in Greenwich Village, *The Seventh Victim* follows Mary Gibson (a young Kim Hunter) on her search for her missing sister, Jacqueline (Jean Brooks). Mary has been at boarding school, while Jacqueline, the owner of a Manhattan cosmetics company, has paid her tuition by mail. Suddenly the payments stop, and the cosmetics firm is taken over by the sinister Esther Redi (Mary Newton). Mary leaves the school, determined to find her sister. Unbeknowst to her, Jacqueline has fallen in with a group of satanists, who meet regularly to conduct their ceremonies and promise death to anyone who betrays the secret of the group's existence. Mary's first attempts to locate Jacqueline end in failure, until she engages the help of Irving August (Lou Lubin), a beaten-down private investigator who tells her, "Sister, I ain't never been off [Manhattan]. Just say the word, and I'll find your sister."

Mary has no money and the private eye demurs, but when a number of people tell him to "lay off" he changes his mind and investigates the case simply out of curiosity. When August and Mary find Jacqueline locked in a room at the cosmetics firm she once controlled, in a pathetic, near-catatonic state, Jacqueline panics and stabs August to death, then flees into the night. In the memorable sequence that follows, Jacqueline wanders desperately through the city, as members of the group follow, attempting to kill or recapture her in a world lit entirely by the glare of streetlamps and the storefronts of rundown all-night cafés. When the satanists succeed in abducting her, they try to force Jacqueline to commit suicide by drinking poison. Val Lewton's embrace of the realm of night is perfectly summarized in the epigram from John Donne's "Holy Sonnets" that prefaces the film: "I run to death, and death meets me as fast, and all my pleasures are like yesterday." The characters in *The Seventh Victim* are a cheerless, foredoomed group, and even the satanists seem powerless to stop the encroaching power of darkness that surrounds the film's protagonists in Manhattan.

New York, in *The Seventh Victim*, is a zone of eternal night, in which the fears, desires, and ambitions of competing factions are inextricably intertwined in a seemingly endless web of failed hopes and dreams. New York at night holds promise, as I noted at the beginning of this essay, but it also holds danger. The night can swallow you up, the night can bring death and disappearance; indeed, at the end of *The Seventh Victim*, Jacqueline commits suicide in a small room she has rented specifically for that purpose, because she can no longer withstand the dominion of the darkness that surrounds her. Nor does anyone try to stop her. Her neighbor, the consumptive Mimi (Elizabeth Russell), who introduces herself to Jacqueline with the words, "I'm Mimi. I'm dying" (echoing, of course, *La Bohème*), encourages Jacqueline to make her final exit from the world, as Mimi sees no point in continuing to struggle against the inevitability of death. The night world, then, is a zone of promise and change, which is nevertheless fraught with genuine peril; the world in which our hopes and dreams must fight to survive until the dawn, when the day once again transforms the city into a place of commerce and social engagement. The night world is the place where we wish for escape, either to avoid the dawn or to eagerly await its appearance. In the darkness of Manhattan everything is readily apparent, even too much so. But in the night world, especially and quintessentially in New York, everything is invisible.

Works Cited and Consulted

Affron, Charles, and Mirella Jona Affron. *Sets in Motion: Art Direction and Film Narrative*. New Brunswick: Rutgers UP, 1995.

Andersen, Thom. "Red Hollywood." *Literature and the Visual Arts in Contemporary Society*. Ed. Suzanne Ferguson and Barbara Groseclose. Columbus: Ohio State UP, 1985. 141–96.

Anderson, Elizabeth. Posting on *http://cinematreasures.org/theater/900*. 14 Dec. 2002.

Baker, Aaron. *Contesting Identities: Sports in American Film*. Urbana: U of Illinois P, 2003.

Battcock, Gregory. "Notes on *The Chelsea Girls*: A Film by Andy Warhol." *Art Journal* 26:4 (Summer 1967): 363–65.

Baudrillard, Jean. "L'Esprit du Terrorisme." *Harper's* (Feb. 2002): 13–18.

Beach, Christopher. *Class, Language, and American Film Comedy*. Cambridge: Cambridge UP, 2002.

Behlmer, Rudy, ed. *Memo from David O. Selznick*. New York: Modern Library, 2000.

Bergin, Paul. "Andy Warhol: The Artist as Machine." *Art Journal* 26:4 (Summer 1967): 359–63.

Berman, Marshall. "The Lonely Crowd: New York After the War." *New York: An Illustrated History*. Ed. Ric Burns and James Sanders with Lisa Ades. New York: Knopf, 1999. 536–41.

——. "Too Much Is Not Enough: Metamorphoses of Times Square." *Impossible Presence: Surface and Screen in the Photogenic Era*. Ed. Terry Smith. Chicago: U of Chicago P, 2001. 39–69.

Blake, Richard A. *Street Smart: The New York of Lumet, Allen, Scorsese, and Lee*. Lexington: UP of Kentucky, 2005.

Bloch, Robert. *Night World*. New York: Simon & Schuster, 1972.

Bockris, Victor. *The Life and Death of Andy Warhol*. New York: Bantam, 1989.

Bordewich, Fergus M. "Manhattan Mayhem." *Smithsonian* (Dec. 2002): 44–54.

Bordwell, David, Janet Staiger, and Kristin Thompson. *The Classical Hollywood Cinema: Film Style & Mode of Production to 1960*. New York: Columbia UP, 1985.

Bouzereau, Laurent. "Guilt Trip: Hitchcock and *The Wrong Man*." DVD Commentary Feature. *The Wrong Man*. Warner Bros. 31866.

Boyarin, Daniel. *Unheroic Conduct: The Rise of Heterosexuality and the Invention of the Jewish Man*. Berkeley: U of California P, 2001.

Boyer, J. *Sidney Lumet*. New York: Twayne, 1993.

Brakhage, Stan. "Metaphors on Vision." *Film Theory and Criticism*. 7th ed. Ed. Leo Braudy and Marshall Cohen. New York: Oxford UP. 199–205.

Braudy, Leo. "The Sacraments of Genre: Coppola, DePalma, and Scorsese." *Film Quarterly* 39:3 (Spring 1986): 17–28.

Brown, Georgia, and Amy Taubin. "Clocking In: Two Critics Rate Spike Lee's Ultimate Hood Movie." *Village Voice* 19 Sep. 1995: 71.

Buhle, Paul, and Dave Wagner. *A Very Dangerous Citizen: Abraham Lincoln Polonsky and the Hollywood Left*. Berkeley: U of California P, 2001.

Bukatman, Scott. "Syncopated City: New York in Musical Films (1929–1961)." *Matters of Gravity: Special Effects and Supermen in the 20th Century*. Durham, N.C.: Duke UP, 2003. 157–83.

Burke, Kenneth. *A Grammar of Motives*. Berkeley: University of California Press, 1969.

Burns, Ric, and James Sanders. *New York: An Illustrated History*. New York: Knopf, 1999.

Caro, Robert. *The Power Broker: Robert Moses and the Fall of New York*. New York: Knopf, 1974.

Cavell, Stanley. *Pursuits of Happiness: The Hollywood Comedy of Remarriage*. Cambridge: Harvard UP, 1981.

Chion, Michel. "Alfred Hitchcock's *Rear Window*: The Fourth Side." Trans. Jane Belton and Alan Williams. *Alfred Hitchcock's Rear Window*. Ed. John Belton. Cambridge: Cambridge UP, 2000. 110–17. Originally published as *"Rear Window* d'Alfred Hitchcock: Le Quatrième coté." *Cahiers du cinéma* 356 (Feb. 1984): 4–7.

——. *Audio-Vision: Sound on Screen*. Ed and trans. Claudia Gorbman. New York: Columbia UP, 1994.

Cogeval, Guy, with Dominique Païni. *Hitchcock and Art: Fatal Coincidences*. Montreal: Montreal Museum of Fine Arts, 2000.

Colacello, Bob. *Holy Terror: Andy Warhol Close Up*. New York: HarperCollins, 1990.

Connelly, Marie Katheryn. *Martin Scorsese: An Analysis of His Feature Films, with a Filmography of His Entire Directorial Career*. Jefferson, N.C.: McFarland, 1998.

Cook, Jim, and Alan Lovell, eds. *Coming to Terms With Hollywood*. London: BFI, 1981.

Corliss, Richard. "Hot Time in Bed-Stuy Tonight." *Time* 3 July 1989: 62.

Cunningham, Frank R. *Sidney Lumet: Film and Literary Vision*. Lexington: UP of Kentucky, 1991.

Curtis, Scott. "The Making of *Rear Window.*" *Alfred Hitchcock's Rear Window*. Ed. John Belton. Cambridge: Cambridge UP, 2000. 21–56.

Deleuze, Gilles. *Cinema 2: The Time-Image*. Trans. Hugh Tomlinson and Robert Galeta. Minneapolis: U of Minnesota P, 1989.

Denby, David. "Viva and Louis." *Film Quarterly* 23:1 (Autumn 1969). 41–44.

Desser, David. "The Kung Fu Craze: Hong Kong Cinema's First American Reception." *The Cinema of Hong Kong: History, Arts, Identity*. Ed. Poshek Fu and David Desser. New York: Cambridge UP, 2000. 19–43.

——. "The Martial Arts Film in the 1990s." *Film Genre 2000: New Critical Essays*. Ed. Wheeler Winston Dixon. Albany: SUNY P, 2000. 77–110.

Desser, David, and Lester D. Friedman. *American Jewish Filmmakers: Traditions and Trends.* Urbana: U of Illinois P, 1993.

DiGirolamo, Vincent. "Such, Such Were the B'hoys . . . ." *Radical History Review* 90 (Fall 2004): 123–41.

Diner, Hasia R. *Lower East Side Memories: A Jewish Place in America.* Princeton: Princeton UP, 2000.

Dixon, Wheeler Winston. Telephone interview with Robert Bloch. 20 Nov. 1985.

Dyer, Richard. *Now You See It: Studies in Lesbian and Gay Film.* London: Routledge, 1990.

——. *White.* London: Routledge, 1997.

East Hampton Star. 26 Aug. 1937, 2 Sep. 1937.

Eberson, John. "A Description of the Capitol Theater, Chicago (1925)." *Moviegoing in America: A Sourcebook in the History of Film Exhibition.* Ed. Gregory A. Waller. Oxford: Blackwell, 2002.

Fiedler, Leslie. *Love and Death in the American Novel.* Rev. ed. New York: Stein & Day, 1966.

Film-makers' Cooperative Catalogue No. 6. New York: n.p., 1975.

Fischer, Lucy. *Designing Women: Cinema, Art Deco and the Female Form.* New York: Columbia UP, 2003.

Flatley, Guy. "He Has Often Walked 'Mean Streets.'" *New York Times* 16 Dec. 1973: 2: 17, 28.

Foucault, Michel. *Discipline and Punish: The Birth of the Modern Prison.* Trans. Alan Sheridan. New York: Vintage, 1979.

Friedman, Lawrence S. *The Cinema of Martin Scorsese.* New York: Continuum, 1999.

Friedman, Lester D. *Hollywood's Image of the Jew.* New York: Frederick Ungar, 1982.

Friedrich, Otto. *City of Nets: A Portrait of Hollywood in the 1940s.* Berkeley: U of California P, 1997.

Gabler, Neal. *An Empire of Their Own: How the Jews Invented Hollywood.* New York: Crown, 1988.

Geisinger, Elliot, dir. *Martin Scorsese: Back on the Block.* Professional Films/Robbins Nest Productions, 1973.

Gerstner, David A. *Manly Arts: Masculinity and Nation in Early American Cinema.* Durham, N.C.: Duke UP, 2006.

——. Personal interview with Charles Henri Ford, n.d.

Giles, James R. *The Naturalistic Inner-City Novel in America: Encounters with the Fat Man.* Columbia: U of South Carolina P, 1995.

Gm_acevedo. Posting on *http://cinematreasures.org/theater/900.* 29 Mar. 2004.

Goldberg, Harold. "Sidney Lumet: The Director Talks about Shooting in Snowstorms." *Sidney Lumet Interviews.* Ed. Joanna E. Rapf. Jackson: UP of Mississippi, 2006.

Goodman, Paul. *The Lordly Hudson: Collected Poems of Paul Goodman.* New York: Macmillan, 1962.

——. "Natural Violence" (part of *Spring 1945, The May Pamphlet*). *Drawing the Line*. New York: Random House, 1962. 3–51.

Goodman, Percival. *Communitas: Means of Livelihood and Ways of Life*. New York: Vintage, 1960.

Grindon, Leger. "Body and Soul: The Structure of Meaning in the Boxing Film Genre." *Cinema Journal* 35:4 (Summer 1996): 54–69.

Grundmann, Roy. *Andy Warhol's Blow Job*. Philadelphia: Temple UP, 2003.

Hackett, Pat, ed. *The Andy Warhol Diaries*. New York: Warner Books, 1989.

Hill, Gladwin. "Hollywood Airs View of Criticism: Film Makers, Though Not Defiant, Counter Bishops' Attack on Moral Tone." *New York Times* 1 Dec. 1960: 40.

Hoberman, J. "Vice City." *Village Voice* 18–24 Dec. 2002: 102, 112.

Houston, Beverle, and Marsha Kinder. "*Rosemary's Baby*." *Sight and Sound* 38:1 (Winter 1969): 17–26.

Howe, Irving. *World of Our Fathers*. New York: Harcourt Brace Jovanovich, 1976.

Jenkins, Henry. *What Made Pistachio Nuts?: Early Sound Comedy and the Vaudeville Aesthetic*. New York: Columbia UP, 1992.

Johnson, Victoria E. "Polyphony and Cultural ExPion: Interpreting Musical Traditions in *Do the Right Thing*." *Film Quarterly* 47:2 (Winter 1993–94): 18–29. Repr. with slight revision in *Spike Lee's Do the Right Thing*. Ed. Mark A. Reid. Cambridge: Cambridge UP, 1997. 50–72.

Joseph, Samuel. *Jewish Immigration in the United States*. Studies in History, Economics and Public Law 59:4. New York: Columbia UP, 1914.

Jowitt, Deborah. *Jerome Robbins: His Life, His Theater, His Dance*. New York: Simon & Schuster, 2004.

Katz, Ephraim. *The Film Encyclopedia*. 2nd ed. New York: HarperCollins, 1994.

Kaufman, Anthony. "An Interview with Sidney Lumet." *Sidney Lumet Interviews*. Ed. Joanna E. Rapf. Jackson: UP of Mississippi, 2006.

Kelly, Mary Pat. *Martin Scorsese: A Journey*. New York: Thunder Mouth's P, 1991.

Kelsey, Carleton. *Amagansett: A Pictorial History 1680–1940*. Amagansett, N.Y.: Amagansett Historical Association, 1986.

Keyser, Les. *Martin Scorsese*. New York: Twayne Publishers, 1992.

Kingsley, Sidney. "It Often Pays to Take a Walk Along the East River." *New York Times* 10 Nov. 1935: 9: 1–2.

Kleeblatt, Norman L. "MERDE! The Caricatural Attack Against Emile Zola." *Art Journal* 52:3 (1993): 54–59.

Knight, Arthur. "1959: Movies and the Racial Divide." *American Cinema of the 1950s: Themes and Variations*. Ed. Murray Pomerance. New Brunswick: Rutgers UP, 2005.

Koch, Stephen. *Stargazer: The Life, World, and Films of Andy Warhol*. New York: Marion Boyars Publishers, 1973; rev. ed., 1991.

Kolker, Robert Phillip. *A Cinema of Loneliness: Penn, Kubrick, Coppola, Scorsese, Altman*. New York: Oxford UP, 1980.

Krauss, Rosalind E. "Carnal Knowledge." *Andy Warhol*. Ed. Annette Michelson. Cambridge: MIT Press, 2001. 111–18.

Lee, Spike. "The Interview: Spike Lee With Nelson George, November 21, 1986." *Spike Lee's Gotta Have It: Inside Guerrilla Filmmaking*. New York: A Fireside Book, 1987. 19–62.

Leff, Leonard. *Hitchcock and Selznick: The Rich and Strange Collaboration of Alfred Hitchcock and David O. Selznick in Hollywood*. New York: Weidenfeld & Nicolson, 1987.

Levin, Ira. *Rosemary's Baby*. 1967; repr., New York: Signet, 1997.

Lewis, Emory. *Cue's New York: A Leisurely Guide to Manhattan*. New York: Duell, Sloan & Pearce, 1963.

Lewis, Jon. "'We Do Not Ask You to Condone This': How the Blacklist Saved Hollywood." *Cinema Journal* 39:2 (Winter 2000): 3–30.

Lindo, Delroy. "Delroy Lindo on Spike Lee." The Independent Film Channel, 1999. *Spike Lee: Interviews*. Ed. Cynthia Fuchs. Jackson: UP of Mississippi, 2002. 161–77.

Lippmann, Walter. *Public Opinion*. New York: Free Press, 1921.

Lombardo, Patrizia. "Warhol as Dandy and Flaneur." *Who Is Andy Warhol?* Ed. Colin MacCabe with Mark Francis and Peter Wollen. London: BFI, 1997. 33–40.

Luhr, William, and Peter Lehman. "*Experiment in Terror*: Dystopian Modernism, The Police Procedural, and the Space of Anxiety." *Cinema and Modernity*. Ed. Murray Pomerance. New Brunswick: Rutgers UP, 2006. 175–93.

Lumet, Sidney. "Keep Them on the Hook." *Sidney Lumet Interviews*. Ed. Joanna E. Rapf. Jackson: UP of Mississippi, 2006.

Mandelbaum, Howard, and Eric Myers. *Screen Deco*. New York: St. Martin's P, 1985.

Marin, Louis. "Frontiers of Utopia: Past and Present." *Critical Inquiry* 19 (1993): 397–420.

Marullo, Glen. Personal interview. 18 June 2005.

Massood, Paula J. *Black City Cinema: African American Urban Experiences in Film*. Philadelphia: Temple UP, 2003.

Mast, Gerald. *Can't Help Singin': The American Musical on Stage and Screen*, New York: Overlook, 1990.

McGilligan, Patrick. *Alfred Hitchcock: A Life in Darkness and Light*. New York: Regan Books, 2003.

McMillan, Terry. "Thoughts on She's Gotta Have It." *The Films of Spike Lee: Five for Five*. Ed. Spike Lee. New York: Stewart, Tabori & Chang, 1991. 19–29.

Miller, Michael. "Loew's Paradise in the Bronx." *Annual of 1975 of the Theatre Historical Society*.

Mitchell, Elvis. "Spike Lee: The *Playboy* Interview." *Playboy* (July 1991): 51–68. Abridged, *Spike Lee Interviews*. Ed. Cynthia Fuchs. Jackson: UP of Mississippi, 2002. 35–64.

Nemerov, Alexander. *Icons of Grief: Val Lewton's Home Front Movies*. Berkeley: U of California P, 2004.

Nowell-Smith, Geoffrey. "Cities: Real and Imagined." *Cinema and the City: Film and Urban Societies in a Global Context*. Ed. Mark Shiel and Tony Fitzmaurice. Oxford: Blackwell, 2001. 99–108.

Oates, Joyce Carol. *On Boxing*. Garden City, N.Y.: Doubleday, 1987.

O'Brien, Geoffrey. *The Times Square Story*. New York: Norton, 1998.

Page, Max. *The Creative Destruction of Manhattan, 1900–1940*. Chicago: U of Chicago P, 1999.

Phillips, McCandlish. "From Little Italy to Big-Time Movies." *New York Times* 18 Oct. 1973: 64.

Plachy, Sylvia. "Lens." *New York Times* 27 Apr. 2005: B2.

Polan, Dana. "Urban Trauma and the Metropolitan Imagination." Unpublished ms., Stanford University. 5–7 May 2005.

Polanski, Roman. *Roman by Polanski*. New York: Morrow, 1984.

——. Interview. *The Film Director as Superstar*. Ed. Joseph Gelmis. Garden City, N.Y.: Doubleday, 1970. 139–55.

——. Interview. *Rosemary's Baby*. DVD. Paramount, 2000.

Pomerance, Murray. *An Eye for Hitchcock*. New Brunswick: Rutgers UP, 2004.

Rainsberger, Todd. *James Wong Howe, Cinematographer*. San Diego: A. S. Barnes, 1981.

Rankin, Jim. Posting on *http://cinematreasures.org/theater/900/*. 28 Sep. 2005.

Rapf, Joanna E. "An Interview with Sidney Lumet." *Sidney Lumet Interviews*. Jackson: UP of Mississippi, 2006.

Ratner, Marc. "A Larger 'Slice of Life': Re-Assessing Literary Naturalism." *College Literature* 24:3 (1997): 169–74.

Rattray, Everett T. *The South Fork: The Land and the People of Eastern Long Island*. New York: Random House, 1979.

Rayns, Tony. "Andy's Hand-jobs." *Who Is Andy Warhol?* Ed. Colin McCabe with Mark Francis and Peter Wollen. London: BFI, 1997. 83–87.

Reed, Kit. *The Attack of the Giant Baby and Other Stories*, New York: Berkeley Books, 1981.

Rice, Elmer. *Minority Report: An Autobiography*. New York: Simon & Schuster, 1963.

Riess, Steven A. *City Games*. Urbana: U of Illinois P, 1991.

——. "Tough Jews: The Jewish American Boxing Experience, 1890–1950." *Sports and the American Jew*. Ed. Steven A. Riess. Syracuse: Syracuse UP, 1999. 60–104.

Riis, Jacob A. *How the Other Half Lives: Studies among the Tenements of New York*. 1890. New York: Dutton, 1971.

Robert R. Posting on *http://cinematreasures.org/theater/900*. 15 June 2005.

Rogin, Michael. *Blackface, White Noise: Jewish Immigrants in the Hollywood Melting Pot*. Berkeley: U of California P, 1996.

Rosen, Alan. "'Teach Me Gold': Pedagogy and Memory in *The Pawnbroker*." *Prooftexts* 22 (2002): 77–117.

Rosenblum, Ralph, and Robert Karen. *When the Shooting Stops . . . the Cutting Begins: A Film Editor's Story.* New York: Viking, 1979.

Rothman, William. *The "I" of the Camera.* 2nd ed. New York: Cambridge UP, 2004.

Rowe, Kathleen. *The Unruly Woman: Gender and the Genres of Laughter.* Austin: U of Texas P, 1995.

Sammons, Jeffrey . *Beyond the Ring: The Role of Boxing in American Society.* Urbana: U of Illinois P, 1990.

Sanders, James. *Celluloid Skyline: New York and the Movies.* New York: Knopf, 2001.

Sarris, Andrew, ed. "Abraham Polonsky in Correspondence with William Pechter, 1962." *Hollywood Voices.* Indianapolis: Bobbs-Merrill, 1971. 135–48.

Schaefer, Dennis, and Larry Salvato. *Masters of Light: Conversations with Contemporary Cinematographers.* Berkeley: U of California P, 1984.

Schatz, Thomas. *The Genius of the System: Hollywood Filmmaking in the Studio Era.* New York: Pantheon, 1988.

Sennett, Ted. *Hollywood Musicals.* New York: Harry Abrams, 1981.

Server, Lee. "If You Don't Get Killed It's a Lucky Day: A Conversation with Abraham Polonsky." *The Big Book of Noir.* Ed. Lee Server, Ed Gorman, and Martin H. Greenberg. New York: Carroll & Graf, 1998. 87–92.

Sharp, Dennis. *The Picture Palace and Other Buildings for the Movies.* London: Hugh Evelyn, 1969.

Shevey, Sandra. "A New York Walk with Alfred Hitchcock." *http://www. theculturedtraveler. com/Archives/NOV2002/Hitchcock.htm.*

Silver, Alain, and Elizabeth Ward. *Film Noir: An Encyclopedic Reference to the American Style.* Rev. expanded ed. Woodstock, N.Y.: 1988.

Simmel, Georg. "The Metropolis and Mental Life." 1905. *The City Cultures Reader.* Ed. Malcolm Miles and Tim Hall (with Iain Borden). 2nd ed. London: Routledge, 2004. 12–19.

Sklar, Robert. *City Boys: Cagney, Bogart, Garfield.* Princeton: Princeton UP, 1992.

Slotkin, Richard. *Regeneration through Violence: The Mythology of the American Frontier, 1600–1860.* Norman: U of Oklahoma P, 1973.

Sobchack, Thomas. "New York Street Gangs or the Warriors of My Mind." *Journal of Popular Film and Television* 10:2 (Summer 1982): 77–85.

Sondheim, Steve. "Review of *Rear Window.*" *Alfred Hitchcock's Rear Window.* Ed. John Belton. Cambridge: Cambridge UP, 2000. 168–170. Originally pub. *Films in Review* 5 (Oct. 1954): 427–29.

Sontag, Susan. "The Imagination of Disaster." *Against Interpretation and Other Essays.* New York: Delta, 1966. 209–25.

Spoto, Donald. *The Dark Side of Genius: The Life of Alfred Hitchcock.* New York: Ballantine Books, 1983.

Staiger, Janet. *Interpreting Films: Studies in the Historical Reception of American Cinema.* Princeton: Princeton UP, 1992.

Stam, Robert, and Roberta Pearson. "Hitchcock's *Rear Window*: Reflexivity and the Critique of Voyeurism." *A Hitchcock Reader.* Ed. Marshall Deutelbaum and Leland Poague. Ames: Iowa State UP, 1986. 193–206. Originally pub. *Enclitic* 7:1 (Spring 1984): 136–45.

Stern, Lesley. *The Scorsese Connection.* Bloomington: Indiana UP, 1995.

Sterritt, David. *"Do the Right Thing." The A List: The National Society of Film Critics' 100 Essential Films.* Ed. Jay Carr. Cambridge, Mass.: Da Capo, 2002. 91–94.

——. "Spike Lee's Hotly Debated New Film." *Christian Science Monitor* 27 June 1989: 15.

Strauss, Bob. "Tale of 'Goodfellas,' Scorsese's Brilliant Cinematic Second Skin." *Telegram and Gazette* (Worcester, Mass.) 21 Sep. 1990: A8.

Swindell, Larry. *Body and Soul: The Story of John Garfield.* New York: Morrow, 1975.

Taubin, Amy. "****." *Who Is Andy Warhol?* Ed. Colin McCabe with Mark Francis and Peter Wollen. London: BFI, 1997. 23–32.

Taylor, John Russell. *Hitch: The Life and Times of Alfred Hitchcock.* New York: Da Capo, 1996.

Theatrefan. Posting on *http://cinematreasures.org/theater/900.* 22 Nov. 2003.

Thompson, David. *A Biographical Dictionary of Film.* 3rd ed. New York: Knopf, 1996.

Thompson, David, and Ian Christie, eds. *Scorsese on Scorsese.* Boston: Faber and Faber, 1989.

Tips on Tables.com. *http://www.tipsontables.com/storkmenu.html.* 5 Aug. 2005.

Tomkins, Calvin. *Duchamp: A Biography.* New York: Henry Holt, 1996.

Truffaut, François. *Hitchcock.* New York: Simon & Schuster, 1967.

Vernon, Raymond. *Metropolis 1985: An Interpretation of the Findings of the New York Metropolitan Region Study.* Cambridge: Harvard UP, 1960.

Wallant, Edward Lewis. *The Pawnbroker.* New York: Macfadden-Bartell, 1961.

Warhol, Andy. *Andy Warhol: America.* New York: Harper & Row, 1985.

——. *The Philosophy of Andy Warhol: From A to B and Back Again.* New York: Harcourt Brace, 1975.

Warhol, Andy, and Pat Hackett. *Popism: The Warhol Sixties.* New York: Harcourt Brace, 1980.

Warner, Frank. Interview. *Sound-on-Film: Interviews with Creators of Film Sound.* Ed. Vincent LoBrutto. Westport, Conn.: Praeger, 1994. 27–40.

Weis, Elisabeth. *The Silent Scream: Alfred Hitchcock's Sound Track.* Rutherford, N.J.: Fairleigh Dickinson UP, 1982.

Wexman, Virginia Wright. *Roman Polanski.* Boston: Twayne, 1985.

Whitfield, Stephen. *American Space, Jewish Time.* Hamden, Conn.: Archon Books, 1988.

——. *In Search of American Jewish Culture.* Hanover, N.H.: Brandeis UP, 1999.

Wollen, Peter. "Note from the Underground: Andy Warhol." *Raiding the Icebox: Reflections on Twentieth-Century Culture.* Bloomington: Indiana UP, 1993. 158–75.

——. *Singin' in the Rain.* London: BFI, 1992.

Wood, Robin. *Hitchcock's Films Revisited.* New York: Columbia UP, 1989.

Notes on Contributors

AARON BAKER is an associate professor of film and media studies at Arizona State University. He is the author of *Contesting Identities: Sports in American Film*, and is currently writing a book on the films of Steven Soderbergh.

SCOTT BUKATMAN is an associate professor in the Film and Media Studies Program at Stanford University. He is the author of *Terminal Identity: The Virtual Subject in Postmodern Science Fiction*, a monograph on *Blade Runner* commissioned by the British Film Institute, and a collection of essays, *Matters of Gravity: Special Effects and Supermen in the 20th Century*.

STEVEN ALAN CARR is an associate professor of communication at Indiana University–Purdue University Fort Wayne and a 2002–2003 Center for Advanced Holocaust Studies Postdoctoral Fellow at the United States Holocaust Memorial Museum in Washington, D.C. He is the author of *Hollywood and Anti-Semitism: A Cultural History up to World War II*.

DAVID DESSER is a professor and the director of the Unit for Cinema Studies, University of Illinois at Urbana-Champaign. He is a former book review editor of *Film Quarterly* and was editor of *Cinema Journal* from 1993 to 1997. He is the author of *The Samurai Films of Akira Kurosawa* and *Eros Plus Massacre: An Introduction to the Japanese New Wave Cinema*; the co-author of *American-Jewish Filmmakers*; the editor of *Ozu's Tokyo Story*, and the co-editor of *The Cinema of Hong Kong: History, Arts, Identity*; *Hollywood Goes Shopping: Consumer Culture and American Cinema*; *Cinematic Landscapes: Observations on the Visual Arts and Cinema in China and Japan*; *Reflections in a Male Eye: John Huston and the American Experience*; and *Reframing Japanese Cinema: Authorship, Genre, History*. He provided the commentary for the Criterion Collection DVD of *Tokyo Story*.

WHEELER WINSTON DIXON is the Ryan Professor of Film Studies and a professor of English at the University of Nebraska, Lincoln, and co-editor-in-chief of the *Quarterly Review of Film and Video*. He is the author or editor of numerous books, including *Visions of Paradise: Images of Eden in the Cinema*; *American Cinema of the 1940s: Themes and Variations*; *Lost in the Fifties: Recovering Phantom Hollywood*; *Film and Television after 9/11*; *Visions of the Apocalypse: Spectacles of Destruction in American Cinema*; *Straight: Constructions of Heterosexuality in the Cinema*; and *Experimental Cinema: The Film Reader*, co-edited with Gwendolyn Audrey Foster.

In April 2003, he was honored with a retrospective of his films at The Museum of Modern Art in New York, and his films were acquired for the permanent collection of the museum, in both print and original format.

GWENDOLYN AUDREY FOSTER teaches film studies, women's studies, and cultural studies in the Department of English at the University of Nebraska, Lincoln. Her most recent book, *Performing Whiteness: Postmodern Re/Constructions in Moving Images*, was named as an Outstanding Title in the Humanities for 2004 by *Choice*. Her other books include *Captive Bodies: Postcolonial Subjectivity in Cinema*; *Troping the Body*; *Experimental Cinema: The Film Reader* (co-edited with Wheeler Winston Dixon); and *Identity and Memory: The Films of Chantal Akerman*. She also co-edits *Quarterly Review of Film and Video*.

DAVID A. GERSTNER is an associate professor of cinema studies at City University of New York, College of Staten Island. He is author of *Manly Arts: Masculinity and Nation in Early American Cinema* and *The Routledge International Encyclopedia of Queer Culture*, and co-author with Janet Staiger of *Authorship and Film*.

PAMELA GRACE teaches film studies at Brooklyn College, City University of New York. She has published essays in *A Companion to Literature and Film*, edited by Robert Stam and Alessandra Raengo; *Joel and Ethan Coen's "Fargo,"* edited by William Luhr; and *Cineaste*; and is currently writing a book on violence and religious heroes in a film genre she has named the "hagiopic."

BARRY KEITH GRANT is a professor of film studies and popular culture at Brock University. He is the author, co-author, or editor of more than a dozen books, including *Five Films by Frederick Wiseman*, *The Film Studies Dictionary*; *Film Genre Reader*; *Documenting the Documentary: Close Readings of Documentary Film and Video*; *John Ford's Stagecoach*; *The Dread of Difference: Gender and the Horror Film*; and *Voyages of Discovery: The Cinema of Frederick Wiseman*. He edits the Contemporary Approaches to Film and Television series for Wayne State University Press and the New Approaches to Film Genre series for Blackwell, and is the editor-in-chief of the *Schirmer Encyclopedia of Film*.

PETER LEHMAN is the director of the Center for Film and Media Research and Film and Media Studies at Arizona State University, Tempe. He is author of *Roy Orbison: The Invention of an Alternative Rock Masculinity* and editor of *Pornography: Film and Culture*. He is co-author with William Luhr of *Thinking about Movies: Watching, Questioning, Enjoying*.

WILLIAM LUHR, a professor of English at Saint Peter's College, is currently completing a book on film noir. His other books include *Raymond Chandler and Film*; *Thinking about Movies: Watching, Questioning, Understanding* (with Peter Lehman); *Joel and Ethan Coen's "Fargo"*; *"The Maltese Falcon": John Huston, Director*;

Blake Edwards (with Peter Lehman); and *World Cinema since 1945*. He is also co-chair of the Columbia University Seminar on Cinema and Interdisciplinary Interpretation.

PAULA J. MASSOOD is an associate professor of film studies in the Department of Film at Brooklyn College, CUNY. She is the author of *Black City Cinema: African American Urban Experiences in Film* and editor of *The Spike Lee Reader*. Her articles have appeared in *Cinema Journal, African American Review, Literature/Film Review, Cineaste*, and anthologies focusing on African American film, the city and film, film adaptation, and Hollywood violence.

JOE McELHANEY is an assistant professor of film studies at Hunter College/City University of New York. He is the author of *The Death of Classical Cinema: Hitchcock, Lang, Minnelli* and *Albert Maysles* and the editor of *Vincente Minnelli: The Art of Entertainment*. His essays have appeared in such publications as the *Journal of Film and Video* and *Millennium Film Journal* and such anthologies as *Hitchcock: Centenary Essays* and *Cinema and Modernity*. He is currently on the editorial advisory board of *The Velvet Light Trap*.

MURRAY POMERANCE is a professor in the Department of Sociology at Ryerson University and the author of *Johnny Depp Starts Here; An Eye for Hitchcock; Savage Time*; and *Magia d'Amore*. He has edited or co-edited numerous anthologies, including *From Hobbits to Hollywood: Essays on Peter Jackson's Lord of the Rings; American Cinema of the 1950s: Themes and Variations; Cinema and Modernity; BAD: Infamy, Darkness, Evil, and Slime on Screen; Where the Boys Are: Cinemas of Masculinity and Youth*; and *Enfant Terrible! Jerry Lewis in American Film*. He edits the Horizons of Cinema series at State University of New York Press, and co-edits both the Screen Decades and Star Decades series at Rutgers University Press.

WILLIAM ROTHMAN is a professor in the Motion Picture Program and the director of graduate studies at the University of Miami. He is the author of *Hitchcock—The Murderous Gaze; The "I" of the Camera; Documentary Film Classics*; and (with Marian Keane) *Reading Cavell's The World Viewed*, and editor of *Cavell on Film*. Since 1985 he has been series editor of Cambridge University Press's Studies in Film series.

DAVID STERRITT, longtime film critic of the *Christian Science Monitor*, is an adjunct professor of language, literature, and culture at the Maryland Institute College of Art, chair of the National Society of Film Critics, and professor emeritus of theater and film at Long Island University. His writing has appeared in *Cahiers du cinéma*, the *New York Times*, the *Journal of Aesthetics and Art Criticism*, the *Chronicle of Higher Education*, and many other periodicals, and he has published several books on film-related subjects, including *Guiltless Pleasures: A David Sterritt Reader*.

RANDY THOM is the director of sound design for Skywalker Sound. He has been nominated for twelve Academy Awards and has received two Oscars, most recently in 2005 for *The Incredibles*.

ELISABETH WEIS is a professor of film and the head of film studies at Brooklyn College and on the faculty of CUNY's Graduate Center. Her books include *Film Sound: Theory and Practice* (co-edited with John Belton) and *The Silent Scream: Alfred Hitchcock's Sound Track*.

Index

(Page numbers in italics denote photographs.)